MINNESOTA
ELEMENTARY EDUCATION
(K-6)

By: Sharon Wynne, M.S.

XAMonline, INC.
Boston

To obtain permission(s) to use the material from this work for any purpose including workshops or seminars, please submit a written request to:

XAMonline, Inc.
25 First Street, Suite 106
Cambridge, MA 02141
Toll Free 1-800-509-4128
Email: info@xamonline.com
Web: www.xamonline.com
Fax: 1-617-583-5552

Library of Congress Cataloging-in-Publication Data

Wynne, Sharon A.
    Minnesota Elementary Education (K-6) Exam / Sharon A. Wynne 1st ed
    ISBN 978-1-60787-076-0
    1. Elementary Education (K-6)
    2. Study Guides
    3. Minnesota
    4. Teachers' Certification & Licensure
    5. Careers

Disclaimer:

The opinions expressed in this publication are the sole works of XAMonline and were created independently from the National Education Association, Educational Testing Service, or any State Department of Education, National Evaluation Systems or other testing affiliates.

Between the time of publication and printing, state specific standards as well as testing formats and Web site information may change and therefore would not be included in part or in whole within this product. Sample test questions are developed by XAMonline and reflect content similar to that on real tests; however, they are not former test questions. XAMonline assembles content that aligns with state standards but makes no claims nor guarantees teacher candidates a passing score. Numerical scores are determined by testing companies such as NES or ETS and then are compared with individual state standards. A passing score varies from state to state.

Printed in the United States of America   œ-1

Minnesota Elementary Education (K-6)
ISBN: 978-1-60787-076-0

Table of Contents

COMPETENCY 3
UNDERSTAND THE DEVELOPMENT OF PHONICS AND OTHER WORD IDENTIFICATION STRATEGIES, SPELLING, AND FLUENCY

COMPETENCY 4
UNDERSTAND VOCABULARY DEVELOPMENT

COMPETENCY 5
UNDERSTAND READING COMPREHENSION AND DEVELOPMENT OF COMPREHENSION STRATEGIES AND INDEPENDENT READING

COMPETENCY 6

UNDERSTAND DIFFERENT TYPES OF TEXTS AND STRATEGIES FOR UNDERSTANDING, ANALYZING, AND RESPONDING TO THEM

COMPETENCY 7

UNDERSTAND ACADEMIC LANGUAGE DEVELOPMENT, INCLUDING ENGLISH LANGUAGE STRUCTURES AND CONVENTIONS

DOMAIN III
MATHEMATICS 145

COMPETENCY 14
UNDERSTAND CONCEPTS AND APPLICATIONS OF DISCRETE MATH 215

COMPETENCY 15
UNDERSTAND MATHEMATICAL PROCESSES AND PERSPECTIVES 221

DOMAIN IV
HEALTH/FITNESS AND FINE ARTS 241

COMPETENCY 16
UNDERSTAND FUNDAMENTAL HEALTH AND PHYSICAL EDUCATION CONCEPTS 243

COMPETENCY 23
UNDERSTAND CHARACTERISTICS OF AND INTERACTIONS AMONG PEOPLE, PLACES, AND ENVIRONMENTS

COMPETENCY 24
UNDERSTAND CHARACTERISTICS OF AND INTERACTIONS AMONG INDIVIDUALS, GROUPS, AND INSTITUTIONS

SAMPLE TEST

MINNESOTA
ELEMENTARY EDUCATION
(K-6)

SECTION 1
ABOUT XAMONLINE

XAMonline—A Specialty Teacher Certification Company

Created in 1996, XAMonline was the first company to publish study guides for state-specific teacher certification examinations. Founder Sharon Wynne found it frustrating that materials were not available for teacher certification preparation and decided to create the first single, state-specific guide. XAMonline has grown into a company of over 1,800 contributors and writers and offers over 300 titles for the entire PRAXIS series and every state examination. No matter what state you plan on teaching in, XAMonline has a unique teacher certification study guide just for you.

XAMonline—Value and Innovation

We are committed to providing value and innovation. Our print-on-demand technology allows us to be the first in the market to reflect changes in test standards and user feedback as they occur. Our guides are written by experienced teachers who are experts in their fields. And our content reflects the highest standards of quality. Comprehensive practice tests with varied levels of rigor means that your study experience will closely match the actual in-test experience.

To date, XAMonline has helped nearly 600,000 teachers pass their certification or licensing exams. Our commitment to preparation exceeds simply providing the proper material for study—it extends to helping teachers **gain mastery** of the subject matter, giving them the **tools** to become the most effective classroom leaders possible, and ushering today's students toward a **successful future**.

SECTION 2
ABOUT THIS STUDY GUIDE

Purpose of This Guide

Is there a little voice inside of you saying, "Am I ready?" Our goal is to replace that little voice and remove all doubt with a new voice that says, "I AM READY. **Bring it on!**" by offering the highest quality of teacher certification study guides.

Organization of Content

You will see that while every test may start with overlapping general topics, each is very unique in the skills they wish to test. Only XAMonline presents custom content that analyzes deeper than a title, a subarea, or an objective. Only XAMonline presents content and sample test assessments along with **focus statements**, the deepest-level rationale and interpretation of the skills that are unique to the exam.

Title and field number of test

→Each exam has its own name and number. XAMonline's guides are written to give you the content you need to know for the specific exam you are taking. You can be confident when you buy our guide that it contains the information you need to study for the specific test you are taking.

Subareas

→These are the major content categories found on the exam. XAMonline's guides are written to cover all of the subareas found in the test frameworks developed for the exam.

Objectives

→These are standards that are unique to the exam and represent the main subcategories of the subareas/content categories. XAMonline's guides are written to address every specific objective required to pass the exam.

Focus statements

→These are examples and interpretations of the objectives. You find them in parenthesis directly following the objective. They provide detailed examples of the range, type, and level of content that appear on the test questions. **Only XAMonline's guides drill down to this level.**

How Do We Compare with Our Competitors?

XAMonline—drills down to the focus statement level.
CliffsNotes and REA—organized at the objective level
Kaplan—provides only links to content
MoMedia—content not specific to the state test

Each subarea is divided into manageable sections that cover the specific skill areas. Explanations are easy to understand and thorough. You'll find that every test answer contains a rejoinder so if you need a refresher or further review after taking the test, you'll know exactly to which section you must return.

How to Use This Book

Our informal polls show that most people begin studying up to eight weeks prior to the test date, so start early. Then ask yourself some questions: How much do you really know? Are you coming to the test straight from your teacher-education program or are you having to review subjects you haven't considered in ten years? Either way, take a **diagnostic or assessment test** first. Also, spend time on sample tests so that you become accustomed to the way the actual test will appear.

This guide comes with an online diagnostic test of 30 questions found online at *www.XAMonline.com*. It is a little boot camp to get you up for the task and reveal things about your compendium of knowledge in general. Although this guide is structured to follow the order of the test, you are not required to study in that order. By finding a time-management and study plan that fits your life you will be more effective. The results of your diagnostic or self-assessment test can be a guide for how to manage your time and point you toward an area that needs more attention.

After taking the diagnostic exam, fill out the **Personalized Study Plan** page at the beginning of each chapter. Review the competencies and skills covered in that chapter and check the boxes that apply to your study needs. If there are sections you already know you can skip, check the "skip it" box. Taking this step will give you a study plan for each chapter.

Week	Activity
8 weeks prior to test	Take a diagnostic test found at www.XAMonline.com
7 weeks prior to test	Build your Personalized Study Plan for each chapter. Check the "skip it" box for sections you feel you are already strong in. ✗ SKIP IT ☐
6-3 weeks prior to test	For each of these four weeks, choose a content area to study. You don't have to go in the order of the book. It may be that you start with the content that needs the most review. Alternately, you may want to ease yourself into plan by starting with the most familiar material.
2 weeks prior to test	Take the sample test, score it, and create a review plan for the final week before the test.
1 week prior to test	Following your plan (which will likely be aligned with the areas that need the most review) go back and study the sections that align with the questions you may have gotten wrong. Then go back and study the sections related to the questions you answered correctly. If need be, create flashcards and drill yourself on any area that you makes you anxious.

SECTION 3
ABOUT THE MINNESOTA ELEMENTARY EDUCATION (K-6) EXAM

What Is the Minnesota Elementary Education (K-6) Exam?

The Minnesota Elementary Education (K-6) exam is meant to assess mastery of the content knowledge required to teach elementary students in Minnesota public schools.

Often **your own state's requirements** determine whether or not you should take any particular test. The most reliable source of information regarding this is your state's Department of Education. This resource should have a complete list of testing centers and dates. Test dates vary by subject area and not all test dates necessarily include your particular test, so be sure to check carefully.

If you are in a teacher-education program, check with the Education Department or the Certification Officer for specific information for testing and testing time-lines. The Certification Office should have most of the information you need.

If you choose an alternative route to certification you can either rely on our website at *www.XAMonline.com* or on the resources provided by an alternative certification program. Many states now have specific agencies devoted to alternative certification and there are some national organizations as well, for example:
National Association for Alternative Certification
http://www.alt-teachercert.org/index.asp

Interpreting Test Results

Contrary to what you may have heard, the results of the Minnesota Elementary Education (K-6) test are not based on time. More accurately, your score will be based on the raw number of points you earn in each section, the proportion of that section to the entire subtest, and the scaling of the raw score. Raw scores are converted to a scale of 100 to 300. It is likely to your benefit to complete as many questions in the time allotted, but it will not necessarily work to your advantage if you hurry through the test.

Scores are available by email if you request this when you register. Score reports are available 21 days after the testing window and posted to your account for 45 days as PDFs. Scores will also be sent to your chosen institution(s).

What's on the Test?

The Minnesota Elementary Education (K-6) exam is a computer-based test and consists of three subtests, each lasting one hour. You can take one, two, or all three subtests at one testing appointment. The breakdown of the questions is as follows:

Category	Approximate Number of Questions	Approximate Percentage of the Test
SUBTEST 1	50	
I: Reading		78%
II: Communication Arts		22%
SUBTEST 2	50	
I: Mathematics		75%
II: Health/Fitness and Fine Arts		25%
SUBTEST 3	50	
I: Science		57%
II: Social Studies		43%

Question Types

You're probably thinking, enough already, I want to study! Indulge us a little longer while we explain that there is actually more than one type of multiple-choice question. You can thank us later after you realize how well prepared you are for your exam.

1. Complete the Statement. The name says it all. In this question type you'll be asked to choose the correct completion of a given statement. For example:

> **The Dolch Basic Sight Words consist of a relatively short list of words that children should be able to:**
>
> A. Sound out
>
> B. Know the meaning of
>
> C. Recognize on sight
>
> D. Use in a sentence

The correct answer is C. In order to check your answer, test out the statement by adding the choices to the end of it.

2. **Which of the Following.** One way to test your answer choice for this type of question is to replace the phrase "which of the following" with your selection. Use this example:

> **Which of the following words is one of the twelve most frequently used in children's reading texts:**
>
> A. There
>
> B. This
>
> C. The
>
> D. An

Don't look! Test your answer. _____ is one of the twelve most frequently used in children's reading texts. Did you guess C? Then you guessed correctly.

3. **Roman Numeral Choices.** This question type is used when there is more than one possible correct answer. For example:

> **Which of the following two arguments accurately supports the use of cooperative learning as an effective method of instruction?**
>
> I.   Cooperative learning groups facilitate healthy competition between individuals in the group.
> II. Cooperative learning groups allow academic achievers to carry or cover for academic underachievers.
> III. Cooperative learning groups make each student in the group accountable for the success of the group.
> IV. Cooperative learning groups make it possible for students to reward other group members for achieving.
>
> A. I and II
>
> B. II and III
>
> C. I and III
>
> D. III and IV

Notice that the question states there are **two** possible answers. It's best to read all the possibilities first before looking at the answer choices. In this case, the correct answer is D.

4. **Negative Questions.** This type of question contains words such as "not," "least," and "except." Each correct answer will be the statement that does **not** fit the situation described in the question. Such as:

> **Multicultural education is not**
>
> A. An idea or concept
>
> B. A "tack-on" to the school curriculum
>
> C. An educational reform movement
>
> D. A process

Think to yourself that the statement could be anything but the correct answer. This question form is more open to interpretation than other types, so read carefully and don't forget that you're answering a negative statement.

5. **Questions that Include Graphs, Tables, or Reading Passages.** As always, read the question carefully. It likely asks for a very specific answer and not a broad interpretation of the visual. Here is a simple (though not statistically accurate) example of a graph question:

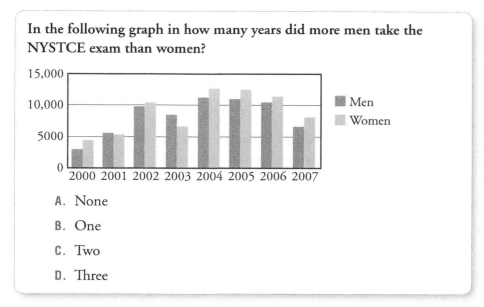

> **In the following graph in how many years did more men take the NYSTCE exam than women?**
>
> A. None
>
> B. One
>
> C. Two
>
> D. Three

It may help you to simply circle the two years that answer the question. Make sure you've read the question thoroughly and once you've made your determination, double check your work. The correct answer is C.

SECTION 4
HELPFUL HINTS

Study Tips

1. You are what you eat. Certain foods aid the learning process by releasing natural memory enhancers called CCKs (cholecystokinin) composed of tryptophan, choline, and phenylalanine. All of these chemicals enhance the neurotransmitters associated with memory and certain foods release memory enhancing chemicals. A light meal or snacks of one of the following foods fall into this category:

   - Milk
   - Rice
   - Eggs
   - Fish
   - Nuts and seeds
   - Oats
   - Turkey

   The better the connections, the more you comprehend!

2. See the forest for the trees. In other words, get the concept before you look at the details. One way to do this is to take notes as you read, paraphrasing or summarizing in your own words. Putting the concept in terms that are comfortable and familiar may increase retention.

3. Question authority. Ask why, why, why? Pull apart written material paragraph by paragraph and don't forget the captions under the illustrations. For example, if a heading reads *Stream Erosion* put it in the form of a question (Why do streams erode? What is stream erosion?) then find the answer within the material. If you train your mind to think in this manner you will learn more and prepare yourself for answering test questions.

4. Play mind games. Using your brain for reading or puzzles keeps it flexible. Even with a limited amount of time your brain can take in data (much like a computer) and store it for later use. In ten minutes you can: read two paragraphs (at least), quiz yourself with flash cards, or review notes. Even if you don't fully understand something on the first pass, your mind stores it for recall, which is why frequent reading or review increases chances of retention and comprehension.

5. Get pointed in the right direction. Use arrows to point to important passages or pieces of information. It's easier to read than a page full of yellow highlights. Highlighting can be used sparingly, but add an arrow to the margin to call attention to it.

6. **The pen is mightier than the sword.** Learn to take great notes. A by-product of our modern culture is that we have grown accustomed to getting our information in short doses. We've subconsciously trained ourselves to assimilate information into neat little packages. Messy notes fragment the flow of information. Your notes can be much clearer with proper formatting. **_The Cornell Method_** is one such format. This method was popularized in *How to Study in College*, Ninth Edition, by Walter Pauk. You can benefit from the method without purchasing an additional book by simply looking up the method online. Below is a sample of how *The Cornell Method* can be adapted for use with this guide.

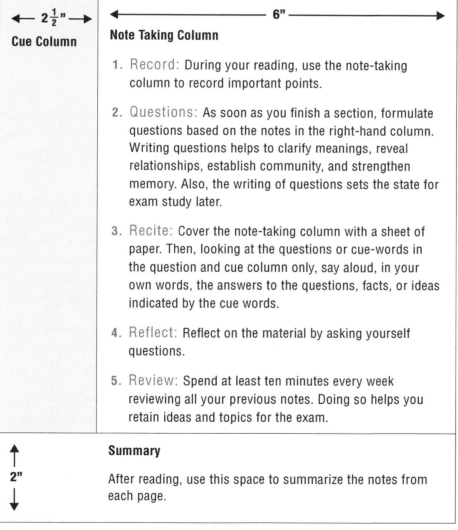

← 2½" →

Cue Column

← 6" →

Note Taking Column

1. Record: During your reading, use the note-taking column to record important points.

2. Questions: As soon as you finish a section, formulate questions based on the notes in the right-hand column. Writing questions helps to clarify meanings, reveal relationships, establish community, and strengthen memory. Also, the writing of questions sets the state for exam study later.

3. Recite: Cover the note-taking column with a sheet of paper. Then, looking at the questions or cue-words in the question and cue column only, say aloud, in your own words, the answers to the questions, facts, or ideas indicated by the cue words.

4. Reflect: Reflect on the material by asking yourself questions.

5. Review: Spend at least ten minutes every week reviewing all your previous notes. Doing so helps you retain ideas and topics for the exam.

↑ 2" ↓

Summary

After reading, use this space to summarize the notes from each page.

Adapted from How to Study in College, Ninth Edition, by Walter Pauk, ©2008 Wadsworth

The proctor will write the start time where it can be seen and then, later, provide the time remaining, typically fifteen minutes before the end of the test.

7. **Place yourself in exile and set the mood.** Set aside a particular place and time to study that best suits your personal needs and biorhythms. If you're a night person, burn the midnight oil. If you're a morning person set yourself up with some coffee and get to it. Make your study time and place as free from distraction as possible and surround yourself with what you need, be it silence or music. Studies have shown that music can aid in concentration, absorption, and retrieval of information. Not all music, though. Classical music is said to work best

8. **Check your budget.** You should at least review all the content material before your test, but allocate the most amount of time to the areas that need the most refreshing. It sounds obvious, but it's easy to forget. You can use the study rubric above to balance your study budget.

Testing Tips

1. **Get smart, play dumb.** Sometimes a question is just a question. No one is out to trick you, so don't assume that the test writer is looking for something other than what was asked. Stick to the question as written and don't overanalyze.

2. **Do a double take.** Read test questions and answer choices at least twice because it's easy to miss something, to transpose a word or some letters. If you have no idea what the correct answer is, skip it and come back later if there's time. If you're still clueless, it's okay to guess. Remember, you're scored on the number of questions you answer correctly and you're not penalized for wrong answers. The worst case scenario is that you miss a point from a good guess.

3. **Turn it on its ear.** The syntax of a question can often provide a clue, so make things interesting and turn the question into a statement to see if it changes the meaning or relates better (or worse) to the answer choices.

4. **Get out your magnifying glass.** Look for hidden clues in the questions because it's difficult to write a multiple-choice question without giving away part of the answer in the options presented. In most questions you can readily eliminate one or two potential answers, increasing your chances of answering correctly to 50/50, which will help out if you've skipped a question and gone back to it (see tip #2).

5. **Call it intuition.** Often your first instinct is correct. If you've been studying the content you've likely absorbed something and have subconsciously retained the knowledge. On questions you're not sure about trust your instincts because a first impression is usually correct.

6. **Graffiti.** Sometimes it's a good idea to mark your answers directly on the test booklet and go back to fill in the optical scan sheet later. You don't get extra points for perfectly blackened ovals. If you choose to manage your test this way, be sure not to mismark your answers when you transcribe to the scan sheet.

7. **Become a clock-watcher.** You have a set amount of time to answer the questions. Don't get bogged down laboring over a question you're not sure about when there are ten others you could answer more readily. If you choose to follow the advice of tip #6, be sure you leave time near the end to go back and fill in the scan sheet.

Do the Drill

No matter how prepared you feel it's sometimes a good idea to apply Murphy's Law. So the following tips might seem silly, mundane, or obvious, but we're including them anyway.

1. **Remember, you are what you eat, so bring a snack.** Choose from the list of energizing foods that appear earlier in the introduction.

2. **You're not too sexy for your test.** Wear comfortable clothes. You'll be distracted if your belt is too tight or if you're too cold or too hot.

3. **Lie to yourself.** Even if you think you're a prompt person, pretend you're not and leave plenty of time to get to the testing center. Map it out ahead of time and do a dry run if you have to. There's no need to add road rage to your list of anxieties.

4. **Bring sharp number 2 pencils.** It may seem impossible to forget this need from your school days, but you might. And make sure the erasers are intact, too.

5. **No ticket, no test.** Bring your admission ticket as well as **two** forms of identification, including one with a picture and signature. You will not be admitted to the test without these things.

6. **You can't take it with you.** Leave any study aids, dictionaries, notebooks, computers, and the like at home. Certain tests **do** allow a scientific or four-function calculator, so check ahead of time to see if your test does.

7. **Prepare for the desert.** Any time spent on a bathroom break **cannot** be made up later, so use your judgment on the amount you eat or drink.

8. Quiet, Please! Keeping your own time is a good idea, but not with a timepiece that has a loud ticker. If you use a watch, take it off and place it nearby but not so that it distracts you. And **silence your cell phone**.

To the best of our ability, we have compiled the content you need to know in this book and in the accompanying online resources. The rest is up to you. You can use the study and testing tips or you can follow your own methods. Either way, you can be confident that there aren't any missing pieces of information and there shouldn't be any surprises in the content on the test.

If you have questions about test fees, registration, electronic testing, or other content verification issues please visit *www.mtle.nesinc.com*.

Good luck!

Sharon Wynne
Founder, XAMonline

DOMAIN I
READING

PERSONALIZED STUDY PLAN

PERSONALIZED STUDY PLAN

KNOWN MATERIAL/ SKIP IT

PAGE	COMPETENCY AND SKILL	
	2.5: Demonstrating knowledge of formal and informal methods for assessing students' development in concepts of print, letter recognition, letter formation, and letter-sound correspondence	☐
	2.6: Applying knowledge of strategies to address the assessed needs of individual students in concepts of print, letter recognition, letter formation, and letter-sound correspondence	☐
29	**3: Understand the development of phonics and other word identification strategies, spelling, and fluency**	☐
	3.1: Demonstrating knowledge of basic concepts related to beginning literacy development and basic terminology used to describe common letter combinations and/or letter-sound relationships in English	☐
	3.2: Applying knowledge of research-based, explicit phonics instruction to promote students' accurate decoding and spelling of regular words of increasing complexity	☐
	3.3: Applying knowledge of research-based, explicit instruction in sight words, common inflectional morphemes, and related orthographic guidelines to promote students' accurate decoding and spelling of irregular and/or inflected words	☐
	3.4: Applying knowledge of research-based, explicit instruction in regular, open and closed syllable patterns and syllabication guidelines; structural analysis skills; and orthographic patterns	☐
	3.5: Demonstrating knowledge of key indicators of reading fluency, common factors that disrupt fluency, and research-based, explicit instruction to promote fluency at all stages of reading development	☐
	3.6: Applying knowledge of the use of appropriate texts and effective, engaging reading and writing activities to motivate and reinforce students' development of phonics and other word identification skills, spelling, and fluency	☐
	3.7: Demonstrating knowledge of formal and informal methods for assessing students' development in phonics and other word identification skills, spelling, and fluency and demonstrating ability to interpret and use the results of these assessments to plan effective instruction in decoding, spelling, and fluency	☐
	3.8: Applying knowledge of strategies to address the assessed needs of individual students in phonics and other word identification skills, spelling, and fluency at all stages of literacy development	☐

PERSONALIZED STUDY PLAN

KNOWN MATERIAL/ SKIP IT

PAGE	COMPETENCY AND SKILL	
46	**4:** **Understand vocabulary development**	☐
	4.1: Demonstrating awareness of the critical role vocabulary plays in reading and the importance of engaging students in early and continual language experiences to promote their vocabulary development	☐
	4.2: Applying knowledge of components of effective vocabulary instruction and criteria for selecting words for vocabulary instruction	☐
	4.3: Applying knowledge of research-based, explicit instruction in independent strategies for building vocabulary and for determining the meaning and pronunciation of unfamiliar or multiple-meaning words encountered through listening and reading	☐
	4.4: Applying knowledge of research-based, explicit instruction in words and their meanings, including the etymology of words, idiomatic expressions, and foreign words and expressions used in English	☐
	4.5: Applying knowledge of the use of appropriate texts and effective, engaging oral language, reading, and writing activities to motivate, augment, and reinforce students' development of robust listening, speaking, reading, and writing vocabularies	☐
	4.6: Demonstrating knowledge of formal and informal methods for assessing students' vocabulary development and demonstrating the ability to interpret and use the results of these assessments to plan effective instruction in vocabulary development	☐
	4.7: Applying knowledge of strategies to address the assessed needs of individual students in vocabulary development	☐
58	**5:** **Understand reading comprehension and development of comprehension strategies and independent reading**	☐
	5.1: Demonstrating knowledge of how proficient readers read, different levels of reading comprehension, and factors that affect reading comprehension	☐
	5.2: Applying knowledge of research-based, explicit instruction in comprehension strategies that students can use to enhance their own comprehension of texts and promote their independence and self-efficacy as readers	☐
	5.3: Applying knowledge of the use of appropriate texts and effective, engaging oral language, reading, and writing activities to facilitate students' comprehension of texts	☐
	5.4: Demonstrating knowledge of the role of independent reading in literacy development and explicit strategies for promoting and motivating students' independent and at-home reading	☐
	5.5: Demonstrating knowledge of formal and informal methods for assessing students' development in reading comprehension and demonstrating the ability to interpret and use the results of these assessments to plan effective comprehension instruction	☐

PERSONALIZED STUDY PLAN

PAGE	COMPETENCY AND SKILL	KNOWN MATERIAL/ SKIP IT
	5.6: Demonstrating knowledge of strategies for determining students' independent, instructional, and frustration reading levels and for using this information to help select appropriate texts for instruction and guide students' independent reading	☐
	5.7: Applying knowledge of strategies to address the assessed needs of individual students in reading comprehension, comprehension strategies, and independent reading	☐
78	**6: Understand different types of texts and strategies for understanding, analyzing, and responding to them**	☐
	6.1: Demonstrating knowledge of children's and young adolescents' literature representing a range of genres, eras, perspectives, and cultures	☐
	6.2: Applying knowledge of explicit instruction in literary response and analysis skills	☐
	6.3: Demonstrating knowledge of various types of informational/expository texts, including key textual features, graphic features, and organizational structures of these texts	☐
	6.4: Applying knowledge of explicit instruction in analysis and response skills for informational/expository texts	☐
	6.5: Applying knowledge of the use of appropriate texts and effective, engaging oral language, reading, and writing activities	☐
	6.6: Demonstrating knowledge of formal and informal methods for assessing students' understanding and analysis of and response to literary/narrative and informational/expository texts	☐
	6.7: Applying knowledge of strategies to address the assessed needs of individual students in literary response and analysis and content-area literacy skills	☐

PERSONALIZED STUDY PLAN

KNOWN MATERIAL/ SKIP IT

PAGE	COMPETENCY AND SKILL	
100	**7: Understand academic language development, including English language structures and conventions**	☐
	7.1: Demonstrating basic knowledge of English language structures and conventions	☐
	7.2: Demonstrating knowledge of strategies for enhancing literacy skills by helping students make connections between oral language and reading and writing	☐
	7.3: Demonstrating knowledge of how to provide explicit instruction and guided practice in language structures and conventions using a range of approaches and motivating activities	☐
	7.4: Demonstrating knowledge of the use of appropriate texts and effective, engaging oral language, reading, and writing activities to facilitate students' ability to interpret and apply English grammar and language conventions	☐
	7.5: Demonstrating knowledge of formal and informal methods for assessing students' academic language development and their understanding and use of English language structures and conventions	☐
	7.6: Applying knowledge of strategies to address the assessed needs of individual students in academic language development	☐

COMPETENCY 1

UNDERSTAND ORAL LANGUAGE FOUNDATIONS OF LITERACY DEVELOPMENT IN ENGLISH, INCLUDING PHONOLOGICAL AND PHONEMIC AWARENESS

> **SKILL 1.1** **Demonstrating knowledge of developmental stages of language, including interrelationships between oral language development and literacy development, and applying knowledge of strategies for promoting students' oral language development** *(e.g., oral vocabulary, listening comprehension skills)* **to support their literacy development**

Development of Oral Language

Oral language begins to develop during the earliest vocal interactions infants experience with their caregivers, and it is an ongoing process. Throughout their youngest years, children observe oral communication in their home, their schools, and their interactions with others. During the preschool years, children acquire cognitive skills in oral language that they later apply to reading comprehension. Reading aloud to young children is one of the most important things that an adult can do because adults are teaching them how to monitor, question, predict, and confirm what they hear in the stories.

Oral language is said to develop in three stages: protolinguistic, transition, and language. Around the time a child learns to crawl, the child is often also in the protolinguistic phase of oral development, which includes baby noises, physical movements, and interactions with others. In the transition phase (around the time the child begins to walk), the child begins to move beyond baby language in order to mimic words and sounds in the child's native tongue. In the final stage, language, the child is able to communicate about shared experiences with another. At this point children are aware that there is more in the world than just what they experience, and they can begin to use language to learn about and share the experiences of others.

Reid (1988) described four metalinguistic abilities that young children acquire through early involvement in reading activities:

1. Word consciousness: Children who have access to books can tell the story through the pictures before they can read. Gradually, they begin to realize the connection between the spoken words and the printed words. The beginning of letter and word discrimination begins in the early years.

> Reading aloud to young children is one of the most important things that an adult can do.

> Once children reach the language phase, they can begin to see how language, in all of its forms, plays a role in the world around them.

2. Language and conventions of print: During this stage children learn how to hold a book, where to begin to read, the left-to-right motion, and how to continue from one line to another.

3. Functions of print: Children discover that print can be used for a variety of purposes and functions, including entertainment and information.

4. Fluency: Through listening to adult models, children learn to read in phrases and use intonation.

SKILL 1.2 Demonstrating knowledge of phonological awareness and research-based, explicit instruction in phonological awareness skills *(e.g., detecting and identifying word boundaries, syllables, rhyming words, onset/rime)*

PHONICS: the connection between the sounds and letters on a page

As opposed to phonemic awareness, the study of **PHONICS** must be done with the eyes open. It is the connection between the sounds and letters on a page. In other words, students learning phonics might see the word "bad" and sound each letter out slowly until they recognize that they just said the word.

Phonological Awareness

PHONOLOGICAL AWARENESS: the ability of the reader to recognize the sounds of spoken language

PHONOLOGICAL AWARENESS means the ability of the reader to recognize the sounds of spoken language. This recognition includes how these sounds can be blended together, segmented (divided up), and manipulated (switched around). This type of awareness then leads to phonics, which is a method for teaching children to read. It helps them to "sound out words."

Development of phonological skills may begin during the pre-K years. Indeed, by the age of five, a child who has been exposed to rhyme can typically recognize another rhyme.

Development of phonological skills may begin during the pre-K years. Indeed, by the age of five, a child who has been exposed to rhyme can typically recognize another rhyme. Such a child can demonstrate phonological awareness by filling in the missing rhyming word in a familiar rhyme or rhymed picture book. It isn't unheard of for children to surprise their parents by filling in missing rhymes in a familiar nursery rhyme book at the age of four or even earlier.

Children are taught phonological awareness when they are taught the sounds made by the letters, the sounds made by various combinations of letters, and the ability to recognize individual sounds in words.

Skills and Strategies with Phonological Awareness

Phonological awareness skills include:

- Rhyming and syllabification

- Blending sounds into words (such as pic-tur-bo-k)

- Identifying the beginning or starting sounds of words and the ending or closing sounds of words

- Breaking words down into sounds (also called "segmenting" words)

- Recognizing small words contained in bigger words by removing starting sounds (hear to ear)

Phonics also involves the spelling of words. Effective spelling strategies should emphasize these principles:

- Knowledge of patterns, sounds, letter-sound association, and syllables

- Memorizing sight words

- Writing those words correctly many times

- Writing the words in personal writing

SKILL 1.3 Demonstrating knowledge of phonemic awareness and research-based, explicit instruction in phonemic awareness skills (e.g., recognizing that words are made up of separate phonemes; distinguishing initial, medial, and final phonemes; orally blending, segmenting, deleting, and substituting phonemes)

Theorist Marilyn Jager Adams, who researches early reading, has outlined five basic types of phonemic awareness tasks.

The five types of phonemic awareness are:

Task 1: Ability to hear rhymes and alliteration. Children would listen to a poem, rhyming picture book or song and identify the rhyming words hear, while the teacher records or lists them on an experiential chart.

Task 2: Ability to do oddity tasks (recognize the member of a set that is different [odd] among the group.) The children would look at the pictures of (a blade of) grass, a garden and a rose and be able to tell which starts with a different sound.

Task 3: **The ability to orally blend words and split syllables.** The children can say the first sound of a word and then the rest of the word and put it together as a single word.

Task 4: **The ability to orally segment words.** This is the ability to count sounds. The children would be asked as a group to count the sounds in "hamburger."

Task 5: **The ability to do phonics manipulation tasks.** The children would replace the "r" sound in rose with a "p" sound to get the word "pose."

Instructional methods that may be effective for teaching phonemic awareness can include:

- Clapping syllables in words

- Distinguishing between a word and a sound

- Using visual cues and movements to help children understand when the speaker goes from one sound to another

- Oral segmentation activities that focus on easily distinguished syllables rather than sounds

- Singing familiar songs (e.g., Happy Birthday, Knick Knack Paddy Wack) and replacing key words in the song with words having a different ending or middle sound (oral segmentation)

- Dealing children a deck of picture cards and having them sound out the words for the pictures on their cards or calling for a picture by asking for its first and second sound.

APPLIED EXAMPLES OF COMMON PHONEMES:			
Phoneme	**Uses**	**Phoneme**	**Uses**
/A/	a (table), a_e (bake), ai (train), ay (say)	/t/	t (time)
/a/	a (flat)	/U/	u (future), u_e (use), ew (few)
/b/	b (ball)	/u/	u (thumb), a (about)
/k/	c (cake), k (Key), ck (back)	/v/	v (voice)

Table continued on next page

Phoneme	Uses	Phoneme	Uses
/d/	d (door)	/w/	w (wash)
/E/	e (me), ee (feet), ea (leap), y (baby)	/gz/	x (exam)
/e/	e (pet), ea (head)	/ks/	x (box)
/f/	f (fix), ph (phone)	/y/	y (yes)
/g/	g (gas)	/z/	z (zoo), s (nose)
/h/	h (hot)	/OO/	oo (boot), u (truth), u_e (rude), ew (chew)
/I/	i (I), i_e (bite), igh (light), y (sky)	/oo/	oo (book), u (put)
/i/	i (sit)	/oi/	oi (soil), oy (toy)
/j/	j (jet), dge (edge), g (gem)	/ou/	ou (out), ow (cow)
/l/	l (lamp)	/aw/	aw (saw), au (caught), al (tall)
/m/	m (map)	/ar/	ar (car)
/n/	n (no), kn (knock)	/sh/	sh (ship), ti (nation), ci (special)
/O/	o (okay), o_e (bone), oa (soap), ow (low)	/hw/	wh (white)
/o/	o (hot)	/ch/	ch (chest), tch (catch)
/p/	p (pie)	/th/	th (thick)
/kw/	qu (quick)	/th/	th (this)
/r/	r (road), wr (wrong), er (her), ir (sir), ur (fur)	/ng/	ng (sing)
/s/	s (say), c (cent)	/zh/	s (measure)

Other Aspects of Language

Choice of the medium through which the message is delivered to the receiver is a significant factor in controlling language. Spoken language relies as much on the gestures, facial expression, and tone of voice of the speaker as on the spoken words. Slapstick comics can evoke laughter without speaking a word. Young children use body language overtly and older children more subtly to convey messages. These refinings of body language are paralleled by an ability to recognize and apply the nuances of spoken language. To work strictly with written work, the writer must use words to imply the body language.

By the time children begin to speak, they have begun to acquire the ability to use language to inform and manipulate. They have already used kinesthetic and verbal cues to attract attention when they seek some physical or emotional gratification. Children learn to apply names to objects and actions. They learn to use language to describe the persons and events in their lives and to express their feelings about the world around them.

Choice of the medium through which the message is delivered to the receiver is a significant factor in controlling language.

For further information on teaching phonemic awareness:

www.ldonline.org/article/6254

> **SKILL 1.4** Applying knowledge of the use of appropriate materials and effective, engaging oral language and writing activities to motivate and reinforce students' development in oral language, phonological awareness, and phonemic awareness and to help them make connections between oral language and reading and writing

Motivation

Readiness for subject-area learning is dependent not only on prior knowledge but also on affective factors such as interest, motivation, and attitude. These factors are often more influential on student learning than the preexisting cognitive base.

Self-motivation is the best tool for learning. Children need to challenge themselves through constant exploration and experimentation. Activities should suit the developmental age of the child so that she can perform them with minimal outside assistance. An adult should act as an assistant who provides help only when it is required.

Self-motivation is the best tool for learning. Children need to challenge themselves through constant exploration and experimentation.

Strategies for promoting awareness of the relationship between spoken and written language

- Write down what the children are saying on a chart.

- Highlight and celebrate the meanings and uses of print products found in the classroom. These products include: posters, labels, yellow sticky-pad notes, labels on shelves and lockers, calendars, rule signs, and directions.

- Read big-print and oversized books to children to teach print conventions such as directionality.

- Use practice exercises in reading to others (for K-1/2), where young children practice how to handle a book, how to turn pages, how to find tops and bottoms of pages, and how to tell the difference between the front and back covers of a book.

- Create search-and-discuss adventures in word awareness and close observation where children are challenged to identify and talk about the length, appearance, and boundaries of specific words and the letters that make them up.

- Have children match oral words to printed words by forming an echo chorus. As the teacher reads the story aloud, children echo the reading. Often this works best with poetry or rhymes.

- Have the children combine, manipulate, switch, and move letters around to change words and spelling patterns.

- Work with letter cards to create messages and respond to the messages that the children create.

Methods used to teach these skills are often featured in a "balanced literacy" curriculum that focuses on the use of skills in various instructional contexts. For example, with independent reading, students independently choose books that are at their reading levels; with guided reading, teachers work with small groups of students to help them with their particular reading problems; with whole-group reading, the entire class reads the same text, and the teacher incorporates activities to help students learn phonics, comprehension, fluency, and vocabulary. In addition to these components of balanced literacy, teachers incorporate writing so students can learn the structures of communicating through text.

> SKILL 1.5 **Demonstrating knowledge of formal and informal methods for assessing students' development in oral language, phonological awareness, and phonemic awareness and demonstrating ability to interpret and use the results of these assessments to plan effective instruction in these areas**

Phonemic Awareness

Phonemic awareness is a critical skill for beginning readers. PHONEMIC AWARENESS involves the understanding that language is made up of sounds and that these sounds can be manipulated to make different words. Often, phonemic awareness skills are described as skills that can be demonstrated in the dark. They are described this way because there is no visual component to them. They are in fact, all oral and auditory in nature.

> **STYLE:** involves the understanding that language is made up of sounds and that these sounds can be manipulated to make different words

Different Phonemic Awareness Skills

Rhyming

The assessment of phonemic awareness skills begins with very young children, even preschool-aged children. One of the earliest phonemic awareness skills is rhyming. Rhyming involves the understanding that words sound the same (cat and hat rhyme but cat and dog do not rhyme because they do not have the same ending sound). To assess this skill teachers use multiple methods. One method is to present the child with two words and have the child identify with a yes or no whether they rhyme. Another method of assessing rhyming skills is to present the child with a word and have him/her produce a word that rhymes with the word presented.

> *The assessment of phonemic awareness skills begins with very young children, even preschool-aged children.*

Following rhyming in the hierarchy of phonemic awareness skills would be segmenting words into syllables (to-mor-ow), onset and rhyme (/c/ /at/), or individual sounds (/d/ /o/ /g/). Teachers assess these skills by asking the students to orally segment to the level they want presented words.

Beginning word sounds

Another phonemic awareness skill involves beginning sounds of words. In this skill, teachers can show a picture or say a word and have the students identify the sound that is said at the beginning of the word/picture. For example, the word fish begins with the sound /f/. This skill can become more complicated when teachers ask the students to make substitutions or deletions of beginning sounds. For example, change the /f/ sound in fish to a /d/ and what new word do you have? The answer would be dish. This is an example of a way to assess the substitution of beginning sounds. The same can be done for deletion. For example, what do you have left if you remove the /d/ sound from drug? The answer would be rug.

Substitutions and deletions are more complex skills within the realm of phonemic awareness. They require the students to manipulate sounds within words and require higher level thinking about phonemic awareness activities. In complexity, it is typically easier for students to make substitutions before they are able to make deletions. Additionally, it is usually less complicated for students to make substitutions and deletions at the beginning or end of a word before they are able to demonstrate this skill in the middle of a word.

How to Assess Phonemic Awareness

In conclusion, the assessment of phonemic awareness skills is almost always an individual oral task. It can be completed in a short period of time and requires no materials other than a record sheet for the teacher. Students with articulation difficulties might need accommodations or support from a speech and language professional in order to have their phonemic awareness skills adequately measured.

> *The assessment of phonemic awareness skills is almost always an individual oral task. It can be completed in a short period of time and requires no materials other than a record sheet for the teacher.*

Phonics

PHONICS is the connection between the sounds of language and the letters. In contradiction to phonemic awareness, phonics requires the student to be able to recognize the sound and match it to the correct letter or group of letters that make that sound. Phonics skills help students to be able to sound out unknown words using the sound symbol correspondence.

> **PHONICS:** the connection between the sounds of language and the letters

Phonics Skills

Phonics skills begin with direct sound to one letter correspondence. For example, recognizing that the sound /d/ is made by the letter d and applying that to reading opportunities. Teachers can assess these skills by having the students write the letters that specific sounds make. Another method for assessing this type of skill would be to show the students pictures and have the students write the first letter of the picture or see if the students are able to write all of the sounds they hear in a word.

Beginning readers and writers will often write words with incorrect spellings because in many English words not all letters needed to spell a word correctly produce a sound that can be heard in the word. For example, the word "team" has four letters to spell it correctly, but only three sounds are heard.

How to assess phonics skills

Assessment of phonics skills can also be completed by watching how students use the skills in the context of reading words in stories. Teachers can take informal notes as to the sounds the student is applying correctly and those that they are not applying to help plan future instruction. This type of formative assessment is critical to help students make continuous progress with their reading skills.

In addition to the informal process of assessing students' phonics use, more formalized approaches can be used. This might be a test which multiple choice questions (i.e., which of the following words is spelled correctly cat or kat?; which two letters combine to make the long a sound? Ay, ao, ab, etc.) or pictures where students are required to label the specific letters that make the sounds of the picture.

Any phonics assessment needs to combine the sounds that make up words with the letters that are used to represent those sounds.

Any phonics assessment needs to combine the sounds that make up words with the letters that are used to represent those sounds. Phonics assessments do not need to be done individually, but certainly can be. Teachers can find many phonics assessments available through commercial companies or Internet sources, or they can create their own assessments specific to the goals and objectives they are teaching their students. Whether formal or informal, phonics skills are important skills for teachers and students alike to consider as a regular component of beginning reading instruction.

> **SKILL 1.6** **Applying knowledge of strategies** (*e.g., differentiated instruction, interventions, enrichment*) **to address the assessed needs of individual students** (*e.g., English language learners, struggling readers through highly proficient readers*) **in oral language, phonological awareness, and phonemic awareness, including recognizing when English phonemes differ from those of other languages and need to be taught explicitly**

Literacy refers to oral language, reading, and writing activities, all of which are intertwined. Emergent literacy is the concept that young children are emerging into reading and writing with no real ending or beginning point. This stage of reading development occurs when the reader understands that print contains a consistent message. Reading to children strengthens oral language and introduces them to various forms of discourse such as stories, fairy tales, and poetry. Reading signs, labels, or thank-you notes helps them understand relationships between oral and written language and emphasizes meaning.

The approach for many emergent readers focuses on the idea that children develop their ability to construct meaning by sharing books they care about with responsive peers and adults. Some characteristics of emerging readers include:

- The reader can attend to left-to-right directionality and features of print.

- The reader can identify some initial sounds and ending sounds in words.

- The reader can recognize some high-frequency words, names, and simple words in context.

- The reader can use pictures to predict meaning.

Children develop their ability to construct meaning by sharing books they care about with responsive peers and adults.

Common Difficulties For Emergent Readers

As young students enter and work through this stage of literacy, the teacher may notice some common difficulties:

- Difficulty in processing information

- Frustration with not being able to understand the text

- Problems with word recognition

- Limited vocabulary hindering comprehension

- Poor visual-motor integration

- Printing difficulties

Strategies for Working with Emergent Readers

Sometimes young students experiencing emergent literacy difficulties do not like being read to because they cannot process all of the information at once. In these cases, parents and teachers should read the pictures and reduce the language level so that the child comprehends the text. The extensive reading of pictures can build vocabulary acquisition, descriptive language, and the basis for simple narratives.

In order to strengthen whole-word recognition, teachers and parents can read to children and ask them to find letters or words that look the same. For an independent activity, students can cut out a page from an old magazine and then circle the words that look the same. Teachers might also highlight a high-frequency word such as *the*, and ask the student to find other words that look the same.

Early writing is also an important part of emergent literacy. Many preschoolers enjoy pretend writing, which is an important part of literacy development. Invented spelling is also encouraged as a part of meaningful writing and is an essential step in developmental spelling. The student is beginning to identify certain sounds and associating them with letters.

From a single action picture (e.g., a child eating a bowl of cereal), a teacher can ask countless questions about the bowl, the cereal, how the cereal might taste, the kinds of cereal the child likes or does not like, as well as simple inferential questions.

The typical variation in literacy backgrounds that children bring to reading can make teaching more difficult. Often a teacher has to choose between focusing on the learning needs of a few students at the expense of the group and focusing on the group at the risk of leaving some students behind academically.

However, many young children with emergent learning difficulties may have problems with visual-motor integration. In this case, teachers may purchase or make templates (stencils) from cardboard so the child can trace inside the boundaries, making basic shapes and simple outlines of figures such as an apple, a kite, or a fish. Parents and teachers can also assist by having children draw figures in sand, make designs with finger paint, etc. Still, some young children may not be able to grasp a pencil or draw even the simplest figures. In these cases, an occupational therapist or specialist in learning disabilities may be needed.

For students experiencing problems with concentration, make sure their desks are away from distractions and that their overall learning environment is comfortable and well lit. Try to encourage the student to work for set amounts of time and, as the student's concentration improves, increase the amounts of time. To help students to select appropriate reading material, it is often helpful to organize your classroom library by level. For example, simpler texts can be labeled with a yellow dot, grade-level texts can be labeled with a red dot, and challenging texts can be labeled with a green dot. This helps students see which books may best suit their comfortable reading needs.

The teacher needs to have an extensive classroom library of books.

Books can be considered one of three levels for each student: easy, just right, or challenging. Students should be encouraged to read mostly books that are a "just right" fit for them. Matching young children with "just right" books fosters their reading independently, no matter how young they are. Books with which emergent readers and early readers can be matched should have fairly large print, appropriate spacing (so the reader can easily see where a word begins and ends), and few words on each page so the young reader can focus on the all-important concerns of top-to-bottom, left-to-right, directionality, and the one-to-one match of spoken word to print.

Students should be permitted to read easy books once in a while, as well as receive support in reading challenging books from time to time. In a reading log or journal, students can record titles of books they've read and the level of the books. This way, teachers can monitor the reading to ensure that a student is meeting individual reading needs.

When students become frustrated and feel they don't understand the text, encourage them to break down the text into chunks. Then, after each chunk, encourage the students to ask themselves questions about what they have read to improve understanding.

Limited vocabulary can often get in the way of a student's comprehension of a text. Have students focus on the structure of words to help decode unfamiliar words. A helpful tip is for students to record new words in a notebook to create a personal glossary. This way, students can refer to a dictionary with their list of words when necessary to help build their vocabulary.

Additional Strategies

Reading aloud to children helps them acquire information and skills such as the meaning of words, how a book works, a variety of writing styles, information about their world, differences between conversations and written language, and the knowledge of printed letters and words along with the relationship between sound and print. Using different types of books assures that all children will find at least a few books that meet their interests and preferences.

Children's storybooks are traditional favorites for many young students. Some children may prefer books that have informational text, such as books about animals, nature, transportation, careers, or travel. Alphabet books, picture dictionaries, and books with diagrams and overlays (such as those about the human body) catch the interest of children as well. Some children particularly enjoy books containing poetry, children's songs and verses, or folktales. Offering different types of books also gives flexibility in choosing one or two languages in which to read a story.

Illustrations for young children should support the meaning of the text and language patterns, and predictable text structures should make these texts appealing to them.

The content of the story should relate to the children's interests and experiences. The story should include lots of monosyllabic and rhyming words. Finally, children, particularly emergent and beginning early readers, benefit from reading books with partners. The partners sit side by side and each one takes turns reading the entire text. Only after all of these considerations have been addressed can the teacher select "just right" books from an already-leveled bin or list.

Children with Special Needs

Introducing language and literacy experiences through concrete, multisensory approaches will provide many children with disabilities with the supports they need to build the necessary foundation for decoding words and understanding meaning. Having access to early literacy activities as part of the curriculum is key to the educational success of all children, including children with mild to severe disabilities. Each child's unique learning needs should be considered in a comprehensive approach to early literacy.

See also Skill 2.6

COMPETENCY 2
UNDERSTAND THE DEVELOPMENT OF CONCEPTS OF PRINT, LETTER RECOGNITION, LETTER FORMATION, AND LETTER-SOUND CORRESPONDENCE

> **SKILL 2.1** Demonstrating knowledge of basic concepts of print and strategies for promoting students' development of concepts of print

EMERGENT LITERACY:
a child's speech and language development

EMERGENT LITERACY refers to a child's speech and language development. It begins at birth and continues into the preschool years, during which time the child learns how to use and understand language in order to communicate. In the school-age years, emergent literacy refers to the way the spoken language relates to reading and writing for the child.

The Concepts of Print

Understanding that print carries meaning is demonstrated every day in the elementary classroom as the teacher holds up a selected book to read it aloud to the class. The teachers explicitly and deliberately think aloud about how to hold the book, how to focus the class on looking at its cover, where to start reading, and in what direction to begin.

Even in writing the morning message on the board, the teacher targets the children on the placement of the message and its proper place at the top of the board to be followed by additional activities and a schedule for the rest of the day.

When a teacher challenges children to make letter posters of a single letter and the items in the classroom, their home, or their knowledge base that start with that letter, the children are making concrete the understanding that print carries meaning.

Teachers should look for five basic behaviors in students:

Do students know how to hold the book?

2. Can students match speech to print?

3. Do students know the difference between letters and words?

4. Do students know that print conveys meaning?

5. Can students track print from left to right?

In order for students to understand concepts of print, they must be able to recognize text and understand the various mechanics that text contains. These include:

- All text contains a message.

- The English language has a specific structure.

- In order to decode words and read text, students must be able to understand that structure.

The structure of the English language consists of rules of grammar, capitalization, and punctuation. For younger children, this means being able to recognize letters and form words. For older children, it means being able to recognize different types of text, such as lists, stories, and signs, and knowing the purpose of each one.

> The structure of the English language consists of rules of grammar, capitalization, and punctuation.

When reading to children, teachers point to words as they read them. Illustrations and pictures also contribute to being able to understand the meaning of the text. Therefore, teachers should also discuss illustrations related to the text. Teachers also discuss the common characteristics of books, such as the author, title page, and table of contents. Asking students to predict what the story might be about is a good strategy to help teach students about the cover and its importance to the story. Pocket charts, big books, and song charts provide ample opportunity for teachers to point to words as they read.

Instructional Strategies

Using Big Books in the Classroom	Gather the children around you in a group with the big book placed on a stand. This allows all children to see the words and pictures. As you read, point to each word. It is best to use a pointer so that you are not covering any other words or part of the page. When students read from the big book on their own, have them also use the pointer for each word. When students begin reading from smaller books, have them transfer what they have learned about pointing to the words by using their finger to track the reading. Observation is a key point in assessing students' ability to track words and speech.

Continued on next page

A Classroom Rich in Print	Having words from a familiar rhyme or poem in a pocket chart lends itself to an activity where the students arrange the words in the correct order and then read the rhyme. This is an instructional strategy that reinforces directionality of print. It also reinforces punctuation, capitalization, and matching print to speech.
	Using highlighters or sticky tabs to locate upper and lower case letters or specific words can help students isolate words and learn about the structure of language they need to have for reading.
	There should be plenty of books in the classroom for children to read on their own or in small groups. As you observe each of these groups, take note of how the child holds the book in addition to how he or she tracks and reads the words.
Word Wall	A word wall is a great teaching tool for words in isolation and for writing. Each of the letters of the alphabet is displayed with words that begin with that letter under each one. Students are able to find the letter on the wall and read the words under each one.
Sounds of the Letters	In addition to teaching the letter names, students should learn the corresponding sound of each letter. This is a key feature of decoding when beginning to read. The use of rhyming words is an effective way to teach letter sounds so that children have a solid background.

Students should be exposed to daily opportunities for viewing and reading texts. Teachers can do this by engaging the students in discussions about books during shared, guided, and independent reading times. The teacher should draw the students' attention to the conventions of print and discuss with them the reasons for choosing different books. For example, teachers should let the students know that it is perfectly acceptable to return a book and select another if they think it is too hard for them.

Predictable books help engage the students in reading. Once the students realize what words are repeated in the text, they will eagerly chime in to repeat the words at the appropriate time during the reading. Rereading of texts helps the students learn the words and helps them to read these lines fluently.

Some things for teachers to observe during reading:

- Students' responses during reading conferences, such as pointing to letters or words

- Students' knowledge about where they should begin reading and how to stop or pause depending on the punctuation

- Students' behavior when holding a book (e.g., holding the book right side up or upside down, reading from left to right, stopping to look at the pictures to confirm meaning)

Sites with information on using word walls:

www.teachingfirst.net /wordwallact.htm

www.theschoolbell.com /Links/word_walls/words .html

SKILL 2.2 Demonstrating knowledge of the development of uppercase and lowercase letter recognition and letter formation skills and research-based, explicit instruction in letter recognition and letter formation

Letter recognition is an essential part of literacy development and the basis for many reading skills. It is often included as part of phonological awareness as children are learning the basics about both spoken and written language. Teachers of young children need to insure that all students have exposure to specific activities for learning upper- and lowercase letters.

These are some of the many strategies that can be used to facilitate letter recognition:

- Creating personalized ABC books

- Playing the letter-a-day game, where many activities are linked to a specific letter

- Matching letters to children's first and last names

- Making an alphabet zoo by drawing pictures or cutting out pictures of animals that start with specific letters

- Letter-matching games, linking upper-and lowercase letters

- Hidden letter worksheets, focusing on one letter at a time

- Using computer-based activities focusing on letter recognition

See also Skill 2.1

SKILL 2.3 Demonstrating knowledge of the alphabetic principle and the nature of letter-sound relationships in English and research-based, explicit instruction in letter-sound correspondence

The alphabetic principle is sometimes called graphophonemic awareness. This multisyllabic technical reading foundation term details the theory that written words are composed of patterns of letters that represent the sounds of spoken words.

Because the English language is dependent on the alphabet, being able to recognize and sound out letters is the first step for beginning readers. Relying simply

There are basically two parts to the alphabetic principle:

- *An understanding that words are made up of letters and that each of these letters has a specific sound.*

- *The correspondence between sounds and letters leads to phonological reading. This consists of reading regular and irregular words and doing advanced analysis of words.*

on memorization of words is just not feasible as a way for children to learn to recognize words. Therefore, decoding is essential. The most important goal of beginning reading teachers is to teach students to decode text so that they can read fluently and with understanding.

There are four basic features of the alphabetic principle:

Students need to be able to take spoken words apart and blend different sounds together to make new words.

2. Students need to apply letter sounds to all their reading.

3. Teachers need to use a systematic effective program in order to teach children to read.

4. The teaching of the alphabetic principle usually begins in kindergarten.

It is important to keep in mind that some children already know the letters and sounds before they come to school. Others may catch on to this quickly and still others need to have one-on-one instruction in order to learn to read.

> *Critical skills that students need to learn are:*
> - *Letter–sound correspondence*
> - *How to sound out words*
> - *How to decode text to make meaning*

> SKILL 2.4 **Applying knowledge of the use of appropriate materials; effective, engaging oral language and writing activities; and multisensory techniques to motivate and reinforce students' development of concepts of print, uppercase and lowercase letter recognition and formation, and letter-sound correspondence**

Materials and Techniques

A "Tale Trail" game

Use a story they have already heard or read. Ask the children to circle certain letters and then reread the story, sharing the letters they have circled. Give the children plenty of opportunities to do letter sorts. Pass out word cards that have the targeted letter on them. Ask the children to come up and display their answers to questions about the letter. As an example, consider the letter "*R*."

> - *R as the first letter—rose, rise, ran*
> - *R as the last letter—car, star, far*
> - *R with a t after it—start, heart, part, smart*
> - *Two Rs in the middle of a word—carry, sorry, starry*

"What's in a Name?"

Select a student's name—for example, William. Write the name on a sentence strip. Have the children count the number of letters in the name and how many of the letters appear twice. Allow them to talk about which letter is uppercase and which letters are lowercase. Have the students chant the name. Then rewrite the name on another sentence strip. Have the strip cut into separate letters, and see if someone from the class can put the name back together correctly.

Single-letter books

Provide children with a sample of a single-letter book (or create one from newspapers, coupons, circulars, magazines, or your own text ideas). Make sure that your selected or created sample includes a printed version of the letter in both upper- and lowercase forms. Make certain that each page contains a picture of something that starts with that specific letter and also has the word for the picture. The book that you select or create should be a predictable one, so that when the picture is identified, the word can be read.

Multi-sensory activities with read-alouds

As you read a book along with or to the children, ask them to show you specific letters, or lowercase or uppercase letters. Read the text first, and encourage as many children as possible to come up and identify the letters. Use a big book and have felt letters available for display as well. If this exercise is grade-, age-, and developmentally appropriate, have the children themselves write the letter they identified.

For even more fun creating letters, make them out of pipe cleaners, craft sticks, or colored markers, using different colors for upper- and lowercase letters.

"Letter Leap"

Have the children look carefully around the room to identify labeled items that begin with a specific letter by "leaping" over to them and placing a large lettered placard next to them. Children who have advanced in letter formation can then be challenged to "leap" through the classroom when called upon to "letter" unlabeled objects.

SKILL 2.5 **Demonstrating knowledge of formal and informal methods for assessing students' development in concepts of print, letter recognition, letter formation, and letter-sound correspondence and demonstrating ability to interpret and use the results of these assessments to plan effective instruction in these areas**

See also Skill 1.5

> **SKILL 2.6** **Applying knowledge of strategies** *(e.g., differentiated instruction, interventions, enrichment)* **to address the assessed needs of individual students** *(e.g., English language learners, struggling readers through highly proficient readers)* **in concepts of print, letter recognition, letter formation, and letter-sound correspondence, including recognizing basic ways in which the writing systems of other languages may differ from English and the importance of helping English language learners transfer relevant skills from their home language to English**

Second Language Learners

Any student who is not in an environment where English phonology operates may have difficulty perceiving and demonstrating the differences between English language phonemes.

Students who are raised in homes where English is not the first language and/or where standard English is not spoken, may have difficulty with hearing the difference between similar sounding words like "send" and "sent." Any student who is not in an environment where English phonology operates may have difficulty perceiving and demonstrating the differences between English language phonemes. If students cannot hear the difference between words that sound the same like "grow" and "glow," they will be confused when these words appear in a print context. This confusion will of course, sadly, impact their comprehension.

Considerations for teaching to English Language Learners (ELL) include recognition by the teacher that what works for the English language speaking student from an English language speaking family, does not necessarily work in other languages.

Research recommends that ELL students learn to read initially in their first language. It has been found that a priority for ELL should be learning to speak English before being taught to read English. Research supports oral language development, since it lays the foundation for phonological awareness.

See also Skills 4.2 and 5.6

COMPETENCY 3

UNDERSTAND THE DEVELOPMENT OF PHONICS AND OTHER WORD IDENTIFICATION STRATEGIES, SPELLING, AND FLUENCY

SKILL 3.1 **Demonstrating knowledge of basic concepts related to beginning literacy development** *(e.g., relationships between beginning stages of reading, writing, and spelling; reciprocity between decoding and encoding)* **and basic terminology used to describe common letter combinations and/or letter-sound relationships in English** *(e.g., consonant digraphs, consonant blends, vowel digraphs, diphthongs, r- and l-controlled vowels)*

See also Skill 3.3

Procedure for letter–sound investigations

The following procedure for letter-sound investigations helps to support beginning decoding.

1. Focus on a particular letter or letters that you want the child to investigate. It is good to choose one from a shared text with which the children are familiar. Make certain that the teacher's directions to the children are clear and either ask them to look for a specific letter or listen for sounds.

2. Begin a list of words that meet the task given to the children. Use chart paper to list the words the children identify. This list can be continued into the next week as long as the children's focus stays on the list. This can be easily done by challenging the children to identify a specific number of letters or sounds and "daring" them as a class team to go beyond those words or sounds.

3. Continue to add to the list. At the beginning of the day, have the children focus on the goal of adding their own words to the list. Give each child an adhesive note (sticky-pad sheet) on which they can write down the words they find. They can then they can attach their newly found words with their names on them to the chart. This provides the children with a sense of ownership and pride in their letter-sounding abilities. During shared reading, discuss the children's proposed additions and have the group decide if they meet the criteria. If all the children agree that they do meet the criteria, include the words on the chart.

4. Do a word sort from all the words generated and have the children put the words into categories that demonstrate similarities and differences. They can be prompted to see if the letter appeared at the beginning of the word or in the middle of the word. They might also be prompted to see that one sound could have two different letter representations. The children can then "box" the word differences and similarities by using colors established in a chart key.

5. Finally, before the children go off to read, ask them to look for new words in the texts, which they can now recognize because of the letter-sound relationships on their chart. During shared reading, make certain that they have time to share the words they were able to decode.

> **SKILL 3.2** **Applying knowledge of research-based, explicit phonics instruction to promote students' accurate decoding and spelling of regular words of increasing complexity** (e.g., VC, CVC, CVCC, CCVC, CVCe, CVVC)

Strategies for Teaching Phonics

The one-letter book

Provide children with a sample of a single letter book (or create one from environmental sources, newspapers, coupons, circulars, magazines, or your own text ideas). Make sure that your already published or created sample includes a printed version of the letter in both upper and lowercase forms. Make certain that each page contains a picture of something that starts with that specific letter and also has the word for the picture. The book you select or create should be a predictable one in that when the picture is identified, the word can be read.

Once the children have been provided with your sample and have listened to it being read, challenge them to each make a one-letter book. Often it is best to focus on familiar consonants for the single letter book or the first letter of the child's first name. Use of the first letter of the child's first name invites the child to develop a book that tells about him or her and the words that he or she finds. This is an excellent way to have the reading workshop aspect of the teacher's instruction of the alphabetic principle complement and enhance the writing workshop. Encourage children to be active writers and readers by finding words for their book on the classroom word wall, in alphabet books in the special alphabet book bin, and in grade- and age-appropriate pictionaries (dictionaries for younger children which are filled with pictures).

Practicing the Four Basic Word Types

Practice techniques for student development of the four basic word types can include speed drills in which they read lists of isolated words with contrasting vowel sounds that are signaled by the syllable type. For example, several closed syllable and vowel-consonant-"e" words containing the vowel a are arranged randomly on pages containing about twelve lines and read for one minute. Individual goals are established and charts are kept of the number of words read correctly in successive sessions. The same word lists are repeated in sessions until the goal has been achieved for several succeeding sessions. When selecting words for these lists, the use of high-frequency words within a syllable category increases the likelihood of generalization to text reading.

Various techniques are useful with students who have acquired some proficiency in decoding skill but whose levels of skill are lower than their oral language abilities. Such techniques have certain, common features:

- Students listen to text as they follow along with the book

- Students follow the print using their fingers as guides

- Reading materials are used that students would be unable to read independently

Teaching Spelling

There are basically four approaches for teaching spelling. These are the traditional spelling instruction, whole language, developmental, and the structured language approaches.

The **TRADITIONAL APPROACH** adheres strictly to a phonics-based approach to spelling. The student uses invented spelling, using known sounds and skipping others. The teacher sequentially teaches phonics rules and their application to spelling, including those words that don't adhere to the rules. In the traditional approach, the student learns to spell by phonemes and word families. Spelling instruction is direct, systematic, and intensive and is believed to be the best way to insure student success. This approach utilizes the traditional basal speller, rote drill, repeated copying, especially of missed words, and weekly spelling tests.

The **WHOLE LANGUAGE APPROACH** for teaching spelling supports the idea that the student learns to spell by remembering what the word looks like rather than by remembering how it sounds. Rebecca Sitton, who has developed a whole spelling series, spearheads this group. Proponents of this group believe student success lies in learning to spell words as they need them for their personal writing. Students are directed in word wall study, both seeing, chanting, writing, and then using the words in their own personal writing. They are then taught to analyze the

> **TRADITIONAL APPROACH:** adheres strictly to a phonics-based approach to spelling

> *In the traditional approach, the student learns to spell by phonemes and word families. Spelling instruction is direct, systematic, and intensive and is believed to be the best way to insure student success.*

> **WHOLE LANGUAGE APPROACH:** supports the idea that the student learns to spell by remembering what the word looks like rather than by remembering how it sounds

It is believed that the student learns spelling best by using the words in his or her own reading/writing tasks.

DEVELOPMENTAL APPROACH: students go through several stages of development from invented spelling to conventional spelling

STRUCTURED LANGUAGE APPROACH: involves an in-depth focus on letter/sound relationships and progresses through letters, phonemes, blended syllables, to whole words

Each method of teaching spelling has shown documented success. It appears that the clue to success is to actively address spelling issues, either in a structured format or based on words needed by individual students.

structure of words and learn what the base words, prefixes, and suffixes look like and mean. Classrooms are print-rich, exposing the student to the sight of many utilitarian words. It is believed that the student learns spelling best by using the words in his or her own reading/writing tasks. Though a few words and word structures are taught, children mainly learn as they use the word.

The **DEVELOPMENTAL APPROACH** suggests several stages of development that students go through in their development from invented spelling to conventional spelling. This approach holds that students should be allowed to just develop without overt instruction, as they will eventually develop to traditional spelling. Different studies have suggested different numbers of stages, but benchmark stages through the continuum are:

- **Precommunicative:** Random letters are heard that may match beginning sound.

- **Semiphonetic:** One or more letters representing sounds are heard, usually without medial vowels.

- **Phonetic:** More letters are included, as are more vowels. They are usually spelled exactly as the child perceives the sounds, i.e., the letter /u might be represented as 'you.'

- **Transitional:** Letters are included for all sounds, words contain the correct number of syllables although some vowels may be misrepresented, i.e., '-er' might be represented as '-ur.'

- **Conventional:** Mostly correct spelling with only errors in difficult spelling patterns.

The **STRUCTURED LANGUAGE APPROACH**, which is considered to have been developed by Samual Orton, involves an in-depth focus on letter/sound relationships and progresses through letters, phonemes, blended syllables, to whole words. There are only 40-plus phonemes used to represent every speech sound made and these are spelled with only 26 letters, so variations have to be learned (as secondary sounds). Orton also identified spelling difficulties with reading difficulties and reasoned that a focus on spelling the 40-plus phonemes would also improve the reading ability of the student.

Each method of teaching spelling has shown documented success. It appears that the clue to success is to actively address spelling issues, either in a structured format or based on words needed by individual students.

SPELLING PATTERN WORD WALL

Create in your classroom a spelling pattern word wall. Wylie and Durrell have identified spelling patterns that are in their classic thirty-seven "dependable" rimes. The spelling word wall can be created by stapling a piece of 3" × 5" butcher block paper to the bulletin board. Then attach spelling pattern cards around the border with thumbtacks, so that the cards can be easily removed to use at the meeting area.

Once you decide on a spelling pattern for instruction, remove the corresponding card from the word wall. Then take a 1" × 3" piece of a contrasting color of butcher block paper and tape the card to the top end of a sheet the children will use for their investigation. Next, read one of Wylie and Durrell's short rimes with the children and have them identify the pattern.

After the pattern is identified, the children can try to come up with other words that have the same spelling pattern. The teacher can write these on the spelling pattern sheet, using a different color marker to highlight the spelling pattern within the word. The children have to add to the list until the sheet is full, which might take two days or more.

After the sheet is full, the completed spelling pattern is attached to the wall.

Spelling in the Classroom

Some of the techniques teachers use to determine the words students need to spell include:

- Lists of misspelled words from student writing
- Lists of theme words
- Lists of words from the content areas
- Word banks

It is important for beginning writers to know that spelling is an important part of the writing process. However, insisting on correct spelling right from the beginning may actually hamper the efforts of beginning writers. In early spelling development, children should be allowed to experiment with words and use invented spelling. Spelling development is something that occurs over time as a developmental process. It does develop in clearly defined stages, which the teacher should take into consideration when planning lessons. Teachers should assess students' spelling knowledge and then plan mini-lessons to whole class and small groups as they are necessary.

Some of the ways teachers can provide spelling instruction in the context of meaningful reading and writing activities include:

- Shared reading
- Guided reading
- Reading chants
- Writing lists

- Shared writing
- Shared reading
- Poetry reading using rhyming words with the same spelling patterns
- Writing daily news in the classroom
- Writing letters
- Writing invitations

By planning spelling instruction, teachers help children recognize word patterns, discern spelling rules, and develop their own tricks for remembering how to spell words.

By planning spelling instruction, teachers help children recognize word patterns, discern spelling rules, and develop their own tricks for remembering how to spell words. Direct instruction is necessary for students to develop the knowledge they need regarding the morphological structure of words and thus the relationships between words. Students also need to be taught graphophonic relationships to know the relationship between letters and sounds, the probability of letter sequences, and the different letter patterns.

See Wylie and Durrell's 37 phonemes:

www.mrs.norris.net /Language/Language /phonograms.htm

Developing visual methods of recognizing correct spelling is also an aid to helping students learn to spell when they can trace around the shape of a word. This helps them develop a visual memory as to whether or not the word looks as if it is spelled correctly. Memory aids (mnemonics) also facilitate spelling development, such as in the word PAINT—Pat Added Ink Not Tar.

Activities for teaching spelling

For more strategies for teaching spelling:

www.readingrockets.org /article/80

Along with direct teaching of spelling, teachers should model the process at all times. By talking about spelling and having students assist in class writing, they will help students develop the awareness that spelling is important. Some activities where teachers can use this approach include:

- Experience charts
- Writing notes to parents
- Writing class poems and stories
- Editing writing with students

Students also need to be encouraged to take risks with spelling. Rather than have students constantly asking how words are spelled, the teacher can use "Have a Go" Sheets. These sheets consist of three columns in which the students write the word as they think it is spelled. Then the student asks the teacher or another student if it spelled correctly. If it is incorrect, the teacher or student approached will tell the student which letters are in the correct place, and the student will try again. After the third try, the teacher can either tell the student how to spell the word and add this to the list of words the student has to learn or work on the necessary spelling strategy.

Have a Go Sheet

HAVE A GO SHEET		This list belongs to: _____
How I spelled the word in my writing	Have a Go	Teacher or helper writes correct words in this column

SKILL 3.3 **Applying knowledge of research-based, explicit instruction in sight words, common inflectional morphemes** *(e.g., -ed, -er, -est, -ing, -s)*, **and related orthographic guidelines** *(e.g., doubling the final consonant or changing y to i when adding an inflection)* **to promote students' accurate decoding and spelling of irregular and/or inflected words**

The Structure of Language

is the study of word structure. When readers develop morphemic skills, they are developing an understanding of patterns they see in words. For example, English speakers realize that cat, cats, and caterpillar share some similarities in structure. This understanding helps readers to recognize words at a faster and easier rate, because each word doesn't need individual decoding.

MORPHOLOGY: the study of word structure

Syntax refers to the rules or patterned relationships that correctly create phrases and sentences from words. When readers develop an understanding of syntax, they begin to understand the structure of how sentences are built, and eventually the beginning of grammar.

Example: "I am going to the movies."

This statement is syntactically and grammatically correct.

Example: "They am going to the movies."

This statement is syntactically correct since all the words are in their correct place, but it is grammatically incorrect with the use of the word "They" rather than "I."

Semantics refers to the meaning expressed when words are arranged in a specific way. This is where connotation and denotation of words eventually will have a role with readers.

All of these skill sets are important to eventually developing effective word recognition skills, which help emerging readers develop fluency.

Phonics

Unlike phonemic awareness, the study of phonics must be done with the eyes open. It's the connection between the sounds and letters on a page. In other words, students learning phonics might see the word "bad" and sound each letter out slowly until they recognize that they just said the word.

Decoding, Word Recognition, and Spelling

WORD ANALYSIS: the process readers use to figure out unfamiliar words based on written patterns

WORD RECOGNITION: the process of automatically determining the pronunciation and some degree of the meaning of an unknown word

DECODE: to change communication signals into messages

(also called phonics or decoding) is the process readers use to figure out unfamiliar words based on written patterns.   is the process of automatically determining the pronunciation and some degree of the meaning of an unknown word. In other words, fluent readers recognize most written words easily and correctly, without consciously decoding or breaking them down. These elements of literacy are skills readers need for word recognition.

To   means to change communication signals into messages. Reading comprehension requires that the reader learn the code within which a message is written and be able to decode it to get the message. Encoding involves changing a message into symbols. For example, to encode oral language into writing (spelling) or to encode an idea into words or to encode a mathematical or physical idea into appropriate mathematical symbols.

Although effective reading comprehension requires identifying words automatically (Adams, 1990, Perfetti, 1985), children do not have to be able to identify every single word or know the exact meaning of every word in a text to understand it. Indeed, Nagy (1988) says that children can read a work with a high level of comprehension even if they do not fully know as many as fifteen percent of the words within a given text. Children develop the ability to decode and recognize words automatically. They then can extend their ability to decode to multisyllabic words.

Spelling instruction should include practicing words misspelled in daily writing, generalizing spelling knowledge, and mastering objectives in progressive phases of development.

The developmental stages of spelling are:

Prephonemic spelling: Children know that letters stand for a message, but they do not know the relationship between spelling and pronunciation.

2. Early phonemic spelling: Children are beginning to understand spelling. They usually write the beginning letter correctly, followed by consonants or long vowels.

3. Letter-name spelling: Some words are consistently spelled correctly. The student is developing a sight vocabulary and a stable understanding of letters as representing sounds. Long vowels are usually used accurately, but silent vowels are omitted. Unknown words are spelled by the child attempting to match the name of the letter to the sound.

4. Transitional spelling: This phase is typically entered in late elementary school. Short vowel sounds are mastered and some spelling rules known. They are developing a sense of which spellings are correct and which are not.

5. Derivational spelling: This is usually reached from high school to adulthood. This is the stage where spelling rules are being mastered.

How Words Are Built

Knowledge of how words are built can help students with basic and more advanced decoding. A   is the primary base of a word. A   is the affix (a morpheme that attaches to a base word) that is placed at the start of a root word, but can't make a word on its own.

> *Examples of prefixes include re-, pre-, and un-.*

A   follows the root word to which it attaches and appears at the end of the word.

> *Examples of suffixes include –s, -es, -ed, -ly, and –tion.*

In the word unlikely, "un" is a prefix, "like" is the root word, and "ly" is a suffix.

ROOT WORD: the primary base of a word

PREFIX: the affix that is placed at the start of a root word, but can't make a word on its own

SUFFIX: follows the root word to which it attaches and appears at the end of the word

High Frequency and Sight Words

High frequency words are the words most often used in the English language. Depending on the list used, these range from 100 to 300 words. It has been estimated that 100 words make up 50 percent of all words used in reading. Other lists, such as Dolch and Fry, use the most frequently encountered words in early childhood reading texts.

Sight words are words that the reader learns to read spontaneously either because of frequency or lack of conformity to orthographic rules. For example, words like 'the', 'what', and 'there' are sight words because they don't conform to rules, and words like 'boy,' 'girl,' and 'book' are sight words because they are seen very frequently in reading texts.

> **SKILL 3.4** Applying knowledge of research-based, explicit instruction in regular, open and closed syllable patterns and syllabication guidelines; structural analysis skills *(e.g., recognizing word roots, derivational affixes, and compound words)*; and orthographic patterns based on etymology to promote students' accurate decoding and spelling of multisyllable words

See also Skills 3.5 and 4.2

> **SKILL 3.5** Demonstrating knowledge of key indicators of reading fluency *(i.e., accuracy, rate, and prosody)*, common factors that disrupt fluency *(e.g., weakness in phonics and other word identification skills, lack of familiarity with academic vocabulary and/or syntactic structures, limited background knowledge)*, and research-based, explicit instruction to promote fluency at all stages of reading development

When students practice fluency, they practice reading connected pieces of text. In other words, instead of looking at a word as just a word, they might read a sentence straight through. Students who are not fluent in reading would sound each letter or word out slowly and pay more attention to the phonics of each word. A fluent reader, on the other hand, might read a sentence out loud using appropriate intonation. The best way to test for fluency, in fact, is to have a student read something out loud, preferably a few sentences in a row. Fluency is considered to be a good predictor of comprehension. A child who is focusing too much on sounding out each word will not be paying attention to the meaning.

A child who is focusing too much on sounding out each word will not be paying attention to the meaning.

Accuracy

One way to evaluate reading fluency is to look at student accuracy, and one way to do this is to keep running records of students during oral reading. Calculating the reading level lets you know if a book is at a level the child can read independently or comfortably with guidance or if the book is at too high a level, which will frustrate the child.

As part of the informal assessment of primary grade reading, it is important to record the child's word insertions, omissions, requests for help, and attempts to get the word. In informal assessment, the rate of accuracy can be estimated from the ratio of errors to total words read.

Results of running record informal assessment can be used for teaching based on accuracy. If a child reads from 95-100 percent correctly, the child is ready for independent reading. If a child reads from 92-97 percent correctly, the child is ready for guided reading. If a child reads below 92 percent correctly, the child needs a read-aloud or shared reading activity.

Automaticity

Fluency in reading depends on automatic word identification, which assists the student in achieving comprehension of the material. Even slight difficulties in word identification can significantly increase the time it takes a student to read material, may require rereading parts or passages of the material, and reduces the level of comprehension. A student who experiences reading as a constant struggle will avoid reading whenever possible and consider it a negative experience. The ability to read for comprehension, and learning in general, will suffer if all aspects of reading fluency are not presented to the student as skills that can be acquired with the appropriate effort.

Fluency in reading depends on automatic word identification.

Automatic reading involves developing strong orthographic representations, which allows fast and accurate identification of whole words made up of specific letter patterns. Most young students move easily from using alphabetic strategies to using orthographic representations, which can be accessed automatically. Initially, word identification is based on the application of phonic word-accessibility strategies (letter-sound associations). These strategies are in turn based on the development of phonemic awareness, which is necessary to learn how to relate speech to print.

Six syllable types

One of the most useful devices for developing automaticity in young students is through the visual pattern provided in the six syllable types.

EXAMPLES OF THE SIX SYLLABLE TYPES	
Not (Closed)	<u>Closed</u> in by a consonant—vowel makes its **short** sound
No (Open)	<u>Ends</u> in a vowel—vowel makes its **long** sound
Note (Silent "E")	<u>Ends</u> in vowel consonant "e"—vowel makes its **long** sound
Nail (Vowel Combination)	<u>Two vowels together</u> make the sound
Bird ("R" Controlled)	<u>Contains</u> a vowel plus 4—vowel sound is changed
Table (Consonant "L"-"E")	<u>Applied</u> at the end of a word

These orthographic (letter) patterns signal vowel pronunciation to the reader. Students must become able to apply their knowledge of these patterns to recognize the syllable types and to see these patterns automatically and ultimately in order to read words as wholes. The move from decoding letter symbols to identify recognizable terms to automatic word recognition is a substantial move toward fluency.

A significant tool for helping students move through this phase was developed by Anna Gillingham, who incorporated an activity using phonetic word cards into the Orton-Gillingham lesson plan (Gillingham and Stillman, 1997). This activity involves having students practice reading words (and some nonwords) on cards as wholes, beginning with simple syllables and moving systematically through the syllable types to complex syllables and two-syllable words. The words are divided into groups that correspond to the specific sequence of skills being taught.

The student's development of the elements necessary for automaticity continually moves through stages. Another important stage involves the automatic recognition of single graphemes as a critical first step to the development of the letter patterns that make up words or word parts.

English orthography is made up of four basic word types:

1. Regular for reading and spelling (e.g., *cat, print*)

2. Regular for reading but not for spelling (e.g., *float, brain*—could be spelled *flote* or *brane*, respectively)

3. Rule-based (e.g., *canning*—doubling rule, *faking*—drop *e* rule)

4. Irregular (e.g., *beauty*)

*Orthography:
the conventional spelling system of a language.*

*graphemes:
a letter or a number of letters that represent a sound (phoneme) in a word.*

Students must be taught to recognize all four types of words automatically in order to be effective readers. Repeated practice in pattern recognition is often necessary. Practice techniques can include speed drills in which students read lists of isolated words with contrasting vowel sounds that are signaled by the syllable type. One way to do this is to randomly arrange several closed syllable and vowel-consonant e words containing the vowel *a* on pages containing about twelve lines and have the child read for one minute. Individual goals are established and charts are kept of the number of words read correctly in successive sessions. The same word lists are repeated in sessions until the goal has been achieved for several succeeding sessions. When selecting words for these lists, the use of high-frequency words in a syllable category increases the likelihood of generalization to text reading.

Rate

A student whose reading rate is slow, or halting and inconsistent, exhibits a lack of reading fluency. According to an article by Mastropieri, Leinart, and Scruggs (1999), some students have developed accurate word pronunciation skills but read at a slow rate. They have not moved to the phase where decoding is automatic, and their limited fluency may affect performance in the following ways:

- They read less text than their peers and have less time to remember, review, or comprehend the text.

- They expend more cognitive energy than their peers trying to identify individual words.

- They may be less able to retain text in their memories and less likely to integrate those segments with other parts of the text.

The simplest means of determining a student's reading rate is to have the student read aloud from a prescribed passage that is at the appropriate reading level for age and grade and contains a specified number of words. The passage should not be too familiar for the student (some will try to memorize or "work out" difficult bits ahead of time), and should not contain more words than can be read comfortably and accurately by a normal reader in one or two minutes.

Count only the words *correctly* pronounced on first reading, and divide this word count into elapsed time to determine the student's reading rate. To determine the student's standing and progress, compare this rate with the norm for the class and the average for all students who read fluently at that specific age/grade level.

The following general guidelines can be applied for reading lists of words with a speed drill and a one-minute timing:

- 30 wpm for first- and second-grade children

- 40 wpm for third-grade children

- 60 wpm for mid-third-grade children

- 80 wpm for students in fourth grade and higher

Various techniques are useful with students who have acquired some proficiency in decoding skill but whose skill levels are lower than their oral language abilities. Such techniques have certain common features:

- Students listen to text as they follow along with the book.

- Students follow the print using their fingers as guides.

- Use reading materials that students would be unable to read independently.

Experts recommend that a beginning reading program incorporate partner reading, practice reading difficult words prior to reading the text, timings for accuracy and rate, opportunities to hear books read, and opportunities to read to others.

> *Experts recommend that a beginning reading program incorporate partner reading, practice reading difficult words prior to reading the text, timings for accuracy and rate, opportunities to hear books read, and opportunities to read to others.*

Prosody

PROSODY: versification of text and involves such matters as which syllable of a word is accented

PROSODY is versification of text and involves such matters as which syllable of a word is accented. With regard to fluency, it is that aspect which translates reading into the same experience as listening in the reader's mind. It involves intonation and rhythm through such devices as syllable accent and punctuation.

In their article for *Perspectives* (Winter 2002), Pamela Hook and Sandra Jones proposed that teachers can begin to develop awareness of the prosodic features of language by introducing a short three-word sentence with each of the three different words underlined for stress (e.g., *He is sick. He is sick. He is sick.*). The teacher can then model the three sentences while discussing the possible meaning for each variation. The students can practice reading them with different stress until they are fluent. These simple three-word sentences can be modified and expanded to include various verbs, pronouns, and tenses (e.g., *You are sick. I am sick. They are sick.*). This strategy can also be used while increasing the length of phrases and emphasizing the different meanings (e.g., *Get out of bed. Get out of bed. Get out of bed now.*) Teachers can also practice fluency with common phrases that frequently occur in text.

Using prepositional phrases

Prepositional phrases are good syntactic structures for this type of work (e.g., *on the _____, in the _____, over the _____*). Teachers can pair these printed phrases with oral intonation patterns that include variations of rate, intensity, and pitch. Students can infer the intended meaning as the teacher presents different prosodic variations of a sentence. For example, when speakers want to stress a concept they often slow their rate of speech and may speak in a louder voice (e.g., *Joshua, get-out-of-bed-**NOW!***). Often, the only text marker for this sentence will be the exclamation point (!), but the speaker's intent will affect the manner in which it is delivered.

Using the alphabet

Practicing oral variations and then mapping the prosodic features onto the text will assist students in making the connection when reading. This strategy can also be used to alert students to the prosodic features present in punctuation marks. In the early stages, using the alphabet helps to focus a student on the punctuation marks without having to deal with meaning. The teacher models for the students and then has them practice the combinations using the correct intonation patterns to fit the punctuation mark (e.g., ABC. DE? FGH! IJKL? or ABCD! EFGHI? KL.).

Using two- or three-word sentences

Teachers can then move to simple two-word or three-word sentences. The sentences are punctuated with a period, question mark and exclamation point and the differences in meaning that occur with each different punctuation mark (e.g., *Chris hops. Chris hops? Chris hops!*) are discussed. It may help students to point out that the printed words convey the fact that someone named Chris is engaged in the physical activity of hopping, but the intonation patterns get their cue from the punctuation mark. The meaning extracted from an encounter with a punctuation mark is dependent upon a reader's prior experiences or background knowledge in order to project an appropriate intonation pattern onto the printed text. Keeping the text static while changing the punctuation marks helps students to attend to prosodic patterns.

Using chunking

Students who read word-for-word may benefit initially from practicing phrasing with the alphabet rather than words because letters do not tax the meaning system. The letters are grouped, an arc is drawn underneath, and students recite the alphabet in chunks (e.g., ABC DE FGH IJK LM NOP QRS TU VW XYZ). Once students understand the concept of phrasing, it is recommended that teachers help students chunk text into syntactic (noun phrases, verb phrases, prepositional phrases) or meaning units until they are proficient. There are no hard and fast rules for chunking, but syntactic units are most commonly used.

Using slashes

For better readers, teachers can mark the phrasal boundaries with slashes for short passages. Eventually, the slashes are used only at the beginning of long passages and then students are asked to continue "phrase reading" even after the marks end. Marking phrases can be done together with students, or those on an independent level may divide passages into phrases themselves. Comparisons can be made to clarify reasons for differences in phrasing. Another way to encourage students to focus on phrase meaning and prosody, in addition to word identification, is to provide tasks that require them to identify or supply a paraphrase of an original statement.

> **SKILL 3.6** Applying knowledge of the use of appropriate texts and effective, engaging reading and writing activities to motivate and reinforce students' development of phonics and other word identification skills, spelling, and fluency

See also Skills 3.2, 3.3, and 3.4

> **SKILL 3.7** Demonstrating knowledge of formal and informal methods for assessing students' development in phonics and other word identification skills, spelling, and fluency and demonstrating ability to interpret and use the results of these assessments to plan effective instruction in decoding, spelling, and fluency

The best way to test for fluency is to have a student read something out loud, preferably a few sentences in a row. Most students just learning to read are probably not fluent right away; with practice, they will increase their fluency. Even though fluency is not the same as comprehension, it is said that fluency is a good predictor of comprehension. Think about it: if a student is focusing too much on sounding out each word, he or she is not going to be paying attention to the meaning.

Assessing Reading Errors

Reading errors or miscues can be classified into one of nine categories. Categorizing the errors helps the teacher determine the appropriate intervention.

CATEGORIES OF READING ERRORS	
Dialect Variation	Pronunciation difference due to dialect, i.e., *caw* for *car*
Intonation Shift or Prosody	Stress or emphasis changes meaning, i.e., *The girl WAS in the house* vs. *The GIRL was in the house*
Graphic Similarity	Word looks similar to correct one, i.e., *horse* for *house*
Sound Similarity	i.e., *cook* for *look*
Grammatical Similarity	i.e., *the blue book* is read as *the red book*
Syntactic Acceptability	Same as grammatical similarity
Semantic Acceptability	Meaning is the same, i.e., *child* is read as *baby*
Meaning Change	i.e., *He rode the horse* read as *he wrote the horse*
Self-Correction with Semantic Acceptability	Self-corrects based on meaning, i.e., as in example above, reader would change *wrote* to *rode* because it doesn't make sense otherwise

If the miscues are due to orthographic mistakes, the teacher should stress phonics instruction. If miscues are due to semantic mistakes, the teacher should teach the child to read for meaning. Syntactic miscues means the teacher needs to address grammar, such as parts of speech and sentence structure.

See also Skills 1.5, 3.5, and 6.6

SKILL **Applying knowledge of strategies** *(e.g., differentiated instruction,*
3.8 *interventions, enrichment)* **to address the assessed needs of individual students** *(e.g., English language learners, struggling readers through highly proficient readers)* **in phonics and other word identification skills, spelling, and fluency at all stages of literacy development, including recognizing basic ways in which the writing systems of other languages may differ from English and the importance of helping English language learners transfer relevant skills from their home language to English**

See also Skills 2.6, 4.2, and 5.6

COMPETENCY 4
UNDERSTAND VOCABULARY DEVELOPMENT

> **SKILL 4.1** **Demonstrating awareness of the critical role vocabulary plays in reading and the importance of engaging students in early and continual language experiences to promote their vocabulary development**

Recognizing and talking about words as "things" to be discovered, collected, enjoyed, and remembered will help foster an appreciation of vocabulary.

The simplest method that teachers can use to increase student vocabulary is exposing students to many new words in the course of frequent reading, speaking, and writing exercises. Students can also learn many words indirectly through independent reading. Teachers should emphasize that words are not separate, disconnected units that need to be learned in isolation, but, rather, are related and interrelated.

Synonyms, antonyms, and root words are three obvious examples of the connections that exist among words. When words are connected together in sentences, their individual meanings change and are enhanced by one another. However, teaching particular words—especially words with multiple meanings—before reading a text helps students with both vocabulary acquisition and reading comprehension. When providing instruction in the definitions of new vocabulary words, teachers should focus on the words' connections to other words.

Student readers comprehend and learn when they are able to connect the new information in their reading material to what they already know. Vocabulary instruction, therefore, should help students make the connections between unknown words and the knowledge they already possess. This is a core element of reading, and vocabulary words are the fundamental building blocks.

Tips for Identifying New Words for Vocabulary Instruction

- Provide opportunities for extensive reading
- Invite students to tell their own stories, using their own words
- Make overt links between oral and written language

- Discuss words in related clusters; help students make connections among words

- Teach key vocabulary words before assigning reading from a text

- Have dictionary and glossary resources available for the precise spelling and meaning of words

SKILL **Applying knowledge of components of effective vocabulary**
4.2 **instruction** *(e.g., explicitly teaching words and word-learning strategies, promoting word consciousness and a love of words, encouraging and supporting wide reading, providing meaningful exposure to and opportunities to use new vocabulary)* **and criteria for selecting words for vocabulary instruction**

Students will be better at comprehension if they have a stronger working vocabulary. Research has shown that students learn more vocabulary when it is presented in context rather than in vocabulary lists. Furthermore, the more students get to use particular words in context, the more they will remember each word and utilize it in the comprehension of sentences that contain the words.

Word Analysis: Identification of Common Morphemes, Prefixes, and Suffixes

The identification of common morphemes, prefixes, and suffixes is an important method of word analysis that students need to know when learning to read. This aspect of vocabulary development helps students look for structural elements in words that they can use to help them determine meaning.

KEY COMPONENTS OF STRUCTURAL ANALYSIS	
Root Words	A word from which another word is developed; the second word has its "root" in the first. This component lends itself to a tree-with-roots illustration. Students may also want to literally construct root words using cardboard trees and roots to create word-family models.
Base Words	A stand-alone linguistic unit, which cannot be deconstructed or broken down into smaller words. For example, in the word *retell*, the base word is *tell*.
Contractions	Shortened forms of two words in which a letter or letters have been deleted. The deleted letters are replaced by an apostrophe.

Continued on next page

Prefixes	Units of meaning that can be added (the word for this type of structural addition is *affixed*) to the beginning of a base word or root word. They are also sometimes known as "bound morphemes," meaning that they cannot stand alone as a base word. An example is *retell*. The prefix in this word is *re*.
Suffixes	Units of meaning that can be "affixed," or added on, to the ends of root or base words. Suffixes transform the original meanings of base and root words. Like prefixes, they are also known as "bound morphemes," because they cannot stand alone as words. In the word *comfortable*, the suffix is *able*.
Compound Words	These occur when two or more base words are connected to form a new word. The meaning of the new word is in some way connected with that of the base words. For example, the word *bedroom* is a compound word made of the two base words *bed* and *room*.
Inflectional Endings	Types of suffixes that impart a new meaning to the base or root word. These endings, in particular, change the gender, number, tense, or form of the base or root words. Like other suffixes, these are also called "bound morphemes." In the word *telling*, the inflectional ending *ing* determines the tense of the verb *tell*.

The National Reading Panel (2000) has published the following conclusions about vocabulary instruction.

1. There is a need for direct instruction of vocabulary items required for a specific text.

2. Repetition and multiple exposure to vocabulary items are important. Students should be given items that are likely to appear in many contexts.

3. Learning in rich contexts is valuable for vocabulary learning. Vocabulary words should be those that the learner will find useful in many contexts. When vocabulary items are derived from content learning materials, the learner will be better equipped to deal with specific reading matter in content areas.

4. Vocabulary tasks should be restructured as necessary. It is important to be certain that students fully understand what is asked of them in the context of reading rather than focusing only on the words to be learned.

5. Vocabulary learning is effective when it entails active engagement in learning tasks.

6. Computer technology can be used effectively to help teach vocabulary.

7. Vocabulary can be acquired through incidental learning. Much of a student's vocabulary will have to be learned in the course of doing things other than explicit vocabulary learning. Repetition, richness of context, and motivation may also add to the efficacy of incidental learning of vocabulary.

8. Dependence on a single vocabulary instruction method will not result in optimal learning. A variety of methods can be used effectively with emphasis on multimedia aspects of learning, richness of context in which words are to be learned, and the number of exposures to words that learners receive.

The panel found that a critical feature of effective classrooms is the teaching of specific words including lessons and activities in which students apply their vocabulary knowledge and strategies to reading and writing. Included in the activities were discussions in which teachers and students talked about words, their features, and strategies for understanding unfamiliar words.

There are many methods for directly and explicitly teaching words. Through its research the panel found twenty-one methods teachers can use in the classroom to teach vocabulary. Many emphasize the underlying concept of a word and its connections to other words, such as semantic mapping and diagrams that use graphics. The keyword method uses words and illustrations that highlight salient features of meaning. Another effective method is visualizing or drawing a picture. Many words cannot be learned in this way, of course, so it should be used as only one method among others. Effective classrooms provide multiple ways for students to learn and interact with words. The panel also found that computer-assisted activities can have a positive role in vocabulary development.

> *Effective classrooms provide multiple ways for students to learn and interact with words.*

Context Clues

When children encounter unknown words in a sentence, they rely on their background knowledge to choose a word that makes sense. Errors of younger children therefore are often substitutions of words in the same syntactic class. Poor readers often fail to make use of context clues to help them identify words or activate the background knowledge that would help them with comprehension. Poor readers also process sentences word by word, instead of "chunking" phrases and clauses, resulting in a slow pace that focuses on the decoding rather than comprehension. They also have problems answering *wh-* questions (who, what, where, when, why?) as a result of these problems with syntax.

One strategy, contextual redefinition, helps children use context more effectively by presenting them with sufficient context *before* they begin reading. It models the use of contextual clues to make informed guesses about word meanings.

To apply this strategy, the teacher should first select two or three unfamiliar words for teaching. The teacher should then write a sentence in which sufficient clues are supplied for the child to successfully figure out the meaning. The types of context clues the teacher can use include compare/contrast, synonyms, and direct definition.

The teacher should then present the words only on the experiential chart or as letter cards and have the children pronounce the words. As they pronounce them, challenge them to come up with a definition for each word. After several definitions have been offered, encourage the children to decide as a group what the definition is. Write down their agreed-upon definition without commenting on it. Then share the contexts (sentences the teacher wrote with the words and explicit context clues). Ask the children to read the sentences aloud and have them come up with a definition for each word. Make sure not to comment as they present their definitions. Ask them to justify their definitions by making specific references to the context clues in the sentences. As the discussion continues, direct the children's attention to their previously agreed-upon definition of the word. Facilitate a discussion of the differences between their guesses about the word when they saw only the word and their guesses about the word when they read it in context. Finally, have the children check their use of context skills to correctly define the word by using a dictionary.

This type of direct teaching of word definitions is useful when children have dictionary skills and the teacher is aware that there are insufficient context clues to help the students define it. In addition, struggling readers and students from ELL backgrounds may benefit tremendously from being walked through this process that successful readers apply automatically.

Choice of Words

Teachers can allow students to develop a personalized vocabulary word journal based on their own interests. Teachers can then encourage them to create their own vocabulary word lists and research their words' various meanings. Teachers can ask students to write down a personal interest, asking the rest of the class for vocabulary words that pertain to the student's answer, and then writing the words on the board. For example, if a student says, "I like to play basketball," ask the class to suggest vocabulary words in that subject area (e.g., basketball, net, slam dunk, hoop). Have students locate definitions in the dictionary, in the thesaurus, or on the computer. Students can then write a story describing their interest using the new words they have learned. Have students meet in groups to share their journals, encouraging them to discuss one another's words.

> SKILL **Applying knowledge of research-based, explicit instruction in**
> 4.3 **independent strategies for building vocabulary** *(e.g., analyzing base morphemes and affixes)* **and for determining the meaning and pronunciation of unfamiliar or multiple-meaning words encountered through listening and reading** *(e.g., using appositives, semantic and syntactic clues, reference materials)*

See also Skill 4.2

> SKILL **Applying knowledge of research-based, explicit instruction in**
> 4.4 **words and their meanings, including the etymology of words** *(e.g., common Latin and Greek roots)*, **idiomatic expressions, and foreign words and expressions used in English**

Root Words

Knowledge of Greek and Latin roots that comprise English words can measurably enhance children's reading skills and can also enrich their writing. Here are several strategies.

> *Knowledge of Greek and Latin roots that comprise English words can measurably enhance children's reading skills and can also enrich their writing.*

Word webs

Taberski (2000) does not advocate teaching Greek and Latin derivatives in the abstract to young children. However, when she comes across specific Greek and Latin roots (which are common) while reading to children, she uses that opportunity to introduce children to these rich resources.

For example, during readings on rodents (a favorite topic of first and second graders), Taberski draws her class's attention to the fact that beavers gnaw at things with their teeth. She then connects the root dent to other words with which the children are familiar. The children then volunteer words like *dentist, dental, denture*. Taberski begins to place these in a graphic organizer, or word web.

When she has tapped the extent of the children's prior knowledge of *dent* words, she tells them that *dens/dentis* is the Latin word for teeth. Then she introduces the word indent, which she has already previewed with them as part of their conventions of print study. She helps them to see that the *indenting* of the first line of a paragraph can even be related to the *teeth* Latin root in that it looks like a print "bite" was taken out of the paragraph.

Taberski displays the resulting word web in the Word Wall Chart section of her room. The class is encouraged throughout, for example, the following week to look for other words to add to the web. Taberski stresses that for her, as an elementary teacher of reading and writing, the key element of the Greek and Latin word root web activity is the children's coming to understand that if they know what a Greek or Latin word root means, they can use that knowledge to figure out what other words mean.

Greek and Latin roots word webs with an assist from the Internet

Older children in grades 3 through 6 can build on this initial activity by searching online for additional words with a particular Greek or Latin root that has been introduced in class.

They can easily do this in a way that authentically ties in with their own interests and experiences by reading online reviews for a book that has been a read-aloud, or by reading online summaries of the day's news and printing out those words that appear in the stories which share the root that has been discussed.

The children can be encouraged to circle these instances of their Latin or Greek root and also to document the exact date and URL for the citation. These can be posted as part of their own online web in the word wall section study area. If the school or class has a website or webpage, the children can post this data there as a special Greek and Latin root word page.

Expanding the concept of the Greek and Latin word web from the printed page to the Internet nicely inculcates the child in the habits of lifelong reading and online researching. This beginning expository research will serve them well in intermediate-level content area work and beyond.

Knowledge of Common Sayings, Proverbs, and Idioms

The Fortune Cookie Strategy (Reissman, 1994)

For grades 3 and up, distribute the fortune cookies to the children. Have them eat the cookies and then draw their attention to the enclosed fortunes.

First, the teacher will model by reading his or her own fortune aloud. After reading the fortune aloud, the teacher will explain what the fortune means, using its vocabulary as a guide. Finally, the teacher can share whether or not the he or she agrees with the statement made in the fortune.

Similarly, children can read their fortunes aloud, explain the saying, and tell whether they agree with the proverb or prediction.

Following this activity, children can be asked to go home and interview their parents or community members to get family proverbs and common sayings.

Once the children return with the sayings and proverbs, they can each share them and explain their meanings. The class as a whole can discuss to what extent

What makes proverbs particularly effective for vocabulary development is the limited number of words in their texts and the fact that these short texts allow for guided and facilitated reading instruction.

these sayings are true for everyone. Proverbs and sayings can become part of a word wall or be included in a special literacy center. The teacher can create fill-in, put-together, and writing activities to go with the proverbs. These tie in nicely with cultural study in grades 3 through 6, including the study of Asian, Latin American, and African nations.

This strategy also highlights, in a positive way, both the uniqueness and commonality of the family proverbs contributed by children from ELL backgrounds. If possible, their proverbs can also be posted in their native languages as well as in English.

Knowledge of Foreign Words and Abbreviations Commonly Used in English (e.g., RSVP)

The English language is replete with abbreviations that are shortened forms of words from other languages. A classic example of this is RSVP, derived from the French phrase *repondez, s'il vous plait*, or, in English, *please reply*. Not only can this be used to expand children's vocabulary and writing variety, it can also help to positively highlight the bilingual and sometimes trilingual abilities of ELL students.

The teacher should develop a word-strip mix-and-match game with commonly found foreign words and abbreviations. These words should, if possible, be cut out of newspapers, flyers, and magazines to highlight their authenticity as items from everyday life and concretely demonstrate the influence of other languages on the English language. Among those common words and abbreviations might be: perfume, latte, cappuccino, brioche, latkes, etc. To get sufficient material to cut out to start the game, just get an extra Sunday newspaper or pick up a few circulars from a large supermarket.

Model for the children how to play the game and use the dictionary to find out the common words' or abbreviations' meanings. Next, have the children work as a whole class or in small groups to identify the derivations of the foreign words and even map them on a world map.

For additional foreign word activities, children can choose from a number of options. These can include maintaining a Big Book of Foreign Words or Abbreviations, to which many contribute; using the weekly food circulars and collecting labels with foreign words, which can then be collaged with an accompanying product list; and authoring stories and true accounts featuring as many foreign words as possible. This, of course, makes the native language talents of the ELL child stand out as positive and important.

What is productive about foreign word activities is that they enhance vocabulary development while also highlighting the extent to which the English language as currently used in the United States is filled with foreign language words and terms.

SKILL 4.5 **Applying knowledge of the use of appropriate texts and effective, engaging oral language, reading, and writing activities to motivate, augment, and reinforce students' development of robust listening, speaking, reading, and writing vocabularies**

Developing the vocabulary of students is important in helping them become lifelong learners as well as improving their understanding of many topics. There are a number of different strategies that can be used to increase the development of students' vocabulary. Some of these strategies are described and detailed below.

Word classification

In this method, the students draw comparisons between different types of words. For younger children, this might begin by looking at parts of speech. Students might classify words as action, describing, nouns, etc. Older students might begin to look at classifying the words in more specific categories based on their content area or another classification system.

Etymology

ETYMOLOGY: the study of the history of words

ETYMOLOGY is the study of the history of words. Understanding the language basis of words can help students determine words' meanings and build the students' general comprehension. It is particularly useful to know the definitions of affixes and root words; these can help determine the meaning of many other words. In science, for example, understanding Latin derivatives can be beneficial for classifying different scientific terms and understanding their meaning.

Semantic mapping

This strategy involves students making the connections between the information they already know about a topic and the new information they are learning. It is typically a graphic representation of the information and is built upon words and ideas. It generally increases knowledge and improves vocabulary development.

Application of vocabulary words in new situations

Students also need to be able to make transfers of knowledge. Understanding what a word means in one context helps the student understand that one reading passage. Being able to transfer that understanding to new and varied situations helps the students become lifelong learners and readers. This transfer of knowledge can be done by asking the students to think of other ways or situations in which the word can be used, or by providing examples from other content areas where that same term is used.

See also Skill 4.7

SKILL **Demonstrating knowledge of formal and informal methods for**
4.6 **assessing students' vocabulary development and demonstrating the ability to interpret and use the results of these assessments to plan effective instruction in vocabulary development**

See also Skills 4.7 and 5.5

SKILL **Applying knowledge of strategies** (e.g., differentiated instruction,
4.7 interventions, enrichment) **to address the assessed needs of individual students** (e.g., English language learners, struggling readers through highly proficient readers) **in vocabulary development**

Strategies for Vocabulary Development

Banking, booking, and filing it: making words their own

Encourage children to create and maintain their own files of words they have learned or are interested in learning. Although they can categorize these files according to their own interests, they should develop files using science, history, physical education, fine arts, dance, and technology content. Newspapers and Web resources approved by the teacher are excellent sources for such words.

Children can realize the goal of making words their own and exploring word structures by creating concrete objects or displays that demonstrate the words they own.

In addition to benefiting the students, this filing activity provides the teacher with the opportunity to instruct children in age-appropriate and grade-level research skills. Even children in grades 2 and 3 can begin simplified bibliographies and Webliographies for their "found" words. They can learn how to annotate and note the page of a newspaper, book, or URL for a particular word.

Children can also copy down words as they appear in the text (print or electronic). If appropriate, they can place the words found for given topics or content in an actual bank of their own making, or print the words on cards. This allows for differentiated word study and appeals to those children who are kinesthetic and spatial learners. Of course, children can also choose to create their own word books showcasing their specialized vocabulary and descriptions of how they identified or hunted down their words.

Write out your words, write with your words

ELL students can share their accounts in their native language first and then translate (with the help of the teacher) these accounts into English with both the native language and the English language versions of the word exploration posted.

Ownership of words can be demonstrated by having the children use the words in their writings. The children can author a procedural narrative (a step-by-step description) of a vocabulary activity, telling how they went about their word searches to compile the words they found. If the children are in grades K–1, or if the children are struggling readers and writers, their procedural narratives can be dictated. Then they can be posted by the teacher.

Children with special needs can model a word box on a specific holiday theme, genre, or science/social studies topic with the teacher. Initially this can be done as a whole class. As the children become more confident, they can work with peers or with a paraprofessional to create their own individual or small team word boxes.

Special needs children can create a storyboard with the support of a paraprofessional, a teacher, or a resource specialist. They can also narrate their story of how they found the words, using a tape recorder.

Word Study Museum in the Classroom

Almost every general education teacher and reading specialist will have to differentiate instruction to address the needs of special education and ELL learners. Family or shared literacy is a major component of all literacy instruction.

This strategy is presented in detail so it can be used by the teachers within their own classrooms. In addition, the way the activity is described and the mention at the end of the description of how the activity can address family literacy, ELL, and special needs children's talents, provides an example of other audiences a teacher should consider in curriculum design.

Children can create a single or multiple museum-style exhibits celebrating their word study within their classrooms. They can build actual representations of the type of study they have done, including word trees (made out of cardboard or foam board), elaborate word boxes and games, word history timelines or murals, and word study maps. They can also develop digital photo essays and PowerPoint presentations to share the words they have identified.

The classroom, gym, or cafeteria can be transformed into a gallery space. Children can author brochure descriptions for their individual, team, or class exhibits. Some children can volunteer to be tour guides or docents for the experience. Other children can work to create a banner for the *Word Study Museum*. The children can name the museum themselves and send out invitations to its opening. Invitations can be sent to parents, community, staff members, peers, and younger classes.

Museum games and quizzes

Depending on their age and grade level, children can also develop interactive games and quizzes focused on particular exhibits. An artist or a team of class artists can design posters for the exhibits while other children build the exhibits. Another small group can work on signage and a catalogue, or register of objects within the exhibit. Greeters who will welcome parents and peers to the exhibit can be trained and can develop their own scripts.

If the children are in grades 4 through 6, they can also develop their own visitor feedback forms and design word-themed souvenirs. The whole museum can be photographed, and the pictures can later be hung near the word walls along with a description of the event. Of course, the children can use many of their newly recognized and owned words to describe the event.

This activity promotes additional writing, researching, discussing, and reading about words. It is also an excellent family literacy strategy, because families can develop their own word exhibits at home. This activity can also support and celebrate learners with disabilities. It can be presented in multiple languages by children who are ELL learners and fluent in more than a single language.

The Word Study Museum *activity can be used with either a phonics-based or a balanced literacy approach.*

COMPETENCY 5
UNDERSTAND READING COMPREHENSION AND DEVELOPMENT OF COMPREHENSION STRATEGIES AND INDEPENDENT READING

> SKILL 5.1 **Demonstrating knowledge of how proficient readers read, different levels of reading comprehension** (i.e., literal, inferential, and evaluative)**, and factors that affect reading comprehension** (e.g., automatic decoding, fluency, vocabulary knowledge, knowledge of academic language structures, background knowledge, comprehension strategies, linguistic and organizational complexity of text, motivation/purpose for reading)

Main Idea

TOPIC: what a paragraph or story is about

MAIN IDEA: the important idea(s) that the author wants the reader to know about a topic

The **TOPIC** of a paragraph or story is what the paragraph or story is about. The **MAIN IDEA** of a paragraph or story is the important idea(s) that the author wants the reader to know about a topic. The topic and main idea of a paragraph or story are sometimes directly stated. There are times, however, when the topic and main idea are not directly stated, but simply implied.

Look at this paragraph:

> *Henry Ford was an inventor who developed the first affordable automobile. The cars that were being built before Mr. Ford created his Model-T were very expensive. Only rich people could afford to have cars.*

The topic of this paragraph is Henry Ford. The main idea is that Henry Ford built the first affordable automobile.

TOPIC SENTENCE: indicates what a passage is about

The **TOPIC SENTENCE** indicates what a passage is about. It is the subject of that portion of the narrative. The ability to identify the topic sentence in a passage will enable the student to focus on the concept being discussed and better comprehend the information provided.

PARAGRAPH: a group of sentences about one main idea

You can find the main ideas by examining how paragraphs are written. A **PARAGRAPH** is a group of sentences about one main idea. Paragraphs usually have two types of sentences: a topic sentence, which contains the main idea, and two or more detail sentences that support, prove, provide more information, explain, or give examples. You can only tell if you have a detail or topic sentence by comparing the sentences with each other.

Look at this sample paragraph:

> *Fall is the best of the four seasons. The leaves change colors to create a beautiful display of golds, reds, and oranges. The air turns crisp and windy. The scent of pumpkin muffins and apple pies fills the air. Finally, Halloween marks the start of the holiday season. Fall is my favorite time of year!*

Breakdown of sentences:

> *Fall is the best of the four seasons. (TOPIC SENTENCE)*
>
> *The leaves change colors to create a beautiful display of golds, reds, and oranges. (DETAIL)*
>
> *The air turns crisp and windy. (DETAIL)*
>
> *The scent of pumpkin muffins and apple pies fill the air. (DETAIL)*
>
> *Finally, Halloween marks the start of the holiday season. (DETAIL)*
>
> *Fall is my favorite time of year! (CLOSING SENTENCE—Often a restatement of the topic sentence)*

The first sentence introduces the main idea and the other sentences support and provide more details and information.

Tips for Finding the Topic Sentence

How can you be sure that you have a topic sentence? Try this trick: Switch the sentence you think is the topic sentence into a question. If the other sentences seem to "answer" the question, then you've got it.

- The topic sentence is usually first, but could be in any position in the paragraph.

- A topic sentence is usually more general than the other sentences; that is, it talks about many things and looks at the big picture. Sometimes it refers to more than one thing. Plurals and the words *many*, *numerous*, or *several* often signal a topic sentence.

- Detail sentences are usually more specific than the topic sentence, that is, they usually talk about one single or small part of an idea. The words *for example, i.e., that is, first, second, third, etc.,* and *finally* often signal a detail.

- Most of the detail sentences support, give examples, prove, talk about, or point toward the topic sentence in some way.

For example, reword the topic sentence "Fall is the best of the four seasons" in one of the following ways:

> "Why is fall the best of the four season?"
>
> "Which season is the best season?"
>
> "Is fall the best season of the year?"

Then, as you read the remaining sentences (the ones you didn't pick), you will find that they answer (support) your question. If you attempt this with a sentence other than the topic sentence, it won't work.

For example, in the sample paragraph about fall, suppose you select "Halloween marks the start of the holiday season," and you reword it in the following way:

> "Which holiday is the start of the holiday season?"

You will find that the other sentences fail to help you answer (support) your question.

Summary Statements

The introductory statement should be at the beginning of the passage. An introductory statement provides a bridge between any previous, relevant text and the content to follow. It provides information about, and sets the tone and parameters for, the text to follow. The old axiom regarding presenting a body of information suggests that you should always "tell them what you are going to tell them; tell it to them; tell them what you just told them." The introductory statement is where the writer tells the readers what he or she is going to tell them.

The summary statement should be at or near the end of the passage, and is a concise presentation of the essential data from the passage. In terms of the old axiom, the content portion (the main body of the narrative) is where the writer "tells it to them." The summary statement is where the writer tells the readers what he or she has just told them.

Restating the main idea

An accurate restatement of the main idea from a passage usually summarizes the concept in a concise manner, and it often presents the same idea from a different perspective. A restatement should always demonstrate complete comprehension of the main idea.

To select an accurate restatement, identifying the main idea of the passage is essential. Once you comprehend the main idea of a passage, evaluate your choices

An accurate restatement of the main idea from a passage usually summarizes the concept in a concise manner, and it often presents the same idea from a different perspective.

to see which statement restates the main idea while eliminating statements that restate a supporting detail. Walk through the steps below the sample paragraph to see how to select the accurate restatement.

Fall is the best of the four seasons. The leaves change colors to create a beautiful display of golds, reds, and oranges. The air turns crisp and windy. The scent of pumpkin muffins and apple pies fill the air. Finally, Halloween marks the start of the holiday season. Fall is my favorite time of year!

Steps

1. Identify the main idea. ("Fall is the best of the four seasons.")

2. Decide which statement below restates the topic sentence:

   A. The changing leaves turn gold, red, and orange.

   B. The holidays start with Halloween.

   C. Of the four seasons, fall is the greatest of them all.

   D. Crisp wind is a fun aspect of fall.

The answer is C because it rephrases the main idea of the first sentence, the topic sentence.

Supporting Details

SUPPORTING DETAILS are sentences that provide more information about the topic and the main idea.

The supporting details in the paragraph about Henry Ford would be that he was an inventor and that before he created his Model T only rich people could afford cars because they were too expensive.

> **SUPPORTING DETAILS:** sentences that provide more information about the topic and the main idea

Fact and Opinion

A fact is something that is true and can be proved.

An opinion is something that a person believes, thinks, or feels.

Consider the following examples:

Joe DiMaggio, a Yankees center fielder, was replaced by Mickey Mantle in 1952.

This is a fact. If necessary, evidence can be produced to support this statement.

> *First-year players are more ambitious than seasoned players.*

This is an opinion. There is no proof to support this statement.

Author's Purpose

> An author may have more than one purpose in writing, such as to entertain, persuade, inform, describe, or narrate.

An author's purpose may be to entertain, to persuade, to inform, to describe, or to narrate.

There are no tricks or rules to follow in attempting to determine an author's purpose. It is up to the reader to use his or her judgment. Read the following paragraph.

> *Charles Lindbergh had no intention of becoming a pilot. He was enrolled in the University of Wisconsin until a flying lesson changed the entire course of his life. He began his career as a pilot by performing daredevil stunts at fairs.*

The author wrote this paragraph primarily to:

A. Describe

B. Inform

C. Entertain

D. Narrate

Since the author is simply telling us or informing us about the life of Charles Lindbergh, the correct answer here is B.

Author's Tone and Point of View

> **AUTHOR'S TONE:**
> attitude reflected in the statement or passage

The AUTHOR'S TONE is attitude reflected in the statement or passage. The author's choice of words helps the reader determine the overall tone of a statement or passage.

Read the following paragraph.

> *I was shocked by your article, which said that sitting down to breakfast was a thing of the past. Many families consider breakfast time to be family time. Children need to realize the importance of having a good breakfast. It is imperative that they be taught this at a young age. I cannot believe that a writer with your reputation has difficulty comprehending this.*

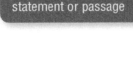

The author's tone in this passage is one of:

A. Concern

B. Anger

C. Excitement

D. Disbelief

Since the author directly states that he "cannot believe" that the writer feels this way, the answer is D, disbelief.

Inferences and Conclusions

In order to draw inferences and make conclusions, a reader must use prior knowledge and apply it to the current situation. A conclusion or inference is never stated. You must rely on your common sense.

Read the following passage.

The Smith family waited patiently around carousel number 7 for their luggage to arrive. They were exhausted after their five-hour trip and were eager to get to their hotel. After about an hour, they realized that they no longer recognized any of the other passengers' faces. Mrs. Smith asked the person who appeared to be in charge if they were at the right carousel. The man replied, "Yes, this is it, but we finished unloading that baggage almost half an hour ago."

From the man's response we can infer that:

A. The Smiths were ready to go to their hotel.

B. The Smiths' luggage was lost.

C. The man had their luggage.

D. They were at the wrong carousel.

Since the Smiths were still waiting for their luggage, we know that they were not yet ready to go to their hotel. From the man's response, we know that they were not at the wrong carousel and that he did not have their luggage. Therefore, though not directly stated, it appears that their luggage was lost. Choice B is the correct answer.

SKILL
5.2
Applying knowledge of research-based, explicit instruction in comprehension strategies (e.g., prediction, making connections to prior knowledge, think-aloud, monitoring, using knowledge of text structure, visual representation, mental imagery, summarization, questions/questioning) **that students can use to enhance their own comprehension of texts and promote their independence and self-efficacy as readers**

The point of comprehension instruction is not to focus simply on the text(s) students are using at the moment of instruction, but rather to help them learn strategies they can use independently with other texts.

COMMON METHODS OF TEACHING COMPREHENSION	
Summarization	When summarizing, either in writing or verbally, students review the main point of the text, along with strategically chosen details that highlight the main point. This is not the same as paraphrasing, which is saying the same thing in different words. Teaching students how to summarize is very important, as it will help them look for the most critical areas in a text. In nonfiction, for example, it helps them distinguish between main arguments and examples. In fiction, it helps them learn how to focus on the main characters and events and distinguish them from the lesser characters and events.
Question Answering	While this method tends to be overused in many classrooms, it is a valid method of teaching comprehension. As the name implies, students answer questions regarding a text, either out loud, in small groups, or individually on paper. The best questions are those that require students to think about the text (rather than just find an answer in the text).
Question Generating	This is the opposite of question answering, although students can then be asked to answer their own questions or the questions of other students. In general, students should be taught to constantly question texts as they read. This is important because it makes them more critical readers. Teaching students to generate questions helps them to learn the types of questions they can ask, and it gets them thinking about how to be critical of texts.
Graphic Organizers	Graphic organizers are visual representations of content within a text. For example, Venn diagrams can be used to highlight the differences between two characters in a novel or two similar political concepts in a social studies textbook. A teacher can use flowcharts with students to talk about the steps in a process (for example, the steps of setting up a science experiment or the chronological events of a story).
Semantic Organizers	These are similar to graphic organizers in that they visually display information. The difference, usually, is that semantic organizers focus on words or concepts. For example, a word web can help students make sense of a word by mapping from the central word all the similar and related concepts to that word.

Continued on next page

Text Structures	In nonfiction, particularly in textbooks, and sometimes in fiction, text structures give readers important clues about what to look for. Often students do not know how to make sense of all the types of headings in a textbook and do not realize that, for example, the sidebar story about a character in history is not the main text on a particular page in the history textbook. Teaching students how to interpret text structures gives them tools they can use to tackle other similar texts.
Monitoring Comprehension	Students need to be aware of their comprehension, or lack of it, in particular texts. It is important to teach students what to do when the text suddenly stops making sense. For example, students can go back and reread the description of a character. They can go back to the table of contents or the first paragraph of a chapter to see where they are headed.
Discussion	Small-group or whole-class discussion stimulates thoughts about texts and gives students a larger picture of their impact. For example, teachers can strategically encourage students to discuss concepts related to the text. This helps students learn to consider texts within larger societal and social contexts. Teachers can also encourage students to provide personal opinions in discussion. Listening to other students' opinions helps all students in a class to see the wide range of interpretations of and thoughts about one text.
Textual Marking	This is when students interact with the text as they read. For example, armed with sticky notes, students can insert questions or comments regarding specific sentences or paragraphs within the text. This helps them focus on the importance of the small things, particularly when they are reading larger works (such as novels in high school). It also gives students a reference point to go back into the text when they need to review something.

Knowledge of Story Structure

Most works of fiction contain a common set of elements that make them come alive to readers. Even though writers do not consciously think about each of these story elements when they sit down to write, all stories essentially contain these "markers" that make them the stories that they are. Even though all stories have these elements, they are a lot like fingerprints: Each story's story elements are just a bit different.

Plot

The most commonly discussed story element in fiction is plot. **PLOT** is the series of events in a story. Typically, but not always, plot moves in a predictable fashion:

PLOT: the series of events in a story

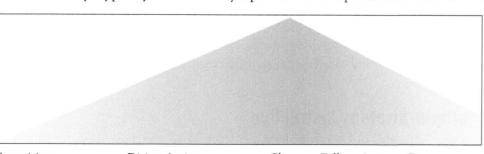

Exposition   Rising Action   Climax   Falling Action   Denouement

Exposition is where characters and their situations are introduced. Rising action is the point at which conflict starts to occur. Climax is the highest point of conflict, often a turning point. Falling action is the result of the climax. Dénouement is the final resolution of the plot.

Character

Character is another commonly studied story element. Stories contain heroes, villains, comedic characters, dark characters, etc. When we examine the characters of a story, we look to see who they are and how their traits contribute to the story. Often, plot elements become more interesting because of the characters' particular traits. For example, authors may pair unlikely characters together who, in turn, create specific conflict.

Setting

SETTING: the place, or location, where a story occurs

The SETTING of a story is the place, or location, where it occurs. Often, the specific place is not as important as some of the specifics about the setting. For example, the setting of F. Scott Fitzgerald's novel *The Great Gatsby* is New York, which is not as significant as the fact that it takes place among extreme wealth. Conversely, John Steinbeck's novel *The Grapes of Wrath*, although it takes place in Oklahoma and California, has a more significant setting of poverty. In fact, as the story takes place *around* other migrant workers, the setting is even more significant. In a way, the setting serves as a reason for various conflicts to occur.

Theme

THEME: the underlying message that a writer wants to convey

The THEME of a story is the underlying message that a writer wants to convey. Common themes in literature are jealousy, money, love, man or woman against corporation or government, etc. These themes are never explicitly stated; rather, they are the result of the portrayal of characters, settings, and plots.

Mood

MOOD: the atmosphere or attitude the writer conveys through descriptive language

Finally, the MOOD of a story is the atmosphere or attitude the writer conveys through descriptive language. Often, mood fits in nicely with theme and setting. For example, in Edgar Allen Poe's stories, we often find a mood of horror and darknes that comes from the descriptions of characters and the setting, as well as from specific plot elements. Mood helps us better understand the writer's theme and intentions through descriptive, stylistic language.

Multiple-Strategy Instruction

Students' attitudes and perceptions about learning are the most powerful factors influencing academic focus and success. When instructional objectives center on students' interests and are relevant to their lives, effective learning occurs. Students must believe that the tasks they are asked to perform have value and that they have the ability and resources to perform them. If a student thinks a task is unimportant, he will not put much effort into it. If a student thinks he lacks the ability or resources to successfully complete a task, even attempting the task becomes too great a risk. The teacher must not only understand the students' abilities and interests but also help students develop positive attitudes and perceptions about tasks and learning.

Good readers do not rely on a single strategy to comprehend what they read. They apply different strategies at different points in a text, switching tactics as the text or reading activity demands. *Reciprocal teaching, concept-oriented reading instruction*, and *transactional strategy instruction* are three examples of multiple-strategy instructional techniques that have demonstrated classroom success.

Reciprocal teaching

This technique begins with the teacher and a group of students discussing a text. The discussion is structured by four strategies: summarizing, questioning, clarifying, and predicting—with the teacher modeling each strategy. After the modeling, students take turns leading the discussion about specific parts of the text.

Teachers should also change instructional strategies based on students' questions and comments. If students express confusion about the content of the lesson, the teacher should immediately take another approach to presenting the lesson. Sometimes this can be accomplished by simply rephrasing an explanation.

Reciprocal teaching, concept-oriented reading instruction, and transactional strategy instruction are three examples of multiple-strategy instructional techniques that have demonstrated classroom success.

Concept-Oriented Reading Instruction (CORI)

CORI integrates comprehension strategies for which the National Reading Panel found firm scientific bases for effectiveness (e.g., cooperative learning, comprehension monitoring, summarizing) with inquiry science. Inquiry science includes hands-on activities such as observation of real-world phenomena and experimentation, designed to support student understanding of scientific concepts. Students use texts to confirm and extend the knowledge they gain through the hands-on activities. The effective teacher uses advanced communication skills such as clarification, reflection, perception, and summarization as a means to facilitate communication. The ability to communicate with students, listen effectively, identify relevant and irrelevant information, and summarize students' messages facilitates establishing and maintaining an optimum classroom learning environment.

Transactional Strategy Instruction (TSI)

TSI takes place in small groups and concerns the transaction among the reader, the text, and the context. Specifically, TSI helps students link their prior knowledge to a text through discussion and involves constructing meaning through group collaboration rather than individual interpretation. The dynamics of the group determine the responses of all group members, including the teacher.

The following are instructional strategy guidelines that teachers may implement:

- Select appropriate text
- Model the strategy
- Select the strategy
- Support student practice
- Give a clear explanation
- Have students apply the strategy

After the teacher has presented a skill or concept lesson, students must be given time to practice the skill or concept. During this time teachers can circulate among students to check for understanding. If the teacher observes that any of the students did not clearly understand the skill or concept, she can immediately readdress the issue using another technique or approach.

See also Skill 5.4

SKILL 5.3 Applying knowledge of the use of appropriate texts and effective, engaging oral language, reading, and writing activities to facilitate students' comprehension of texts before, during, and after reading and to motivate and reinforce their development of comprehension strategies

Making Predictions

One theory or approach to the teaching of reading that gained currency in the late 1960s and the early 1970s was the importance of asking inferential and critical thinking questions, which would challenge and engage the children to read text. This approach to reading went beyond the literal level of what was stated in the text to an inferential level of using text clues to make predictions and to a critical level of involving the child in evaluating the text. While asking engaging and thought-provoking questions is still viewed as part of the teaching of reading, it is currently viewed as just one of several components of the teaching of reading.

Prior Knowledge

PRIOR KNOWLEDGE can be defined as all of an individual's prior experiences, learning, and development that precede his or her entering a specific learning situation or attempting to comprehend a specific text. Sometimes prior knowledge can be erroneous or incomplete. Obviously, if there are misconceptions in a child's prior

Sites on teaching reading comprehension:

www.readingrockets.org /article/3479

web001.greece.k12 .ny.us/academics .cfm?subpage=930

PRIOR KNOWLEDGE: all of an individual's prior experiences, learning, and development that precede entering a specific learning situation or attempting to comprehend a specific text

knowledge, these must be corrected so that the child's overall comprehension skills can progress.

Even the prior knowledge of kindergarteners includes their accumulated positive and negative experiences both in and out of school. These might range from wonderful family travels, watching television, visiting museums and libraries, to visiting hospitals, prisons, and surviving poverty. Whatever prior knowledge that the child brings to the school setting, the independent reading and writing the child does in school immeasurably expands his prior knowledge and, hence, broadens that child's reading comprehension capabilities.

Literary response skills are dependent on prior knowledge, schemata, and background. SCHEMATA (the plural of schema) are those structures that represent generic concepts stored in our memory. Readers who effectively comprehend text, whether they are adults or children, use both their schemata and prior knowledge plus the ideas from the printed text for reading comprehension. Graphic organizers help organize this information.

> **SCHEMATA:** those structures that represent generic concepts stored in our memory

Graphic Organizers

Graphic organizers solidify in a chart or diagram format a visual relationship among various reading and writing ideas including: sequence, timelines, character traits, fact and opinion, main idea and details, and differences and likenesses (generally done using a Venn diagram of interlocking circles, KWL chart, etc). These charts and diagrams are essential for providing scaffolding for instruction through activating pertinent prior knowledge.

KWL CHARTS aid reading comprehension by outlining what readers *KNOW*, what they *WANT* to know, and what they've *LEARNED* after reading. Students are asked to activate prior knowledge about a topic and further develop their knowledge about a topic using this organizer. Teachers often opt to display and maintain KWL charts throughout the reading of a text to continually record pertinent information about a student's reading.

> **KWL CHARTS:** aid reading comprehension by outlining what readers KNOW, what they WANT to know, and what they've LEARNED after reading

When the teacher first introduces the KWL strategy, the children should be allowed sufficient time to brainstorm in response to the first question, listing what all of them in the class or small group actually know about the topic. The children should have a three-columned KWL worksheet template for their journals and the teacher should use a KWL chart to record the responses from class or group discussion. The children can write under each column in their own journal and should also help the teacher with notations on the chart. This strategy allows the children to gain experience in note taking and in creating a concrete record of new data and information they have gleaned from the passage about the topic.

Depending on the grade level of the participating children, the teacher may also want to ask them to consider categories of information they hope to find out from the expository passage. For instance, they may be reading a book on animals to find out more about the animal's habitats during the winter or about the animal's mating habits.

Use this chart during your study of spiders. First write what you know about spiders. Then write what you would like to know about spiders. At the end of your study write the most important things you learned.

SPIDER KWL		
What I know	**What I want to know**	**What I have learned**
• • •	• • •	• • •
The most interesting fact I learned was: _____ _____		

When children are working on the middle section of their KWL strategy sheet—What I want to know—the teacher may want to give them a chance to share what they would like to learn further about the topic and help them to express it in question format.

KWL is useful and can even be introduced as early as Grade 2 with extensive teacher discussion support. It not only serves to support the child's comprehension of a particular expository text, but also models for children a format for note taking. Beyond note taking, when the teacher wants to introduce report writing, the KWL format provides excellent outlines and question introductions for at least three paragraphs of a report.

Cooper (2004) recommends this strategy for use with thematic units and with reading chapters in required science, social studies, or health text books.

In addition to its usefulness with thematic unit study, KWL is wonderful for providing the teacher with a concrete format to assess how well children have absorbed pertinent new knowledge within the passage by looking at the third section—What I have learned. Ultimately, it is hoped that students will learn to use this strategy, not only under explicit teacher direction with templates of KWL sheets, but also on their own by informally writing questions they want to find out about in their journals and then going back to their own questions and answering them after the reading.

Note taking

Older children take notes in their reading journals, while younger children and those more in need of explicit teacher support contribute their ideas and responses as part of the discussion in class. Their responses are recorded on the experiential chart.

Connecting texts

The concept of readiness is generally regarded as a developmentally based phenomenon. Various abilities, whether cognitive, affective, or psychomotor, are perceived to be dependent upon the mastery or development of certain prerequisite skills or abilities.

Readiness for subject area learning is dependent not only on prior knowledge, but also on affective factors such as interest, motivation, and attitude. These factors are often more influential on student learning than the preexisting cognitive base.

When texts relate to a student's life or other reading materials or areas of study, they become more meaningful and relevant to the student's learning. Students enjoy seeing reading material connect to their lives, other subject areas, and other reading material.

Discussing the text

Discussion is an activity in which the children (and this activity works well from grades 3–6 and beyond) consider a particular text. Among the prompts, the teacher–coach might suggest that the children focus on words of interest they encountered in the text. These can also be words that they heard if the text was read aloud. Children can be asked to share something funny or upsetting or unusual about the words they have read. Through this focus on children's response to words as the center of the discussion circle, peers become more interested in word study.

Literacy, reading, writing, thinking, listening, viewing, and discussing are not viewed as separate activities or components of instruction. Instead they are developed and nurtured simultaneously and interactively.

SKILL 5.4 **Demonstrating knowledge of the role of independent reading in literacy development and explicit strategies for promoting and motivating students' independent and at-home reading to consolidate and reinforce their reading competence and promote their personal growth and lifelong learning** (e.g., applying knowledge of students' interests; reading aloud to students; providing access to a variety of reading materials, including materials in students' home languages; encouraging and providing support for parents/guardians to read to their children)

Reading comprehension is not a passive process. When we read for understanding, we are consciously focused on obtaining meaning through a variety of methods.

For instance, we might access background knowledge to help us understand new ideas or we might go back and re-read a few sentences to clarify a confusing concept.

When we apply various strategies to make sense of text, we first have to monitor our levels of comprehension. In other words, we need to know when comprehension is breaking down; we need to notice that we aren't actually understanding something. Furthermore, we need to know what it is that is causing our confusion. By understanding what we do not understand, as well as why we do not understand, we will be in a better position to pick the right strategy to fix our comprehension. There are various ways to teach students how to monitor their comprehension. Below is a brief description of two of the most common methods.

THINK-ALOUDS: deliberate explanations of comprehension strategies provided to students out-loud by the teacher

THINK-ALOUDS are deliberate explanations of comprehension strategies provided to students out-loud by the teacher. Basically, the teacher models to students his or her own comprehension strategies as he or she reads aloud some text. For example, the teacher might run across a confusing idea and mention to the class that an ideal strategy would be to go back and re-read a section of text. Or, the teacher might come across a difficult word and look at the rest of the sentence to see if meaning can be derived from context. This strategy helps students in a few ways. First, students see that reading is not necessarily a continuous process, but rather one that takes multiple strategies to successfully understand what is written. Second, it actually gives students specific strategies they can use when they come across similar situations.

SELF-QUESTIONING: reminders to students to keep comprehension visible as they read by asking themselves common questions about their text

Another way to teach the monitoring of comprehension is by teaching students to use **SELF-QUESTIONING** strategies. Self-questioning strategies simply are active reading cues—essentially, reminders to students that they can keep comprehension visible as they read by asking themselves common questions about their text. For example, at the end of each section of a long story, students can be trained to self-predict about the next section. They can also ask themselves continuously, "why?" In other words, as events unfold in a story, they can constantly ask themselves, "Why did this occur?" or "Why did the character do this or that?" These types of questions greatly assist in the comprehension of text simply because they force readers to be more aware of what is going on within the text. In essence, they cause readers to be less lazy as they read.

SKILL Demonstrating knowledge of formal and informal methods for
5.5 assessing students' development in reading comprehension and
demonstrating the ability to interpret and use the results of these
assessments to plan effective comprehension instruction

Retelling

RETELLING needs to be very clearly defined so that the child reader does not think
that the teacher wants him or her to repeat verbatim the WHOLE story back in
the retelling. A child should be able to talk comfortably and fluently about the
story he/she has just read. He/she should be able to tell the main things that have
happened in the story.

When a child retells a story to a teacher, the teacher needs ways to help in assessing the child's understanding. Ironically, the teacher can use some of the same
strategies he/she suggests to the child to assess the child's understanding of a book
with which the teacher is not familiar. These strategies include:

- Back cover reading

- Scanning the table of contents

- Looking at the pictures

- Reading the book jacket

If the child can explain how the story turned out and provide examples to support
these explanations, the teacher should try not to interrupt the child with too many
questions. Children can use the text of the book to reinforce what they are saying
and they can even read from it if they wish. It is also important to note that some
children need to reread the text twice with the second reading being for enjoyment.

Assessing a student's retelling

When the teacher plans to use the retelling as a way of assessing the child, then
the following ground rules have to be set and made clear to the child. The teacher
explains the purpose of the retelling to determine how well the child is reading at
the outset of the conference.

The teacher maintains in the child's assessment notebook or in his/her assessment
record what the child is saying in phrases, not sentences. Just enough is recorded
to indicate whether the child actually understood the story. The teacher also tries
to analyze from the retelling why the child cannot comprehend a given text. If
the child's accuracy rate with the text is below 95 percent, then the problem
is at the word level, but if the accuracy rate for the text is above 95 percent, the
difficulty lies at the text level.

> **RETELLING:** a compre-
> hension assessment strat-
> egy in which the student
> retells a story that he or
> she has read to highlight
> the main themes

Word Map Strategy

Although also a teaching strategy, this approach provides useful assessment data for teachers. This strategy is helpful for children in grades 3–6 and beyond. The target group of children for the **WORD MAP STRATEGY** includes those who need to improve their independent vocabulary acquisition abilities. The strategy is essentially teacher-directed learning where children are "walked through" the process. The teacher helps the children to identify the type of information that makes a definition. Children are also assisted in using context clues and background understanding to construct meaning.

The word map graphic organizer is the tool teachers use to complete this strategy with children. Word map templates are available online from the Houghton Mifflin Web site and from *ReadWriteThink*, the Web site of the NCTE. The word map helps children to visually represent the elements of a given concept.

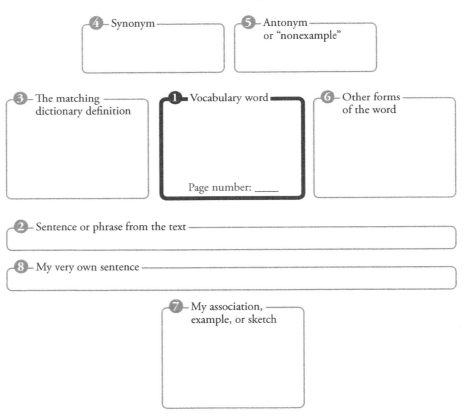

Word Map

Example of word mapping

The children's literal articulation of the concept can be prompted by three key questions:

- What is it?
- What is it like?
- What are some examples?

For instance, the word "oatmeal" might yield a word map with boxes that have the answers to each of the three key questions. What is it? (A hot cereal) What's it like? (Mushy and Salty) What are some examples? (Plain or Apple-Flavored)

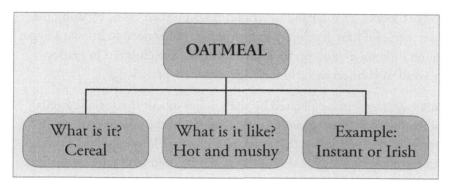

Implementing mapping in class

To share this strategy with children, the teacher selects three concepts familiar to the children and shows them the template of a word map with the three questions asked on the map. The teacher then helps the children to fill in at least two word maps with the topic in the top box and the answers in the three question boxes. The children should then independently complete the word map for the third topic. To reinforce the lesson, the teacher has the children select a concept of their own to map either independently or in a small group. As the final task for this first part of the strategy, the children, in teams or individually, write a definition for at least one of the concepts using the key things about it listed on the map. The children share these definitions aloud and talk about how they used the word maps to help them with the definitions.

For the next part of this strategy, the teacher picks an expository text or a textbook the children are already using to study mathematics, science, or social studies. The teacher either locates a short excerpt where a particular concept is defined or uses the content to write original model passages of definition.

After the passages are selected or authored, the teacher duplicates them. Then they are distributed to the children along with blank word map templates. The children will be asked to read each passage and then to complete the word map for the concept in each passage. Finally, the children share the word maps they have developed for each passage, and explain how they used the word in the passage to help them fill out their word map. Lastly, the teacher reminds the children that the three components of the concept—class, description, and example—are just three of the many components for any given concept.

Word mapping as assessment

This strategy has assessment potential because the teacher can literally see how the students understand specific concepts by looking at their maps and hearing their explanations. The maps that the students develop on their own demonstrate whether they have really understood the concepts in the passages. This strategy serves to ready students for inferring word meanings on their own. By using the word map strategy, children develop concepts of what they need to know to begin to figure out an unknown word on their own. It assists the children in grades three and beyond to connect prior knowledge with new knowledge.

This word map strategy can be adapted by the teacher to suit the specific needs and goals of instruction. Illustrations of the concept and the comparisons to other concepts can be included in the word mapping for children grades five and beyond. This particular strategy is also one that can be used with a research theme in other content areas.

> Word mapping can be adapted by the teacher to suit the specific needs and goals of instruction.

> **SKILL 5.6** Demonstrating knowledge of strategies for determining students' independent, instructional, and frustration reading levels and for using this information to help select appropriate texts for instruction and guide students' independent reading

Independent, Instructional, and Frustration Reading Levels

Instructional reading is generally judged to be at the 95 percent accuracy level, although Taberski places it between 92 and 97 percent. Taberski tries to enhance the independent reading levels by making sure that readers on the instructional reading levels read a variety of genres and have a range of available and interesting books of a particular genre to read.

Taberski's availability for reading conferences helps her to both assess first-hand her children's frustration levels and to model ongoing teacher/reader book conversations by scheduling child-initiated reading conferences where she personally replenishes their book bags.

In order to allay children's frustration levels in their reading and to foster their independent reading, it is important to some children that the teacher personally take time out to hear them read aloud and to check for fluency and expression. Children's frustration levels can be immeasurably lessened if they are explicitly told by the teacher after they have read aloud that they need to read without pointing and that they should try chunking words into phrases that mimic their natural speech.

Assessment of the reading development of individual students

Using pictures and illustrations

For young readers who are from ELL backgrounds, even if they were born in the United States, the use of pictures validates their story-authoring and story-telling skills and provides them with access and equity to the literary discussion and book talk of their native English-speaking peers. These children can also demonstrate their story-telling abilities by drawing sequels or prequels to the story detailed in the illustrations alone. They might even be given the opportunity to share the story aloud in their native language or to comment on the illustrations in their native language.

Since many stories today are recorded in two or even three languages discussing story events or analyzing pictures in a different native language is a beneficial practice.

Use of pictures and illustrations can also help the K–3 educator assess the capabilities of children who are struggling readers because they are children whose learning strength is spatial. Through targeted questions about how the pictures would change if different plot twists occurred, or how the child might transform the story through changing the illustrations, the teacher can begin to assess struggling reader deficits and strengths.

Using recorded readings

Children from ELL backgrounds can benefit from listening to a recorded version of a particular story with which they can read along. This gives them another opportunity to "hear" the story correctly pronounced and presented and to begin to internalize its language structures. In the absence of recorded versions of some key stories or texts, the teacher may want to make sound recordings.

Highly proficient readers can also be involved in creating these literature recordings for use with ELL peers or younger peers. This, of course, develops oral language proficiency, but also introduces these skilled readers to the intricacies of supporting ELL English language reading instruction. When they actually see their tapes being used by children they will be tremendously gratified.

In order to allay children's frustration levels in their reading and to foster their independent reading, it is important to some children that the teacher personally take time out to hear them read aloud and to check for fluency and expression.

Use of pictures and illustrations can help the K-3 educator assess the capabilities of children who are struggling readers because they are children whose learning strength is spatial.

> SKILL 5.7 **Applying knowledge of strategies** (e.g., differentiated instruction, interventions, enrichment) **to address the assessed needs of individual students** (e.g., English language learners, struggling readers through highly proficient readers) **in reading comprehension, comprehension strategies, and independent reading, including helping English language learners transfer relevant skills from their home language to English**

See also Skills 4.7 and 5.6

COMPETENCY 6
UNDERSTAND DIFFERENT TYPES OF TEXTS AND STRATEGIES FOR UNDERSTANDING, ANALYZING, AND RESPONDING TO THEM

> SKILL 6.1 **Demonstrating knowledge of children's and young adolescents' literature representing a range of genres, eras, perspectives, and cultures, including key characteristics and elements of literary/ narrative texts** (e.g., story elements such as character and plot, stylistic elements such as figurative language)**, and applying knowledge of explicit instruction in key features, genres, and elements of literary/ narrative texts to promote students' understanding of these texts**

The major literary genres include allegory, ballad, drama, epic, epistle, essay, fable, novel, poem, romance, and the short story.

MAJOR LITERARY GENRES	
Allegory	A story in verse or prose with characters representing virtues and vices. There are two meanings, symbolic and literal. John Bunyan's *The Pilgrim's Progress* is the most well-known text of this genre.

Continued on next page

Ballad	An *in medias res* story, told or sung, usually in verse and accompanied by music. Literary devices found in ballads include the refrain, or repeated section, and incremental repetition, or anaphora, for effect. Earliest forms were anonymous folk ballads. Later forms include Coleridge's Romantic masterpiece, "The Rime of the Ancient Mariner."
Drama	Plays—comedy, modern, or tragedy—typically in five acts. Traditionalists and neoclassicists adhere to Aristotle's unities of time, place, and action. Plot development is advanced via dialogue. Literary devices include asides, soliloquies, and the chorus representing public opinion. Greatest of all dramatists/playwrights is William Shakespeare. Other well-known playwrights include Ibsen, Williams, Miller, Shaw, Stoppard, Racine, Moliére, Sophocles, Aeschylus, Euripides, and Aristophanes.
Epic	Long poem usually of book length reflecting values inherent in the generative society. Epic devices include an invocation to a Muse for inspiration, purpose for writing, universal setting, protagonist and antagonist who possess supernatural strength and acumen, and interventions of a god or gods. Understandably, there are very few epics: Homer's *Iliad* and *Odyssey*, Virgil's *Aeneid*, Milton's *Paradise Lost*, Spenser's *The Fairie Queene*, Barrett Browning's *Aurora Leigh*, and Pope's mock-epic, *The Rape of the Lock*.
Epistle	A letter that is not always originally intended for public distribution, but due to the fame of the sender and/or recipient, becomes public. Paul wrote epistles that were later placed in the Bible.
Essay	Typically a limited length prose work focusing on a topic and propounding a definite point of view and authoritative tone. Great essayists include Carlyle, Lamb, DeQuincy, Emerson, and Montaigne, who is credited with defining this genre.
Fable	Terse tale offering up a moral or exemplum. Chaucer's "The Nun's Priest's Tale" is a fine example of a *bête fabliau* or beast fable in which animals speak and act characteristically human, illustrating human foibles.
Legend	A traditional narrative or collection of related narratives, popularly regarded as historically factual but actually a mixture of fact and fiction.
Myth	Stories that are more or less universally shared within a culture to explain its history and traditions.
Novel	The longest form of fictional prose containing a variety of characterizations, settings, and regionalism. Most have complex plots, expanded description, and attention to detail. Some of the great novelists include Austin, the Brontes, Twain, Tolstoy, Hugo, Hardy, Dickens, Hawthorne, Forster, and Flaubert.
Poem	The only requirement is rhythm. Subgenres include fixed types of literature such as the sonnet, elegy, ode, pastoral, and villanelle. Unfixed types of literature include blank verse and dramatic monologue.

Continued on next page

Romance	A highly imaginative tale set in a fantastical realm dealing with the conflicts between heroes, villains and/or monsters. "The Knight's Tale" from Chaucer's *Canterbury Tales*, *Sir Gawain and the Green Knight* and Keats' "The Eve of St. Agnes" are prime representatives.
Short Story	Typically a terse narrative, with less developmental background about characters than a novel. Short stories may include description, author's point of view, and tone. Poe emphasized that a successful short story should create one focused impact. Hemingway, Faulkner, Twain, Joyce, Shirley Jackson, Flannery O'Connor, de Maupassant, Saki, Edgar Allen Poe, and Pushkin are considered to be great short story writers.
Children's Literature	A genre of its own that emerged as a distinct and independent form in the second half of the eighteenth century. *The Visible World in Pictures* by John Amos Comenius, a Czech educator, was one of the first printed works and the first picture book. For the first time, educators acknowledged that children are different from adults in many respects. Modern educators acknowledge that introducing elementary students to a wide range of reading experiences plays an important role in their mental/social/psychological development.

LITERATURE SPECIFICALLY FOR CHILDREN	
Traditional Literature	Traditional literature opens up a world where right wins out over wrong, where hard work and perseverance are rewarded, and where helpless victims find vindication—all worthwhile values that children identify with even as early as kindergarten. In traditional literature, children will be introduced to fanciful beings, humans with exaggerated powers, talking animals, and heroes that will inspire them. For younger elementary children, these stories in Big Book format are ideal for providing predictable and repetitive elements that can be grasped by these children.
Folktales/ Fairy Tales	Adventures of animals or humans and the supernatural characterize these stories. The hero is usually on a quest and is aided by other-worldly helpers. More often than not, the story focuses on good and evil and reward and punishment. Some examples: *The Three Bears*, *Little Red Riding Hood*, *Snow White*, *Sleeping Beauty*, *Puss-in-Boots*, *Rapunzel*, and *Rumpelstiltskin*.
Fables	Animals that act like humans are featured in these stories, which usually reveal human foibles or sometimes teach a lesson. Example: Aesop's *Fables*.
Myths	These stories about events from the earliest times, such as the origin of the world, are considered true in their own societies.
Legends	These are similar to myths except that they tend to deal with events that happened more recently. Example: Arthurian legends.
Tall Tales	These are purposely exaggerated accounts of individuals with superhuman strength. Examples: Paul Bunyan, John Henry, and Pecos Bill.

Continued on next page

Modern Fantasy	Many of the themes found in these stories are similar to those in traditional literature. The stories start out based in reality, which makes it easier for the reader to suspend disbelief and enter worlds of unreality. Little people live in the walls in *The Borrowers* and time travel is possible in *The Trolley to Yesterday*. Including some fantasy tales in the curriculum helps elementary-grade children develop their senses of imagination. These often appeal to ideals of justice and issues having to do with good and evil; and because children tend to identify with the characters, the message is more likely to be retained.
Science Fiction	Robots, spacecraft, mystery, and civilizations from other ages often appear in these stories. Most presume advances in science on other planets or in a future time. Most children like these stories because of their interest in space and the "what if" aspect of the stories. Examples: *Outer Space and All That Junk* and *A Wrinkle in Time*.
Modern Realistic Fiction	These stories are about real problems that real children face. By finding that their hopes and fears are shared by others, young children can find insight into their own problems. Young readers also tend to experience a broadening of interests as the result of this kind of reading. It's good for them to know that a child can be brave and intelligent and can solve difficult problems.
Historical Fiction	The stories are presented in a historically accurate setting. One example of this kind of story is *Rifles for Watie*. This story is about a young boy who serves in the Union army. He experiences great hardship but discovers that his enemy is an admirable human being. It provides a good opportunity to introduce younger children to history.
Biography	Reading about inventors, explorers, scientists, political and religious leaders, social reformers, artists, sports figures, doctors, teachers, writers, and war heroes helps children to see that one person can make a difference. They also open new vistas for children to think about when they choose an occupation to fantasize about.
Informational Books	These are ways to learn more about something you are interested in or something that you know nothing about. Encyclopedias are good resources, of course, but a book like *Polar Wildlife* by Kamini Khanduri shows pictures and facts that will capture the imaginations of young children.

Living in a multicultural society, it is important that teachers think beyond the classics of literature (or even simply the works of literature they personally enjoy and are familiar with) and consider literature that is representative of the various cultures in this country and their particular classrooms, and instructive to students about how to interact with people who are not like themselves.

When selecting multicultural literature, a few things need to be considered:

- Is the literature, in general, appropriate?

- Does the literature accurately portray a particular culture?

- Will students be able to utilize the literature for a greater social purpose?

When selecting a piece of literature for classroom use, teachers need to ensure that it is appropriate. Has the board of education in the teacher's district approved the text for classroom use? If it is up to the teacher to decide whether the text is appropriate, the teacher must determine whether the text contains violence, vulgar language, sexual explicitness, negative values, or racism. If so, the text is probably not appropriate. In addition, is the text at the appropriate reading level for the class? These considerations are necessary for all texts, whether or not they are multicultural selections.

The next issue to consider is the extent to which the text accurately portrays other cultures. Often, in general literature, there are gross misrepresentations of some cultures, which can give students incorrect perceptions of those cultures. In addition, teachers should consider whether students who are members of the cultures portrayed feel that the portrayals are accurate. If not, it could be damaging to those students, as well as to their relationships with other students.

Finally, the literature should help students learn how to live in a multicultural society. The literature students read in school may provide one of the few opportunities they have to learn how to interact with people in different cultures. Teachers need to make sure that students have good role models in the literature and that the literature assists in positively developing their habits of mind. While not all literature must serve this purpose, it is important that, at various times throughout the school year, students get some "life instruction" through their classroom reading materials.

> SKILL 6.2 **Applying knowledge of explicit instruction in literary response and analysis skills** (e.g., using evidence from a text to support responses, analyzing story elements, interpreting figurative language, evaluating tone and mood, recognizing that texts can reflect diverse cultural perspectives)

Imagery

IMAGERY: a word or sequence of words that refers to any sensory experience; anything that can be seen, tasted, smelled, heard, or felt on the skin or with the fingers

IMAGERY can be described as a word or sequence of words that refers to any sensory experience—that is, anything that can be seen, tasted, smelled, heard, or felt on the skin or with the fingers. While writers of prose also use imagery, it is most common in poetry. The poet intends to make an experience available to the reader. In order to do that, the poet must choose words that appeal to one of the senses. The poet will deliberately paint a scene in such a way that the reader can see it. However, the purpose is not simply to stir the visceral feeling, but also to stir the emotions.

A good example is "The Piercing Chill" by Taniguchi Buson (1715-1783):

> *The piercing chill I feel:*
> *My dead wife's comb, in our bedroom,*
> *Under my heel . . .*

In only a few short words, the reader can feel many things: the shock that might come from touching the corpse, a literal sense of death, and the contrast between the death of the wife and the memories the husband has of her when she was alive. Imagery might be defined as speaking of the abstract in concrete terms, a powerful device in the hands of a skilful poet.

Symbols

A **SYMBOL** is an object or action that can be observed with the senses and that suggests other things. The lion is a symbol of courage; the color green, a symbol of envy. Symbols used in literature are usually of a different sort. They tend to be private and personal; their significance is only evident in the context of the work in which they are used. A good example is the huge pair of spectacles on a billboard in *The Great Gatsby* by F. Scott Fitzgerald. They are interesting as a part of the landscape, but they also symbolize divine myopia. A symbol can certainly have more than one meaning, and the meaning may be as personal as the memories and experiences of the particular reader. In analyzing a poem or a story, it is important to identify symbols and their possible meanings.

> **SYMBOL:** an object or action that can be observed with the senses and that suggests other things

Looking for symbols is often challenging, especially for novice poetry readers. However, these suggestions may be useful: First, pick out all references to concrete objects, such as a newspaper or a black cat. Note any that the poet emphasizes by describing them in detail, repeating, or by placing them at the very beginning or end of a poem. Ask yourself, "What is the poem about? What does it mean?" Paraphrase the poem and determine whether the meaning depends on certain concrete objects. Then think about what the concrete object symbolizes in this particular poem. A symbol may be a part of a person's body, such as the eye of the murder victim in Edgar Allan Poe's short story "The Tell-Tale Heart," or a look, a voice, or a mannerism.

The following are some things a symbol is *not*: an abstraction such as truth, death, or love; in narrative, a well developed character who is not at all mysterious; or the second term in a metaphor. In Emily Dickinson's "The Lightning Is a Yellow Fork," the symbol is the lightning, not the fork.

An **ALLUSION** is very much like a symbol. In *Merriam-Webster's Encyclopedia of Literature*, an allusion is defined as "an implied reference to a person, event, thing, or a part of another text." Allusions are based on the assumption that there

> **ALLUSION:** an implied reference to a person, event, thing, or a part of another text

is a common body of knowledge shared by the poet and the reader and that a reference to that body of knowledge will be immediately understood. Allusions to the Bible and classical mythology are common in Western literature on the assumption that they will be immediately understood. This is not always the case, of course. T. S. Eliot's *The Waste Land* requires research and annotation for understanding. The author assumed more background on the part of the average reader than actually exists. However, when Michael Moore headlines an article on the war in Iraq: "Déjà Fallouja: Ramadi surrounded, thousands of families trapped, no electricity or water, onslaught impending," we understand immediately that this refers to a repeat of the human disaster in New Orleans, although the "onslaught" is not a storm but an invasion by American and Iraqi troops.

The use of allusion is a sort of shortcut for poets. They can use fewer words and count on meaning to come from the reader's own experience.

Figures of Speech

Figurative language is also called figures of speech. If all figures of speech that have ever been identified were listed, it would be a very long list. However, for purposes of analyzing poetry, a few are sufficient:

1. Simile: Direct comparison between two things. "My love is like a red-red rose."

2. Metaphor: Indirect comparison between two things; the use of a word or phrase denoting one kind of object or action in place of another to suggest a comparison between them. While poets use them extensively, they are also integral to everyday speech. For example, it is said that chairs have "legs" and "arms," although everyone knows that inanimate objects do not have limbs.

3. Parallelism: The arrangement of ideas in phrases, sentences, and paragraphs that balance one element with another of equal importance and similar wording. An example from Francis Bacon's "Of Studies:" "Reading maketh a full man, conference a ready man, and writing an exact man."

4. Personification: Attributing human characteristics to an inanimate object, an abstract quality, or an animal. John Bunyan exemplified this by writing about characters named Death, Knowledge, Giant Despair, Sloth, and Piety in his Pilgrim's Progress. The metaphor of "an arm of a chair" is a form of personification.

5. Euphemism: The substitution of an agreeable or inoffensive term for one that might offend or suggest something unpleasant. Many euphemisms, such as "passed away," "crossed over," or "passed," are used to refer to death to avoid using the real word.

6. Hyperbole: Deliberate exaggeration for effect or comic effect. Seen here is an example from Shakespeare's *The Merchant of Venice*:

> *Why, if two gods should play some heavenly match*
> *And on the wager lay two earthly women,*
> *And Portia one, there must be something else*
> *Pawned with the other, for the poor rude world*
> *Hath not her fellow.*

7. Climax: A number of phrases or sentences are arranged in ascending order of rhetorical forcefulness. Here is an example from Melville's *Moby Dick*:

> *All that most maddens and torments; all that stirs up the lees of things; all truth with malice in it; all that cracks the sinews and cakes the brain; all the subtle demonisms of life and thought; all evil, to crazy Ahab, were visibly personified and made practically assailable in Moby Dick.*

8. Bathos: A ludicrous attempt to portray pathos; that is, to evoke pity, sympathy, or sorrow. It may result from inappropriately dignifying the commonplace, elevated language to describe something trivial, or greatly exaggerated pathos.

9. Oxymoron: A contradiction in terms deliberately employed for effect. It is usually seen in a qualifying adjective whose meaning is contrary to that of the noun it modifies, such as "wise folly."

10. Irony: Expressing something other than and particularly opposite the literal meaning, such as words of praise when the author or speaker intends blame. In poetry, it is often used as a sophisticated or resigned awareness of contrast between what is and what ought to be and expresses a controlled pathos without sentimentality. This form of indirection avoids overt praise or censure. An early example is the Greek comic character Eiron, a clever underdog who by his wit repeatedly triumphs over the boastful character Alazon.

11. Alliteration: The repetition of consonant sounds in two or more neighboring words or syllables. In its simplest form, it reinforces one or two consonant sounds, for example, Shakespeare's "Sonnet #12:" "When I do count the clock that tells the time."

> *Some poets have used more complex patterns of alliteration by creating consonants both at the beginning of words and at the beginning of stressed syllables within words; for example, Shelley's "Stanzas Written in Dejection Near Naples:" "The City's voice itself is soft like Solitude's."*

12. Onomatopoeia: The naming of a thing or action by a vocal imitation of the sound associated with it, such as *buzz* or *hiss* or the use of words whose sound suggests the sense. The following is a good example from "The Brook" by Tennyson:

> I chatter over stony ways,
> In little sharps and trebles,
> I bubble into eddying bays,
> I babble on the pebbles.

13. Malapropism: A verbal blunder in which one word is replaced by another that is similar in sound but different in meaning. Thinking of the geography of contiguous countries, Mrs. Malaprop in Richard Brinsley Sheridan's *The Rivals* (1775) spoke of the "geometry" of "contagious countries."

Poets use figures of speech to sharpen the effect and meaning of their poems and to help readers see things in ways they have never seen them before. In her poem "A Grave," Marianne Moore observes that a fir tree has "an emerald turkey-foot at the top." This poem makes the reader aware of something not previously noticed. The sudden recognition of the likeness yields pleasure in the reading.

Figurative language allows for the statement of truths that literal language cannot.

Figurative language allows for the statement of truths that literal language cannot. Skillfully used, figures of speech will help the reader see more clearly and focus upon particulars. They add dimensions of richness to our reading and understanding of a poem; they also provide many opportunities for analysis. In analyzing a poem on the basis of its figures of speech, one should ask the questions: What do they do for the poem? Do they underscore meaning? Do they intensify understanding? Do they increase the intensity of our response?

SKILL 6.3 **Demonstrating knowledge of various types of informational/expository texts, including key textual features** (e.g., indexes and headings), **graphic features** (e.g., charts and diagrams), **and organizational structures** (e.g., descriptive, chronological, cause/effect, comparison/contrast, problem/solution) **of these texts, and applying knowledge of explicit instruction in key features and organizational structures of various print and digital informational/expository texts to promote students' understanding of these texts**

While the teaching of writing undoubtedly involves an enormous amount of work on the composition of text, it also involves the general concept of ideas conveyed in the best possible manner. In other words, the results of a survey could be explained in words, but it might be easier to understand in a graph or chart. If that is the case, why would we want to present it in words? The important point is for the information to be conveyed effectively.

So, as students write reports and respond to ideas in writing, they can learn how to incorporate multiple representations of information, including various graphic representations, into written text. While this is seemingly fairly easy to do considering the word processing technology we have available to us, students struggle with knowing how to appropriately and successfully do this. They can learn to do this in three primary ways: explanation, observation/modeling, and practice.

First, students need to have clear explanations from teachers on appropriate forms of graphical representations in text, as well as the methods in which to include those representations. They need to see plenty of examples of how it is done.

Second, they need to be able to see teacher-modeled examples where text has been replaced or enhanced by graphical representations. The more they see of examples, the clearer the concepts will be to them.

Finally, students need to get a chance to practice incorporating graphical representations in their writing. This, of course, will require technology and plenty of feedback.

Students will most likely appreciate the ability to utilize graphical representations in place of text, but they will soon realize that deciding which type of representation to use and how to actually use it will be very challenging.

Quantitative data is often easily presented in graphs and charts in many content areas. However, if students are unable to decipher the graph, its use is limited. Because information can clearly be displayed in a graph or chart form, accurate interpretation of the information is an important skill for students.

For graphs, students should be taught to evaluate all the features of the graph, including main title, what the horizontal axis represents, and what the vertical axis represents. Also, students should locate and evaluate the graph's key (if there is one) in the event there is more than one variable on the graph. For example, line graphs are often used to plot data from a scientific experiment. If more than one variable was used, a key or legend would indicate what each line on the line graph represented. Then, once students have evaluated the axes and titles, they can begin to assess the results of the experiment.

There are two good reasons for using a graph:

- To present a model or theory visually in order to show how two or more variables interrelate

Generally, graphical representations should be used only if they can convey information better than written text can. This is an important principal that students will need to learn through constant practice.

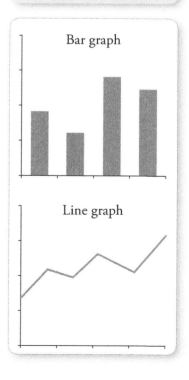

Bar graph

Line graph

• To present real world data visually in order to show how two or more variables interrelate

GRAPHS are most useful when one wishes to demonstrate the sequential increase or decrease of a variable or to show specific correlations between two or more variables in a given circumstance. In all graphs, an upward sloping line represents a direct relationship between the two variables. A downward slope represents an inverse relationship between the two variables. In reading any graph, you must be very careful to understand what is being measured, what can be deduced, and what cannot be deduced from the given graph.

For charts (such as a pie chart), the process is similar to interpreting bar or line graphs. The key which depicts what each section of the pie chart represents is very important to interpreting the pie chart. Be sure to provide students with lots of assistance and practice with reading and interpreting graphs and charts so their experience with, and confidence in, reading them develops.

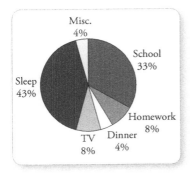

Information can be gained looking at a map that might take hundreds of words to explain otherwise. To show such a variety of information, maps are made in many different ways. Because of this variety, maps must be understood in order to make the best sense of them. Once they are understood, maps provide a meaningful and useful tool in communicating a particular point of view.

To use charts correctly, you should remember the reasons for using graphs. The general ideas are similar. It is usually a question as to which is more capable of adequately portraying the information you want to illustrate. You can see the difference between them and realize that in many ways graphs and charts are interrelated. One of the most common types, because it is easiest to read and understand, even for the lay person, is the pie chart. Pie charts get a lot of use, especially for illustrating the differences in percentages among various items or when the divisions of a whole are being demonstrated.

To interpret data in tables, we read across rows and down columns. Each item of interest has different data points listed under different column headings.

TABLE 1: SAMPLE PURCHASE ORDER				
Item	**Unit**	**$/Unit**	**Qty**	**Tot $**
Coffee	lb.	2.79	45	125.55
Milk	gal.	1.05	72	75.60
Sugar	lb.	0.23	150	34.50

In this table the first column on the left contains the items in a purchase order. The other columns contain data about each item labeled with column headings. The second column from the left gives the unit of measurement for each item, the third column gives the price per unit, the fourth column gives the quantity of each item ordered, and the fifth column gives the total cost of each item.

> **SKILL Applying knowledge of explicit instruction in analysis and response**
> **6.4 skills for informational/expository texts** (e.g., analyzing an author's point
> of view or argument, evaluating a text with respect to credibility, analyzing a text's
> internal consistency or logic, paraphrasing information from a text, summarizing a
> text's main ideas)

Teachers should have a toolkit of instructional strategies, materials, and technologies to encourage and teach students how to problem solve and think critically about subject content. There is an established level of academic performance and proficiency in public schools that students are required to master. Research of national and state standards indicates that there are benchmarks and learning objectives in the subject areas of science, foreign language, English language arts, history, art, health, civics, economics, geography, physical education, mathematics, and social studies that students are required to master in state assessments (Marzano & Kendall, 1996).

A critical thinking skill is a skill target that teachers help students develop to sustain learning in specific subject areas that they can apply in other subject areas. For example, when learning algebraic concepts to solve a math word problem on how much fencing material is needed to build a fence around a an 8' x 12' backyard area, a math student must understand the order of numerical expression to simplify algebraic expressions. Teachers can provide instructional strategies that show students how to group the fencing measurements into an algebraic word problem that, with minor addition, subtraction, and multiplication, can produce a simple number equal to the amount of fencing materials needed to build the fence.

Higher-Order Thinking Skills

Developing critical thinking skills in students is not as simple as developing other, simpler, skills. Critical thinking skills must be taught within the context of specific subject matter. For example, language arts teachers can teach critical thinking skills through novels; social studies teachers can teach critical thinking skills through primary source documents or current events; and science teachers

Developing critical thinking skills in students is not as simple as developing other, simpler, skills.

can teach critical thinking skills by having students develop hypotheses prior to conducting experiments.

The three main types of critical thinking skills are: analysis, synthesis, and evaluation.

Analysis

ANALYSIS is the systematic exploration of a concept, event, term, piece of writing, element of media, or any other complex item. Usually, people think of analysis as the exploration of the parts that make up a whole. For example, when someone analyzes a piece of literature, that person might focus on small pieces of the novel; yet, as they focus on the small pieces, they also call attention to the big picture and show how the small pieces create significance for the whole novel.

> **ANALYSIS:** the systematic exploration of a concept, event, term, piece of writing, element of media, or any other complex item

To carry this example further, if one were to analyze a novel, she might investigate a particular character to determine how that character adds significance to the novel. In something more concrete like biology, one could analyze the findings of an experiment to see if the results might be of significance for something even larger than the experiment itself. It can be easier to analyze political events. For example, a social studies teacher might ask students to analyze the events leading up to World War II; doing so would require that students look at the small pieces (e.g., smaller world events prior to World War II) and determine how those small pieces, when added together, caused the war.

Synthesis

SYNTHESIS is usually thought of as the opposite of analysis. In analysis, one takes a whole, breaks it up into pieces, and looks at the pieces. With synthesis, one takes different things and makes them one whole thing. A language arts teacher could ask students to synthesize two works of literature. For example, *The Scarlett Letter* and *The Crucible* are two works featuring Puritan life in America, written about a century apart. A student could synthesize the two works and come to conclusions about Puritan life. An art teacher could ask students to synthesize two paintings from the Impressionist era and come to conclusions about the features that distinguish that style of art.

> **SYNTHESIS:** examining different concepts and drawing a global conclusion

Evaluation

Finally, **EVALUATION** involves making judgments. Whereas analysis and synthesis seek answers and hypotheses based on investigations, evaluation is based on opinions. A social studies teacher could ask students to evaluate the quality of Richard Nixon's resignation speech. To do so, they would judge whether or not they felt it was good. In contrast, analysis would keep judgment out of the assignment. Rather, it might have students focus on the structure of the speech (i.e., does the argument move from emotional to logical?).

> **EVALUATION:** drawing conclusions based on judgments

When evaluating a speech, a novel, a movie, or a painting, one must determine whether it is good or not. However, teaching evaluation skills requires not just that students learn how to determine whether something is good. It requires that students learn how to support their evaluations. If a student claims that Nixon's speech was effective in what the president intended the speech to do, the student would need to explain how this is so. Notice that evaluation often utilizes the skills of analysis and/or synthesis, but that the purpose is ultimately different.

Encouraging Independent Critical Thinking

Questioning is an effective tool to build students up to these higher-level thinking skills. Low-order questions are useful to begin the process. If the objective is for students to be able to read and understand the story "Goldilocks and the Three Bears," the teacher may wish to start with low-order questions, for example, "What are some things Goldilocks did while in the bears' home?" (knowledge) or "Why didn't Goldilocks like the Papa Bear's chair?" (analysis).

Through a series of questions, the teacher can move students up the taxonomy: For example, "If Goldilocks had come to your house, what are some things she might have used?" (application); "How might the story have differed if Goldilocks had visited the three fishes?" (synthesis); or "Do you think Goldilocks was good or bad? Why?" (evaluation). The teacher can control the thinking process of the class through questioning. As students become more involved in the discussion they are systematically led to higher-level thinking.

To develop a critical-thinking approach to the world, children need to know enough about valid and invalid reasoning to ask questions. Bringing speeches or essays that demonstrate examples of both valid and invalid reasoning into the classroom can be useful in helping students develop the ability to question the reasoning of others. These examples should be by published writers or televised speakers so students can see that they are able to question even ideas that are accepted by some adults and talk about what is wrong in the thinking of those apparently successful communicators.

If the teacher stays on the cutting edge of children's experience, children will become more and more curious about things they don't know. A good way to introduce the outside world could be a lesson on a foreign country that the children may not know exists. This kind of lesson would reveal what life is like in other countries for children their own age. The lesson could use different types of media for variety and greater impact. In such lessons, positive aspects of the lives of those "other" children should always be included. Perhaps correspondence with children in a foreign country could be established.

> Because most teachers want their students to develop higher-level thinking skills, they need to direct students to these higher levels on the taxonomy.

Political speeches are a good example of texts to use in the classroom. Students will become better analyzers, synthesizers, and evaluators if they understand some of the basics of political speeches. Therefore, a teacher might introduce concepts such as rhetoric, style, persona, audience, diction, imagery, and tone. The best way to introduce these concepts would be to provide students with good examples of these things. Once they are familiar with these critical tools, students will be better able to apply them individually to political speeches—and then be able to analyze, synthesize, and evaluate political speeches on their own.

> **SKILL 6.5** Applying knowledge of the use of appropriate texts and effective, engaging oral language, reading, and writing activities, including teacher read-alouds, to motivate and reinforce students' understanding and analysis of and response to various literary/ narrative and informational/expository texts

At some point it is crucial that the early reader integrate graphophonic cues with semantic and structural cues and move toward fluency. Before this happens, early readers sound stilted when they read aloud, which, does not promote the enjoyment of reading.

Expressive Reading

The teacher needs to be theatrical to model for children so they can hear the beauty and nuances that are contained in the texts whose print they are tracking so anxiously. Children love to mimic their teachers and will do so if the teacher takes time each day to recite a poem with them. The poem might be posted on chart paper and stay up on the board for a week.

First, the teacher can model the fluent and expressive reading of the poem. Then, with the use of a pointer, the class can recite it with the teacher. As the week progresses, students can recite it on their own.

Illustrations

Illustrations can be key supports for emergent and early readers. Teachers should not only use wordless stories (books that tell their stories through pictures alone), but can also make targeted use of Big Books for read-alouds, so that young children become habituated to illustrations as an important tool for constructing meaning. The teacher should teach children how to reference an illustration for help in identifying a word the child does not recognize in the text.

Of course, children can also go on a picture walk with the teacher as part of a mini-lesson or guided reading and anticipate the story (narrative) using the pictures alone to construct meaning.

Decodability

Use literature that contains examples of letter-sound correspondences you wish to teach. First, read the literature with the children or read it aloud to them. Take a specific example from the text and have the children reread it as you point out the letter-sound correspondence. Then ask the children to go through the now-familiar literature to find other letter-sound correspondences. Once the children have correctly made the text-sound correspondence, have them share other similar correspondences they find in other works of literature.

Cooper (2004) suggests that children can be taught to become word detectives so they can independently and fluently decode on their own. The child should learn the following word detective routines in order to function as an independent fluent reader who can decode words on his own:

- First, the child should read to the end of the sentence.

- Next, the child should search for known word parts and also try to decode the word from the letter sounds.

- As a last resort, the child should ask someone for help or look up the word in the dictionary.

> SKILL 6.6 **Demonstrating knowledge of formal and informal methods for assessing students' understanding and analysis of and response to literary/narrative and informational/expository texts, and demonstrating the ability to interpret and use the results of these assessments to plan effective instruction in literary response and analysis and content-area literacy skills**

Evaluation of student progress has two primary purposes: *summative*, to measure student progress or achievement, and *formative*, to provide feedback to students to help them learn. The types of assessment discussed below represent many of the more common types, but the list is not comprehensive.

Anecdotal Records

These are notes recorded by the teacher concerning an area of interest in or concern about a particular student. These records should focus on observable behaviors and should be descriptive in nature. They should not include assumptions or speculations regarding effective areas such as motivation or interest. These records are usually compiled over a period of several days to several weeks.

Rating Scales and Checklists

These assessments are generally self-appraisal instruments completed by the students or observation-based instruments completed by the teacher. The focus of these is frequently on behavior or effective areas such as interest and motivation.

Informal Reading Inventories

The setting in which you administer the informal reading inventory (IRI) should be as quiet and isolated as possible. Speak in a relaxed tone and reassure the student that this is not for a "grade." An informal reading inventory can be used to estimate a student's reading level and also to assess a student's ability to use word identification strategies. Specifically, the IRI will help you assess a student's strengths and needs in these areas:

- Word recognition

- Word meaning

- Reading strategies

- Comprehension

The IRI can assist a teacher in determining reading fluency as well as strengths and weaknesses in the progress of reading comprehension.

The IRI can assist a teacher in determining reading fluency as well as strengths and weaknesses in the progress of reading comprehension. It may suggest directions for instruction or complete a profile of a student's reading ability. The inventory provides graded word lists and graded passages that assess oral reading, silent reading, and listening comprehension. Some IRIs provide narrative and expository passages with longer-passage options. After reading a passage, the student answers questions or retells the passage.

Fluency Checks

Fluency is a student's ability to read a text accurately and quickly. Students can make connections among the ideas in the text and their background knowledge. In other words, fluent readers recognize words and comprehend at the same time.

Fluent readers read aloud effortlessly and with expression. Readers who have not yet developed fluency read slowly, word by word. Their oral reading is choppy and plodding.

To complete a fluency check, teachers should have a student read independently during a teacher-student conference. The teacher will select a passage (100 words) from the student's independent reading book. The student will then read the passage while the teacher times her and takes a running record of the student's oral reading. The student will be assessed using the fluency standard expectations for that grade level. The number of words read correctly per minute is an indicator of a student's progress in all aspects of reading: decoding, fluency, and comprehension.

Minimum fluency rates

An expected quantitative level of 60 words per minute (wpm) for first grade and 90 wpm for second grade is to be met by the end of the year. The expected quantitative level of 110 wpm is required for the third grade and 118 wpm for the fourth grade. To put these rates into perspective, fluent adults read about 200 wpm during oral passage reading.

Think-Alouds

Poor readers are often delayed at the basic level of comprehension as they concentrate on decoding words and sentences. They often don't see how various parts of a whole text relate to each other and work together to create a larger meaning. Struggling readers often cannot draw on background knowledge or make predictions as they read. They frequently cannot visualize the events of a text as they are reading. These students often have trouble thinking about the text while they are reading it.

Think-alouds can be used to improve reading comprehension by getting students to reflect on the process of thinking aloud as they read. Teachers can encourage students to recognize the difference between reading the words and comprehending the text by implementing coached practice.

Have students read a short passage to you. Tell them to continually pause and ask themselves, "Does this make sense to me?" Remind them that you will be stopping occasionally to ask them what they are thinking about as they are reading. When students share their thoughts, and the connection to the text is not clear, encourage the students to explain themselves. If students are having trouble with this task, focus on a single strategy, for example, prediction.

Running Records

Running records permit teachers to determine students' reading strengths, weaknesses, readability levels, and fluency. A teacher can do a running record by asking a student to read a book he has never seen before or one that has been read only once or twice. This will often give a more accurate measure of a child's ability to handle text at the assessed level. The running record, for example, requires that each child read 100 words of text out loud to the teacher. The teacher notes the time it takes the child to read the passage and the accuracy with which the child reads the passage.

The teacher tallies the errors during the reading whenever a child does any of the following:

- Substitutes a word

- Omits a word

- Inserts an erroneous word

- Has to be told a word by the person administering the running record

Teachers can administer this type of assessment multiple times during the year to note progress in fluency as well as accuracy in reading.

> Running records should be administered with greater frequency at the earlier stages of reading.

Storytelling

After the student has read the target book and the teacher has done a running record, have the child do an oral retelling of the story. Ask the student to close the book and then tell you about the story in as much detail as he can remember. If the child has difficulty retelling parts of the story or remembering certain details, the teacher can use prompts such as, "Tell me more about Character X" or "What happened after…?"

Retelling checklist

- Can the child tell you what happened in the story or what the factual book was about in his or her own words?

- Does the child include details about the characters in the retelling? Can she explain the relationships between the characters?

- Can the child describe the setting? How detailed is the description?

- Can the child recall the events of the story, and can she place them in the correct sequence?

Portfolio Assessment

The use of student portfolios for some aspects of assessment has become quite common. The purpose, nature, and policies of portfolio assessment vary greatly from one setting to another. In general, a student's portfolio contains samples of work collected over an extended period of time. The nature of the subject, age of the student, and scope of the portfolio all contribute to the specific mechanics of analyzing, synthesizing, and otherwise evaluating the portfolio contents.

In most cases, the student and teacher make joint decisions regarding which work samples go into the student's portfolio. A collection of work compiled over an extended time period allows teacher, student, and parents to view the student's progress from a unique perspective. Qualitative changes over time can be readily apparent from work samples. Such changes are difficult to establish with strictly quantitative records like the scores recorded in the teacher's grade book.

Questioning

One of the most frequently used forms of assessment in the classroom is oral questioning by the teacher. As the teacher questions students, he can collect a considerable amount of information about how much students have learned and potential sources of confusion for students. While questioning is often viewed as a component of instructional methodology, it is also a powerful assessment tool.

Tests

Tests and similar direct-assessment methods are the most easily identified types of assessment. Thorndike (1997) identifies three types of assessment instruments:

1. Standardized achievement tests

2. Assessment material packaged with curricular materials

3. Teacher-made assessment instruments:
    - Pencil-and-paper tests
    - Oral tests
    - Product evaluations
    - Performance tests
    - Effective measures

Kellough and Roberts (1991) take a slightly different perspective. They describe "three avenues for assessing student achievement: a) what the learner says, b) what the learner does, and c) what the learner writes…" (p. 343).

Types of tests

Formal tests are tests that have been standardized on a large sample population. The process of standardization provides various comparative norms and scales for the assessment instrument. The term informal test includes all other tests. Most publisher-provided tests and teacher-made tests are informal tests by this definition. Note clearly that an "informal" test is not necessarily unimportant. A teacher-made final exam, for example, is informal by definition because it has not been standardized, but is a very important assessment tool.

> Formal tests are tests that have been standardized on a large sample population. The process of standardization provides various comparative norms and scales for the assessment instrument.

SKILL 6.7 **Applying knowledge of strategies** (e.g., differentiated instruction, interventions, enrichment) **to address the assessed needs of individual students** (e.g., English language learners, struggling readers through highly proficient readers) **in literary response and analysis and content-area literacy skills**

One of the common fallacies students have about reading comes from the ways in which students are taught to read. Sure, as students are being taught to read, they must learn the strategies of careful reading, which includes sounding out words, focusing on fluency, obtaining meaning, etc. However, at points in the learning-to-read process, teachers can help students learn that there are various reasons why people read. Sometimes people read for pleasure, in which case they can decide whether to skim through quickly for the content or read slowly to savor ideas and language. Other times, people simply want to find information quickly, in which case they will skim or scan. In some texts, rereading is necessary to fully comprehend information.

READING STRATEGIES	
Skimming	Skimming is when readers read quickly while paying little attention to specific words. This is often done when readers want a full picture of a text but do not want to focus on the details. Skimming can be done as a preview or a review. When done as a preview, often readers will look to see what it is they can expect from the text. When done as a review, readers will hope to be reminded of the main points through the skim.
Scanning	Scanning is a bit different from skimming. In skimming, readers read connected text quickly. In scanning, readers go straight to specific ideas, words, sections, or examples. They pick and choose what they will read within a text. This is done when the reader does not need to know everything from a text.
In-Depth Reading	In-depth reading is the reading most people think is the only legitimate type of reading. Strangely, though, all types of reading are done by all types of people—all the time! In-depth reading is done when readers want to enjoy a text or learn from it thoroughly. For the most part, in this type of reading, readers will move forward quickly and not stop to focus on a specific word or idea, although sometimes this is necessary. The main idea of this type of reading, though, is that readers do not skip over or read fast to get information. They read everything carefully and thoroughly.
Rereading	Rereading is the final type of reading, which comes in many forms. Sometimes, whole texts must be reread for the concepts. This is usually the case when the text is difficult. Rereading can also be done as someone is doing regular in-depth reading. For example, a word, concept, or a few ideas may need to be reviewed before the reader can go on. Another method of rereading is rereading a whole text months or years after reading it the first time. This is done when readers realize that through their life experiences since the first reading, they will view the text in a different light.

All these methods are acceptable forms of reading, however, all must be done with specific purposes in mind. Generally, it is not a good idea to skim or scan a class novel, but skimming and scanning through a textbook may be acceptable if only a few ideas are crucial.

See also Skill 5.3

COMPETENCY 7

UNDERSTAND ACADEMIC LANGUAGE DEVELOPMENT, INCLUDING ENGLISH LANGUAGE STRUCTURES AND CONVENTIONS

> **SKILL 7.1** **Demonstrating basic knowledge of English language structures and conventions** (i.e., sentence structure, grammar, punctuation, capitalization, spelling, syntax, and semantics)

Candidates should be cognizant of proper rules and conventions of punctuation, capitalization, and spelling. Competency exams generally test the ability to apply the more advanced skills; thus, a limited number of more frustrating rules are presented here. Rules should be applied according to the American style of English, i.e., spelling *theater* instead of *theatre* and placing terminal marks of punctuation almost exclusively within other marks of punctuation.

Subject-Verb Agreement

A verb should always agree in number with its subject. Making them agree relies on the ability to properly identify the subject.

> *One of the boys was playing too rough.*
>
> *No one in the class, not the teacher nor any student, was listening to the message from the intercom.*
>
> *The candidates, including a grandmother and a teenager, are debating some controversial issues.*

If two singular subjects are connected by *and*, the verb must be plural.

> *A man and his dog were jogging on the beach.*

If two singular subjects are connected by *or* or *nor*, a singular verb is required.

> *Neither Dot nor Joyce has missed a day of school this year. Either Fran or Paul is missing.*

If one singular subject and one plural subject are connected by *or* or *nor*, the verb agrees with the subject nearest to the verb.

> *Neither the coach nor the players were able to sleep on the bus.*

If the subject is a collective noun, its sense of number in the sentence determines the verb: It is singular if the noun represents a group or unit and plural if the noun represents individuals.

> *The House of Representatives has adjourned for the holidays.*

Pronoun-Antecedent Agreement

A noun is any word that names a person, place, thing, idea, quality, or activity. A pronoun is a word that is used in place of a noun or other pronoun. The word or word group that a pronoun stands for (or refers to) is called its **ANTECEDENT**.

We use pronouns in many of the sentences that we write. Pronouns enable us to avoid monotonous repetition of nouns. They also help us maintain coherence within and among sentences. Pronouns must agree with their antecedents in number and person. Therefore, if the antecedent is plural, use a plural pronoun; if the antecedent is feminine, use a feminine pronoun.

> **ANTECEDENT:** the word or word group that a pronoun stands for (or refers to)

Specific types of pronouns include: personal, possessive, indefinite, reflexive, reciprocal, intensive, interrogative, relative, and demonstrative.

To help students revise their work to correct errors, have them complete the following steps:

- Read focusing only on pronouns.

- Circle each pronoun, and draw an arrow to its antecedent.

- Replace the pronoun with a noun to eliminate a vague pronoun reference.

- Supply missing antecedents where needed.

- Place the pronoun so that the nearest noun is its antecedent.

After students have focused on pronoun-antecedent agreement a few times, they will progress from correcting errors to avoiding errors. The only way to develop their skill with pronoun references, however, is sufficient focused practice.

Verbs (Tense)

PRESENT TENSE is used to express that which is currently happening or is always true.

> *Randy is playing the piano.*
> *Randy plays the piano like a pro.*

PAST TENSE is used to express action that occurred in a past time.

> *Randy learned to play the piano when he was six years old.*

FUTURE TENSE is used to express action or a condition of future time.

> *Randy will probably earn a music scholarship.*

PRESENT PERFECT TENSE is used to express action or a condition that started in the past and is continued or completed in the present.

> *Randy has practiced the piano every day for the last ten years.*
> *Randy has never been bored with practice.*

PAST PERFECT TENSE expresses action or a condition that occurred as a precedent to some other past action or condition.

> *Randy had considered playing clarinet before he discovered the piano.*

FUTURE PERFECT TENSE expresses action that started in the past or the present and will conclude at some time in the future.

> *By the time he goes to college, Randy will have been an accomplished pianist for more than half of his life.*

Use of verbs: mood

Indicative mood is used to make unconditional statements; subjunctive mood is used for conditional clauses or wish statements that pose conditions that are untrue. Verbs in subjunctive mood are plural with both singular and plural subjects.

> *If I <u>were</u> a bird, I would fly.*
> *I wish I <u>were</u> as rich as Donald Trump.*

PRESENT TENSE: expresses that which is currently happening or is always true

PAST TENSE: expresses action that occurred in a past time

FUTURE TENSE: expresses action or a condition of future time

PRESENT PERFECT TENSE: expresses action or a condition that started in the past and is continued or completed in the present

PAST PERFECT TENSE: expresses action or a condition that occurred as a precedent to some other past action or condition

FUTURE PERFECT TENSE: expresses action that started in the past or the present and will conclude at some time in the future

Conjugation of verbs

The conjugation of verbs follows the patterns used in the discussion of tense above. However, the most common errors in verb use stem from the improper formation of the past and past participial forms.

Regular verb:	believe, believed, (have) believed
Irregular verbs:	run, ran, run; sit, sat, sat; teach, taught, taught

Other errors stem from the use of verbs that are the same in some tenses but have different forms and different meanings in other tenses.

I lie on the ground. I lay on the ground yesterday. I have lain down. I lay the blanket on the bed. I laid the blanket there yesterday. I have laid the blanket down every night.

The sun rises. The sun rose. The sun has risen.

He raises the flag. He raised the flag. He had raised the flag.

I sit on the porch. I sat on the porch. I have sat in the porch swing.

I set the plate on the table. I set the plate there yesterday. I had set the table before dinner.

Two other common verb problems stem from misusing the preposition *of* for the verb auxiliary *have* and misusing the verb *ought* (now rare).

Incorrect: *I should of gone to bed.*

Correct: *I should have gone to bed.*

Incorrect: *He hadn't ought to get so angry.*

Correct: *He ought not to get so angry.*

Adjectives

An adjective should agree in number with the word it modifies.

Those apples are rotten. This one is ripe. These peaches are hard.

With some exceptions, comparative adjectives end in *-er* and superlatives in *-est*, like *worse* and *worst*. Some adjectives that cannot easily make comparative inflections are preceded by *more* and *most*.

Mrs. Carmichael is the better of the two basketball coaches. That is the hastiest excuse you have ever contrived.

Avoid double comparatives and superlatives.

Incorrect: *This is the worstest headache I ever had.*

Correct: *This is the worst headache I ever had.*

When comparing one thing to others in a group, exclude the thing under comparison from the rest of the group.

Incorrect: *Joey is larger than any baby I have ever seen. (Since you have seen him, he cannot be larger than himself.)*

Correct: *Joey is larger than any other baby I have ever seen. (Include all necessary words to make a comparison clear in meaning.)*

> I am as tall as my mother. I am as tall as she (is).
> My cats are better behaved than those of my neighbor.

Plurals

The multiplicity and complexity of spelling rules based on phonics, letter doubling, and exceptions to rules that are not mastered by adulthood should be replaced by a good dictionary. As spelling mastery is also difficult for adolescents, the recommendation is the same: Learning the uses of a dictionary and a thesaurus are strategic solutions to this common problem.

Most plurals of nouns that end in hard consonants or in hard consonant sounds followed by a silent *e* are made by adding -*s*. Plurals of some words ending in vowels are formed by adding only -*s*.

> fingers, numerals, banks, bugs, riots, homes, gates, radios, bananas

For nouns that end in soft consonant sounds—*s, j, x, z, ch,* and *sh*—the plurals are formed by adding -*es*. Plurals of some nouns ending in *o* are formed by adding -*es*.

> dresses, waxes, churches, brushes, tomatoes

For nouns ending in *y* preceded by a vowel, just add -*s*.

> boys, alleys

For nouns ending in *y* preceded by a consonant, change the *y* to *i* and add *-es*.

> *babies, corollaries, frugalities, poppies*

Some nouns' plurals are formed irregularly or remain the same.

> *sheep, deer, children, leaves, oxen*

Some nouns derived from foreign words, especially Latin words, are made plural in two different ways. Sometimes the meanings are the same; other times the two plural forms are used in slightly different contexts. It is always wise to consult the dictionary.

> *appendices, appendixes*   *criterion, criteria*
>
> *indexes, indices*   *crisis, crises*

Make the plurals of closed (solid) compound words in the usual way.

> *timelines, hairpins*
>
> *cupfuls, handfuls*

Make the plurals of open or hyphenated compounds by adding the change in inflection to the word that changes in number.

> *fathers-in-law, courts-martial, masters of art, doctors of medicine*

Make the plurals of letters, numbers, and abbreviations by adding *-s*.

> *fives and tens, IBMs, 1990s, ps and qs (Note that letters are italicized.)*

Possessives

Make the possessives of singular nouns by adding an apostrophe followed by the letter *s* (*'s*).

> *baby's bottle, mother's job, elephant's eye, teacher's desk,*
>
> *sympathizer's protests, week's postponement*

Make the possessives of singular nouns ending in *s* by adding either an apostrophe or an apostrophe followed by the letter *s*, depending upon common usage or sound. When the possessive sounds awkward, use a prepositional phrase instead.

Even with the sibilant ending, with a few exceptions, it is advisable to use the 's construction.

> dress's color, species' characteristics (or characteristics of the species),
> James' hat (or James's hat), Dolores's shirt

Make the possessives of plural nouns ending in *s* by adding an apostrophe after the *s*.

> horses' coats, jockeys' times, four days' time

Make the possessives of plural nouns that do not end in s by adding 's, just as with singular nouns.

> children's shoes, deer's antlers, cattle's horns

Make the possessives of compound nouns by adding the inflection at the end of the word or phrase.

> the mayor of Los Angeles' campaign, the mailman's new truck, the mailmen's new trucks, my father-in-law's first wife, the keepsakes' values, several daughters-in-law's husbands

Pronouns

A pronoun used as a direct object, indirect object, or object of a preposition requires the objective case form.

> The teacher praised him. She gave him an A on the test. Her praise of him was appreciated. The students whom she did not praise will work harder next time.

Common pronoun errors occur from misuse of reflexive pronouns:

Singular: *myself, yourself, herself, himself, itself*
Plural: *ourselves, yourselves, themselves.*

Incorrect: *Jack cut hisself shaving.*

Correct: *Jack cut himself shaving.*

Incorrect: *They backed theirselves into a corner.*

Correct: *They backed themselves into a corner.*

Note: *Because a gerund functions as a noun, any noun preceding it and operating as a possessive adjective must reflect the necessary inflection. However, if the gerundive following the noun is a participle, no inflection is added.*

The general was perturbed by the private's sleeping on duty. (The word sleeping *is a gerund, the object of the preposition* by.*)*
–BUT–
The general was perturbed to see the private sleeping on duty. (The word sleeping *is a participle modifying* private.*)*

Capitalization

Capitalize all proper names of persons (including specific organizations or agencies of government), places (countries, states, cities, parks, and specific geographical areas), things (political parties, structures, historical and cultural terms, and calendar and time designations), and religious terms (deities, revered persons or groups, and sacred writings).

> Percy Bysshe Shelley, Argentina, Mount Rainier National Park, Grand Canyon, League of Nations, the Sears Tower, Birmingham, Lyric Theater, Americans, Midwesterners, Democrats, Renaissance, Boy Scouts of America, Easter, Bible, Dead Sea Scrolls, Koran

Capitalize proper adjectives and titles used with proper names.

> California gold rush, President John Adams, French fries, Homeric epic, Romanesque architecture, Senator John Glenn

Note: Some words that represent titles and offices are not capitalized unless used with a proper name.

Capitalized	Not Capitalized
Congressman McKay	the congressman from Hawaii
Commander Alger	the commander of the Pacific Fleet
Queen Elizabeth	the queen of England

Capitalize all main words in titles of works of literature, art, and music.

Punctuation

Quotation marks

In a quoted statement that is either declarative or imperative, place the period inside the closing quotation marks.

> "The airplane crashed on the runway during takeoff."

If other words in the sentence follow the quotation, place a comma inside the closing quotations marks and a period at the end of the sentence.

> "The airplane crashed on the runway during takeoff," said the announcer.

Usually, when a quoted title or expression occurs at the end of a sentence, the period is placed before the single or double quotation marks.

> *"The middle school readers were unprepared to understand Bryant's poem 'Thanatopsis.'"*
>
> *Early book-length adventure stories such as* Don Quixote *and* The Three Musketeers *were known as "picaresque novels."*

The final quotation mark precedes the period if the content of the sentence is about a speech or quote.

> *The first thing out of his mouth was "Hi, I'm home."*
>
> *—BUT—*
>
> *The first line of his speech began: "I arrived home to an empty house".*

In interrogatory or exclamatory sentences, the question mark or exclamation point should be positioned outside the closing quotation marks if the quote itself is a statement, command, or cited title.

> *Who decided to lead us in the recitation of the "Pledge of Allegiance"?*
>
> *Why was Tillie shaking as she began her recitation, "Once upon a midnight dreary. . ."?*
>
> *I was embarrassed when Mrs. White said, "Your slip is showing"!*

In declarative sentences, where the quotation is a question or an exclamation, place the question mark or exclamation point inside the quotation marks.

> *The hall monitor yelled, "Fire! Fire!"*
>
> *"Fire! Fire!" yelled the hall monitor.*
>
> *Cory shrieked, "Is there a mouse in the room?" (In this instance, the question supersedes the exclamation.)*

Quotations—whether words, phrases, or clauses—should be punctuated according to the rules of the grammatical function they serve in the sentence.

> *The works of Shakespeare, "the Bard of Avon," have been contested as originating with other authors.*
>
> *"You'll get my money," the old·man warned, "when 'hell freezes over'."*
>
> *Sheila cited the passage that began "Four score and seven years ago . . . ." (Note the ellipsis followed by an enclosed period.)*
>
> *"Old Ironsides" inspired the preservation of the U.S.S. Constitution.*

Use quotation marks to enclose the titles of shorter works: songs, short poems, short stories, essays, and chapters of books. (See "Dashes and Italics" for rules on punctuating longer titles.)

> "The Tell-Tale Heart" "Casey at the Bat" "America the Beautiful"

Using Periods with Parentheses

Place the period inside the parentheses or brackets if they enclose a complete sentence that is independent of the other sentences around it.

> Stephen Crane was a confirmed alcohol and drug addict. (He admitted as much to other journalists in Cuba.)

If the parenthetical expression is a statement inserted within another statement, the period in the enclosure is omitted.

> Mark Twain used the character Indian Joe (he also appeared in The Adventures of Tom Sawyer) as a foil for Jim in The Adventures of Huckleberry Finn.

Commas

Separate two or more coordinate adjectives that modify the same word and three or more nouns, phrases, or clauses in a list.

> It was a dank, dark day.
>
> Maggie's hair was dull, dirty, and lice-ridden.
>
> Dickens portrayed the Artful Dodger as a skillful pickpocket, loyal follower of Fagin, and defender of Oliver Twist.
>
> Ellen daydreamed about getting out of the rain, taking a shower, and eating a hot dinner.
>
> In Elizabethan England, Ben Johnson wrote comedy, Christopher Marlowe wrote tragedies, and William Shakespeare composed both.

Use commas to separate antithetical or complementary expressions from the rest of the sentence.

> The veterinarian, not his assistant, would perform the delicate surgery.
>
> The more he knew about her, the less he wished he had known.
>
> Randy hopes to, and probably will, get an appointment to the Naval Academy.
>
> His thorough, though esoteric, scientific research could not easily be understood by high school students.

Semicolons

Use semicolons to separate independent clauses when the second clause is introduced by a transitional adverb. (These clauses may also be written as separate
sentences, preferably by placing the adverb within the second sentence.)

> *The Elizabethans modified the rhyme scheme of the sonnet; thus, it was called the
> English sonnet.*
>
> or
>
> *The Elizabethans modified the rhyme scheme of the sonnet. Thus, it was called the
> English sonnet.*

Use semicolons to separate items in a series that are long and complex or have
internal punctuation.

> *The Italian Renaissance produced masters in the fine arts: Dante Alighieri, author of the*
> Divine Comedy; *Leonardo da Vinci, painter of* The Last Supper; *and Donatello, sculptor
> of the* Quattro Coronati, *the four saints.*
>
> *The leading scorers in the WNBA were Zheng Haixia, averaging 23.9 points per game;
> Lisa Leslie, 22; and Cynthia Cooper, 19.5.*

Colons

Place a colon at the beginning of a list of items. (Note its use in the sentence
about Renaissance Italians in the previous section.)

> *The teacher directed us to compare Faulkner's three symbolic novels:* Absalom,
> Absalom; As I Lay Dying; *and* Light in August.

Do not use a colon if the list is preceded by a verb.

> *Three of Faulkner's symbolic novels are* Absalom, Absalom; As I Lay Dying; *and* Light in
> August.

Dashes and Italics

Place **EM DASHES** to denote sudden breaks in thought.

> *Some periods in literature—the Romantic Age, for example—spanned different periods
> in different countries.*

EM DASHES: used to
denote sudden breaks in
thought or, if commas
are already used in the
sentence, for amplification
or explanation

Use dashes instead of commas if commas are already used elsewhere in the sentence for amplification or explanation.

> *The Fireside Poets included three Brahmans—James Russell Lowell, Henry David
> Wadsworth, and Oliver Wendell Holmes.*

Use **ITALICS** to punctuate the titles of long works of literature, names of periodical publications, musical scores, works of art, and motion picture, television, and radio programs. (If italic type is unavailable, students should be instructed to use underlining where italics would be appropriate.)

The Idylls of the King	*Hiawatha*	*The Sound and the Fury*
Mary Poppins	*Newsweek*	*The Nutcracker Suite*

ITALICS: used to punctuate the titles of long works of literature, names of periodical publications, musical scores, works of art, and motion picture, television, and radio programs

SKILL 7.2 Demonstrating knowledge of strategies for enhancing literacy skills by helping students make connections between oral language and reading and writing, including helping them understand similarities and differences between language structures and conventions used in spoken and written English, and applying knowledge of strategies and activities for integrating reading and the communication arts

Fact and Opinion

FACTS are statements that are verifiable. **OPINIONS** are statements that must be supported in order to be accepted. Facts are used to support opinions. For example, "Jane is a bad girl" is an opinion. However, "Jane hit her sister with a baseball bat" is a fact upon which the opinion is based.

Judgments are opinions—decisions or declarations based on observation or reasoning that express approval or disapproval. Facts report what has happened or exists and come from observation, measurement, or calculation. Facts can be tested and verified whereas opinions and judgments cannot. They can only be supported with facts.

Most statements cannot be so clearly distinguished. "I believe that Jane is a bad girl" is a fact. The speaker knows what he or she believes. However, it obviously includes a judgment that could be disputed by another person who might believe otherwise. Judgments are not usually so firm. They are, rather, plausible opinions that provoke thought or lead to factual development.

FACTS: statements that are verifiable

OPINIONS: statements that must be supported in order to be accepted

Resources for teaching fact/opinion:

www.dowlingcentral.com/MrsD/area/readingcomp/terms/factfeeling.html

www.kidport.com/Grade5/TAL/G5-TAL-FactOpinion.htm

Valid and invalid arguments

An **ARGUMENT** is a generalization that is proven or supported with facts. If the facts are not accurate, the generalization remains unproven. Using inaccurate "facts" to support an argument is called a fallacy in reasoning. Some factors to consider in judging whether the facts used to support an argument are accurate

ARGUMENT: a generalization that is proven or supported with facts

follow:

- Are the facts current or are they out of date? For example, if the proposition is "birth defects in babies born to drug-using mothers are increasing," then the data must be the most current available.

- Where were the data obtained, and is that source reliable?

- Are the calculations on which the facts are based reliable? It is a good idea to run one's own calculations before using a piece of derived information.

Even facts that are true and have a profound effect on the argument may not be relevant to the case at hand. For example, health statistics from an entire state may have no or little relevance to a particular county or zip code. Statistics from an entire country are not likely to prove very much about a particular state or county.

An analogy can be useful in making a point, but the comparison must match up in all characteristics or it will not be relevant. Analogy should be used very carefully. It is often just as likely to destroy an argument as it is to strengthen it.

The importance or significance of a fact may not be sufficient to strengthen an argument. For example, of the millions of immigrants in the United States, using a single family to support a solution to the immigration problem will not make much difference overall even though those single-example arguments are often used to support one approach or another. They may achieve a positive reaction, but they will not prove that one solution is better than another. If enough cases were cited from a variety of geographical locations, the information might be significant.

How much is enough? Generally speaking, three strong supporting facts are sufficient to establish the thesis of an argument. For example:

Three strong supporting facts are sufficient to establish the thesis of an argument.

> ### Conclusion: Teenagers are bad drivers.
> 1 When I was a teenager, I was not a good driver.
> 2. Many teenagers receive speeding tickets.
> 3. Teenagers do not have a lot of experience driving.

Sometimes more than three arguments are too many. On the other hand, it's not unusual to hear public speakers, particularly politicians, cite a long litany of facts to support their positions.

A very good example of the omission of facts in an argument is the resumé of an applicant for a job. The applicant is arguing that she should be chosen to be awarded a particular job. The application form will ask for information about past employment; the applicant may omit positions that resulted in an unfavorable dismissal. Employers are usually suspicious of periods of time when the applicant has not listed an employer.

A writer makes choices about which facts will be used and which will be discarded in developing an argument. He may exclude anything that is not supportive of the point of view the he is taking. It's always a good idea for the reader to do some research to identify the omissions and to consider whether they affect the point of view presented in the argument.

Judgments are seldom black or white. If the argument seems too neat or too compelling, it is reasonable to assume that relevant facts have not been included.

See also Skill 5.1

SKILL 7.3 **Demonstrating knowledge of how to provide explicit instruction and guided practice in language structures and conventions using a range of approaches and motivating activities to develop students' facility in comprehending and using academic language in spoken and written English**

See also Skill 5.3

SKILL 7.4 **Demonstrating knowledge of the use of appropriate texts and effective, engaging oral language, reading, and writing activities to facilitate students' ability to interpret and apply English grammar and language conventions in authentic reading, writing, listening, and speaking contexts; and applying strategies for helping students consolidate knowledge of English grammar to improve their reading fluency and comprehension** *(e.g., by providing frequent opportunities to listen to, read, and reread materials that use academic language)*

It used to be that when teachers would think about varying instruction, they would be thinking mainly about content. Methods of instruction were fairly constant. In older grade levels, lecture—and possibly some discussion—was the primary method of instructional delivery. In younger grades, independent work, as well as some group work, was standard fare for most instructional topics. Today, however, teachers know that for the enormous variety of content to be taught, there are multiple varieties of instructional methods they can use. A good way to think about the variety of instructional methods is to classify them into organizational formats. While there are literally hundreds of instructional ideas for just about any K-12 curricular topic, teachers can make the job easier by thinking of how organizational formats essentially organize their instructional ideas.

As the standard states, widely used organizational formats include literature circles, small groups, individual work, workshops, reading centers, and multiage groups. These formats are described in the table below. It is important to remember, however, that other ideas are possible; for example, whole-class drama. In whole-class drama, after reading a book or story, the entire class acts out various portions of the text.

CLASSROOM ORGANIZATIONAL FORMATS	
Literature Circles	Group activities in which each individual in the group has a particular "job." Jobs may include discussion leader, artist (for representing the discussion through art, perhaps), word leader (someone who looks up definitions and informs the group about specific vocabulary words), and many others. The point of these jobs is to keep a student-centered conversation of literature alive. These jobs assist the group in maintaining a conversation without teacher assistance.
Small-Group Activities	Activities that allow a few students to work together. While teachers circulate around the room and assist where necessary, small-group activities give students a chance to help each other and work together on a common problem. Often, small groups are beneficial because they can be prearranged by the teacher to serve various purposes. Sometimes teachers want to have homogeneous groups (groups of the same ability); other times, it is preferable to mix groups up so that highly skilled students can assist less-skilled students.
Individual Work	This format should not be ruled out, although there is a movement to get away from it. Individual work is beneficial when the teacher wants to ensure that all students get the practice they need to become proficient on their own in a certain area.
Workshops	Structures that allow students to work on different products simultaneously. Writing workshops are common in language arts classrooms. While there may be times when, for example, teachers want all students to work on the same writing assignment (which would be considered individual work), at other times teachers want students to have choices about what they write. In workshops, one student might be writing a short story while another student is writing an essay. Students can get feedback from one another in a workshop, and they can also get assistance from the teacher.

Continued on next page

Reading Centers	Structured places in the room where, while the teacher is working with an individual or a small group, students can complete certain reading activities without teacher assistance. Usually, students spend a little time at each center and then rotate to the next center. Common centers include computer terminals (so students can use reading instruction software), student desks (so students can read silently), and reading activity tables (where students, in groups, can do a reading activity together).
Multiage Groups	These groups are coordinated among teachers. Sometimes it is preferable to have homogeneous groups on certain topics. Thus, a third-grade teacher might have some of his students go to the fourth-grade class if they read at a fourth-grade level, and the fourth-grade teacher would send his third-grade readers to the third-grade room. This allows teachers to work with students on their specific reading difficulties.

When classroom organizational concepts are considered, teachers are then free to expand their repertoire of classroom activities for the variety of content they teach.

> **SKILL 7.5** **Demonstrating knowledge of formal and informal methods for assessing students' academic language development and their understanding and use of English language structures and conventions, and demonstrating the ability to interpret and use the results of these assessments to plan effective instruction in these areas**

Guidelines for Assessing Student Writing

When assessing and responding to student writing, there are several guidelines to remember:

1. Use a rating system—for example, a scale from 1 to 4 (where 1 = unsatisfactory and 4 = excellent)

2. Monitor the students' use of source material

3. Evaluate the structure and development of the writing

4. Ensure that the writing style is appropriate for the task assigned

5. Check for grammatical correctness

6. Provide follow-up support for any weaknesses detected

Responding to nongraded writing (formative)

1. Avoid using a red pen; whenever possible, use a #2 pencil

2. Explain in advance the criteria that will be used for assessment

3. Read the writing once while asking the question, "Is the student's response appropriate for the assignment?"

4. Reread and note at the end whether the student met the objective of the writing task

5. Responses should be noncritical and use supportive and encouraging language

6. Resist writing on or over the students' writing

7. Highlight the ideas you wish to emphasize, question, or verify

8. Encourage students to take risks

Responding to and evaluating graded writing (summative)

1. Ask students to submit prewriting and rough-draft materials, including all revisions with their final draft

2. For the first reading, use a holistic method, examining the work as a whole

3. When reading the draft for the second time, assess it using the standards previously established

4. Responses to the writing should be written in the margin and should use supportive language

5. Make sure to address the process as well as the product; it is important that students value the learning process as well as the final product

6. After scanning the piece a third time, write final comments at the end of the draft

Rubrics

Holistic scoring involves assessing a child's ability to construct meaning through writing. It uses a scale called a rubric, with grades ranging from 0 to 4:

0. This grade is for a piece of writing that cannot be scored. It does not respond to the topic or is illegible.

Holistic scoring involves assessing a child's ability to construct meaning through writing.

1. This grade is for writing that does respond to the topic but does not cover it accurately.

2. This grade is for writing that adresses the question but lacks sufficient details to convey the purpose and to accomplish the writing task requested.

3. This grade is for writing which, in general, fulfills the purpose of the writing assignment and demonstrates that the reader correctly constructed meaning. The reader showed that he or she understands the writer's purpose and message.

4. This grade is for writing that has the most details, the best organization, and that presents a well-crafted reaction to the original writer's piece.

Subjective tests put the student in the driver's seat. These types of assessments usually consist of short answers, longer essays, or problem solving that involves critical-thinking skills requiring definitive proof from the short reading passages to support the student's answer. Sometimes teachers provide rubrics that include assessment criteria for high-scoring answers and projects. Sometimes the rubric is as simple as a checklist, and other times a maximum point value is awarded for each item on the rubric. Either way, rubrics provide a guideline of the teacher's expectations for the specifics of the assignment. The teacher usually discusses and/or models what is expected to fulfill each guideline and provides a detailed outline of these expectations for reference.

For example, students being asked to write a research paper might be provided with a rubric. An elementary teacher may assign a total of fifty points for the entire paper. The rubric might award ten points for note-taking quality, ten points for research skills, twenty points for content covered, five points for creative elements, and five points for organization and presentation. Then a certain number of points are awarded in accordance with the students' performance.

Rubrics allow students to score in multiple areas, rather than simply on a final product.

SKILL 7.6 **Applying knowledge of strategies** (*e.g., differentiated instruction, interventions, enrichment*) **to address the assessed needs of individual students** (*e.g., English language learners, struggling writers through highly proficient writers*) **in academic language development, including recognizing ways in which language structures and written language conventions of other languages may differ from English and the importance of helping English language learners transfer language skills from their home language to English**

See also Skill 8.3

DOMAIN II
COMMUNICATION ARTS

PERSONALIZED STUDY PLAN

KNOWN MATERIAL/ SKIP IT

COMPETENCY 8
UNDERSTAND THE DEVELOPMENT OF WRITING SKILLS

SKILL Demonstrating knowledge of the structure and key elements of
8.1 various modes of writing *(e.g., expository, persuasive)*

Different Types of Writing

Most nonfiction writing falls into one of four different forms:

1. Narrative

2. Descriptive

3. Expository

4. Persuasive

Persuasive writing

PERSUASION is a piece of writing, a poem, a play, or a speech whose purpose is to change the minds of the audience members or to get them to do something. This is achieved in a variety of ways:

1. The credibility of the writer/speaker might lead the listeners/readers to a change of mind or a recommended action.

2. Reasoning is important in persuasive discourse. No one wants to believe that he or she accepts a new viewpoint or goes out and takes action just because he or she likes and trusts the person who recommended it. Logic comes into play in reasoning that is persuasive.

3. The third and most powerful force that leads to acceptance or action is emotional appeal. Even if audience members have been persuaded logically and reasonably that they should believe in a different way, they are unlikely to act on it unless moved emotionally. A person with resources might be convinced that people suffered in New Orleans after Katrina, but he or she will not be likely to do anything about it until he or she feels a deeper emotional connection to the disaster. Sermons are good examples of persuasive discourse.

> **PERSUASION:** a piece of writing, a poem, a play, or a speech whose purpose is to change the minds of the audience members or to get them to do something

Expository writing

In contrast to persuasion, the only purpose of exposition is to inform. EXPOSITORY WRITING is not interested in changing anyone's mind or getting anyone to take a certain action. It exists to give information. Some examples include directions to a particular place or the directions for putting together a toy that arrives unassembled. The writer doesn't care whether you do or don't follow the directions. He or she only wants to be sure you have the information in case you do decide to use it.

> **EXPOSITORY WRITING:** a form of writing where the only purpose is to inform

Narrative writing

NARRATION is discourse that is arranged chronologically—something happened, and then something else happened, and then something else happened. It is also called a story. News reports are often narrative in nature, as are records of trips or experiences.

> **NARRATION:** discourse that is arranged chronologically

Descriptive writing

DESCRIPTIVE WRITING has the purpose of making an experience available through one of the five senses—seeing, smelling, hearing, feeling (as with the fingers), and tasting. Descriptive words are used to make it possible for readers to "see" with their own mind's eye, "hear" through their own mind's ear, "smell" through their own mind's nose, "taste" with their own mind's tongue, and "feel" with their own mind's fingers. This is how language moves people. Only by experiencing an event can the emotions become involved. Poets are experts in descriptive language. Descriptive writing is typically used to make sure the point is established emotionally.

> **DESCRIPTIVE WRITING:** making an experience available through one of the five senses—seeing, smelling, hearing, feeling (as with the fingers), and tasting

Understanding Nonfiction

Students often misrepresent the differences between fiction and nonfiction. They mistakenly believe that stories are always examples of fiction. The simple truth is that stories are both fiction and nonfiction. The primary difference is that fiction is imaginary, and nonfiction is generally true (or an opinion). It is harder for students to understand that non-fiction entails an enormous range of material from textbooks to true stories and newspaper articles to speeches. Fiction, on the other hand, is fairly simple—imaginary stories, novels, etc. But it is also important for students to understand that most of fiction throughout history has been based on true events. In other words, authors use their own life experiences to help them to create works of fiction.

> *Students often misrepresent the differences between fiction and nonfiction. They mistakenly believe that stories are always examples of fiction. The simple truth is that stories are both fiction and nonfiction.*

Opinion versus truth

The artistry in telling a story to convey a point is important in understanding nonfiction. Realizing what is truth and what is perspective is important in understanding nonfiction. Often, a nonfiction writer will present an opinion, and that opinion is very different from a truth. Knowing the difference between the two is very crucial.

Comparing fiction and nonfiction

In comparing fiction to nonfiction, students need to learn about the conventions of each. In fiction, students can generally expect to find plot, characters, setting, and themes. In nonfiction, students may find a plot, characters, settings, and themes, but they will also experience interpretations, opinions, theories, research, and other elements.

Overall, students can begin to see patterns that identify fiction from nonfiction. Often, the more fanciful or unrealistic a text or story is, the more likely it is fiction, or contains facts that have been "fictionalized."

Nonfiction comes in a variety of styles. While many students simplify nonfiction as being true (as opposed to fiction, which is make-believe), nonfiction is much deeper than that. The following are various types of nonfiction; students should be exposed to all of these.

TYPES OF NONFICTION	
Informational Texts	These types of books explain concepts or phenomena. An informational text might explain the history of a state or the idea of photosynthesis. These types of text are usually based on research.
Newspaper Articles	These short texts rely completely on factual information and are presented in a very straightforward, sometimes choppy manner. The purpose of these texts is to present information to readers in a quick and efficient manner.
Essays	Usually, essays take an opinion (whether it is about a concept, a work of literature, a person, or an event) and describe how the opinion was arrived at or why the opinion is a good one.
Biographies	These texts explain the lives of individuals. They are usually based on extensive research.
Memoirs	In a way, a memoir is like an autobiography, but memoirs tend to be based on a specific idea, concept, issue, or event in life. For example, most presidents of the United States write memoirs about their time in office.

Continued on next page

| Letters | When letters are read and analyzed in the classroom, students are generally studying the writer's style or the writer's true opinions and feelings about certain events. Often, students will find letters of famous individuals in history reprinted in textbooks. |
| Journals | Similar to letters, journals present very personal ideas. When available (as most people rarely want their journals published), they give students the opportunity to see peoples' thought processes about various events or issues. |

SKILL 8.2 Applying knowledge of techniques for generating topics and developing ideas (e.g., brainstorming, using graphic organizers) and for organizing written presentations

See also Skill 8.3

Students can learn specific techniques for generating ideas and for organizing their writing. Encourage students to ask questions such as "Who is my audience?" and "How can I introduce my topic?" Strategies they can use to generate topics and organize their thoughts include journal writing and reading aloud. More specific strategies are below.

TEACHING-LEARNING STRATEGIES		
Teacher-Guided	Student Empowerment	Specific Strategies
BEFORE		
• Discovering what to say about a particular topic • Considering the variables of purpose, audience, and form • Planning	• What is my topic? My purpose? • Who is my audience? • What should I say? • What form should I use? • How should I organize my ideas?	• Talking, interviewing, reading, researching • Brainstorming, listing, clustering, mapping, webbing, flowcharting, outlining • Focused free writing • Heuristics (questions/prompts/leads) • Reading and examining models • Viewing, visualization, guided imagery • Journal writing

Continued on next page

DURING		
• Saying what is meant as directly and clearly as possible • Finding an appropriate voice and point of view • Telling the reader about the topic	• How can I introduce my topic? • How can I develop each part? • How can I conclude my topic?	• Mapping thoughts • Writing off a lead • Fast or free writing • Personal letter • Conferencing • Reflecting and questioning self
REVISING		
• Editing for ideas and organization • Proofreading for conventions other than content	• Have I edited and proofread? • Have I practiced a variety of editing and proofreading methods? Which work best for me?	• Reading aloud to another • Using revision checklists • Check and question marks • Using a "pass" strategy • Self-monitoring • Peer conferencing

See also Skill 5.3

SKILL 8.3 **Demonstrating knowledge of the steps in the writing process** *(e.g., drafting, editing)* **and strategies for developing students' use of a process to write competently with confidence, accuracy, and imagination**

The Writing Process

Learning to write is generally a sequential process. Research confirms that children develop spelling strategies in predictable stages. There is a continuous growth in writing, but the children vary in the development of these stages. A child's writing may show evidence of more than one stage. Children may even skip levels on their way to developing writing competency.

Stage progression

Children progress as writers from one phase to the next, with one set of skills building on the skills acquired earlier. Writing, however, combines many skills, and relies on development in many areas not specific to writing. A child's fine motor control and vocabulary, for example, must improve in order for writing to progress normally.

Cognitive theories of understanding state that learning only takes place when the new learning is based upon previous learning. Struggling students may often lack essential background knowledge necessary to successfully complete a task or use a strategy.

Task analysis

The best way to identify the basic terms and skills necessary for the strategy is to do a task analysis. The task analysis will help teachers to determine if students possess the prerequisite skills necessary to advance to the next stage of writing. After the task analysis is complete, there are many ways that teachers can check students' skills. These include observing student performance, using curriculum-based measures, or simply asking students.

Writing is a process that flows gradually. As you give your students time to explore and experiment with writing, you will begin to see evidence of growth. Since writing is a process and stages are connected. Students may show evidence of more than one stage in a single piece of writing.

DEVELOPING EMERGENT WRITING SKILLS	
Assessment	The first step in developing young writers skills is to know where they are in developmental writing stages. Though skills are overlapping, at any one time a child will fall predominately into one or more skill areas. While the child may be an emergent writer in content, the same child may be a role player writer in penmanship. Teachers need to be aware of where each student falls at any one time in each area of writing. The best means of assessment are writing samples and/or portfolios and journals. Assessment should be ongoing, as a child's writing stage is not static.
Teaching Strategies	Invented spelling is an early writing skill. Teachers should encourage and teach the child invented spelling. The child's name is usually the first meaningful writing the child does. The teacher should focus intensely on teaching the child to write her name. Teachers can develop an interest in writing in a young child by providing and guiding the student through meaningful writing tasks such as letters home to parents, thank you notes, and journal writing to share experiences.

Continued on next page

Environment	Teachers should set up their classroom environment to encourage meaningful writing, such as having a sign-in sheet, providing pencils and pads for play, for writing traffic tickets, menus, taking restaurant orders, etc. Meaningful writing opportunities should also be provided such as journaling and writing centers, observation journals in science centers, and providing reference charts for alphabet and pattern sentences. Outside writing opportunities should be encouraged with sidewalk chalk, nature journals, and signing library books in and out.
Materials	Teachers should provide a variety of writing materials to inspire all students. Markers and construction paper provide inspiration to some students, while others prefer paints. Sponges cut into letter shapes, stamps, stencils, and hole punchers are some writing materials that can be made available. Shaving cream, sand, jello, rice, and other manipulative materials should be available for those students who need or enjoy the tactile stimulation for writing.

Stages of the Writing Process

Writing is a recursive process. As students engage in the various stages of writing, they develop and improve not only their writing skills, but their thinking skills as well. Students must understand that writing is a process and typically involves many steps when writing quality work. No matter the level of writer, students should be experienced in the following stages of the writing process.

Prewriting

Students gather ideas before writing. **PREWRITING** may include clustering, listing, brainstorming, mapping, free writing, and charting. Providing many ways for a student to develop ideas on a topic will increase his/her chances for success.

Remind students that as they prewrite, they need to consider their audience.

Prewriting strategies assist students in a variety of ways. Listed below are the most common prewriting strategies students can use to explore, plan and write on a topic. It is important to remember when teaching these strategies that not all prewriting must eventually produce a finished piece of writing. In fact, in the initial lesson of teaching prewriting strategies, it might be more effective to have students practice prewriting strategies without the pressure of having to write a finished product.

- Keep an idea book so that they can jot down ideas that come to mind.

- Write in a daily journal.

- Write down whatever comes to mind; this is called free writing. Students do not stop to make corrections or interrupt the flow of ideas. A variation of this technique is focused free writing—writing on a specific topic—to prepare for an essay.

- Make a list of all ideas connected with their topic; this is called brainstorming

> *Writing is a recursive process. As students engage in the various stages of writing, they develop and improve not only their writing skills, but their thinking skills as well.*

> **PREWRITING:** a stage of the writing process during which students gather ideas; this stage may include clustering, listing, brainstorming, mapping, free writing, and charting

- Make sure students know that this technique works best when they let their minds work freely. After completing the list, students should analyze the list to see if a pattern or way to group the ideas emerges.

- Ask the questions Who? What? When? Where? When? and How? Help the writer approach a topic from several perspectives.

- Create a visual map on paper to gather ideas. Cluster circles and lines to show connections between ideas. Students should try to identify the relationship that exists between their ideas. If they cannot see the relationships, have them pair up, exchange papers and have their partners look for some related ideas.

- Observe details of sight, hearing, taste, touch, and taste.

- Visualize by making mental images of something and write down the details in a list.

After students have practiced each of these prewriting strategies, ask them to pick out the ones they prefer and ask them to discuss how they might use the techniques to help them with future writing assignments. It is important to remember that they can use more than one prewriting strategy at a time. Also they may find that different writing situations may suggest certain techniques.

Drafting

Students compose the first draft. Students should follow their notes/writing plan from the prewriting stage.

Revision and editing

Revision

Revise comes from the Latin word *revidere*, meaning "to see again." **REVISION** is probably the most important step for the writer in the writing process. Here, students examine their work and make changes in wording, details, and ideas. So many times, students write a draft and then feel they're done. On the contrary, students must be encouraged to develop, change, and enhance their writing as they go, as well as once they've completed a draft.

> **REVISION:** a stage of the writing process where students examine their work and make changes in wording, details, and ideas

When discussing revision, begin with discussing the definition of revise. Also, state that all writing must be revised to improve it. After students have revised their writing, it is time for the final editing and proofreading.

Editing

Both teachers and students should be aware of the difference between these two writing processes. Revising typically entails making substantial changes to a written draft, and it is during this process that the look, idea, and feel of a draft may be altered, sometimes significantly. Like revising, **EDITING** continues to make changes to a draft. However the changes made during the editing process do more to enhance the ideas in the draft, rather than change or alter them. Finally, **PROOFREADING** is the stage where grammatical and technical errors are addressed.

Effective teachers realize that revision and editing go hand-in-hand and students often move back and forth between these stages during the course of one written work. Also, these stages must be practiced in small groups, pairs and/or individually. Students must learn to analyze and improve their own work as well as the works of their peers. Some methods to use include:

1. Students, working in pairs, analyze sentences for variety.

2. Students work in pairs or groups to ask questions about unclear areas in the writing or to help students add details, information, etc.

3. Students perform final edit.

Students need to be trained to become effective at proofreading, revising, and editing strategies. Begin by training them using both desk-side and scheduled conferences. Listed below are some strategies to use to guide students through the final stages of the writing process.

• Provide some guide sheets or forms for students to use during peer responses.

• Allow students to work in pairs and limit the agenda.

• Model the use of the guide sheet or form for the entire class.

• Give students a time limit or number of written pieces to be completed in a specific amount of time.

• Have the students read their partners' papers and ask at least three who, what, when, why, how questions; the students answer the questions and use them as a place to begin discussing the piece.

• At this point in the writing process, a mini-lesson that focuses on some of the problems your students are having would be appropriate.

To help students revise, provide students with a series of questions that will assist them in revising their writing:

• Do the details give a clear picture? Add details that appeal to more than just the sense of sight.

• How effectively are the details organized? Reorder the details if it is needed.

• Are the thoughts and feelings of the writer included? Add personal thoughts and feelings about the subject.

EDITING: a stage of the writing process where students continue to make changes to a draft, enhancing the ideas rather than altering or changing them

PROOFREADING: a stage of the writing process where grammatical and technical errors are addressed

Grammar needs to be taught in the context of the students' own work.

Grammar needs to be taught in the context of the students' own work. Listed below is a series of classroom practices that encourage meaningful context-based grammar instruction, combined with occasional mini-lessons and other language strategies that can be used on a daily basis.

- Connect grammar with the student's own writing while emphasizing grammar as a significant aspect of effective writing.

- Emphasize the importance of editing and proofreading as an essential part of classroom activities.

- Provide students with an opportunity to practice editing and proofreading cooperatively.

- Give instruction in the form of fifteen- to twenty-minute mini-lessons.

- Emphasize the sound of punctuation by connecting it to pitch, stress, and pause.

- Involve students in all facets of language learning including reading, writing, listening, speaking and thinking; good use of language comes from exploring all forms of it on a regular basis.

There are a number of approaches that involve grammar instruction in the context of the writing.

APPROACHES TO GRAMMAR INSTRUCTION	
Sentence Combining	Try to use the student's own writing as much as possible. The theory behind combining ideas and the correct punctuation should be emphasized.
Sentence and Paragraph Modeling	Provide students with the opportunity to practice imitating the style and syntax of professional writers.
Sentence Transforming	Give students an opportunity to change sentences from one form to another, i.e. from passive to active, inverting the sentence order, change forms of the words used.
Daily Language Practice	Introduce or clarify common errors using daily language activities. Use actual student examples whenever possible. Correct and discuss the problems with grammar and usage.

Proofreading

Students proofread the draft for punctuation and mechanical errors. There are a few key points to remember when helping students learn to edit and proofread their work.

- It is crucial that students are not taught grammar in isolation, but in context of the writing process.

- Ask students to read their writing and check for specific errors such as whether or not every sentence starts with a capital letter and has the correct punctuation at the end.

- Provide students with a proofreading checklist to guide them as they edit their work.

Publishing

PUBLISHING is the last stage of the process. Students may have their work displayed on a bulletin board, read aloud in class, or printed in a literary magazine or school anthology.

It is important to realize that these steps are recursive, as a student engages in each aspect of the writing process. The students may begin with prewriting, then write, revise, write, revise, edit, and publish. They do not engage in this process in a lockstep manner; it is more circular.

> **PUBLISHING:** a stage in the writing process at which students may have their work displayed on a bulletin board, read aloud in class, or printed in a literary magazine or school anthology

---

SKILL 8.4 **Analyzing and revising written work in relation to organization, unity, clarity, and style** *(e.g., adding topic sentences, reordering sentences, deleting unnecessary information)*

See also Skill 8.3

Writing Introductions

It is important to remember that in the writing process, the introduction should be written last. Until the body of the paper has been determined—thesis, development—it's difficult to make strategic decisions regarding the introduction. The Greek rhetoricians called this part of a discourse *exordium*, a "leading into." The basic purpose of the introduction, then, is to lead the audience into the discourse. It can let the reader know what the purpose of the discourse is and it can condition the audience to be receptive to what the writer wants to say. It can be very brief or it can take up a large percentage of the total word count. Aristotle said that the introduction could be compared to the flourishes that flute players make before their performance—an overture in which the musicians display what they can play best in order to gain the favor and attention of the audience for the main performance.

> *In the writing process, the introduction should be written last. It can let the reader know what the purpose of the discourse is and it can condition the audience to be receptive to what the writer wants to say.*

In order to do this, we must first of all know what we are going to say; who the readership is likely to be; what the social, political, economic, climate is; what preconceived notions the audience is likely to have regarding the subject; and how long the discourse is going to be.

There are many ways to do this:

- Show that the subject is important

- Show that although the points we are presenting may seem improbable, they are true

- Show that the subject has been neglected, misunderstood, or misrepresented

- Explain an unusual mode of development

- Forestall any misconception of the purpose

- Apologize for a deficiency

- Arouse interest in the subject with an anecdotal lead-in

- Ingratiate oneself with the readership

- Establish one's own credibility

The introduction often ends with the thesis, the point or purpose of the paper. However, this is not set in stone. The thesis may open the body of the discussion or it may conclude the discourse. The most important thing to remember is that the purpose and structure of the introduction should be deliberate if it is to serve the purpose of "leading the reader into the discussion."

Writing Conclusions

It is easier to write a conclusion after the decisions regarding the introduction have been made. Aristotle taught that the conclusion should strive to do five things:

Inspire the reader with a favorable opinion of the writer

2. Amplify the force of the points made in the body of the paper

3. Reinforce the points made in the body

4. Rouse appropriate emotions in the reader

5. Restate in a summary way what has been said

The conclusion may be short or it may be long depending on its purpose in the paper. Recapitulation, a brief restatement of the main points or certainly of the thesis, is the most common form of effective conclusion. A good example is the closing argument in a court trial.

Text Organization

In studies of professional writers and how they produce their successful works, it has been revealed that writing is a process that can be clearly defined although in practice it must have enough flexibility to allow for creativity. The teacher must be able to define the various stages that a successful writer goes through in order to make a statement that has value. There must be a discovery stage when ideas, materials, supporting details, etc., are deliberately collected. These may come from many possible sources: the writer's own experience and observations, deliberate research of written sources, interviews of live people, television presentations, or the Internet.

The next stage is organization, where the purpose, thesis, and supporting points are determined. Most writers will put forth more than one possible thesis and in the next stage—the writing of the paper—settle on one as the result of trial and error. Once the paper is written, the editing stage is necessary and is probably the most important stage. This is not just the polishing stage. At this point, decisions must be made regarding whether the reasoning is cohesive: Does it hold together? Is the arrangement the best possible one or should the points be rearranged? Are there holes that need to be filled in? What form will the introduction take? Does the conclusion lead the reader out of the discourse or is it inadequate or too abrupt?

It's important to remember that the best writers engage in all of these stages recursively. They may go back to discovery at any point in the process. They may go back and rethink the organization. To help students become effective writers, the teacher needs to give them adequate practice in the various stages and encourage them to engage deliberately in the creative thinking that makes writers successful.

> **SKILL 8.5** Applying knowledge of strategies for developing students' writing vocabulary and their ability to use written language to communicate effectively with a variety of audiences and for different purposes

See also Skill 8.1

In writing, students can be taught to express their points of view either implicitly or explicitly, depending on the situation, the intended audience, and purpose. Often, in a clear-cut argumentative essay, students should portray their points of view and opinions explicitly. In other words, they should make it very clear what their belief or argument is. However, in persuasive or critical essays that are intended to slowly draw someone from one perspective to the student's perspective, it is often a better idea to hide the argument within the examples and other areas of support. For an audience who may already agree with the writer's perspective, it is useful to clearly state the argument; for an audience who may not agree with the writer's perspective, it is safer to ease the audience into the argument with examples and support first.

Logical organization for a **supportive audience** looks like this:

- Argument

- Weak example

- Adequate example

- Strong example

By organizing in this fashion, the writer clearly states the opinion up front (so to keep the audience interested). Then, the writer arranges the weakest arguments first, so that the strong examples at the end assist in a strong, emphasis-filled conclusion.

Logical organization for a **nonsupportive audience** looks like this:

- Example

- Example

- Example

- Argument

Or

- Argument (stated very lightly)

- Strong example

- Adequate example

- Weak example

The reason for this approach is that we want the audience to be drawn in by the facts of the case first. Then, once they have, in essence, agreed on the facts, the writer can suggest that, "If you believe X, you must also believe Y." And hence, Y is the argument that they first did not accept.

This type of approach works for persuasive writing, argumentation, critical analysis, and evaluation. In each type of writing, we are trying to convince the reader of our thesis. Even with critical analysis, where opinions might not be as heated, if we propose out of the ordinary ideas, we might be better off using the approach for a nonsupportive audience.

Finally, in order to write—either for or against an idea—and not utilize biased language, we need to write as much as possible in an active voice and be concise. If a word is not needed, it should be eliminated. Writers can further remove bias by putting themselves in the frames of mind of various people for or against an issue and rereading the essay. Even if we are arguing for a particular topic, we want to remain bias-free, so that we look like we are simply presenting the best possible solution to any problem, for example. Let's say we are arguing for gun control. We want to write not as if we have always been gun control supporters, but rather as unbiased people who have simply come to the best decision about the topic.

SKILL 8.6 Demonstrating knowledge of formal and informal methods for assessing students' writing development and demonstrating the ability to interpret and use the results of these assessments to plan effective writing instruction

Literacy Portfolios

Compiling LITERACY PORTFOLIOS is an increasingly popular and meaningful form of informal assessment. It is particularly compelling because artists, television directors, authors, architects, and photographers use portfolios in their careers and jobs. It is also a most authentic format for documenting children's literacy growth over time. The portfolio is not only a significant professional informal assessment tool for the teacher, but a vehicle and format for the child reader to take ownership of his/her progress over time. It models a way of compiling one's reading and writing products as a lifelong learner, which is the ultimate goal of reading instruction.

> **LITERACY PORTFOLIOS:** a student assessment strategy where students collect all of their reading and writing products so that teachers can track growth

FOUR CATEGORIES OF MATERIALS IN LITERACY PORTFOLIOS	
Work Samples	These can include children's story maps, webs, KWL charts, pictures, illustrations, storyboards, and writings about the stories they have read.
Records of Independent Reading and Writing	These can include the children's journals, notebooks, or logs of books read with the names of the authors, titles of the books, date completed, and pieces related to books completed or in progress.
Checklists and Surveys	These include checklists designed by the teacher for reading development, writing development, ownership checklists, and general interest surveys.

Continued on next page

Self-Evaluation Forms	These are the children's own evaluations of their reading and writing process framed in their own words. They can be simple templates with starting sentences such as: • I am really proud of the way I • I feel one of my strengths as a reader is • To improve the way I read aloud I need to • To improve my reading I should

Generally, a child's portfolio in grade three or above begins with a letter to the reader explaining the work that will be found in the portfolio. In grade four and up, children write a brief reflection detailing their feelings and judgments about their growth as readers and writers.

Uses for Literacy Portfolios

When teachers maintain student portfolios for mandated school administrative review, district review, or even for their own research, they often prepare portfolio summary sheets. These provide identifying data on the children and then a timeline of their review of the portfolio contents. The summary sheets also contain professional comments on the extent to which the portfolio documents satisfactory and ongoing growth in reading.

Portfolios can be used beneficially for child-teacher and parent/teacher conversations to:

- Review the child's progress.

- Discuss areas of strength.

- Set future goals.

- Make plans for future learning activities.

- Evaluate what should remain in the portfolio and what needs to be cleared out for new materials.

See also Skill 7.5

> SKILL **Applying knowledge of strategies** (e.g., differentiated instruction,
> 8.7 interventions, enrichment) **to address the assessed needs of individual students** (e.g., English language learners, struggling writers through highly proficient writers) **in writing**

See also Skills 8.3, 8.4, and 8.5

COMPETENCY 9
UNDERSTAND THE DEVELOPMENT OF LISTENING, SPEAKING, VIEWING, AND MEDIA LITERACY SKILLS

**SKILL Demonstrating knowledge of how to provide explicit instruction
9.1 and guided practice using a range of approaches and activities to
develop students' facility in communicating information, opinions,
and ideas orally and visually to different audiences for a variety of
purposes**

Analyzing the speech of others is a very good technique for helping students improve their own public speaking abilities. Because in most circumstances, students cannot view themselves as they give speeches and presentations, when they get the opportunity to critique, question, and analyze others' speeches, they begin to learn what works and what doesn't work in effective public speaking. However, a very important word of warning: DO NOT have students critique each others' public speaking skills. It could be very damaging to a student to have his or her peers point out what did not work in a speech. Instead, video is a great tool teachers can use. Any appropriate source of public speaking can be used in the classroom for students to analyze and critique.

Some of the things students can pay attention to include:

- Volume: A speaker should use an appropriate volume—not too loud to be annoying, but not too soft to be inaudible.

- Pace: The rate at which words are spoken should be appropriate—not too fast to make the speech nonunderstandable, but not too slow so as to put listeners to sleep.

- Pronunciation: A speaker should make sure words are spoken clearly. Listeners do not have a text to go back and reread things they didn't catch.

- Body language: While animated body language can help a speech, too much of it can be distracting. Body language should help convey the message, not detract from it.

- Word choice: The words speakers choose should be consistent with their intended purpose and the audience.

- Visual aids: Visual aids, like body language, should enhance a message. Many visual aids can be distracting, and that detracts from the message.

Overall, instead of telling students to keep these factors in mind when presenting information orally, having them view speakers who do these things well and poorly will help them know and remember the next time they give a speech.

FEATURES OF SPOKEN LANGUAGE	
Voice	Many people fall into one of two traps when speaking: using a monotone or talking too fast. These are both caused by anxiety. A monotone restricts your natural inflection, but can be remedied by releasing tension in upper and lower body muscles. Talking fast, on the other hand, is not necessarily a bad thing if the speaker is exceptionally articulate. If not, or if the speaker is talking about very technical things, it becomes far too easy for the audience to become lost. When you talk too fast and begin tripping over your words, consciously pause after every sentence you say. Don't be afraid of brief silences. The audience needs time to absorb what you are saying.
Volume	Problems with volume, whether too soft or too loud, can usually be combated with practice. If you tend to speak too softly, have someone stand the back of the room and give you a signal when your volume is strong enough. If possible, have someone in the front of the room as well to make sure you're not overcompensating with excessive volume. Conversely, if you have a problem with speaking too loudly, have the person in the front of the room signal you when your voice is soft enough and check with the person in the back to make sure it is still loud enough to be heard. In both cases, note your volume level for future reference. Don't be shy about asking your audience, "Can you hear me in the back?" Suitable volume is beneficial for both you and the audience.
Pitch	Pitch refers to the length, tension, and thickness of a person's vocal bands. As your voice gets higher, the pitch gets higher. In oral performance, pitch reflects upon the emotional arousal level. More variation in pitch typically corresponds to more emotional arousal, but can also be used to convey sarcasm or highlight specific words.
Posture	Maintain a straight, but not stiff posture. Instead of shifting weight from hip to hip, point your feet directly at the audience and distribute your weight evenly. Keep shoulders orientated toward the audience. If you have to turn your body to use a visual aid, turn 45 degrees and continue speaking toward the audience.
Movement	Instead of staying glued to one spot or pacing back and forth, stay within four to eight feet of the front row of your audience, and take maybe a step or half-step to the side every once in a while. If you are using a lectern, feel free to move to the front or side of it to engage your audience more. Avoid distancing yourself from the audience—you want them to feel involved and connected.
Gestures	Gestures are a great way to keep a natural atmosphere when speaking publicly. Use them just as you would when speaking to a friend. They shouldn't be exaggerated, but they should be utilized for added emphasis. Avoid keeping your hands in your pockets or locked behind your back, wringing your hands and fidgeting nervously, or keeping your arms crossed.
Eye Contact	Many people are intimidated by using eye contact when speaking to large groups. Interestingly, eye contact usually helps the speaker overcome speech anxiety by connecting with their attentive audience and easing feelings of isolation. Instead of looking at a spot on the back wall or at your notes, scan the room and make eye contact for one to three seconds per person.

SKILL 9.2 Recognizing the principles of effective listening and viewing and strategies for enhancing listening and viewing skills

When complex or new information is provided to us orally, we must analyze and interpret that information. What is the author's most important point? How do figures of speech affect meaning? How are conclusions determined? Often, making sense of information can be difficult when it is presented orally—first, because we have no way to go back and review material already stated; second, because oral language is so much less predictable and even than written language. However, when we focus on extracting the meaning, message, and speaker's purpose, rather than just "listening" and waiting for things to make sense to us, then we have greater success in interpreting speech.

> When we are more active in our listening, then we have greater success in interpreting speech.

In the classrooms of exceptional teachers, students are captivated by the reading aloud of good literature. It is refreshing and enjoyable to just sit and soak in language, stories, and poetry being read aloud. Therefore, we must teach students how to listen and enjoy such work. We do this by making it fun and providing many opportunities and alternatives to appeal to the wide array of interests in each classroom.

Large- and small-group conversation requires more than just listening. It involves feedback and active involvement. This can be particularly challenging because, in our culture, we are trained to move conversations along and to avoid silences in a conversation. This poses significant problems for the art of listening. In a discussion, for example, when we are preparing our next response instead of listening to what others are saying, we do a large disservice to the entire discussion. Students need to learn how listening carefully to others in discussions actually promotes better responses on the part of subsequent speakers. One way teachers can encourage this in both large- and small-group discussions is to expect students to respond directly to previous comments before moving ahead with their new comments. This will encourage them to add their new comments in light of the comments that came before their turn.

Listening to Messages

Speech can be difficult to follow. First, we have no written record by which to "reread" things we didn't hear or understand. Second, it can be much less structured and have far more variation in volume, tone, and rate than written language. Yet, aside from rereading, many of the skills and strategies that help us in reading comprehension can help us in listening comprehension. For example, as soon as we start listening to something new, we can tap into our prior knowledge in order to attach new information to what we already know. This not only helps

> Speech can be difficult to follow. First, we have no written record by which to "reread" things we didn't hear or understand. Second, it can be much less structured and have far more variation in volume, tone, and rate than written language.

us understand the new information more quickly, it also helps us remember the material.

We can also look for transitions between ideas. Sometimes, we can notice voice tone or body language changes. Of course, we don't have the luxury of looking at paragraphs in oral language, but we do have the animation that comes along with live speech. Human beings have to try very hard to be completely nonexpressive in their speech. Listeners should pay attention to the way speakers change character and voice in order to signal a transition of ideas.

Listeners can also better comprehend the underlying intent of a speaker when they attend to the nonverbal cues of the speaker. The expression on a speaker's face can do more to communicate irony, for example, than the actual words.

One good way to follow speech is to take notes and outline major points. Because speech can be less linear than written text, notes and outlines can be of great assistance in keeping track of a speaker's message. Students can practice this strategy in the classroom by taking notes of teachers' oral messages and of other students' presentations and speeches.

Other classroom methods can help students learn good listening skills. For example, teachers can have students practice following complex directions. They can also have students retell stories or retell oral presentations of stories or other materials. These activities give students direct practice in important listening skills.

Oral language (listening and speaking) involves receiving and understanding messages sent by other people and also expressing our own feelings and ideas. Students must learn that listening is a communication process and that they must be *active participants* in the process.

Often, in speech, elements like irony are not indicated at all by the actual words, but rather through tone and nonverbal cues.

In active listening, students must determine and evaluate the meaning of a message before they can respond appropriately.

Responding to Messages

The way students respond to messages is more than communication going from a student's mouth to a teacher's ear. In addition to the words, messages are transmitted by eye contact, physical closeness, tone of voice, visual cues, and overall body language. Speech employs gestures, visual clues, and vocal dynamics to convey information between teachers and students. Children first learn to respond to messages by listening to and understanding what they hear (supported by overall body language); next, they experiment with expressing themselves through speaking.

As children become proficient in language, they expect straight messages from teachers. A straight message is one in which words, vocal expression, and body movements are all congruent. Students need to feel secure and safe. If the message is not straight—if the words say one thing but the tone and facial expression say another—children get confused. When they are confused, they often feel threatened.

Remembering Message Content

Reading is more than pronouncing words correctly; readers have to gain meaning from the words. A competent reader can pronounce the words on a page, remember what the words mean, and learn from them.

Processes that enhance students' ability to remember include:

- **Association:** When you associate, you remember things by relating them to each other in some way.

- **Visualization:** Visualization helps you create a strong, vivid memory. Try to picture in your mind what you wish to remember.

- **Concentration:** Concentration can be defined as focusing attention on one thing only. When you read for a particular purpose, you will concentrate on what you read.

- **Repetition:** When you have difficulty remembering textbook information, you should repeat the procedures for association, visualization, and concentration. The repetition helps store the information in your memory.

SKILL 9.3 **Demonstrating knowledge of strategies for evaluating a variety of media** *(e.g., television, magazines, Web sites)* **with regard to purpose, message, audience, bias, and accuracy of information**

Searching for information from printed and electronic sources is a critical literacy-related activity. Increasingly, teachers realize that it is impossible to memorize or even be exposed to the majority of basic facts in our world today. Information is produced so rapidly that knowing **how to access, judge, and synthesize information will help students throughout their lives**.

To understand what this standard means, let's take it apart piece by piece. First, the gathering of information requires that students are competent with everything from a traditional library catalog system to Web-based collections. The best way to get students to feel comfortable with these sources of information is simply to have to search for specific items with proper teacher guidance. It is usually not a good idea to set students out on a journey for information without first explaining the tools and modeling how information can be found from them.

One of the most important parts of gathering information is judging the sources.

One simple cause of the rapid increase in information is that it is easier now than it has ever been for anyone to provide information to the public. For example, anyone can post wikis, blogs, and Web sites. Print material is no safer: more journals and magazines are published today, and many have very uncertain records of reliability. While even the best teacher can fall prey to bad sources of information, generally, experienced adult readers will know when quality is not sufficient. A good way to teach students how to evaluate the quality of an information source is to model how decisions are made in the judging process. For example, a teacher can show students a variety of Web sites on a particular topic. While showing students these sites, the teacher can do a "think aloud," whereby he or she expresses her opinions about the ways in which the information presented demonstrates quality or a lack thereof.

Interpreting information from a variety of sources can be challenging, as well. Many students who have experienced little nonfiction will tend to view information sources in much the same way they view their textbooks: objective and straightforward. Experienced readers will note that information sources are often opinionated, embedded in other ideas or works, part of a greater dialogue, or highly slanted. Often, the sources found are not necessarily meant for extraction of ideas from students; rather, intended audiences vary incredibly for each work. Even though we may have access to quite a bit, we may not be the anticipated audience of the writer. To teach students how to interpret nonfiction sources, have them focus on these components of the work:

- Purpose: The author's intended purpose in writing the piece

- Audience: The author's intended audience (for example, an article about a scientific phenomenon could be written for other scientists, the general public, a source of funding for an experiment, etc.)

- Argument: It is important for students to determine if the author has an argument, and what that argument is; all the information in the piece will make better sense when this is figured out.

Finally, synthesizing information is a complex task. When multiple sources regarding the same concept are used, students can outline the main points of each source and look at how the pieces differ. Students can also trace similar ideas through each of the pieces to see how authors treat subjects differently or similarly. Graphic organizers can be very helpful in the synthesis of a variety of sources.

SKILL
9.4
Demonstrating knowledge of formal and informal methods for assessing students' development of listening, speaking, viewing, and media literacy skills and demonstrating the ability to interpret and use the results of these assessments to plan effective instruction in these areas

See also Skill 6.6

SKILL
9.5
Applying knowledge of strategies (e.g., differentiated instruction, interventions, enrichment) **to address the assessed needs of individual students** (e.g., English language learners) **in the development of listening, speaking, viewing, and media literacy skills**

See also Skill 9.1

Organizing a Presentation

Class presentations are an opportunity for students to demonstrate their understanding of a topic and to explain it to an audience. Teachers can emphasize these main points for organizing a presentation:

- State your main point clearly.

- Explain your main point.

- Support your main point with evidence from credible sources.

- Conclude and restate your main point.

Audience Feedback

After a presentation, audience members are often allowed to give feedback to the presenter. Teachers should emphasize that while students are listening to feedback about their presentation, they should not be overly sensitive to their classmates' comments because other students may feel uncomfortable about giving feedback and may not phrase their comments properly.

Teacher Feedback

Teachers should instruct students about the distinction between criticism and feedback. Feedback describes what took place and what did not take place in terms of goals. Teachers should not offer feedback as critical examination, but should include a variety of comments. Feedback can be in the form of suggestions, questions, or in response to a student-generated form.

Feedback describes what took place and what did not take place in terms of goals.

DOMAIN III
MATHEMATICS

PERSONALIZED STUDY PLAN

PAGE	COMPETENCY AND SKILL	KNOWN MATERIAL/ SKIP IT
149	**10: Understand concepts of numerical literacy**	☐
	10.1: Demonstrating knowledge of number sense	☐
	10.2: Translating among equivalent representations of numbers and using them to solve problems	☐
	10.3: Demonstrating knowledge of concepts of number theory and of models, methods, and tools for exploring number relationships	☐
	10.4: Demonstrating the ability to apply a variety of computational procedures to model and solve problems and to examine the reasonableness of solutions	☐
	10.5: Demonstrating knowledge of the properties of numerical operations and the relationship of integers to other numbers	☐
166	**11: Understand concepts of mathematical patterns, relations, and functions**	☐
	11.1: Identifying and extending number and geometric patterns	☐
	11.2: Using patterns, tables, graphs, and function rules to solve real-world and mathematical problems	☐
	11.3: Recognizing relationships between varying quantities using different representations and translating between any two of these representations	☐
	11.4: Interpreting and solving equations and inequalities involving variables and rational numbers	☐
	11.5: Recognizing types and properties of functions	☐
178	**12: Understand concepts of space and shape**	☐
	12.1: Recognizing properties of planes, lines, and angles	☐
	12.2: Applying knowledge of the properties of and relationships between geometric figures	☐
	12.3: Applying knowledge of symmetry and transformations to geometric shapes and figures	☐
	12.4: Demonstrating knowledge of the concepts of direct and indirect measurement of two- and three-dimensional figures and of real-world applications of these concepts	☐
	12.5: Selecting appropriate units of measurement, converting measurements within measurement systems, and solving real-world problems	☐
	12.6: Applying knowledge of the characteristics and uses of geometric learning tools	☐

PERSONALIZED STUDY PLAN

![x checkmark] **KNOWN MATERIAL/ SKIP IT**

PAGE	COMPETENCY AND SKILL	KNOWN MATERIAL/ SKIP IT
207	**13: Understand concepts and techniques of data investigations and the concepts of randomness and uncertainty**	☐
	13.1: Demonstrating knowledge of conceptual and procedural tools for collecting, organizing, and reasoning about data	☐
	13.2: Applying knowledge of statistical measures for analyzing data	☐
	13.3: Applying knowledge of techniques for representing and summarizing data graphically	☐
	13.4: Interpreting and drawing inferences from data and making decisions in applied problem situations	☐
	13.5: Using principles of probability to solve real-world and mathematical problems involving simple and compound events	☐
	13.6: Demonstrating knowledge of randomness and sampling in surveys and experimental studies	☐
215	**14: Understand concepts and applications of discrete math**	☐
	14.1: Applying knowledge of set theory and its real-world applications	☐
	14.2: Applying knowledge of permutations and combinations and their real-world applications	☐
	14.3: Demonstrating knowledge of graph theory and its real-world applications	☐
	14.4: Applying knowledge of sequences, series, and iterative processes to solve problems	☐
221	**15: Understand mathematical processes and perspectives**	☐
	15.1: Demonstrating the ability to apply reasoning to make conjectures, justify ideas or arguments, and solve mathematical and nonmathematical problems	☐
	15.2: Demonstrating knowledge of the connections among mathematical concepts and procedures and the relationships between mathematics and other fields	☐
	15.3: Demonstrating the ability to communicate mathematically by translating between different representations of mathematical concepts and at different levels of formality	☐
	15.4: Selecting appropriate strategies to solve a variety of problems	☐
	15.5: Demonstrating knowledge of the history of mathematics and the interaction between different cultures and mathematics	☐
	15.6: Demonstrating knowledge of methods for integrating technological and nontechnological tools in mathematics	☐
	15.7: Applying mathematical language to solve problems and communicate understanding	☐

COMPETENCY 10
UNDERSTAND CONCEPTS OF NUMERICAL LITERACY

Demonstrating knowledge of number sense *(e.g., place value, rounding, comparing and ordering numbers, estimation, equality)*

Place Value

Place value is the basis of our entire number system. A **PLACE VALUE SYSTEM** is one in which the position of a digit in a number determines its value. In the standard system, called base ten, each place represents ten times the value of the place to its right. You can think of this as making groups of ten of the smaller unit and combining them to make a new unit.

PLACE VALUE SYSTEM: one in which the position of a digit in a number determines its value

Base ten

Ten ones make up one of the next larger unit, tens. Ten of those units make up one of the next larger unit, hundreds. This pattern continues for greater values (ten hundreds = one thousand, ten thousands = one ten thousand, etc.), and lesser, decimal values (ten tenths = 1, ten hundredths = one tenth, etc.).

Hundreds 10×10	Tens $10 = 10 \times 1$	Ones 1

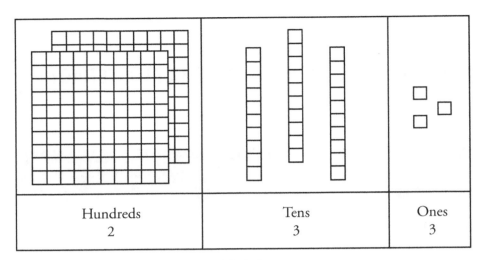

Hundreds 2	Tens 3	Ones 3

In standard form, the number modeled above is 233.

Teaching place value

A place value chart is a way to make sure digits are in the correct places. The value of each digit depends on its position or place. A great way to see the place value relationships in a number is to model the number with actual objects (place value blocks, bundles of craft sticks, etc.), write the digits in the chart, and then write the number in the usual, or standard, form.

Place value is vitally important to all later mathematics. Without it, keeping track of greater numbers rapidly becomes impossible. (Can you imagine trying to write 999 with only ones?) A thorough mastery of place value is essential to learning the operations with greater numbers. It is the foundation for regrouping ("borrowing" and "carrying") in addition, subtraction, multiplication, and division.

Preschool children and place value

Preschool children should develop an understanding of one-to-one correspondence, being able to link a single number name with one object, and only one, at a time. This concept is needed in order for children to formalize the meaning of a whole number. An example would be for a child to count four blocks in a row, saying the number as each block is touched. Another example would be for a child to get a carton of milk for each of the other children at a table.

Preschool children should also be able to use one-to-one correspondence to compare the size of a group of objects. For example, students should be able to compare the number of cars they have with the number another child has and say, "I have more...or less."

Preschool children should develop an understanding of one-to-one correspondence, being able to link a single number name with one object, and only one, at a time.

Number sense

Number sense develops into the further understanding of place value and how numbers are related. This involves identifying and explaining how numbers can be grouped into tens, ones, and eventually hundreds or more. Using trading games, place value mats, and base ten blocks students can develop these skills. These activities will progress until the student understands that the one in sixteen represents ten, not simply one.

Children first learn to count using the counting numbers (1, 2, 3 . . .). Preschool children should be able to recite the names of the numerals in order or sequence (rote counting). This might be accomplished by singing a counting song. This should progress to being able to attach a number name to a series of objects. A preschool child should understand that the last number spoken when counting a group of objects represents the total number of objects.

In kindergarten, children should learn to read the numbers 0 through 10, and in first grade, they should be able to read through the number 20. At first, this could involve connecting a pictorial representation of the number with a corresponding number of items. This exercise may or may not involve assistive technology. As students advance, they should be able to read the numbers as sight words.

> In kindergarten, children should learn to read the numbers 0 through 10, and in first grade, they should be able to read through the number 20.

Naming procedure

Students should be taught that there is a naming procedure for our number system. The numbers 0, 1 . . . 12 all have unique names. The numbers 13, 14 . . . 19 are the "teens." These names are a combination of earlier names, with the ones place named first. For example, fourteen is short for "four ten" which means "ten plus four." The numbers 20, 21 . . . 99 are also combinations of earlier names, but the tens place is named first. For example, 48 is "forty-eight," which means "four tens plus eight." The numbers 100, 101 . . . 999 are combinations of hundreds and previous names. Once a number has more than three digits, groups of three digits are usually set off by commas.

Real-life application of numbers

As students gain an understanding of numbers and are able to read them, they should be taught to apply these concepts to everyday life applications. For example, once children can read the numbers 1 through 12, they can begin to learn how to tell time. At the very basic level, if shown a clock or a diagram of a clock, a child needs to understand that the big hand represents minutes and the little hand represents hours. The child begins to recognize that when the big hand is on the twelve and the little hand is on the two, it is 2 o'clock. As the child learns to count by fives, the concept may be expanded so that the child understands that the distance between two consecutive numbers is an interval of five minutes. The child

> As students gain an understanding of numbers and are able to read them, they should be taught to apply these concepts to everyday life applications.

then begins to recognize by counting by fives that when the big hand is on the 4 and the little hand is on the 2, it is twenty minutes after the hour of 2 o'clock.

Money

Another real-life application is money. In kindergarten, students learn to recognize a penny, nickel, dime, quarter, and one-dollar bill. In first grade, they learn how different combinations of coins have equivalent values, for example, that 10 pennies are the same as 1 dime and 10 dimes are the same as 1 dollar. Teaching children that money has value can start with a simple exercise of counting pennies to understand their monetary value. From here, students can advance to counting nickels, dimes, and so on. The next step might be to have students combine different coins and compute the value of the combination. As students advance in their understanding of the value of money, shopping math can be introduced where students see that money has value in exchange for goods. They can also learn to make change and count change.

Number Systems

The real number system includes all rational and irrational numbers.

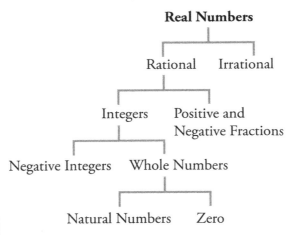

RATIONAL NUMBERS can be expressed as the ratio of two integers, $\frac{a}{b}$, where $b \neq 0$. For example: $\frac{2}{3}, -\frac{4}{5}, \frac{5}{1} = 5$.

The rational numbers include integers, fractions and mixed numbers, and terminating and repeating decimals. Every rational number can be expressed as a repeating or terminating decimal and can be shown on a number line.

INTEGERS are the positive and negative whole numbers and zero.

...-6, -5, -4, -3, -2, -1, 0, 1, 2, 3, 4, 5, 6,...

WHOLE NUMBERS are the natural numbers and zero.

0, 1, 2, 3, 4, 5, 6...

RATIONAL NUMBERS: can be expressed as the ratio of two integers, $\frac{a}{b}$, where $b \neq 0$

INTEGERS: the positive and negative whole numbers and zero

WHOLE NUMBERS: the natural numbers and zero

NATURAL NUMBERS are the counting numbers.

1, 2, 3, 4, 5, 6...

IRRATIONAL NUMBERS are real numbers that cannot be written as the ratio of two integers. They are infinite, nonrepeating decimals.

Examples:

$\sqrt{5} = 2.2360$, pi $= \pi = 3.1415927...$

PERCENT = per 100 (written with the symbol %). Thus $10\% = \frac{10}{100} = \frac{1}{10}$.

DECIMALS = deci = part of ten. To find the decimal equivalent of a fraction, use the denominator to divide the numerator as shown in the following examples.

Example: Find the decimal equivalent of $\frac{7}{10}$:

$$
\begin{array}{r}
.7 \\
10\overline{)7.0} \\
\underline{70} \\
00
\end{array}
$$

Since 10 cannot divide into 7 evenly, put a decimal point in the answer row on top; put a 0 behind 7 to make it 70. Continue the division process. If a remainder occurs, put a 0 by the last digit of the remainder and continue the division.

Thus $\frac{7}{10} = 0.7$

It is a good idea to write a 0 before the decimal point so that the decimal point is emphasized.

Example: Find the decimal equivalent of $\frac{7}{25}$:

$$
\begin{array}{r}
.056 \\
125\overline{)7.000} \\
\underline{625} \\
750 \\
\underline{750} \\
0
\end{array}
$$

Example: Convert 0.056 to a fraction.

Multiplying 0.056 by $\frac{1000}{1000}$ to get rid of the decimal point:

$0.056 \times \frac{1000}{1000} = \frac{56}{1000} = \frac{7}{25}$

Example: Find 23% of 1000.

$\frac{23}{100} \times \frac{1000}{1} = 23 \times 10 = 230$

NATURAL NUMBERS: the counting numbers

IRRATIONAL NUMBERS: real numbers that cannot be written as the ratio of two integers

PERCENT: a base-ten positional notation system for numbers

DECIMAL: a number written with a whole-number part, a decimal point, and a decimal part

Example: Convert 6.25% to a fraction and to a mixed number.

$$6.25\% = 0.0625 = 0.0625 \times \frac{10000}{10000} = \frac{625}{10000} = \frac{1}{16}$$

A decimal can be converted to a percent by multiplying by 100, or merely moving the decimal point two places to the right. A percent can be converted to a decimal by dividing by 100, or moving the decimal point two places to the left.

A decimal can be converted to a percent by multiplying by 100, or merely moving the decimal point two places to the right. A percent can be converted to a decimal by dividing by 100, or moving the decimal point two places to the left.

Examples:

$0.375 = 37.5\%$	$84\% = 0.84$
$0.7 = 70\%$	$3\% = 0.03$
$0.04 = 4\%$	$60\% = 0.6$
$3.15 = 315\%$	$110\% = 1.1$
	$\frac{1}{2}\% = 0.5\% = 0.005$

A percent can be converted to a fraction by placing it over 100 and reducing to simplest terms.

Examples:

$$32\% = \frac{32}{100} = \frac{8}{25}$$
$$6\% = \frac{6}{100} = \frac{3}{50}$$
$$111\% = \frac{111}{100} = 1\frac{11}{100}$$

Common Equivalents

COMMON EQUIVALENTS				
$\frac{1}{2}$	=	0.5	=	50%
$\frac{1}{3}$	=	$0.33\frac{1}{3}$	=	$33\frac{1}{3}\%$
$\frac{1}{4}$	=	0.25	=	25%
$\frac{1}{5}$	=	0.2	=	20%
$\frac{1}{6}$	=	$0.16\frac{2}{3}$	=	$16\frac{2}{3}\%$
$\frac{1}{8}$	=	$0.12\frac{1}{2}$	=	$12\frac{1}{2}\%$
$\frac{1}{10}$	=	0.1	=	10%
$\frac{2}{3}$	=	$0.66\frac{2}{3}$	=	$66\frac{2}{3}\%$

Table continued on next page

$\frac{5}{6}$	=	$0.83\frac{1}{3}$	=	$83\frac{1}{3}\%$
$\frac{3}{8}$	=	$0.37\frac{1}{2}$	=	$37\frac{1}{2}\%$
$\frac{5}{8}$	=	$0.62\frac{1}{2}$	=	$62\frac{1}{2}\%$
$\frac{7}{8}$	=	$0.87\frac{1}{2}$	=	$87\frac{1}{2}\%$
1	=	1.0	=	100%

CARDINAL NUMBERS are also known as "counting" numbers because they indicate quantity. Examples of cardinal numbers are 1, 2, and 10.

ORDINAL NUMBERS indicate the order of things in a set; for example, 1st, 2nd, 10th. They do not show quantity, only position.

CARDINAL NUMBERS: also known as "counting" numbers because they indicate quantity

ORDINAL NUMBERS: indicate the order of things in a set

SKILL 10.2 **Translating among equivalent representations of numbers and using them to solve problems**

To convert a fraction to a decimal, simply divide the numerator (top) by the denominator (bottom). Use long division if necessary.

If a decimal has a fixed number of digits, the decimal is said to be terminating. To write such a decimal as a fraction, first determine what place value the farthest right digit is in, for example: tenths, hundredths, thousandths, ten thousandths, hundred thousands, etc. Then drop the decimal and place the string of digits over the number given by the place value.

If a decimal continues forever by repeating a string of digits, the decimal is said to be repeating. To write a repeating decimal as a fraction, follow these steps.

1. Let $x =$ the repeating decimal
   ($x = 0.716716716...$)

2. Multiply x by the multiple of ten that will move the decimal just to the right of the repeating block of digits.
   ($1000x = 716.716716...$)

3. Subtract the first equation from the second.
   ($1000x - x = 716.716716... - 0.716716...$)

4. Simplify and solve this equation. The repeating block of digits will subtract out.
$(999x = 716$ so $x = \frac{716}{999})$

5. The solution will be the fraction for the repeating decimal.

In ordering and comparing fractions, the student needs to be introduced to the concept that the larger the denominator, the smaller the fraction. This is best done using manipulative and graphic representation. Cutting an actual object, or a card stock or paper representation, into more and more equal pieces shows the student that the larger the number of pieces, the smaller each piece will be. This is a hard concept for the student just beginning work with fractions, because normally the larger number is the largest.

An important concept for teaching comparing and ordering decimals is the concept of the zero placed at the end of a number following the decimal. Such a zero doesn't change the value. However, a zero added before the decimal does change the number. Resorting to using base ten blocks to teach decimal concepts will help the student visualize the concept.

Percentage Problems

Word problems involving percents can be solved by writing the problem as an equation, then solving the equation. Keep in mind that "**of**" means "*multiplication*" and "**is**" means "*equals*."

Example: The Ski Club has 85 members; 80% of the members are able to attend the meeting. How many members attended the meeting?

Restate the problem: What is 80% of 85?
Write an equation: $n = 0.8 \times 85$
Solve: $n = 68$

Sixty-eight members attended the meeting.

Example: There are 64 dogs in the kennel. 48 are collies. What percentage are collies?

Restate the problem: 48 is what percentage of 64?
Write an equation: $48 = n \times 64$
Solve: $48 \div 64 = n$
                          $n = 75\%$

75% of the dogs are collies.

Example: The auditorium was filled to 90% capacity. There were 558 seats occupied. What is the capacity of the auditorium?

Restate the problem: 90% of what number is 558?

Write an equation: $0.9n = 558$

Solve: $n = \frac{558}{.09}$

$n = 620$

The capacity of the auditorium is 620 people.

Example: Shoes cost $42.00. Sales tax is 6%. What is the total cost of the shoes?

Restate the problem: What is 6% of 42?

Write an equation: $n = 0.06 \times 42$

Solve: $n = 2.52$

Add the sales tax: $42.00 + $2.52 = 44.52

The total cost of the shoes, including sales tax, is $44.52.

PRIME NUMBERS are numbers that can only be factored into 1 and the number itself. When factoring into prime factors, all the factors must be numbers that cannot be factored again (without using 1). Initially numbers can be factored into any 2 factors. Check each resulting factor to see if it can be factored again. Continue factoring until all remaining factors are prime. This is the list of prime factors. Regardless of what way the original number was factored, the final list of prime factors will always be the same.

> **PRIME NUMBERS:**
> numbers that can only be factored into 1 and the number itself

Example:

Factor 30 into prime factors.

Factor 30 into any two factors.

5×6 Now factor the 6.

$5 \times 2 \times 3$ These are all prime factors.

or

Factor 30 into any two factors.

3×10 Now factor the 10.

$3 \times 2 \times 5$ These are the same prime factors, even though the
                original factors were different.

Example:

Factor 240 into prime factors.

Factor 240 into any two factors.

24×10 Now factor both 24 and 10.

$4 \times 6 \times 2 \times 5$ Now factor both 4 and 6.

$2 \times 2 \times 2 \times 3 \times 2 \times 5$ These are the prime factors.

This can also be written as $2^4 \times 3 \times 5$.

SKILL 10.3 **Demonstrating knowledge of concepts of number theory** *(e.g., divisibility rules, factors, multiples, perfect numbers, prime numbers)* **and of models, methods, and tools for exploring number relationships**

See also Skill 10.2

Greatest Common Factor

> **GREATEST COMMON FACTOR:** the largest number that is a factor of all the numbers in a problem

GCF is the abbreviation for **GREATEST COMMON FACTOR**. The GCF is the largest number that is a factor of all the numbers given in a problem. The GCF can be no larger than the smallest number given in the problem. If no other number is a common factor, then the GCF will be the number 1.

To find the GCF, list all possible factors of the smallest number (include the number itself). Starting with the largest factor (which is the number itself), determine if that factor is also a factor of all the other given numbers. If so, that factor is the GCF. If that factor doesn't divide evenly into the other given numbers, try the same method on the next smaller factor. Continue until a common factor is found. That factor is the GCF.

Note: There can be other common factors besides the GCF.

Example: Find the GCF of 12, 20, and 36.
The smallest number in the problem is 12. The factors of 12 are 1, 2, 3, 4, 6, and 12. 12 is the largest of these factors, but it does not divide evenly into 20. Neither does 6. However, 4 will divide into both 20 and 36 evenly.

Therefore, 4 is the GCF.

Example: Find the GCF of 14 and 15.
The factors of 14 are 1, 2, 7 and 14. 14 is the largest factor, but it does not divide evenly into 15. Neither does 7 or 2. Therefore, the only factor common to both 14 and 15 is the number 1, the GCF.

Least Common Multiple

> **LEAST COMMON MULTIPLE:** the smallest number of a group of numbers that all the given numbers will divide into evenly

LCM is the abbreviation for **LEAST COMMON MULTIPLE**. The least common multiple of a group of numbers is the smallest number that all of the given numbers will divide into. The LCM will always be the largest of the given numbers or a multiple of the largest number.

Example: Find the LCM of 20, 30, and 40.

The largest number given is 40, but 30 will not divide evenly into 40. The next multiple of 40 is 80 (2 × 40), but 30 will not divide evenly into 80 either. The next multiple of 40 is 120 (3 × 40). 120 is divisible by both 20 and 30, so 120 is the LCM.

Example: Find the LCM of 96, 16, and 24.

The largest number is 96. 96 is divisible by both 16 and 24, so 96 is the LCM.

Rules of Divisibility

1. A number is divisible by 2 if it is an even number (which means it ends in 0, 2, 4, 6 or 8).

   1,354 ends in 4 so it is divisible by 2. The number 240,685 ends in 5 so it is not divisible by 2.

2. A number is divisible by 3 if the sum of its digits is evenly divisible by 3.

   The sum of the digits of 964 is 9 + 6 + 4 = 19. Since 19 is not divisible by 3, neither is 964. The sum of the digits of 86,514 is 8 + 6 + 5 + 1 + 4 = 24. Since 24 is divisible by 3, then 86,514 is also divisible by 3.

3. A number is divisible by 4 if the number formed by its last two digits is evenly divisible by 4.

   The number 113,336 ends with the number 36 in the last two places. Since 36 is divisible by 4, then 113,336 is also divisible by 4. The number 135,627 ends with the number 27 in the last two places. Since 27 is not evenly divisible by 4, then 135,627 is not divisible by 4 either.

4. A number is divisible by 5 if the number ends in either a 5 or a 0.

   The number 225 ends with a 5 so it is divisible by 5. The number 470 is also divisible by 5 because its last digit is 0. The number 2,358 is not divisible by 5 because its last digit is 8, not 5 or 0.

5. A number is divisible by 6 if the number is even and the sum of its digits is evenly divisible by 3.

   The number 4,950 is an even number and its digits add up to 18 (4 + 9 + 5 + 0 = 18). Since the number is even, and the sum of its digits is 18 (which is divisible by 3), then 4,950 is divisible by 6. The number 326 is even, but its digits add up to 11. Since 11 is not divisible by 3, then 326 is not divisible by 6. The number 698,135 is not an even number so it cannot possibly be divided evenly by 6.

6. A number is divisible by 8 if the number in its last 3 digits is evenly divisible by 8.

The number 113,336 ends with the three-digit number 336 in the last three places. Since 336 is divisible by 8, then 113,336 is also divisible by 8. The number 465,627 ends with the number 627 in the last three places. Since 627 is not evenly divisible by 8, then 465,627 is not divisible by 8 either.

7. A number is divisible by 9 if the sum of its digits is evenly divisible by 9.

The sum of the digits of 874 is $8 + 7 + 4 = 19$. Since 19 is not divisible by 9, neither is 874. The digits of 116,514 are $1 + 1 + 6 + 5 + 1 + 4 = 18$. Since 18 is divisible by 9, the number 116,514 is also divisible by 9.

8. A number is divisible by 10 if the number ends in the digit 0.

The number 305 ends with 5 so it is not divisible by 10. The number 2,030,270 is divisible by 10 because its last digit is 0. The number 42,978 is not divisible by 10 because its last digit is 8, not 0.

9. Why these rules work:

All even numbers are divisible by 2, by definition. A two-digit number (with T representing the tens digit and U representing the ones digit) has as its sum of the digits, $T + U$. Suppose this sum of $T + U$ is divisible by 3. Then it equals 3 times some constant, K. So, $T + U = 3K$. Solving for U, $U = 3K - T$. The original two-digit number would be represented by $10T + U$. Substituting $3K - T$ in place of U, this two-digit number becomes $10T + U = 10T + (3K - T) = 9T + 3K$. This two-digit number is clearly divisible by 3, since each term is divisible by 3. Therefore, if the sum of the digits of a number is divisible by 3, then the number itself is also divisible by 3. Since 4 divides evenly into 100, 200, or 300, it will divide evenly into any number of hundreds. The only part of a number that determines whether 4 will divide into it evenly is the number in the last two places. Numbers divisible by 5 end in 5 or 0. This is clear if you look at the answers to the multiplication table for 5.

Answers to the multiplication table for 6 are all even numbers. Since 6 factors into 2 times 3, the divisibility rules for 2 and 3 must both work. Any number of thousands is divisible by 8. Only the last three places of the number determine whether it is divisible by 8. A two-digit number (with T representing the tens digit and U representing the ones digit) has as its sum of the digits, $T + U$. Suppose this sum of $T + U$ is divisible by 9. Then it equals 9 times some constant, K. So, $T + U = 9K$.

Solving this for U, $U = 9K - T$. The original two-digit number would be represented by $10T + U$. Substituting $9K - T$ in place of U, this two-digit number becomes $10T + U = 10T + (9K - T) = 9T + 9K$. This two-digit number is clearly divisible by 9 since each term is divisible by 9. Therefore, if the sum of the digits of a number is divisible by 9, then the number itself is also divisible by 9. Numbers divisible by 10 must be multiples of 10, which all end in zero.

COMPOSITE NUMBERS are whole numbers that have more than two different factors. For example, 9 is composite because, besides the factors of 1 and 9, 3 is also a factor. 70 is composite because, besides the factors of 1 and 70, the numbers 2, 5, 7, 10, 14, and 35 are also all factors. The number 1 is neither prime nor composite.

> **COMPOSITE NUMBERS:** whole numbers that have more than two different factors

A pattern of numbers arranged in a particular order is called a number sequence. Pre-K children should be able to recognize and extend simple repeating patterns using objects and pictures. By patterns, we mean a sequence of symbols, sounds, movements, or objects that follow a simple rule, such as ABBABBABB. Students should be presented with a simple pattern that they try to understand. Once they have an understanding of the pattern, they should copy and extend it. Students at this age are capable of assigning letters to their patterns to verbalize how the pattern repeats. These are the very early fundamental stages of algebra.

Many of the traditional ways of talking about this in algebra would certainly not be appropriate. However, many types of patterns and relationships can be addressed. In arithmetic, first do the traditional counting with students by 2s, 5s and 10s. Then have them start at a different number. For example, tell them to count by 5s beginning with 3. As they get better with their addition skills, use larger numbers for the starting number You might also explain how the even and odd counting numbers follow a sequence. Then give them the first few numbers of a sequence and ask them to tell you the pattern. Finally, let them make up some sequences themselves and give them to the other students to guess what the pattern is. The possibilities are endless here. Students in the upper elementary grades should be taught how looking for a pattern or sequence is an important problem-solving tool.

> SKILL 10.4 **Demonstrating the ability to apply a variety of computational procedures to model and solve problems and to examine the reasonableness of solutions**

Ratios

Problems involving ratios are solved using multiplication and division.

Example: The ratio of the length of a rectangle to its width is 3:2. If the length of the rectangle is 12 meters, what is the width?

Set up the ratios: $\frac{3}{2} = \frac{\text{length}}{\text{width}}$

Substitute: $\frac{3}{2} = \frac{12}{x}$

Cross-multiply: $3x = 24$

Solve by dividing: $x = 8$

Proportions

Problems involving proportions are solved in the same manner as those involving ratios, since proportions are two ratios set equal to each other.

Example: The weight of artificial sweetener in a box of 400 identical sweetener bags is 14 ounces. What is the weight, in ounces, of the sweetener in 12 bags?

Set up two ratios: $\frac{12}{400} = \frac{x}{14}$

Cross-multiply: $400x = 168$

Solve by dividing: $x = 0.42$

Percentages

Percentages are also ratios; for example $75\% = \frac{75}{100}$. Therefore, problems involving percentages are solved in a manner similar to those involving ratios and proportions.

Example: 15 is what percentage of 75?

Set up two ratios: $\frac{15}{75} = \frac{x}{100}$

Cross-multiply: $75x = 1500$

Solve by dividing: $x = 0.20$ or 20%

Rational Numbers

Addition and subtraction

If fractions have the same denominators, only addition and subtraction are necessary. However, if a common denominator must be determined, then multiplication is needed to convert the fractions.

Multiplication and division

Multiplication of fractions is the easiest operation involving fractions. You merely multiply the numerators by each other and the denominators by each other.

Division of fractions, on the other hand, calls for multiplication. To divide two fractions, you must multiply the dividend by the reciprocal of the divisor.

Example:

$$\frac{2}{3} \div \frac{3}{4} =$$
$$\frac{2}{3} \times \frac{4}{3} =$$
$$\frac{8}{9}$$

Estimation

Estimation and approximation can be used to check the reasonableness of answers.

Example: Estimate the answer.

$$\frac{58 \times 810}{1989}$$

58 becomes 60, 810 becomes 800, and 1989 becomes 2000.

$$\frac{60 \times 800}{2000} = 24$$

For word problems, an estimate may sometimes be all that is needed to find the solution.

Example: Janet goes into a store to purchase a CD that is on sale for $13.95. While shopping, she sees two pairs of shoes priced at $19.95 and $14.50. She only has $50. Can she purchase everything?

Solve by rounding:

$19.95 \rightarrow$ $20.00
$14.50 \rightarrow$ $15.00
$13.95 \rightarrow$ $14.00
$49.00

Yes, she can purchase the CD and the shoes.

Demonstrating knowledge of the properties of numerical operations (e.g., associative, distributive) **and the relationship of integers to other numbers** (e.g., real, rational)

Field Properties

Real numbers exhibit the following addition and multiplication properties, where a, b, and c are real numbers.

Note: Multiplication is implied when there is no symbol between two variables. Thus,

$a \times b$ can be written ab.

Multiplication can also be indicated by a raised dot $\cdot$ $(a \cdot b)$.

Closure

$a + b$ is a real number

Example: Since 2 and 5 are both real numbers, 7 is also a real number.
ab is a real number.

Example: Since 3 and 4 are both real numbers, 12 is also a real number.
The sum or product of two real numbers is a real number.

Commutative

$a + b = b + a$

Example:
$5 + -8 = -8 + 5 = -3$
$ab = ba$

Example:
$-2 \times 6 = 6 \times -2 = -12$
The order of the addends or factors does not affect the sum or product.

Associative

$(a + b) + c = a + (b + c)$

Example:

$(-2 + 7) + 5 = -2 + (7 + 5)$

$5 + 5 = -2 + 12 = 10$

$(ab)c = a(bc)$

Example:

$(3 \times -7) \times 5 = 3 \times (-7 \times 5)$

$-21 \times 5 = 3 \times -35 = -105$

The grouping of the addends or factors does not affect the sum or product.

Distributive

$a(b + c) = ab + ac$

Example:

$6 \times (-4 + 9) = (6 \times -4) + (6 \times 9)$

$6 \times 5 = -24 + 54 = 30$

To multiply a sum by a number, multiply each addend by the number, then add the products.

Additive Identity (Property of Zero)

$a + 0 = a$

Example:

$17 + 0 = 17$

The sum of any number and zero is that number.

Multiplicative Identity (Property of One)

$a \times 1 = a$

Example:

$-34 \times 1 = -34$

The product of any number and one is that number.

Additive Inverse (Property of Opposites)

$a + -a = 0$

Example:
$$25 + {-}25 = 0$$
The sum of any number and its opposite is zero.

Multiplicative Inverse (Property of Reciprocals)

$$a \times \frac{1}{a} = 1$$

Example:
$$5 \times \frac{1}{5} = 1$$
The product of any number and its reciprocal is one.

Property of Denseness

Between any pair of rational numbers, there is at least one rational number. The set of natural numbers is *not* dense because between two consecutive natural numbers there may not exist another natural number.

Example: Between 7.6 and 7.7, there is the rational number 7.65 in the set of real numbers.
Between 3 and 4 there exists no other natural number.

COMPETENCY 11
UNDERSTAND CONCEPTS OF MATHEMATICAL PATTERNS, RELATIONS, AND FUNCTIONS

SKILL 11.1 Identifying and extending number and geometric patterns

The function or relationship between two quantities may be analyzed to determine how one quantity depends on the other. For example, the function below shows a relationship between y and x:

$$y = 2x + 1.$$

The relationship between two or more variables can be analyzed using a table, graph, written description, or symbolic rule. The function $y = 2x + 1$ is written as a symbolic rule. The same relationship is also shown in the table below:

x	0	2	3	6	9
y	1	5	7	13	19

This relationship could be written in words by saying that the value of y is equal to two times the value of x, plus one. This relationship could be shown on a graph by plotting given points such as the ones shown in the table above.

Another way to describe a function is as a process in which one or more numbers are input into an imaginary machine that produces another number as the output. If 5 is input (x) into a machine with a process of $x + 1$, then the output (y) will equal 6.

In real situations, relationships can be described mathematically. The function $y = x + 1$, can be used to describe the idea that people age one year on their birthday. To describe the relationship in which a person's monthly medical costs are 6 times a person's age, we could write $y = 6x$. The monthly cost of medical care could be predicted using this function. A 20-year-old person would spend $120 per month ($120 = 20 \times 6$). An 80-year-old person would spend $480 per month ($480 = 80 \times 6$). Therefore, one could analyze the relationship as follows: As you get older, medical costs increase by a factor of $6.00 each year.

SKILL 11.2 Using patterns, tables, graphs, and function rules to solve real-world and mathematical problems

A relationship between two quantities can be shown using a table, graph, or rule. In this example, the rule $y = 9x$ describes the relationship between the total amount earned, y, and the total number of $9.00 sunglasses sold, x.

A table using these data would appear as:

Number of Sunglasses Sold	1	5	10	15
Total Dollars Earned	9	45	90	135

Each (*x, y*) relationship between a pair of values is called the coordinate pair that can be plotted on a graph. The coordinate pairs (1, 9), (5, 45), (10, 90), and (15, 135) are plotted on the graph below.

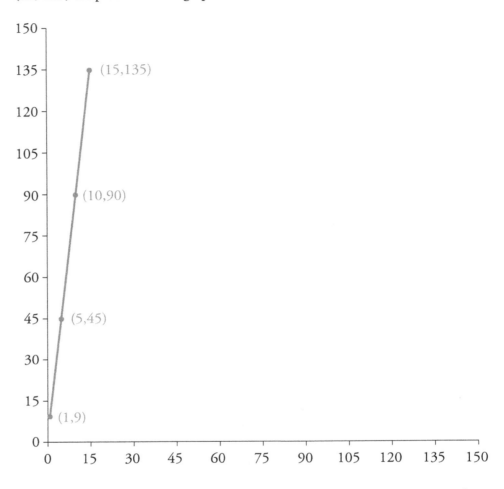

The graph above shows a linear relationship. A **LINEAR RELATIONSHIP** is a relationship in which two quantities are proportional to each other. Doubling *x* also doubles *y*. On a graph, a straight line depicts a linear relationship.

Another type of relationship is a **NONLINEAR RELATIONSHIP**. This is a relationship in which change in one quantity does not affect the other quantity to the same extent. Nonlinear graphs have a curved line, as in the graph below.

LINEAR RELATIONSHIP: a relationship in which two quantities are proportional to each other

NONLINEAR RELATION-SHIP: a relationship in which change in one quantity does not affect the other quantity to the same extent

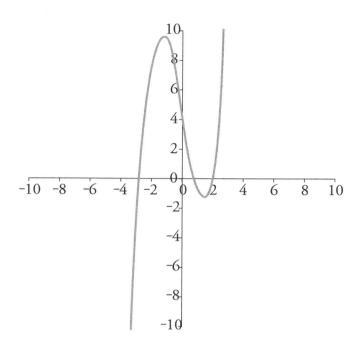

Recognizing relationships between varying quantities using
11.3 **different representations** *(e.g., function rules, graphs, tables)* **and**
translating between any two of these representations

The **ORDER OF OPERATIONS** is to be followed when evaluating algebraic expressions. Follow these steps in order:

1. Simplify inside grouping characters such as parentheses, brackets, square root, and fraction bars.

2. Multiply out expressions with exponents

3. Do multiplication and/or division, from left to right

4. Do addition and/or subtraction, from left to right

> **ORDER OF OPERATIONS:** the order in which mathematical operations should be performed

SIMPLIFIED EXPRESSIONS WITH EXPONENTS			
$(-2)^3$	=	-8	$-2^3 = -8$
$(-2)^4$	=	16	$-2^4 = 16$ Note change of sign.
$\left(\frac{2}{3}\right)^3$	=	$\frac{8}{27}$	

Continued on next page

5^0	=	1	
4^{-1}	=	$\frac{1}{4}$	

EXPONENT FORM: a shortcut method to write repeated multiplication

BASE: the factor

EXPONENT: tells how many times the base is multiplied by itself

The **EXPONENT FORM** is a shortcut method to write repeated multiplication. The **BASE** is the factor. The **EXPONENT** tells how many times that number is multiplied by itself.

Example: 3^4 is $3 \times 3 \times 3 \times 3 = 81$ where 3 is the base and 4 is the exponent.

x^2 is read "x squared"

y^3 is read "y cubed"

$a^1 = a$ for all values of a; thus $17^1 = 17$

$b^0 = 1$ for all values of b; thus $24^0 = 1$

When 10 is raised to any power, the exponent tells the numbers of zeroes in the product.

Example: $10^7 = 10,000,000$

To simplify a radical, follow these steps:

1. Factor the number or coefficient completely.

2. For square roots, group like factors in pairs. For cube roots, arrange like factors in groups of three. For n^{th} roots, group like factors in groups of n.

3. For each of these groups, put one of that number outside the radical. Any factors that cannot be combined in groups should be multiplied together and left inside the radical.

4. The index number of a radical is the little number on the front of the radical. For a cube root, the index is 3. If no index appears, then the index is 2 for square roots.

5. For variables inside the radical, divide the index number of the radical into each exponent. The quotient (the answer to the division) is the new exponent to be written on the variable outside the radical. The remainder from the division is the new exponent on the variable remaining inside the radical sign. If the remainder is zero, then the variable no longer appears in the radical sign.

If the index number is an odd number, you can still simplify the radical to get a negative solution.

Examples:

$$\sqrt{50a^4b^7} = \sqrt{5 \times 5 \times 2 \times a^4 \times b^7} = 5a^2b^3\sqrt{2b}$$

$$7x\sqrt[3]{16x^5} = 7x\sqrt[3]{2 \times 2 \times 2 \times 2 \times x^5} = 7x \times 2x\sqrt[3]{2x^2} = 14x^2\sqrt[3]{2x^2}$$

A mnemonic devise to help the student keep the order of operations straight is the saying, "**P**lease **E**xcuse **M**y **D**ear **A**unt **S**ally." Another is to teach the acronym PEMDAS, or parenthesis, exponents, multiplication/division, and addition/subtraction. Explain that multiplication/division and addition/subtraction are done left to right, without reference to which comes first in the acronym.

See also Skill 10.2

SKILL 11.4 Interpreting and solving equations and inequalities involving variables and rational numbers

Word problems can sometimes be solved by using a system of two equations in two unknowns. This system can then be solved using substitution, or the addition-subtraction method.

Example: Farmer Greenjeans bought 4 cows and 6 sheep for $1,700. Mr. Ziffel bought 3 cows and 12 sheep for $2,400. If all the cows were the same price and all the sheep were another fixed price, find the price charged for a cow and the price charged for a sheep.

Let x = price of a cow

Let y = price of a sheep

Then Farmer Greenjeans's equation would be:	$4x + 6y = 1700$
Mr. Ziffel's equation would be:	$3x + 12y = 2400$

To solve by **addition-subtraction**:

Multiply the first equation by -2:	$-2(4x + 6y = 1700)$
Keep the other equation the same:	$(3x + 12y = 2400)$

Now the equations can be added to each other to eliminate one variable, and you can solve for the other variable.

$$-8x - 12y = -3400$$
$$\underline{3x + 12y = \ \ 2400} \qquad \text{Add these equations.}$$
$$-5x \qquad \ \ = -1000$$

$x = 200$ ← the price of a cow was $200.

Solving for y, $y = 150$ ← the price of a sheep was $150.

To solve by **substitution**:

Solve one of the equations for a variable. (Try to make an equation without fractions if possible.) Substitute this expression into the equation that you have not yet used. Solve the resulting equation for the value of the remaining variable.

$$4x + 6y = 1700$$
$$3x + 12y = 2400 \leftarrow \text{Solve this equation for } x.$$

It becomes $x = 800 - 4y$. Now substitute $800 - 4y$ in place of x in the *other* equation. $4x + 6y = 1700$ now becomes:

$$4(800 - 4y) + 6y = 1700$$
$$3200 - 16y + 6y = 1700$$
$$3200 - 10y = 1700$$
$$-10y = -1500$$
$$y = 150, \text{ or } \$150 \text{ for a sheep.}$$

Substituting 150 back into an equation for y, find x.

$$4x + 6(150) = 1700$$
$$4x + 900 = 1700$$
$$4x = 800 \text{ so } x = 200, \text{ or } \$200 \text{ for a cow.}$$

Word problems can sometimes be solved by using a system of three equations in 3 unknowns. This system can then be solved using substitution or the addition-subtraction method.

Example: Mrs. Allison bought 1 pound of potato chips, a 2 pound beef roast, and 3 pounds of apples for a total of $8.19. Mr. Bromberg bought a 3 pound beef roast and 2 pounds of apples for $9.05. Kathleen Kaufman bought 2 pounds of potato chips, a 3 pound beef roast, and 5 pounds of apples for $13.25. Find the per pound price of each item.

Let x = price of a pound of potato chips

Let y = price of a pound of roast beef

Let z = price of a pound of apples

Mrs. Allison's equation would be: $1x + 2y + 3z = 8.19$

Mr. Bromberg's equation would be: $3y + 2z = 9.05$

K. Kaufman's equation would be: $2x + 3y + 5z = 13.25$

To solve by **substitution**:

Take the first equation and solve it for x. (This was chosen because x is the easiest variable to get alone in this set of equations.) This equation would become:

$$x = 8.19 - 2y - 3z$$

Substitute this expression into the other equations in place of the letter x:

$3y + 2z = 9.05$ Equation 2

$2(8.19 - 2y - 3z) + 3y + 5z = 13.25$ Equation 3

Simplify the equation by combining like terms:

$3y + 2z = 9.05$ Equation 2

$x - 1y - 1z = -3.13$ Equation 3

Solve equation 3 for either y or z:

$y = 3.13 - z$

Substitute this into equation 2 for y:

$3(3.13 - z) + 2z = 9.05$ Equation 2

$-1y - 1z = -3.13$ Equation 3

Combine like terms in equation 2:

$9.39 - 3z + 2z = 9.05$

$z = .34$ per pound price of apples

Substitute .34 for z in the starred equation above to solve for y:

$y = 3.13 - z$ becomes $y = 3.13 - .34$, so

$y = 2.79$ per pound price of roast beef

Substituting .34 for z and 2.79 for y in one of the original equations, solve for x:

$1x + 2y + 3z = 8.19$

$1x + 2(2.79) + 3(.34) = 8.19$

$x + 5.58 + 1.02 = 8.19$

$x + 6.60 = 8.19$

$x = 1.59$ per pound of potato chips

$(x, y, z) = (1.59, 2.79, .34)$

To solve by **addition-subtraction**:

Choose a letter to eliminate. Since the second equation is already missing an x, let's eliminate x from equations 1 and 3.

1) $1x + 2y + 3x = 8.19$ Multiply by -2 below.

2) $3y + 2z = 9.05$

3) $2x + 3y + 5z = 13.25$

$-2(1x + 2y + 3z = 8.19) = -2x - 4y - 6z = -16.38$

Keep equation 3 the same: $\underline{2x + 3y + 5z = 13.25}$

By doing this, the equations $-y - z = -3.13$ Equation 4 can be added to each other to eliminate one variable.

The equations left to solve are equations 2 and 4:

$-y - z = -3.13$ Equation 4

$3y + 2z = 9.05$ Equation 2

Multiply equation 4 by 3: $3(y - z = -3.13)$

Keep equation 2 the same: $3y + 2z = 9.05$

$3y - 3z = -9.39$

$\underline{3y + 2z = 9.05}$ Add these equations.

$-1z = -.34$

$z = .34$ per pound price of apples

solving for y, $y = 2.79$ per pound roast beef price

solving for x, $x = 1.59$ potato chips, per pound price

To solve by **substitution**:

Solve one of the 3 equations for a variable. (Try to make an equation without fractions if possible.) Substitute this expression into the other 2 equations that you have not yet used.

1) $1x + 2y + 3x = 8.19$ Solve for x.

2) $3y + 2z = 9.05$

3) $2x + 3y + 5z = 13.25$

Equation 1 becomes $x = 8.19 - 2y - 3z$.

Substituting this into equations 2 and 3, they become:

2) $3y + 2z = 9.05$

3) $2(8.19 - 2y - 3z) + 3y + 5z = 13.25$

     $16.38 - 4y - 6z + 3y + 5z = 13.25$

     $-y - z = -3.13$

The equations left to solve are:

$3y + 2z = 9.05$

$-y - z = -3.13$ Solve for either y or z.

It becomes $y = 3.13 - z$. Now substitute $3.13 - z$ in place of y in the OTHER equation. $3y + 2z = 9.05$ now becomes:

$3(3.13 - z) + 2z = 9.05$

$9.39 - 3z + 2z = 9.05$

$9.39 - z\, 9.05$

$-z = -.34$

$z = .34$, or \$.34/lb of apples

Substituting .34 back into an equation for z, find y.

$3y + 2z = 9.05$

$3y + 2(.34) = 9.05$

$3y + .68 = 9.05$, so $y = 2.79$/lb of roast beef

Substituting .34 for z and 2.79 for y into one of the original equations, it becomes:

$2x + 3y + 5z = 13.25$

$2x + 3(2.79) + 5(.34) = 13.25$

$2x + 8.37 + 1.70 = 13.25$

$2x + 10.07 = 13.25$, so $x = 1.59$/lb of potato chips

To graph an inequality, solve the inequality for y. This gets the inequality in **slope intercept form**, (for example: $y < mx + b$). The point (0,b) is the **y**-intercept and m is the line's slope.

If the inequality solves to $x \geq$ any number, then the graph includes a **vertical line**.

If the inequality solves to $y \leq$ any number, then the graph includes a **horizontal line**.

When graphing a linear inequality, the line will be dotted if the inequality sign is $<$ or $>$. If the inequality signs are either $\geq$ or $\leq$, the line on the graph will be a solid line. Shade above the line when the inequality sign is $\geq$ or $>$. Shade below the line when the inequality sign is $\leq$ or $<$. For inequalities of the forms $x >$ number, $x \leq$ number, $x <$ number, or $x \geq$ number, draw a vertical line (solid or dotted). Shade to the right for $>$ or $\geq$. Shade to the left for $<$ or $\leq$.

Use these rules to graph and shade each inequality. The solution to a system of linear inequalities consists of the part of the graph that is shaded for each inequality. For instance, if the graph of one inequality was shaded with red, and the graph of another inequality was shaded with blue, then the overlapping area would be shaded purple. The purple area would be the points in the solution set of this system.

Example: Solve by graphing:

$x + y \leq 6$

$x - 2y \leq 6$

Solving the inequalities for y, they become:

$y \leq -x + 6$ (y-intercept of 6 and slope $= -1$)

$y \geq 1.2x - 3$ (y-intercept of -3 and slope $= \frac{1}{2}$)

A graph with shading is shown below:

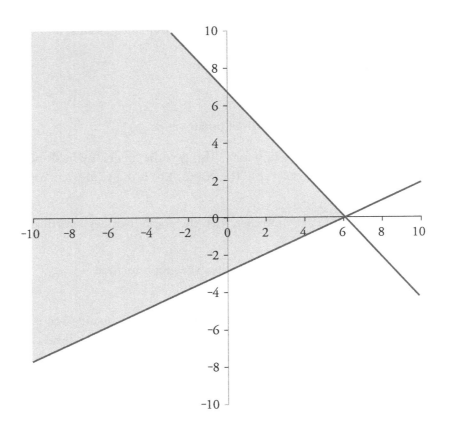

SKILL 11.5 **Recognizing types and properties of functions**

Example: Conjecture about pattern presented in tabular form.

Kepler discovered a relationship between the average distance of a planet from the sun and the time it takes the planet to orbit the sun.

The following table shows the data for the six planets closest to the sun:

	Mercury	Venus	Earth	Mars	Jupiter	Saturn
Average distance, x	0.387	0.723	1	1.523	5.203	9.541
x^3	0.058	0.378	1	3.533	140.852	868.524

Continued on next page

Time, y	0.241	0.615	1	1.881	11.861	29.457
y^2	0.058	0.378	1	3.538	140.683	867.715

Looking at the data in the table, we see that $x^3 = y^2$. We can conjecture the following function for Kepler's relationship:

$$y = \sqrt{x^3}.$$

Example: Find the recursive formula for the sequence 1, 3, 9, 27, 81...
We see that any term other than the first term is obtained by multiplying the preceding term by 3. Then, we may express the formula in symbolic notation as

$$a_n = 3a_{n-1}, \, a_1 = 1,$$

where a represents a term, the subscript n denotes the place of the term in the sequence and the subscript $n - 1$ represents the preceding term.

Identification of Patterns of Change Created by Functions

A **LINEAR FUNCTION** is a function defined by the equation $f(x) = mx + b$. This equation can be used to represent patterns in animals, people, and technology.

> **LINEAR FUNCTION:** a function defined by the equation $f(x) = mx + b$

Example: A model for the distance traveled by a migrating monarch butterfly looks like f(t) = 80t, where t represents time in days.
We interpret this to mean that the average speed of the butterfly is 80 miles per day, and distance traveled may be computed by substituting the number of days traveled for t. In a linear function, there is a constant rate of change.

The standard form of a quadratic function is $f(x) = ax^2 + bx + c$

Example: What patterns appear in a table for $y = x^2 - 5x + 6$?

x	0	1	2	3	4	5
y	6	2	0	0	2	6

We see that the values for y are symmetrically arranged.

An **EXPONENTIAL FUNCTION** is a function defined by the equation $y = ab^x$, where a is the starting value, b is the growth factor, and x tells how many times to multiply by the growth factor.

> **EXPONENTIAL FUNCTION:** a function defined by the equation $y = ab^x$, where a is the starting value, b is the growth factor, and x tells how many times to multiply by the growth factor

Example: $y = 100(1.5)^x$

x	0	1	2	3	4
y	100	150	225	337.5	506.25

This is an exponential, or multiplicative, pattern of growth.

Iterative and Recursive Functional Relationships

The **ITERATIVE PROCESS** involves repeated use of the same steps. A recursive function is an example of the iterative process. A recursive function requires the computation of all previous terms in order to find a subsequent term. Perhaps the most famous recursive function is the Fibonacci sequence. This is the sequence of numbers 1,1, 2, 3, 5, 8,13, 21, 34 . . . , for which the next term is found by adding the previous two terms.

> **ITERATIVE PROCESS:** involves repeated use of the same steps

COMPETENCY 12
UNDERSTAND CONCEPTS OF SPACE AND SHAPE

SKILL 12.1 Recognizing properties of planes, lines, and angles

The classifying of angles refers to the angle measure. The naming of angles refers to the letters or numbers used to label the angle.

Example:

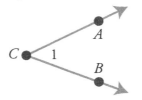

$\overrightarrow{CA}$ (read ray *CA*) and $\overrightarrow{CB}$ are the sides of the angle.
The angle can be called $\angle ACB$, $\angle BCA$, $\angle C$, or $\angle 1$.

Angles are classified according to their size as follows:

- Acute: greater than 0 and less than 90 degrees

- Right: exactly 90 degrees

- Obtuse: greater than 90 and less than 180 degrees

- Straight: exactly 180 degrees

Angles can be classified in a number of ways. Some of those classifications are outlined here.

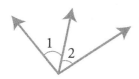

Adjacent angles have a common vertex and one common side but no interior points in common.

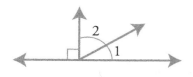

Complementary angles add up to 90 degrees.

Supplementary angles add up to 180 degrees.

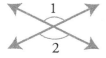

Vertical angles have sides that form two pairs of opposite rays.

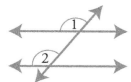

Corresponding angles are in the same corresponding position on two parallel lines cut by a transversal.

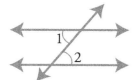

Alternate interior angles are diagonal angles on the inside of two parallel lines cut by a transversal.

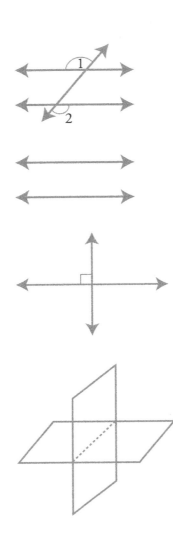

Alternate exterior angles are diagonal on the outside of two parallel lines cut by a transversal.

Parallel lines or planes do not intersect.

Perpendicular lines or planes form a 90 degree angle to each other.

Intersecting lines share a common point, and intersecting planes share a common set of points, or line.

Skew lines do not intersect and do not lie on the same plane.

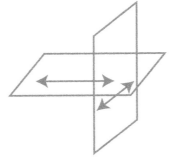

Examining the change in area or volume of a given figure requires you first to find the existing area, given the original dimensions, and then the new area, given the increased dimensions.

Example: Given the rectangle below, determine the change in area if the length is increased by 5 and the width is increased by 7.

7

4

Draw and label a sketch of the new rectangle.

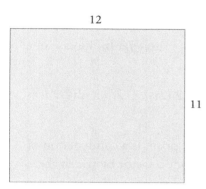

12

11

Find the areas.

Area of original $= lw$ Area of enlarged shape $= lw$

$= (7)(4)$ $= (12)(11)$

$= 28$ units² $= 132$ units²

The change in area is $132 - 28 = 104$ units².

The perimeter of a figure is found by adding the sides of a figure. For a rectangle, this would be $l + w + l + w$.

If we add 2 units to the length, we get $l + 2 + w + l + 2 + w$ or $2l + 2w + 4$.

The perimeter of a figure will change by the total number of units added or subtracted from each side.

The area of a polygon is a product of the length, width, and height. Therefore, a change in any of those dimensions has multiple effects on the area.

Example: The area of a triangle is equal to $\frac{1}{2}bh$ where b is the base and h is the height.

If we double the height, the area becomes $\frac{1}{2}b(2h) = bh$.

Doubling the height doubles the area.

Circumference and area of a circle are products involving the radius. As in the case of polygons, the factor by which the radius changes will be the factor by which the circumference changes.

> The formula for circumference is $2\pi r$.
> If we multiply the radius by 3, we get $2\pi(3r) = 6\pi r$.
> Tripling the radius triples the circumference.
> The formula for area is πr^2.
> If we multiply the radius by 3, we get $\pi(3r)^2 = 9r^2\pi$.

The area of a circle changes by a factor equal to the square of the number by which we multiply the radius.

SURFACE AREA is the sum of all of the faces of a prism or sphere. In the case of a rectangular prism, this is $2lw + 2lh + 2wh$.

> If we double the width, the surface area becomes $2l(2w) + 2lh + 2(2w)h = 4lw + 2lh + 4wh$.

Since the formula for the surface area of a rectangular prism is a combination of addition and multiplication, we cannot easily determine a factor by which the surface area changes.

However, we can determine a factor of change for the surface area of a sphere. The surface area of a sphere is equal to $4\pi r^2$.

> If we triple the radius, the surface area becomes $4\pi(3r)^2 = 4\pi(9r^2) = 36\pi r^2$.

The surface area changes by a factor equal to the square of the number by which we multiply the radius.

Volume is a three-dimensional measurement. The volume of a rectangular prism is equal to lwh.

> If we double the width, we get $l(2w)h = 2lwh$.

The volume has doubled. The volume changes by the factor that the length, width, or height changes.

> The volume of a sphere is equal to $\frac{4}{3}\pi r^3$.
> If we double the radius, we get $\frac{4}{3}\pi(2r)^3 = \frac{4}{3}\pi(8r^3) = \frac{32\pi r^3}{3}$.

SURFACE AREA: the sum of the area of all of the faces of a prism or sphere

The volume changes by a factor equal to the cube of the number by which we multiply the radius.

SKILL Applying knowledge of symmetry and transformations to geometric
12.3 shapes and figures

A **TESSELLATION** is an arrangement of closed shapes that completely covers the plane without overlapping or leaving gaps. Unlike tilings, tessellations do not require the use of regular polygons. In art, the term is used to refer to pictures or tiles mostly in the form of animals and other life forms, which cover the surface of a plane in a symmetrical way without overlapping or leaving gaps. M. C. Escher is known as the "father" of modern tessellations. Tessellations are used for tiling, mosaics, quilts, and art.

If you look at a completed tessellation, you will see the original motif repeats in a pattern. There are seventeen possible ways that a pattern can be used to tile, or "wallpaper," a flat surface.

There are four basic transformational symmetries that can be used in tessellations: translation, rotation, reflection, and glide reflection. The transformation of an object is called its image. If the original object was labeled with letters, such as *ABCD*, the image may be labeled with the same letters followed by a prime symbol, *A'B'C'D'*.

The tessellation below is a combination of the four types of transformational symmetry we have discussed:

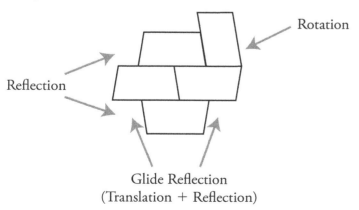

Glide Reflection
(Translation + Reflection)

A **TRANSFORMATION** is a change in the position, shape, or size of a geometric figure. **TRANSFORMATIONAL GEOMETRY** is the study of manipulating objects by flipping, twisting, turning, and scaling them. **SYMMETRY** is exact similarity between two parts or halves, as if one were a mirror image of the other. A **TRANSLATION** is

TESSELLATION: an arrangement of closed shapes that completely covers the plane without overlapping or leaving gaps

TRANSFORMATION: a change in the position, shape, or size of a geometric figure

TRANSFORMATIONAL GEOMETRY: the study of manipulating objects by flipping, twisting, turning, and scaling them

SYMMETRY: exact similarity between two parts or halves, as if one were a mirror image of the other

TRANSLATION: a transformation that "slides" an object a fixed distance in a given direction

a transformation that "slides" an object a fixed distance in a given direction. The original object and its translation have the same shape and size, and they face in the same direction.

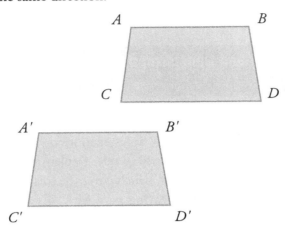

An example of a translation in architecture is stadium seating. The seats are the same size and the same shape, and they face in the same direction.

> **ROTATION:** a transformation that turns a figure about a fixed point called the center of rotation

A **ROTATION** is a transformation that turns a figure about a fixed point called the center of rotation. An object and its rotation are the same shape and size, but the figures may be turned in different directions. Rotations can occur in either a clockwise or a counterclockwise direction.

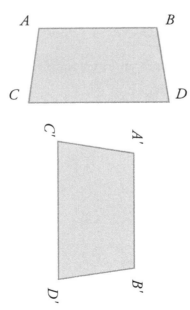

Rotations can be seen in wallpaper and art, and a Ferris wheel is an example of rotation.

An object and its **REFLECTION** have the same shape and size, but the figures face in opposite directions.

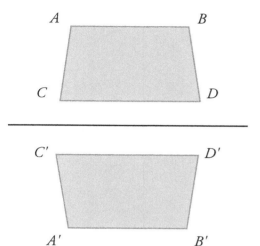

> **REFLECTION:** objects have the same shape and size, but the figures face in opposite directions

The line (where a mirror may be placed) is called the **LINE OF REFLECTION**. The distance from a point to the line of reflection is the same as the distance from the point's image to the line of reflection.

A **GLIDE REFLECTION** is a combination of a reflection and a translation.

> **LINE OF REFLECTION:** the line where a mirror may be placed; the distance from a point to this line is the same as the distance from the point's image to this line

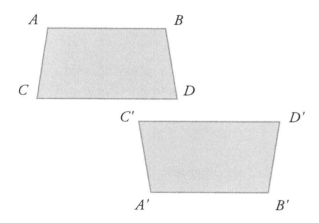

> **GLIDE REFLECTION:** a combination of a reflection and a translation

Another type of transformation is dilation. Dilation is a transformation that "shrinks" an object or makes it bigger.

Example: Use dilation to transform a diagram.
Starting with a triangle whose center of dilation is point *P*,

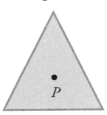

we dilate the lengths of the sides by the same factor to create a new triangle.

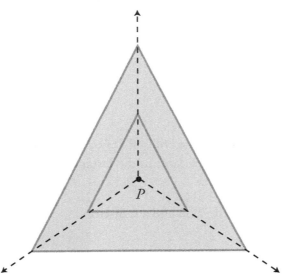

Congruent figures have the same size and shape. If one is placed above the other, they will fit exactly. Congruent lines have the same length. Congruent angles have equal measures.

The symbol for congruence is ≅.

Polygons (pentagons) *ABCDE* and *VWXYZ* are congruent. They are exactly the same size and shape.

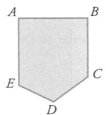
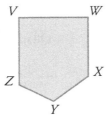

ABCDE ≅ *VWXYZ*

Corresponding parts are the congruent angles and congruent sides. They are:

Corresponding Angles	Corresponding Sides
$\angle A \leftrightarrow \angle V$	$AB \leftrightarrow VW$
$\angle B \leftrightarrow \angle W$	$BC \leftrightarrow WX$
$\angle C \leftrightarrow \angle X$	$CD \leftrightarrow XY$
$\angle D \leftrightarrow \angle Y$	$DE \leftrightarrow YZ$
$\angle E \leftrightarrow \angle Z$	$AE \leftrightarrow VZ$

Two triangles can be proven congruent by comparing pairs of appropriate congruent corresponding parts.

SSS Postulate

If three sides of one triangle are congruent to three sides of another triangle, then the two triangles are congruent.

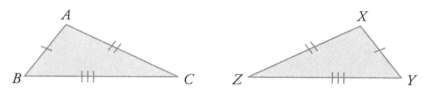

Since $AB \cong XY$, $BC \cong YZ$, and $AC \cong XZ$, then $\triangle ABC \cong \triangle XYZ$.

Example: Given isosceles triangle ABC, with D the midpoint of base AC, prove the two triangles formed by BD are congruent.

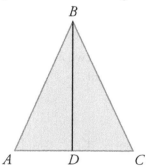

Proof:

1. Isosceles triangle ABC,
   D midpoint of base AC Given

2. $AB \cong BC$ An isosceles triangle has two congruent sides

3. $AD \cong DC$ A midpoint divides a line into two equal parts

4. $BD \cong BD$ Reflexive

5. $\triangle ABD \cong \triangle BCD$ SSS

SAS Postulate

If two sides and the included angle of one triangle are congruent to two sides and the included angle of another triangle, the two triangles are congruent.

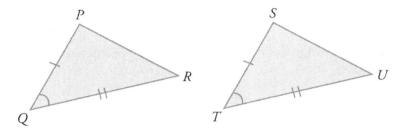

Example:

The two triangles are congruent by SAS.

ASA Postulate

If two angles and the included side of one triangle are congruent to two angles and the included side of another triangle, the triangles are congruent.

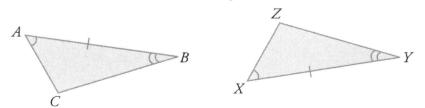

$\angle A \cong \angle X$, $\angle B \cong \angle Y$, $AB \cong XY$, then $\triangle ABC \cong \triangle XYZ$ by ASA

Example: Given two right triangles with one leg of each measuring 6 cm and the adjacent angle 37°, prove the triangles are congruent.

1. Right triangles *ABC* and *KLM*
   $AB = KL = 6$ cm
   $\angle A = \angle K = 37°$ Given

2. $AB \cong KL$ Figures with the same measure
   $\angle A \cong \angle K$ are congruent

3. $\angle B \cong \angle L$ All right angles are congruent

4. $\triangle ABC \cong \triangle KLM$ ASA

Example: Which method would you use to prove the triangles congruent?

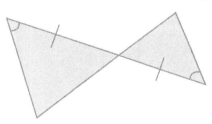

ASA, because vertical angles are congruent.

AAS Theorem

If two angles and a nonincluded side of one triangle are congruent to the corresponding parts of another triangle, then the triangles are congruent.

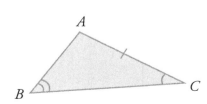 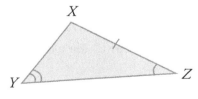

$\angle B \cong \angle Y$, $\angle C \cong \angle Z$, $AC \cong XZ$, then $\triangle ABC \cong \triangle XYZ$ by AAS.

We can derive this theorem because if two angles of the triangles are congruent, then the third angle must also be congruent. Therefore, we can use the ASA postulate.

HL Theorem

If the hypotenuse and a leg of one right triangle are congruent to the corresponding parts of another right triangle, the triangles are congruent.

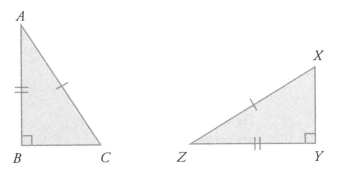

Since $\angle B$ and $\angle Y$ are right angles and $AC \cong XZ$ (hypotenuse of each triangle), $AB \cong YZ$ (corresponding leg of each triangle), then $\triangle ABC \cong \triangle XYZ$ by the HL theorem.

Example: Which method would you use to prove the triangles congruent?

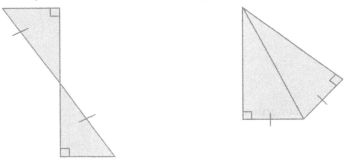

Answer: AAS   Answer: HL

Similar solids share the same shape but are not necessarily the same size. The ratio of any two corresponding measurements of similar solids is the scale factor. For example, the scale factor for two square pyramids, one with a side measuring 2 inches and the other with a side measuring 4 inches, is 2:4.

 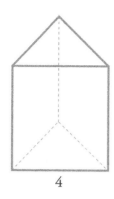

2   4

The base perimeter, the surface area, and the volume of similar solids are directly related to the scale factor. If the scale factor of two similar solids is a:b, then

the ratio of base perimeters = a:b

the ratio of areas = a^2:b^2

the ratio of volumes = a^3:b^3

Thus, for the above example,

the ratio of base perimeters = 2:4

the ratio of areas = 2^2:4^2 = 4:16

the ratio of volumes = 2^3:4^3 = 8:64

Sample problem:

What happens to the volume of a square pyramid when the lengths of the sides of the base are doubled?

Scale factor = a:b = 1:2

Ratio of volume = 13:26 = 1:2 (the volume is increased 2 times)

SKILL 12.4 **Demonstrating knowledge of the concepts of direct and indirect measurement** *(e.g., volume, surface area, scale, similarity, Pythagorean theorem)* **of two- and three-dimensional figures and of real-world applications of these concepts**

Most numbers in mathematics are "exact" or "counted," but measurements are "approximate." They usually involve interpolation, or figuring out which mark on the ruler is closest. Any measurement acquired with a measuring device is approximate. These variations in measurement are called precision and accuracy.

A measurement's **PRECISION** tells us how exactly a measurement is made, without reference to a true or real value. If a measurement is precise, it can be made again and again with little variation in the result. The precision of a measuring device is

PRECISION: how exactly a measurement is made, without reference to a true or real value

the smallest fractional or decimal division on the instrument. The smaller the unit or fraction of a unit on the measuring device, the more precisely it can measure.

The greatest possible error of measurement is always equal to one-half the smallest fraction of a unit on the measuring device. A measurement's **ACCURACY** tells us how close the result of measurement comes to the "true" value.

In the game of throwing darts, the true value is the bull's eye. If the three darts land on the bull's eye, the dart thrower is both precise (all the darts land near the same spot) and accurate (the darts all land on the "true" value).

The greatest measure of error allowed is called the **TOLERANCE**. The least acceptable limit is called the **LOWER LIMIT**, and the greatest acceptable limit is called the **UPPER LIMIT**. The difference between the upper and lower limits is called the **TOLERANCE INTERVAL**. For example, a specification for an automobile part might be 14.625 ± 0.005 mm. This means that the smallest acceptable length of the part is 14.620 mm and the largest acceptable length is 14.630 mm. The tolerance interval is 0.010 mm. One can see how it would be important for automobile parts to be within a set of limits in terms of length. If the part is too long or too short, it will not fit properly, and vibrations that weaken the part will occur, which might eventually cause damage to other parts.

ACCURACY: how close the result of measurement comes to the "true" value

TOLERANCE: the greatest measure of error allowed

LOWER LIMIT: the least acceptable limit

UPPER LIMIT: the greatest acceptable limit

TOLERANCE INTERVAL: the difference between the upper and lower limits

PERIMETER: the sum of the lengths of the sides of any polygon

Measuring Perimeter, Area, and Volume

The **PERIMETER** of any polygon is the sum of the lengths of the sides.

$P = $ sum of sides

Since the opposite sides of a rectangle are congruent, the perimeter of a rectangle equals twice the sum of the length and width or

$P_{rect} = 2l + 2w$ or $2(l + w)$

Similarly, since all the sides of a square have the same measure, the perimeter of a square equals four times the length of one side or

$P_{square} = 4s$

The **AREA** of a polygon is the number of square units covered by the figure.

$A_{rect} = l \times w$

$A_{square} = s^2$

AREA: the number of square units covered by a polygon

Example: Find the perimeter and the area of this rectangle.

16 cm

9 cm

$P_{\text{rect}} = 2l + 2w$
$\quad = 2(16) + 2(9)$
$\quad = 32 + 18 = 50 \text{ cm}$

$A_{\text{rect}} = l \times w$
$\quad = 16(9)$
$\quad = 144 \text{ cm}^2$

Example: Find the perimeter and area of this square.

3.6 in.

$P_{\text{square}} = 4s$
$\quad = 4(3.6)$
$\quad = 14.4 \text{ in.}$

$A_{\text{square}} = s^2$
$\quad = (3.6)(3.6)$
$\quad = 12.96 \text{ in}^2$

In the following formulas, $b =$ the base and $h =$ the height of an altitude drawn to the base.

$$A_{\text{parallelogram}} = bh \qquad A_{\text{triangle}} = \tfrac{1}{2}bh \qquad A_{\text{trapezoid}} = \tfrac{1}{2}h(b_1 + b_2)$$

Example: Find the area of a parallelogram whose base is 6.5 cm and the height of the altitude to that base is 3.7 cm.

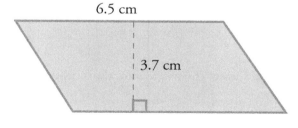

6.5 cm

3.7 cm

$A_{\text{parallelogram}} = bh$
$\quad = (3.7)(6.5)$
$\quad = 24.05 \text{ cm}^2$

Example: Find the area of this triangle.

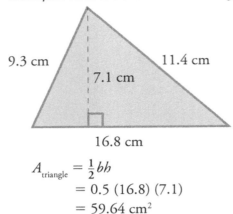

$$A_{triangle} = \tfrac{1}{2}bh$$
$$= 0.5\,(16.8)\,(7.1)$$
$$= 59.64 \text{ cm}^2$$

Note that the altitude is drawn to the base measuring 16.8 cm. The lengths of the other two sides are unnecessary information.

Example: Find the area of a right triangle whose sides measure 10 inches, 24 inches, and 26 inches.

Since the hypotenuse of a right triangle must be the longest side, then the two perpendicular sides must measure 10 and 24 inches.

$$A_{triangle} = \tfrac{1}{2}bh$$
$$= \tfrac{1}{2}(10)\,(24)$$
$$= 120 \text{ sq. in.}$$

Example: Find the area of this trapezoid.

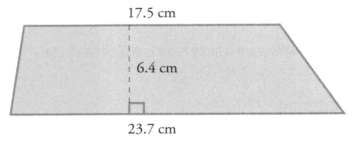

The area of a trapezoid equals one-half the sum of the bases times the altitude.

$$A_{trapezoid} = \tfrac{1}{2}h(b_1 + b_2)$$
$$= 0.5\,(6.4)\,(17.5 + 23.7)$$
$$= 131.84 \text{ cm}^2$$

Compute the area remaining when sections are cut out of a given figure composed of triangles, squares, rectangles, parallelograms, trapezoids, or circles.

Example: You have decided to fertilize your lawn. The shapes and dimensions of your lot, house, pool, and garden are given in the diagram below. The shaded area will not be fertilized. If each bag of fertilizer costs $7.95 and covers 4,500 square feet, find the total number of bags needed and the total cost of the fertilizer.

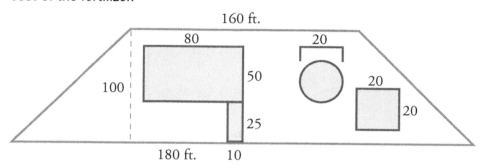

Area of lot

$A = \frac{1}{2}h(b_1 + b_2)$

　　$= \frac{1}{2}(100)(180 + 160)$

　　$= 17,000$ sq ft

Area of house

$A = lw$

　　$= (80)(50)$

　　$= 4,000$ sq ft

Area of driveway

$A = lw$

　　$= (10)(25)$

　　$= 250$ sq ft

Area of pool

$A = \pi r^2$

　　$= \pi(10)^2$

　　$= 314.159$ sq ft

Area of garden

$A = s^2$

　　$= (20)^2$

　　$= 400$ sq ft

Total area to fertilize = Lot area − (house + driveway + pool + garden)

　　　　　　$= 17,000 − (4,000 + 250 + 314.159 + 400)$

　　　　　　$= 12,035.841$ sq ft

Number of bags needed = Total area to fertilize/4,500 sq ft. bag

　　　　　　$= 12,035.841/4,500$

　　　　　　$= 2.67$ bags

Since we cannot purchase 2.67 bags we must purchase 3 full bags.

Total cost = Number of bags × $7.95

　　　　$= 3 × \$7.95$

　　　　$= \$23.85$

The Pythagorean Theorem

Pythagorean theorem states that the square of the length of the hypotenuse is equal to the sum of the squares of the lengths of the legs. Symbolically, this is stated as:

　　$c^2 = a^2 + b^2$

Example: Given the right triangle below, find the missing side.

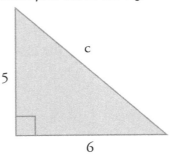

$c^2 = a^2 + b^2$ 1. Write formula.

$c^2 = 5^2 + 6^2$ 2. Substitute known values.

$c^2 = 61$ 3. Take square root.

$c = \sqrt{61}$ or 7.81   4. Solve.

The converse of the Pythagorean Theorem states that if the square of one side of a triangle is equal to the sum of the squares of the other two sides, then the triangle is a right triangle.

Example: Given △XYZ, with sides measuring 12, 16, and 20 cm. Is this a right triangle?

$c^2 = a^2 + b^2$

$20^2 \underline{\ ?\ } 12^2 + 16^2$

$400 \underline{\ ?\ } 144 + 256$

$400 = 400$

Yes, the triangle is a right triangle.

This theorem can be expanded to determine if triangles are obtuse or acute.

If the square of the longest side of a triangle is greater than the sum of the squares of the other two sides, then the triangle is an obtuse triangle.

and

If the square of the longest side of a triangle is less than the sum of the squares of the other two sides, then the triangle is an acute triangle.

Example: Given △LMN with sides measuring 7, 12, and 14 inches. Is the triangle right, acute, or obtuse?

$14^2 \underline{\ ?\ } 7^2 + 12^2$

$196 \underline{\ ?\ } 49 + 144$

$196 > 193$

Therefore, the triangle is obtuse.

Real-world example: Find the area and perimeter of a rectangle if its length is 12 inches and its diagonal is 15 inches.

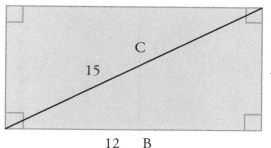

1. Draw and label sketch.
2. Since the height is still needed, use Pythagorean formula to find missing leg of the triangle.

$A^2 + B^2 = C^2$

$A^2 + 12^2 = 15^2$

$A^2 = 15^2 - 12^2$

$A^2 = 81$

$A = 9$

Now use this information to find the area and perimeter.

A = LW	P = 2(L + W)	1. Write formula.
A = (12)(9)	P = 2(12 + 9)	2. Substitute.
A = 108 in²	P = 42 inches	3. Solve.

Real-world example: Given the figure below, find the area by dividing the polygon into smaller shapes.

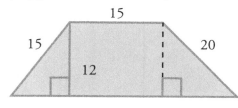

1. Divide the figure into two triangles and a rectangle.
2. Find the missing lengths.
3. Find the area of each part.
4. Find the sum of all areas.

Find base of both right triangles using Pythagorean Formula:

$a^2 + b^2 = c^2$	$a^2 + b^2 = c^2$
$a^2 + 12^2 = 15^2$	$a^2 + 12^2 = 20^2$
$a^2 = 225 - 144$	$a^2 = 400 - 144$
$a^2 = 81$	$a^2 = 256$
$a = 9$	$a = 16$

Area of triangle 1
$A = \frac{1}{2}bh$
$= \frac{1}{2}(9)(12)$
$= 54$ sq units

Area of triangle 2
$A = \frac{1}{2}bh$
$= \frac{1}{2}(16)(12)$
$= 96$ sq units

Area of triangle 3
$A = lw$
$= (15)(12)$
$= 180$ sq units

Find the sum of all three figures.

$54 + 96 + 180 = 330$ sq units

Given triangle right *ABC*, the adjacent side and opposite side can be identified for each angle *A* and *B*.

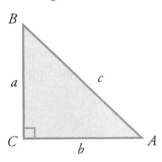

Looking at angle *A*, it can be determined that side *b* is adjacent to angle *A* and side *a* is opposite angle *A*.

If we now look at angle *B*, we see that side a is adjacent to angle *B* and side *b* is opposite angle *B*.

Trigonometric Ratios

The longest side (opposite the 90° angle) is always called the hypotenuse.

The basic trigonometric ratios are listed below:

$$\text{Sine} = \frac{\text{opposite}}{\text{hypotenuse}} \qquad \text{Cosine} = \frac{\text{adjacent}}{\text{hypotenuse}} \qquad \text{Tangent} = \frac{\text{opposite}}{\text{adjacent}}$$

Sample problem: Use triangle ABC to find the sin, cos, and tan for angle A.

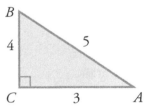

$$\sin = \frac{4}{5}$$
$$\cos = \frac{3}{5}$$
$$\tan = \frac{4}{3}$$

Use the **basic trigonometric ratios** of sine, cosine, and tangent to solve for the missing sides of right triangles when given at least one of the acute angles.

In the triangle *ABC*, an acute angle of 63° and the length of the hypotenuse (12). The missing side is the one adjacent to the given angle.

The appropriate trigonometric ratio to use would be cosine since we are looking for the adjacent side and we have the length of the hypotenuse.

$$\cos x = \frac{\text{adjacent}}{\text{hypotenuse}}$$ 1. Write formula.

$$\cos 63 = \frac{x}{12}$$ 2. Substitute known values.

$$0.454 = \frac{x}{12}$$

$$x = 5.448$$ 3. Solve.

Example: Find the missing side or angle.

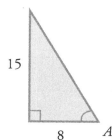

$\tan A = \text{opposite/adjacent}$

$\tan A = \frac{15}{8} = 1.875$

Looking on the trigonometric chart, the angle whose tangent is closest to 1.875 is 62°.

Thus $\measuredangle A \approx 62°$.

Example:

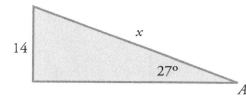

$$\sin A = \frac{\text{opposite}}{\text{hypotenuse}}$$

$$\sin 27° = \frac{14}{x}$$

$$0.4540 \approx \frac{14}{x}$$

$$x \approx \frac{14}{.454}$$

$$x \approx 30.8$$

Example:

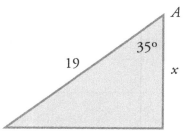

$$\cos A = \frac{\text{adjacent}}{\text{hypotenuse}}$$

$$\cos 35° = \frac{x}{19}$$

$$x \approx 19 \times .5636$$

$$x \approx 10.9$$

Selecting appropriate units of measurement, converting measurements within measurement systems, and solving real-world problems

Solving Problems Involving Measurement

The units of length in the customary system are inches, feet, yards, and miles.

12 inches (in.)	=	1 foot (ft.)
36 in.	=	1 yard (yd.)
3 ft.	=	1 yd.
5280 ft.	=	1 mile (mi.)
1760 yd.	=	1 mi.

To change from a larger unit to a smaller unit, multiply.

To change from a smaller unit to a larger unit, divide.

Example:

4 mi. = _____ yd.
Since 1760 yd. = 1 mile, multiply $4 \times 1760 = 7040$ yd.

Example:

21 in. = _____ ft.
$21 \div 12 = 1.75$ ft. (or 1 foot and 9 inches)

The units of weight are ounces, pounds, and tons.

16 ounces (oz.)	=	1 pound (lb.)
2000 lb.	=	1 ton (T.)

Example:

$2\frac{3}{4}$ T. = _____ lb.
$2\frac{3}{4} \times 2000 = 5500$ lb.

The units of capacity are fluid ounces, cups, pints, quarts, and gallons.

8 fluid ounces (fl. oz.)	=	1 cup (c.)
2 c.	=	1 pint (pt.)
4 c.	=	1 quart (qt.)
2 pt.	=	1 qt.
4 qt.	=	1 gallon (gal.)

Example:

3 gal. = _____ qt.

$3 \times 4 = 12$ qt.

Example:

$1\frac{1}{4}$ cups = _____ oz.

$1\frac{1}{4} \times 8 = 10$ oz.

Example:

7 c. = _____ pt.

$7 \div 2 = 3\frac{1}{2}$ pt.

Square Units

Square units can be derived with knowledge of basic units of length by squaring the equivalent measurements.

1 square foot (sq. ft.)	=	144 sq. in.
1 sq. yd.	=	9 sq. ft.
1 sq. yd.	=	1296 sq. in.

Example:

14 sq. yd. = _____ sq. ft.

$14 \times 9 = 126$ sq. ft.

Metric Units

The metric system is based on multiples of ten. Conversions are made by simply moving the decimal point to the left or right.

METRIC PREFIXES AND THEIR MEANING		
kilo-	1000	thousands
hecto-	100	hundreds
deca-	10	tens
deci-	.1	tenths
centi-	.01	hundredths
milli-	.001	thousandths

The basic unit for length is the meter. One meter is approximately one yard.

The basic unit for weight or mass is the gram. A paper clip weighs about one gram.

The basic unit for volume is the liter. One liter is approximately a quart.

These are the most commonly used units.

1 m = 100 cm	1000 mL = 1 L
1 m = 1000 mm	1 kL = 1000 L
1 cm = 10 mm	1000 mg = 1 g
1000 m = 1 km	1 kg = 1000 g

The prefixes are commonly listed from left to right for ease in conversion.

K   H   D   U   D   C   M

Example: 63 km = _____ m
Since there are 3 steps from **K**ilo to **U**nit, move the decimal point 3 places to the right.

63 km = 63,000 m

Example: 14 mL = _____ L

Since there are 3 steps from **M**illi to **U**nit, move the decimal point 3 places to the left.

   14 mL = 0.014 L

Example: 56.4 cm = _____ mm

   56.4 cm = 564 mm

Example: 9.1 m = _____ km

   9.1 m = 0.0091 km

Solve Word Problems with Rational Algebraic Expressions and Equations

Some problems can be solved using equations with rational expressions. First write the equation. To solve it, multiply each term by the LCD of all fractions. This will cancel out all of the denominators and give an equivalent algebraic equation that can be solved.

Some problems can be solved using equations with rational expressions.

Example: The denominator of a fraction is two less than three times the numerator. If 3 is added to both the numerator and denominator, the new fraction equals $\frac{1}{2}$.

   Original fraction: $\frac{x}{3x - 2}$ Revised fraction: $\frac{x + 3}{3x + 1}$

   $$\frac{x + 3}{3x + 1} = \frac{1}{2}$$ $$2x + 6 = 3x + 1$$

                                          $$x = 5$$

   So the original fraction is $\frac{5}{13}$.

Example: Elly Mae can feed the animals in 15 minutes. Jethro can feed them in 10 minutes. How long will it take them to feed the animals if they work together?

If Elly Mae can feed the animals in 15 minutes, then she could feed $\frac{1}{15}$ of them in 1 minute, $\frac{2}{15}$ of them in 2 minutes, and $\frac{x}{15}$ of them in x minutes. In the same fashion, Jethro could feed $\frac{x}{10}$ of them in x minutes. Together they complete 1 job. The equation is:

   $$\frac{x}{15} + \frac{x}{10} = 1$$

Multiply each term by the LCD (least common denominator) of 30:

   $$2x + 3x = 30$$
   $$x = 6 \text{ minutes}$$

Example: A salesman drove 480 miles from Pittsburgh to Hartford. The next day he returned the same distance to Pittsburgh in half an hour less time than his original trip took, because he increased his average speed by 4 mph. Find his original speed.

Since distance = rate × time, then time = $\frac{\text{distance}}{\text{rate}}$.

The form of the equation is original time $-\frac{1}{2}$ hour = shorter return time.

$$\frac{480}{x} - \frac{1}{2} = \frac{480}{x+4}$$

Multiplying by the LCD of $2x(x + 4)$, the equation becomes:

$480[2(x + 4)] - 1[x(x + 4)] = 480(2x)$

$960x + 3840 - x^2 - 4x = 960x$

$x^2 + 4x - 3840 = 0$

$(x + 64)(x - 60) = 0$

$x = 60$

60 mph is the original speed, 64 mph is the faster return speed.

Try these:

1. Working together, Larry, Moe, and Curly can paint an elephant in 3 minutes. Working alone, it would take Larry 10 minutes or Moe 6 minutes to paint the elephant. How long would it take Curly to paint the elephant if he worked alone?

2. The denominator of a fraction is 5 more than twice the numerator. If the numerator is doubled, and the denominator is increased by 5, the new fraction is equal to $\frac{1}{2}$. Find the original number.

3. A trip from Augusta, Maine, to Galveston, Texas, is 2,108 miles. If one car drove 6 mph faster than a truck and got to Galveston 3 hours before the truck, find the speeds of the car and truck.

Here is an example of a real-world problem for which an estimate is more appropriate than an exact measurement:

Ms. Jackson wants to make a 5-by-10-foot braided rug using 1-inch-wide braid.

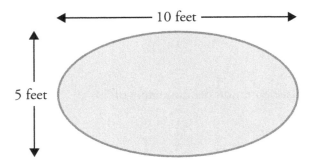

10 feet

5 feet

She can estimate how much braid she will need by determining the approximate area of the rug. If the rug were rectangular, the area would be 50 square feet, or 7,200 square inches (50 by 144). Ms. Jackson can use this estimate to make or purchase the amount of braid she needs for the rug.

Here is an example of a real-world problem where an exact measurement is more appropriate than an estimate:

A carpenter is building a staircase to the second floor of a house. If the carpenter estimates instead of using an exact measurement and overestimates the length of the staircase, the staircase will not fit against the second floor. If he underestimates the length, it will not reach to the second floor.

SKILL 12.6 Applying knowledge of the characteristics and uses of geometric learning tools *(e.g., geoboard, protractor, ruler)*

Scales

If students are using a scale with a needle that has a mirrored plate behind it, the scale should be viewed so that the needle's reflection is hidden behind the needle itself. Students should not look at the needle from an angle. In order to read a balance scale accurately, it is necessary to place the scale on a level surface and make sure that the hand points precisely at 0. Objects should be placed on the plate gently and taken away gently. The dial should be viewed straight-on to read the graduation accurately. Students should read from the large graduation to smaller graduation. If the dial hand points between two graduations, they should choose the number that is closest to the hand.

> When reading an instrument, students should first determine the interval of scale on that particular instrument. To achieve the greatest accuracy, they should read the scale to the nearest measurement mark.

Rulers

When reading inches on a ruler, the student needs to understand that each inch is divided into halves by the longest mark in the middle; into fourths by the next-longest marks; into eighths by the next; and into sixteenths by the shortest marks. When the measurement falls between two inch marks, they can give the whole number of inches, count the additional fractional marks, and give the answer as the number and fraction of inches. Remind students that the convention is always to express a fraction with its lowest possible denominator.

If students are using the metric system on a ruler, have them focus on the marks between the whole numbers (centimeters). Point out that each centimeter is broken into tenths, with the longer mark in the middle indicating the halfway mark. Students should learn to measure things accurately to the nearest tenth of a centimeter, then to the nearest hundredth, and, finally, to the nearest thousandth. Measurements using the metric system should always be written using the decimal system; for example, 3.756 centimeters.

Protractors

PROTRACTORS: instruments that measure angles in degrees

PROTRACTORS measure angles in degrees. To measure accurately, students must find the center hole on the straight edge of the protractor and place it over the vertex of the angle they wish to measure. They should line up the zero on the straight edge with one of the sides of the angle and then find the point where the second side of the angle intersects the curved edge of the protractor. They can then read the number that is written at the point of intersection.

Thermometers

When reading a thermometer, one should hold it vertically at eye level. Students should check the scale of the thermometer to make certain that they read as many significant digits as possible. Thermometers with heavy or extended lines that are marked 10, 20, 30, and so on should be read to the nearest 0.1 degree. Thermometers with fine lines every two degrees can be read to the nearest 0.5 degree.

Measuring Liquids

In order to get an accurate reading in a liquid measuring container, students should set the container on a level surface and read it at eye level. The measurement should be read at the bottom of the concave arc at the liquid's surface (the meniscus). When measuring dry ingredients, dip the appropriately sized measuring cup into the ingredient, and sweep away the excess across the top with a straight-edged object.

COMPETENCY 13

UNDERSTAND CONCEPTS AND TECHNIQUES OF DATA INVESTIGATIONS AND THE CONCEPTS OF RANDOMNESS AND UNCERTAINTY

SKILL 13.1 Demonstrating knowledge of conceptual and procedural tools for collecting, organizing, and reasoning about data

See also Skills 18.2 and 18.3

SKILL 13.2 Applying knowledge of statistical measures *(e.g., mean, median, mode)* for analyzing data

Mean, median, and mode are three measures of central tendency. The **MEAN** is the average of the data items. The **MEDIAN** is found by putting the data items in order from smallest to largest and selecting the item in the middle (or the average of the two items in the middle). The **MODE** is the most frequently occurring item. **RANGE** is a measure of variability. It is found by subtracting the smallest value from the largest value.

Example: Find the mean, median, mode, and range of the test scores listed below:

85	77	65
92	90	54
88	85	70
75	80	69
85	88	60
72	74	95

Mean = sum of all scores ÷ number of scores = 78

Median = Put the numbers in order from smallest to largest. Pick the middle number.

54 60 65 69 70 72 74 75 | 77 80 | 85 85 85 88 88 90 92 95

both in middle

MEAN: the sum of the numbers given, divided by the number of data values

MEDIAN: the middle number of a set of data values

MODE: the number that occurs with the greatest frequency in a set of numbers

RANGE: the difference between the highest and lowest value

Therefore, the median is the average of two numbers in the middle, 78.5.

Mode = most frequent number
        = 85

Range = the largest number minus the smallest number
         = 95 − 54
         = 41

SKILL 13.3 **Applying knowledge of techniques for representing and summarizing data graphically** *(e.g., histogram, frequency distribution, stem-and-leaf plot, Venn diagram)*

To read a bar graph or a pictograph, read the explanation of the scale that was used in the legend. Compare the length of each bar with the dimensions on the axes and calculate the value each bar represents.

BAR GRAPHS: used to compare various quantities

BAR GRAPHS are used to compare various quantities.

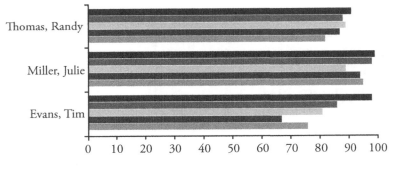

PICTOGRAPHS: show comparison of quantities using symbols; each symbol represents a number of items

A **PICTOGRAPH** shows comparison of quantities using symbols. Each symbol represents a number of items.

CIRCLE GRAPHS: show the relationship of various parts to each other and the whole as percentages

CIRCLE GRAPHS show the relationship of various parts to each other and the whole. Percentages are used to create circle graphs. To read a circle graph, find the total of the amounts represented on the entire graph. To determine the amount that each sector of the graph represents, multiply the percentage in a sector by the number representing the total amount.

Julie spends eight hours each day in school, two hours doing homework, one hour eating dinner, two hours watching television, ten hours sleeping, and the rest of the time doing other things.

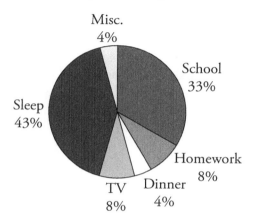

Stem-and-leaf plots are visually similar to line plots. The stems are the digits in the greatest place value of the data values, and the leaves are the digits in the next greatest place value. Stem-and-leaf plots are best suited for small sets of data and are especially useful for comparing two sets of data. The following is an example using test scores:

4	9
5	4 9
6	1 2 3 4 6 7 8 8
7	0 3 4 6 6 6 7 7 7 7 8 8 8 8
8	3 5 5 7 8
9	0 0 3 4 5
10	0 0

To read a chart, read the row and column headings on the table. Use this information to evaluate the information in the chart.

	Test 1	Test 2	Test 3	Test 4	Test 5
Evans, Tim	75	66	80	85	97
Miller, Julie	94	93	88	97	98
Thomas, Randy	81	86	88	87	90

**HISTOGRAMS: ** summarize information from large sets of data that can be naturally grouped into intervals

**FREQUENCY: ** the number of times any particular data value occurs

**FREQUENCY OF THE INTERVAL: ** the number of data values in any interval

HISTOGRAMS are used to summarize information from large sets of data that can be naturally grouped into intervals. The vertical axis indicates **FREQUENCY** (the number of times any particular data value occurs), and the horizontal axis indicates data values or ranges of data values. The number of data values in any interval is the **FREQUENCY OF THE INTERVAL**.

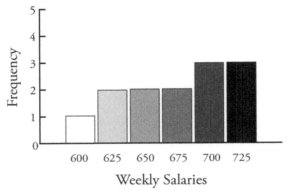

Graphical representations of data sets, like box-and-whisker plots, help relate the measures of central tendency to data outliers, clusters, and gaps. Consider the hypothetical box-and-whisker plot with one outlier value on each end of the distribution.

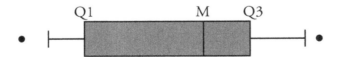

Note the beginning of the box is the value of the first quartile of the data set and the end is the value of the third quartile. We represent the median as a vertical line in the box. The "whiskers" extend to the last point that is not an outlier (i.e., within $\frac{3}{2}$ times the range between Q1 and Q3). The points beyond the figure represent outlier values.

Box-and-whisker graphs are useful when handling large amounts of data. They allow students to explore the data and arrive at an informal conclusion when two or more variables exist. Another name for the visual representation of a box-and-whisker graph is a five-number summary. This consists of the median, the quartiles, and the least and greatest numbers in the representation.

In order to create a box-and-whisker graph, one first has to find the median in a list of numbers. Then look at the numbers only to the left of the median and find the median of this set of numbers. This is the lower quartile of the list. Repeat the procedure with the set of numbers to the right of the main median. This is the upper quartile. Use the two medians from the quartile to find the interquartile range by subtracting the lowest from the highest numbers. Then draw the graph on a number line.

Example: Fifteen girls own different numbers of hair elastics.
21 25 30 36 38 42 45 50 51 55 64 66 70 75 80

The median is the number in the middle: 50.
The median of the numbers to the left of 50 (the lower quartile) is 36, and the median of the numbers to the right of 50 (the upper quartile) is 66.
When you subtract (66 − 50), the interquartile range is 16.
Then you plot these numbers on a number line.

SKILL 13.4 Interpreting and drawing inferences from data and making decisions in applied problem situations

The absolute probability of some events cannot be determined. For instance, one cannot assume the probability of winning a tennis match is $\frac{1}{2}$ because, in general, winning and losing are not equally likely. In such cases, past results of similar events can be used to help predict future outcomes. The **RELATIVE FREQUENCY** of an event is the number of times an event has occurred divided by the number of attempts.

$$\text{Relative frequency} = \frac{\textbf{Number of successful trials}}{\textbf{Total number of trials}}$$

RELATIVE FREQUENCY: the number of times an event has occurred divided by the number of attempts

For example, if a weighted coin flipped fifty times lands on heads forty times and tails ten times, the relative frequency of heads is $\frac{40}{50} = \frac{4}{5}$. Thus, one can predict that if the coin is flipped one hundred times, it will land on heads eighty times.

Example:
Two tennis players, John and David, have played each other twenty times. John has won fifteen of the previous matches and David has won five.

A. Estimate the probability that David will win the next match.

B. Estimate the probability that John will win the next three matches.

Solution:

A. David has won five out of twenty matches. Thus, the relative frequency of David winning is $\frac{5}{20}$ or $\frac{1}{4}$. We can estimate that the probability of David winning the next match is $\frac{1}{4}$.

B. John has won fifteen out of twenty matches. The relative frequency of John winning is $\frac{15}{20}$ or $\frac{3}{4}$. We can estimate that the probability of John winning a future match is $\frac{3}{4}$. Thus, the probability that John will win the next three matches is $\frac{3}{4} \times \frac{3}{4} \times \frac{3}{4} = \frac{27}{64}$.

SKILL 13.5 **Using principles of probability** *(e.g., counting, sample space, independence)* **to solve real-world and mathematical problems involving simple and compound events**

The **Addition Principle of Counting** states:
  If A and B are events, $n(A \text{ or } B) = n(A) + n(B) - n(A \cap B)$.

Example: In how many ways can you select a black card or a Jack from an ordinary deck of playing cards?
Let B denote the set of black cards and let J denote the set of Jacks.
Then, $n(B) = 26$, $n(J) = 4$, $n(B \cap J) = 2$ and
$$n(B \text{ or } J) = n(B) + n(J) - n(B \cap J)$$
$$= 26 + 4 - 2$$
$$= 28$$

The **Addition Principle of Counting for Mutually Exclusive Events** states:
If A and B are mutually exclusive events, $n(A \text{ or } B) = n(A) + n(B) - n(A \cap B)$.

Example: A travel agency offers 40 possible trips: 14 to Asia, 16 to Europe and 10 to South America. In how many ways can you select a trip to Asia or Europe through this agency?
Let A denote trips to Asia and let E denote trips to Europe. Then, $A \cap E = \varnothing$ and
$$n(A \text{ or } E) = 26 + 4 - 2$$
$$= 28$$
Therefore, the number of ways you can select a trip to Asia or Europe is 30.

The **Multiplication Principle of Counting for Dependent Events** states:
Let A be a set of outcomes of Stage 1 and B a set of outcomes of Stage 2. Then the number of ways $n(A \text{ and } B)$, that A and B can occur in a two-stage experiment is given by:

$n(A \text{ and } B) = n(A)n(B|A)$,

where $n(B|A)$ denotes the number of ways can occur given that has already occurred.

Example: How many ways from an ordinary deck of 52 cards can two Jacks be drawn in succession if the first card is drawn but not replaced in the deck and then the second card is drawn?

This is a two-stage experiment for which we wish to compute $n(A \text{ and } B)$, where A is the set of outcomes for which a Jack is obtained on the first draw and B is the set of outcomes for which a Jack is obtained on the second draw.

If the first card drawn is a Jack, then there are only three remaining Jacks left to choose from on the second draw. Thus, drawing two cards without replacement means the events A and B are dependent.

$n(A \text{ and } B) = n(A)n(B|A) = 4 \cdot 3 = 12$

The **Multiplication Principle of Counting for Independent Events** states:
Let A be a set of outcomes of Stage 1 and B a set of outcomes of Stage 2. If A and B are independent events then the number of ways $n(A \text{ and } B)$, that A and B can occur in a two-stage experiment is given by: $n(A \text{ and } B) = n(A)n(B)$

Example: How many six-letter code "words" can be formed if repetition of letters is not allowed?

Since these are code words, a word does not have to look like a word; for example, abcdef could be a code word. Since we must choose a first letter and a second letter and a third letter and a fourth letter and a fifth letter and a sixth letter, this experiment has six stages

Since repetition is not allowed there are 26 choices for the first letter; 25 for the second; 24 for the third; 23 for the fourth; 22 for the fifth; and 21 for the sixth. Therefore, we have:

n(six-letter code words without repetition of letters)
$= 26 \cdot 25 \cdot 24 \cdot 23 \cdot 22 \cdot 21$
$= 165,765,600$

SKILL 13.6 Demonstrating knowledge of randomness and sampling in surveys and experimental studies

> **SAMPLING or SURVEYING:** collecting data on a small percentage of a population with the goal of obtaining the same results that would result from collecting data on the entire population

In cases where the number of events or individuals is too large to collect data on each one, scientists collect information from only a small percentage. This is known as **SAMPLING** or **SURVEYING**. If sampling is done correctly, it should give the investigator nearly the same information he would have obtained by testing the entire population. The survey must be carefully designed, considering both the sampling technique and the size of the sample.

Types of Samples

> *Bias occurs in a sample when some members or opinions of a population are less likely to be included than others. The method by which a survey is taken can contribute to bias in a survey.*

There are a variety of sampling techniques: random, systematic, stratified, cluster, and quota are just a few. Truly **RANDOM SAMPLING** chooses events or individuals without regard to time, place, or result. Random samples are least likely to be biased because they are most likely to represent the population from which they are taken.

> **RANDOM SAMPLING:** chooses events or individuals without regard to time, place, or result

Stratified sampling, quota sampling, and cluster sampling all involve the definition of subpopulations. Those subpopulations are then sampled randomly in an attempt to represent many segments of a data population evenly. While random sampling is typically viewed as the "gold standard," sometimes compromises must be made to save time, money, or effort. For instance, when conducting a phone survey, calls are typically only made in a certain geographical area and at a certain time of day. This is an example of cluster sampling. There are three stages to cluster or area sampling:

1. The target population is divided into many regional clusters (groups)

2. A few clusters are randomly selected for study

3. A few subjects are randomly chosen from within a cluster

> **SYSTEMATIC SAMPLING:** the collection of a sample at defined intervals

SYSTEMATIC SAMPLING involves the collection of a sample at defined intervals (for instance, every tenth part to come off a manufacturing line).

> **CONVENIENCE SAMPLING:** the method of choosing items arbitrarily and in an unstructured manner from the frame

CONVENIENCE SAMPLING is the method of choosing items arbitrarily and in an unstructured manner from the frame. Convenience samples are most likely to be biased because they are likely to exclude some members of a population.

Accuracy of Samples

Another important consideration in sampling is sample size. Again, a large sample will yield more accurate information that a smaller sample, but other factors often limit possible sample size. Statistical methods may be used to determine how large a sample is necessary to give an investigator a specified level of certainty (95% is a typical confidence interval).

Conversely, if a scientist has a sample of certain size, those same statistical methods can be used to determine how confident the scientist can be that the sample accurately reflects the whole population. The smaller the sample size, the more likely the sample is biased.

Example: Brittany called 500 different phone numbers from the phone book to ask people which candidate they were voting for. Which type of sample did Brittany use? Is the sample biased?

Brittany used a random sample. The sample is not biased because it is random and the sample size is appropriate.

Example: Jacob surveyed the girls' softball team on their favorite foods. Which type of sample did he use? Is the sample biased?

Jacob used a convenience sample. The sample is biased because it only sampled a small population of girls.

COMPETENCY 14

UNDERSTAND CONCEPTS AND APPLICATIONS OF DISCRETE MATH

SKILL 14.1 **Applying knowledge of set theory** (e.g., *Venn diagrams, union*) **and its real-world applications**

Conditional statements can be diagrammed using a Venn diagram. A diagram can be drawn with one figure inside another figure. The inner figure represents the hypothesis. The outer figure represents the conclusion. If the hypothesis is taken to be true, then you are located inside the inner figure. If you are located in the inner figure then you are also inside the outer figure, so that proves the conclusion is true. Sometimes that conclusion can then be used as the hypothesis for another conditional, which can result in a second conclusion.

Suppose that these statements were given to you, and you are asked to try to reach a conclusion. The statements are:

All swimmers are athletes.

All athletes are scholars.

In "if-then" form, these would be:

If you are a swimmer, then you are an athlete.

If you are an athlete, then you are a scholar.

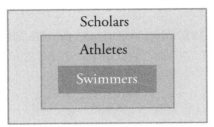

Clearly, if you are a swimmer, then you are also an athlete. This includes you in the group of scholars.

Suppose that these statements were given to you, and you are asked to try to reach a conclusion. The statements are:

All swimmers are athletes.

All wrestlers are athletes.

In "if-then" form, these would be:

If you are a swimmer, then you are an athlete.

If you are a wrestler, then you are an athlete.

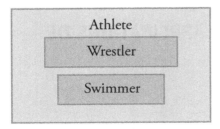

Clearly, if you are a swimmer or a wrestler, then you are also an athlete. This does NOT allow you to come to any other conclusions.

A swimmer may or may NOT also be a wrestler. Therefore, NO CONCLUSION IS POSSIBLE.

Suppose that these statements were given to you, and you are asked to try to reach a conclusion. The statements are:

All rectangles are parallelograms.

Quadrilateral *ABCD* is not a parallelogram.

In "if-then" form, the first statement would be:

If a figure is a rectangle, then it is also a parallelogram.

Note that the second statement is the negation of the conclusion of statement one. Remember also that the contrapositive is logically equivalent to a given conditional. That is, "**If ~ q, then ~ p.**" Since "*ABCD* is NOT a parallelogram" is like saying "**If ~ q,**" then you can come to the conclusion "**then ~ p.**" Therefore, the conclusion is *ABCD* is not a rectangle.

Looking at the Venn diagram below, if all rectangles are parallelograms, then rectangles are included as part of the parallelograms. Since quadrilateral *ABCD* is not a parallelogram, that it is excluded from anywhere inside the parallelogram box. This allows you to conclude that *ABCD* cannot be a rectangle either.

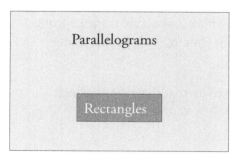

Permutations

In order to understand permutations, the concept of factorials must be addressed.

n factorial, written $n!$, is represented by $n! = n(n-1)(n-2) \ldots (2)(1)$.

$5! = (5)(4)(3)(2)(1) = 120$

$3! = 3(2)(1) = 6$

By definition: $0! = 1$

$\qquad\qquad\qquad 1! = 1$

$\frac{6!}{6!} = 1$ but $\frac{6!}{2!} \neq 3!$

$\frac{6!}{2!} = \frac{6 \times 5 \times 4 \times 3 \times 2}{2!} = 6 \times 5 \times 4 \times 3 = 360$

The **NUMBER OF PERMUTATIONS** represents the number of ways in which r items can be selected from n items and arranged in a specific order. It is written as $_nP_r$ and is calculated using the following relationship.

$$_nP_r = \frac{n!}{(n-r)!}$$

NUMBER OF PERMUTATIONS: the number of ways in which r items can be selected from n items and arranged in a specific order

When we are calculating permutations, order counts. For example, 2, 3, 4 and 4, 3, 2 are counted as two different permutations. Calculating the number of permutations is not valid with experiments where replacement is allowed.

Example: How many different ways can a president and a vice president be selected from a math class if 7 students are available?

We know we are looking for the number of permutations, since the positions of president and vice president are not equal.

$$_7P_2 = \frac{7!}{(7-2)!} = \frac{7!}{5!} = \frac{7 \times 6 \times 5}{5!} = 7 \times 6 = 42$$

It is important to recognize that the number of permutations is a special case of the counting principle. Unless specifically asked to use the permutation relationship, use the counting principle to solve problems dealing with the number of permutations. For instance, in this example, we have 7 available students from whom to choose a president. After a president is chosen, we have 6 available students from whom to choose a vice president.

Hence, by using the counting principle, we discover that the ways in which a president and a vice president can be chosen = $7 \times 6 = 42$.

Combinations

NUMBER OF COMBINA-TIONS: the number of ways in which *r* elements can be selected from *n* elements (in no particular order)

When we are dealing with the **NUMBER OF COMBINATIONS**, the order in which elements are selected is not important. For instance, 2, 3, 4 and 4, 2, 3 are considered one combination.

The number of combinations represents the number of ways in which r elements can be selected from n elements (in no particular order). The number of combinations is represented by $_nC_r$ and can be calculated using the following relationship.

$$_nC_r = \frac{n!}{(n-r)!r!}$$

Example: In how many ways can 2 students be selected from a class of 7 students to represent the class?

Since both representatives have the same position, the order is not important, and we are dealing with the number of combinations.

$$_7C_2 = \frac{7!}{(7-2)!2!} = \frac{7 \times 6 \times 5!}{5!2 \times 1} = 21$$

Example: In a club, there are 6 women and 4 men. A committee of 2 women and 1 man is to be selected. How many different committees can be selected?

This problem has a sequence of two events. The first event involves selecting 2 women out of 6 women, and the second event involves selecting 1 man out of 4 men. We use the combination relationship to find the number of ways in events 1 and 2, and we use the counting principle to find the number of ways the sequence can happen.

$$\text{Number of committees} = {}_6C_2 \times {}_4C_1$$
$$\frac{6!}{(6-2)!2!} \times \frac{4!}{(4-1)!1!}$$
$$= \frac{6 \times 5 \times 4!}{4! \times 2 \times 1} \times \frac{4 \times 3!}{3! \times 1}$$
$$= (15) \times (4) = 60$$

SKILL 14.3 **Demonstrating knowledge of graph theory and its real-world applications**

See also Skill 11.2

SKILL 14.4 **Applying knowledge of sequences, series, and iterative processes to solve problems**

Arithmetic Sequences

When given a set of numbers where the common difference between the terms is constant, use the following formula:

$a_n = a_1 + (n - 1)d$

where $a_1 = $ the first term

$n = $ the *nth* term (general term)

$d = $ the common difference between the terms

Example: Find the eighth term of the arithmetic sequence 5, 8, 11, 14, ...

$a_n = a_1 + (n - 1)d$	
$a_1 = 5$	Identify the 1st term.
$d = 8 - 5 = 3$	Find *d*.
$a_n = 5 + (8 - 1)3$	Substitute.
$a_n = 26$	

Example: Given two terms of an arithmetic sequence, find a_1 and d.

$$a_4 = 21 \qquad\qquad a_6 = 32$$
$$a_n = a_1 + (n-1)d \qquad a_4 = 21, n = 4$$
$$21 = a_1 + (4-1)d \qquad a_6 = 32, n = 6$$
$$32 = a_1 + (6-1)d$$

$$21 = a_1 + 3d \qquad\qquad \text{Solve the system of equations.}$$
$$32 = a_1 + 5d$$

$$21 = a_1 + 3d$$
$$-32 = -a_1 - 5d \qquad\qquad \text{Multiply by -1.}$$
$$\overline{-11 = \qquad -2d} \qquad\qquad \text{Add the equations.}$$
$$5.5 = d$$

$$21 = a_1 + 3(5.5) \qquad\qquad \text{Substitute } d = 5.5 \text{ into one of the equations.}$$
$$21 = a_1 + 16.5$$
$$a_1 = 4.5$$

The sequence begins with 4.5 and has a common difference of 5.5 between numbers.

Geometric Sequences

When using geometric sequences, consecutive numbers are compared to find the common ratio.

$$r = \frac{a_{n+1}}{a_n}$$

where r = common ratio

a = the *nth* term

The ratio is then used in the geometric sequence formula:

$$a_n = a_1 r^{n-1}$$

Example: Find the eighth term of the geometric sequence 2, 8, 32, 128 ...

$$r = \frac{a_{n+1}}{a_n} \qquad\qquad \text{Use common ratio formula to find ratio.}$$

$$r = \qquad\qquad \text{Substitute } a_n = 2 a_{n+1} = 8.$$

$$r = 4$$

$$a_n = a_1 \times r^{n-1} \qquad\qquad \text{Use } r = 4 \text{ to solve for the 8th term.}$$

$$a_n = 2 \times 4^{8-1}$$

$$a_n = 32,768$$

COMPETENCY 15
UNDERSTAND MATHEMATICAL PROCESSES AND PERSPECTIVES

SKILL 15.1 **Demonstrating the ability to apply reasoning to make conjectures, justify ideas or arguments, and solve mathematical and nonmathematical problems**

INDUCTIVE THINKING is the process of finding a pattern from a group of examples. That pattern is the conclusion that this set of examples seemed to indicate. It may be a correct conclusion, or it may be an incorrect conclusion because other examples may not follow the predicted pattern.

DEDUCTIVE THINKING is the process of arriving at a conclusion on the basis of other statements that are all known to be true, such as theorems, axioms, or postulates. Conclusions found by deductive thinking based on true statements will always be true.

Examples:

Suppose:

 On Monday Mr. Peterson eats breakfast at McDonald's.
 On Tuesday Mr. Peterson eats breakfast at McDonald's.
 On Wednesday Mr. Peterson eats breakfast at McDonald's.
 On Thursday Mr. Peterson eats breakfast at McDonald's.

Conclusion:

 On Friday Mr. Peterson will eat breakfast at McDonald's again.

This is a conclusion based on inductive reasoning. On the basis of several days' observations, it can be concluded that Mr. Peterson will eat at McDonald's the next day as well. This may or may not be true, but it is a conclusion developed by inductive thinking.

CONDITIONAL STATEMENTS are frequently written in **"if-then"** form. The "if" clause of the conditional is known as the hypothesis, and the "then" clause is called the conclusion. In a proof, the hypothesis is the information that is assumed to be true, while the conclusion is what is to be proven true. A conditional is considered to be of the form:

 If p, then q
 p is the hypothesis. q is the conclusion.

> **INDUCTIVE THINKING:** the process of finding a pattern from a group of examples

> **DEDUCTIVE THINKING:** the process of arriving at a conclusion on the basis of other statements that are all known to be true, such as theorems, axioms, or postulates

> **CONDITIONAL STATEMENTS:** frequently written in "if-then" form

Conditional statements can be diagrammed using a Venn diagram. A diagram can be drawn with one figure inside another figure. The inner portion represents the hypothesis. The outer portion represents the conclusion. If the hypothesis is taken to be true, then you are located inside the inner circle. If you are located in the inner circle then you are also inside the outer circle, so that proves the conclusion is true.

Example: If an angle has a measure of 90°, then it is a right angle.
In this statement "an angle has a measure of 90°" is the hypothesis.
In this statement "it is a right angle" is the conclusion.

Example: If you are in Pittsburgh, then you are in Pennsylvania.
In this statement "you are in Pittsburgh" is the hypothesis.
In this statement "you are in Pennsylvania" is the conclusion.

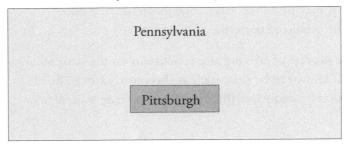

Conditional: If p, then q
   p is the hypothesis. q is the conclusion.

Inverse: If ~ p, then ~ q.
   Negate both the hypothesis (If not p, then not q) and the conclusion from the original conditional.

Converse: If q, then p.
   Reverse the two clauses.
   The original hypothesis becomes the conclusion.
   The original conclusion then becomes the new hypothesis.

Contrapositive: If ~ q, then ~ p.
   Reverse the two clauses. The "If not q, then not p" original hypothesis becomes the conclusion.
   The original conclusion then becomes the new hypothesis.
   THEN negate both the new hypothesis and the new conclusion.

Example: Given the conditional: If an angle has 60°, then it is an acute angle.
Its **inverse**, in the form "If ~ p, then ~ q," would be:

    If an angle doesn't have 60°, then it is not an acute angle.

    Notice that the inverse is not true, even though the conditional statement was true.

Its **converse**, in the form "If q, then p," would be:

    If an angle is an acute angle, then it has 60°.

    Notice that the converse is not true, even though the conditional statement was true.

Its **contrapositive**, in the form "If ~ q, then ~ p," would be:

    If an angle isn't an acute angle, then it doesn't have 60°.

    Notice that the contrapositive is true, assuming original conditional statement was true.

> **Tip:** *If you are asked to pick a statement that is logically equivalent to a given conditional, look for the contrapositive. The inverse and converse are not always logically equivalent to every conditional. The contrapositive is ALWAYS logically equivalent.*

Find the inverse, converse, and contrapositive of the following conditional statement. Also determine if each of the four statements is true or false.

Conditional: If $x = 5$, then $x^2 - 25 = 0$. TRUE

Inverse: If $x \neq 5$, then $x^2 - 25 \neq 0$. FALSE, x could be -5

Converse: If $x^2 - 25 = 0$, then $x = 5$. FALSE, x could be -5

Contrapositive: If $x^2 - 25 \neq 0$, then $x \neq 5$. TRUE

Conditional: If $x = 5$, then $6x = 30$. TRUE

Inverse: If $x \neq 5$, then $6x \neq 30$. TRUE

Converse: If $6x = 30$, then $x = 5$. TRUE

Contrapositive: If $6x \neq 30$, then $x \neq 5$. TRUE

Sometimes, as in this example, all four statements can be logically equivalent; however, the only statement that will always be logically equivalent to the original conditional is the contrapositive.

> **SKILL 15.2** Demonstrating knowledge of the connections among mathematical concepts and procedures and the relationships between mathematics and other fields

Exercise: Interpreting Slope as a Rate of Change

Connection: Social Sciences/Geography

Real-life Application: Slope is often used to describe a constant or average rate of change. These problems usually involve units of measure such as miles per hour or dollars per year.

Problem: The town of Verdant Slopes has been experiencing a boom in population growth. By the year 2000, the population had grown to 45,000, and by 2005, the population had reached 60,000.

Communicating about Algebra:

a. Using the formula for slope as a model, find the average rate of change in population growth, expressing your answer in people per year.

Extension:

b. Using the average rate of change determined in a., predict the population of Verdant Slopes in the year 2010.

Solution:

a. Let t represent the time and p represent population growth. The two observances are represented by (t_1, p_1) and (t_2, p_2).

$\quad$ 1st observance = (t_1, p_1) = (2000, 45,000)

$\quad$ 2nd observance = (t_2, p_2) = (2005, 60,000)

Use the formula for slope to find the average rate of change.

$\quad$ Rate of change $= \dfrac{p_2 - p_1}{t_2 - t_1}$

Substitute values.

$\quad \dfrac{60000 - 45000}{2005 - 2000}$

Simplify.

$\quad \dfrac{15000}{5} = 3{,}000$ people/year

The average rate of change in population growth for Verdant Slopes between the years 2000 and 2005 was 3,000 people/year.

$\quad$ 3,000 people/year $\times$ 5 years = 15,000 people

$\quad$ 60,000 people/year + 15,000 people = 75,000 people

At a continuing average rate of growth of 3,000 people/year, the population of Verdant Slopes could be expected to reach 75,000 by the year 2010.

SKILL Demonstrating the ability to communicate mathematically by
15.3 translating between different representations (e.g., verbal, tabular, graphic, symbolic) **of mathematical concepts and at different levels of formality**

	Word Name	Standard Numeral	Pictorial Model
Decimal	Three-tenths	0.3	
Fraction	One-half	$\frac{1}{2}$	
Integer or Whole Number	Three	3	

The expanded form of a number can be expressed in words or numbers. In words, the expanded form of 4,213 would be 4 thousands and 2 hundreds and 1 ten and 3 ones. In numeric form, it would be $4 \times 1000 + 2 \times 100 + 1 \times 10 + 3 \times 1$.

$$x^3 = x \times x \times x$$
$$x^{-2} = \frac{1}{x^2}$$
$$x^{\frac{1}{2}} = \sqrt{x}$$

Following are different representations of expressions with exponents and square roots:

If we compare numbers in various forms, we see the following:

The integer $400 = \frac{800}{2}$ (fraction)

$= 400.0$ (decimal) $= 100\%$ (percentage of integer) $= 20^2$ (number with exponent)

$= 4 \times 10^2$ (scientific notation), and

$1 > \frac{7}{8} > 0.65 > 60\% > 2^{-2} > 1 \times 10^{-2}$

Scientific Notation

SCIENTIFIC NOTATION is a convenient method for writing very large and very small numbers. It employs two factors. The first factor is a number between 1 and 10. The second factor is a power of 10. This notation is considered "shorthand" for expressing very large numbers (such as the weight of 100 elephants) or very small numbers (such as the weight of an atom in pounds).

SCIENTIFIC NOTATION:
a convenient method for writing very large and very small numbers

Recall that:

10^n	=	Ten multiplied by itself n times
10^n	=	Any nonzero number raised to the zero power is 1
10^1	=	10
10^2	=	$10 \times 10 = 100$
10^3	=	$10 \times 10 \times 10 = 1000$
10^{-1}	=	$\frac{1}{10}$ (deci)
10^{-2}	=	$\frac{1}{100}$ (centi)
10^{-3}	=	$\frac{1}{1000}$ (milli)
10^{-6}	=	$\frac{1}{1,000,000}$ (micro)

KEY EXPONENT RULES: FOR 'a' NONZERO AND 'm' AND 'n' REAL NUMBERS	
Product Rule	$a^m \times a^n = a^{(m+n)}$
Quotient Rule	$\frac{a^m}{a^n} = a^{(m-n)}$
Rule of Negative Exponents	$\frac{a^{-m}}{a^{-n}} = \frac{a^n}{a^m}$

Scientific Notation Format

Convert a number to a form of $b \times 10^n$, where b is a number between -9.9 and 9.9 and n is an integer.

Example: 356.73 can be written in various forms.

$$
\begin{aligned}
356.73 &= 3567.3 \times 10^{-1} \\
&= 35673 \times 10^{-2} \\
&= 35.673 \times 10^{1} \\
&= 3.5673 \times 10^{2} \\
&= 0.35673 \times 10^{3}
\end{aligned}
$$

Only (4) is written in proper scientific notation format. The following examples illustrate how to write a number in scientific notation format:

Example: Write 46,368,000 in scientific notation.

1. Introduce a decimal point and decimal places.
   46,368,000 = 46,368,000.0000

2. Make a mark between the two digits that give a number between -9.9 and 9.9.
   4 ^ 6,368,000.0000

3. Count the number of digit places between the decimal point and the ^ mark. This number is the nth power of ten.
   So, $46,368,000 = 4.6368 \times 10^{7}$.

Example: Write 0.00397 in scientific notation.

1. Decimal point is already in place.

2. Make a mark between the 3 and the 9 to obtain a number between -9.9 and 9.9.

3. Move decimal place to the mark (three hops).
   0.003 ^ 97
   Motion is to the right, so n of 10^n is negative.
   Therefore, $0.00397 = 3.97 \times 10^{-3}$.

Example: Evaluate $\dfrac{3.22 \times 10^{-3} \times 736}{0.00736 \times 32.2 \times 10^{-6}}$.

Since we have a mixture of large and small numbers, convert each number to scientific notation:

$736 = 7.36 \times 10^2$

$0.00736 = 7.36 \times 10^{-3}$

$32.2 \times 10^{-6} = 3.22 \times 10^{-5}$ $\qquad$ thus we have,

$\dfrac{3.22 \times 10^{-3} \times 7.36 \times 10^2}{7.36 \times 10^{-3} \times 3.22 \times 10^{-5}}$

$= \dfrac{3.22 \times 7.36 \times 10^{-3} \times 10^2}{7.36 \times 3.22 \times 10^{-3} \times 10^{-5}}$

$= \dfrac{3.22 \times 7.36}{7.36 \times 3.22} \times \dfrac{10^{-1}}{10^{-8}}$

$= \dfrac{3.22 \times 7.36}{7.36 \times 3.22} \times 10^{-1} \times 10^8$

$= \dfrac{23.6992}{23.6992} \times 10^7$

$= 1 \times 10^7 = 10,000,000$

SKILL 15.4 Selecting appropriate strategies to solve a variety of problems

> *From the very beginning, children need to experience a variety of mathematical situations across all subject areas.*

For very young children, almost any mathematical question posed is a problem to be solved. Too often, the term problem solving is misrepresented as word problems. In fact, any problem presented to a child where they are unaware of the answer is a problem to be solved. From the very beginning, children need to experience a variety of mathematical situations across all subject areas. Exposing children to a variety of contexts in which to solve problems allows the child to develop their own constructs upon which they can build new learning.

Problem Solving in the Classroom

More than one way

> *Problem solving is not about finding the "correct" strategy, but rather about allowing students of varying mathematical skills and abilities to look at the same situation presented and find a way to solve it.*

Problem solving is not about one strategy or right way, but rather about allowing students of varying mathematical skills and abilities to look at the same situation presented and find a way to solve it. In a group of five, it may be reasonable to expect five different methods to reach the solution. Providing students with the means to investigate a problem allows them to be flexible in their approach. Often times, teachers limit the abilities of their students to solve problems by restricting them to one mode of reaching a solution.

Incorporating real-world problems

Problem solving needs to be incorporated in a real way for students to understand, appreciate, and value the process. Using daily activities or problems can help make problem solving a regular part of a child's day. As situations arise in any subject area, it is important for the teacher to incorporate problem-solving activities. Some examples of ways to include realistic problem solving in the classroom are:

- Having the students help with lunch count

- Attendance

- Counting the number of days left in the school year

- Calculating the time left until recess

- Other daily types of activities

Problem solving in all subject areas

Additionally, problem-solving activities should be incorporated into all subject areas.

POSSIBLE PROBLEM-SOLVING ACTIVITIES	
SUBJECT	**POSSIBLE ACTIVITIES**
Science	Children can graph the daily temperatures and make predictions for future temperatures.
Social Studies	Children can gather, tabulate, and calculate the data related to the topic presented (e.g., how many classmates agree that drugs are bad for your body).
Language Arts	Children can solve problems that occur in all types of children's literature.

Charting favorite books, calculating ages of characters in stories, and drawing maps of the setting(s) of books are some beginning ways to connect the two subjects. There are also numerous exciting books written with a mathematical basis that can be used to cover both subjects in a fun manner.

It is important for the teacher to be a role model. Thinking aloud as you come across a problem in the course of the day will help the students begin to realize the necessity and real-world implications of solving problems. Encouraging students to be reflective will also help in building the necessary mathematical language. Also, students can begin to share their ideas and methods with each other, which is an excellent strategy for learning about problem solving.

Four steps for problem solving

Typically, there are four steps to problem solving. Teachers will need to teach each of the steps explicitly and model them regularly. The steps are:

THE FOUR STEPS OF PROBLEM SOLVING	
Understand the Problem	This involves, among other things, understanding all the words in the problem, understanding what you are being asked to find, possibly being able to draw a picture or diagram, knowing if there is enough information, and knowing if there is too much information.
Devise a Plan	This involves being able to choose an appropriate strategy to solve the problem. These strategies include, but are not limited to, guessing and checking, looking for a pattern, using a model, and working backward.
Carry Out the Plan	This is the actual solving of the problem using whatever strategy you have chosen.
Look Back	Included in this step is checking the answer, if possible, to make sure it is correct. This step may be extended to include determining if there might have been an easier way to find the solution.

Nondirect methods for problem solving

The **GUESS-AND-CHECK STRATEGY** calls for making an initial guess of the solution, checking the answer, and using the outcome of this check to inform the next guess. With each successive guess, one should get closer to the correct answer. Constructing a table from the guesses can help organize the data.

> **GUESS-AND-CHECK STRATEGY:** calls for making an initial guess of the solution, checking the answer, and using the outcome of this check to inform the next guess

Example: There are 100 coins in a jar: 10 are dimes, and the rest are pennies and nickels. If there are twice as many pennies as nickels, how many pennies and nickels are in the jar?

Based on the given information, there are 90 total nickels and pennies in the jar (100 coins − 10 dimes = 90 nickels and pennies). Also, there are twice as many pennies as nickels. Using this information, guess results that fulfill the criteria and then adjust the guess in accordance with the result. Continue this iterative process until the correct answer is found: 60 pennies and 30 nickels. The table below illustrates this process.

Number of Pennies	40	80	70	60
Number of Nickels	20	40	35	30
Total Number of Pennies and Nickels	60	120	105	90

Another nondirect approach to problem solving is **WORKING BACKWARD**. If the result of a problem is known (for example, in problems that involve proving a particular result), it is sometimes helpful to begin from the conclusion and attempt to work backwards to a particular known starting point. A slight variation of this approach involves both working backward and working forward until a common point is reached somewhere in the middle. The following example from trigonometry illustrates this process.

> **WORKING BACKWARD:** a nondirect problem-solving method where students begin from the conclusion and attempt to work backwards to a particular known starting point

Example:

Prove that $\sin^2\theta = \frac{1}{2} - \frac{1}{2}\cos^2\theta$.

If the method for proving this result is not clear, one approach is to work backward and forward simultaneously. The following two-column approach organizes the process. Judging from the form of the result, it is apparent that the Pythagorean identity is a potential starting point.

$\sin^2\theta + \cos^2\theta = 1$ $\qquad\qquad$ $\sin^2\theta = \frac{1}{2} - \frac{1}{2}\cos^2\theta$

$\sin^2\theta = 1 - \cos^2\theta$ $\qquad\qquad$ $\sin^2\theta = \frac{1}{2} - \frac{1}{2}(2\cos^2\theta - 1)$

$\qquad\qquad\qquad\qquad\qquad$ $\sin^2\theta = \frac{1}{2} - \cos^2\theta + \frac{1}{2}$

$\qquad\qquad\qquad\qquad\qquad$ $\sin^2\theta = 1 - \cos^2\theta$

Thus, a proof is apparent based on the combination of the reasoning in these two columns.

Selection of an appropriate problem-solving strategy depends largely on the type of problem being solved and the particular area of mathematics with which the problem deals. For instance, problems that involve proving a specific result often require different approaches than do problems that involve finding a numerical result.

Estimation as a problem-solving strategy

In order to estimate measurements, it is helpful to have a familiar reference with a known measurement. For instance, you can use the knowledge that a dollar bill is about six inches long or that a nickel weighs about 5 grams to make estimates of weight and length without actually measuring with a ruler or a balance.

Some common equivalents include:

ITEM	APPROXIMATELY EQUAL TO	
	Metric	Customary
large paper clip	1 gram	0.1 ounce
capacity of sports bottle	1 liter	1 quart
average sized adult	75 kilograms	170 pounds
length of an office desk	1 meter	1 yard
math textbook	1 kilogram	2 pounds
length of dollar bill	15 centimeters	6 inches
thickness of a dime	1 millimeter	0.1 inches
area of football field		6,400 sq. yd
temperature of boiling water	100°C	212°F
temperature of ice	0°C	32°F
1 cup of liquid	240 mL	8 fl oz
1 teaspoon	5 ml	

Example: Estimate the measurement of the following items:

The length of an adult cow = ____3____ meters

The thickness of a compact disc = ____2____ millimeters

Your height = ____1.5____ meters

The length of your nose = ____4____ centimeters

The weight of your math textbook = ____1____ kilogram

The weight of an automobile = ____1,000____ kilogram

The weight of an aspirin = ____1____ gram

Depending on the degree of accuracy needed, an object may be measured to different units.

For example, a pencil may be 6 inches to the nearest inch, or $6\frac{3}{8}$ inches to the nearest eighth of an inch. Similarly, it might be 15 cm to the nearest cm or 154 mm to the nearest mm.

Estimation and approximation may be used to check the reasonableness of answers.

Example: Estimate the answer.

$$\frac{58 \times 810}{1989}$$

58 becomes 60, 810 becomes 800, and 1989 becomes 2000.

$$\frac{60 \times 800}{2000} = 24$$

An estimate may sometimes be all that is needed to solve a word problem.

Example: Janet goes into a store to purchase a CD on sale for $13.95. While shopping, she sees two pairs of shoes, prices $19.95 and $14.50. She only has $50. Can she purchase everything, assuming no sales tax?

Solve by rounding:

$19.95 \rightarrow$ $20.00
$14.50 \rightarrow$ $15.00
$13.95 \rightarrow$ $14.00
$49.00   Yes, she can purchase the CD and the shoes.

Solving number problems

Rational numbers include integers, fractions and mixed numbers, and terminating and repeating decimals. Every rational number can be expressed as a repeating or terminating decimal and can be shown on a number line.

Proportions can be used to solve word problems whenever relationships are compared. Some situations include scale drawings and maps, similar polygons, speed, time and distance, cost, and comparison shopping.

Example: Which is the better buy, 6 items for $1.29 or 8 items for $1.69?
Find the unit price.

$6x = 1.29$ $8x = 1.69$
$x = 0.215$ $x = 0.21125$

Thus, 8 items for $1.69 is the better buy.

Example: A car travels 125 miles in 2.5 hours. How far will it go in 6 hours?

Write a proportion comparing the distance and time.

Let x represent distance in miles. Then,

$\frac{125}{2.5} = \frac{x}{6}$	Set up the proportion.
$2.5x = 6 \times 125$	Cross-multiply.
$2.5x = 750$	Simplify.
$2.5x = \frac{750}{2.5}$	Divide both sides of the equation by 2.5
$2.5x = 750$ miles	Simplify.

Example: The scale on a map is one inch = 6 miles. What is the actual distance between two cities if they are 2 inches apart on the map?

Write a proportion comparing the scale to the actual distance.

Scale		Actual
x	$=$	1×6
x	$=$	6
$2x$	$=$	12

Thus, the actual distance between the cities is twelve miles.

Word problems involving percentages can be solved by writing the problem as an equation, then solving the equation. Keep in mind that *of* means multiplication and *is* means equals.

See also Skills 10.2 and 12.5

> *Word problems involving percentages can be solved by writing the problem as an equation, then solving the equation.*

SKILL 15.5 Demonstrating knowledge of the history of mathematics and the interaction between different cultures and mathematics

Early mathematicians

Pythagoras (born in 580 BCE) was a mathematician and physician who wrote the significant piece on the principle of the "Golden Mean," Euclid (born in 300 BCE) is considered the father of geometry; Archimedes (born in 287 BCE) made the first real progress on the estimation of π, and Apollonius and Ptolemy (85 CE) also made significant contributions to the development of mathematics.

During the 5th century CE in China, Tsu Ch'ung-Chih estimated π, as Archimedes did, using circumscribed and inscribed polygons. In India, Brahmagupta made valuable contributions to geometry during the 6th century CE, and Arabs played an important role in preserving the work of the Greeks through translations and expansion of that knowledge.

Development of Mathematics

Archeological digs in Babylonia and Greece have uncovered counting boards. These include the Chinese abacus, whose current form dates from approximately 1200 CE. Prior to the development of the concept of zero, a counting board or abacus was the common method used for all types of calculations. In fact, the abacus is still taught in Asian schools and is used by some Asian proprietors. Blind children learn to use the abacus, which is an equivalent method of learning basic mathematical calculations.

Islamic culture from the 6th through 12th centuries drew knowledge from areas ranging from Africa and Spain to India. Al-Khowarizmi introduced Hindu numerals to the West for the first time during the 9th century, and wrote a significant article on algebra. At the beginning of the 15th century, notable Muslim mathematician Al-Kashi wrote the book *Key to Arithmetic*, in which he used decimals instead of fractions. Fibonacci made important contributions to algebra and geometry during the 13th century CE.

In the Americas, the Mayan civilization contributed significantly with regard to calendars and mathematics. The Mayan calendars were the most accurate on the planet until the sixteenth century CE. The Mayas also invented the idea of zero, something that no other culture, aside from India, had considered.

It was after the Renaissance era, during the 17th century, however, that some of the most significant contributions were made. Newton, along with Leibniz, developed calculus, and Descartes formulated analytical geometry. Maria Gaetana Agnesi is known for the "Witch of Agnesi": the modern version of the curve called the Cartesian equation.

During this period, John Napier developed a theory of logarithms and Pascal and Fermat broadened knowledge of number theory. The 18th century saw contributions by Gauss in arithmetic, algebra, and number theory. Gauss insisted that every area of mathematics must apply rigorous proofs, and this influenced Cauchy in the 19th century to develop a more comprehensible theory of limits, the definite integral, continuity and the derivative. David Hilbert laid the foundations of geometry in the 19th century.

This mix of cultures, gender, and ethnicities have culminated in substantial developments in many areas of mathematics, including algebra, our current numbering system, geometry, trigonometry, calculus, statistics, and discrete mathematics.

Recent History of Mathematics

A number of present-day individuals have also made significant contributions to the field of mathematics. David Blackwell was the first African-American to be named to the National Academy of Sciences, and he won the von Neumann Theory Prize in 1979 for his contributions to the field of statistics. African-American Etta Falconer (1933–2002) received numerous awards and recognitions during her lifetime for her contributions to furthering the opportunities for minorities and women in the fields of mathematics and science. Margaret Wright is well-known in such fields as linear algebra and numerical and scientific computing. She has received several awards recognizing her contributions to mathematics. Sijue Wu received two awards in 2001 for her part in finding a solution to a long-standing problem in the water-wave equation.

SKILL 15.6 Demonstrating knowledge of methods for integrating technological and nontechnological tools in mathematics

The use of supplementary materials in the classroom can greatly enhance the learning experience by stimulating student interest and satisfying different learning styles. Manipulatives, models, and technology are examples of tools available to teachers.

MANIPULATIVES: materials that students can physically handle and move

MANIPULATIVES are materials that students can physically handle and move. They allow students to understand mathematical concepts by allowing them to see concrete examples of abstract processes. Manipulatives are attractive to students because they appeal to the visual and tactile senses. Available for all levels of math, manipulatives are useful tools for reinforcing operations and concepts.

Models are another means of representing mathematical concepts by relating the concepts to real-world situations. Teachers must choose wisely when devising and selecting models. For example, a building with floors above and below ground is a good model for introducing the concept of negative numbers. It would be difficult, however, to use the building model in teaching subtraction of negative numbers.

Finally, there are many forms of technology available to math teachers. For example, students can test their understanding of math concepts by working on skill-specific computer programs and Web sites. Math games on the computer or the smart board can supplement and reinforce learning. Graphing calculators can help students visualize the graphs of functions. Teachers can also enhance their lectures and classroom presentations by creating multimedia presentations.

Manipulatives

Example: Using tiles to demonstrate both geometric ideas and number theory.

Give each group of students 12 tiles and instruct them to build rectangles. Students draw their rectangles on paper.

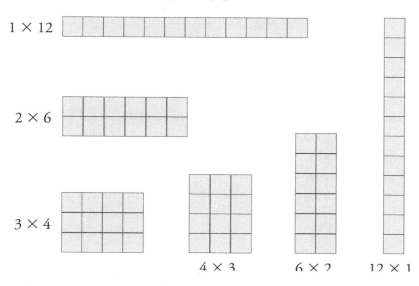

Encourage students to describe their reactions. Extend to 16 tiles. Ask students to form additional problems.

Technology

There are many forms of technology available to math teachers. Calculators are important tools. They should be encouraged in the classroom and at home. They do not replace basic knowledge, but they can relieve the tedium of mathematical computations, allowing students to explore mathematical directions that are more challenging. Even so, at times, it may be appropriate to have students complete the calculations themselves and then check it with a calculator. Some special needs students rely on calculators to complete computation, and all students are allowed to use calculators on certain standardized tests. An important thing to remember is that students will be able to use calculators more intelligently if they are taught how to do so. Students always need to check their work by estimating. The goal of mathematics is to prepare the child to survive in the real world.

Computers are now commonplace, and some schools can now afford DVD players to bring alive the content of a reference book in text, motion, and sound. Textbook publishers often provide films, recordings, and software to accompany the text, as well as maps, graphics, and colorful posters to help students visualize what is being taught. Teachers can usually scan the educational publishers' brochures that arrive at their principal's or department head's office on a frequent basis. Another way to stay current in the field is by attending workshops or conferences. Teachers will be enthusiastically welcomed on those occasions when educational publishers are asked to display their latest productions and revised editions.

In addition, yesterday's libraries are today's media centers. Teachers can usually have projectors delivered to the classroom to project print or images (including student work) onto a screen for classroom viewing. Some teachers have chosen to replace chalkboards with projectors that reproduce the print or images on transparencies, which the teacher can write on during a presentation or have machine-printed in advance. In either case, the transparency can easily be stored for later use. In an art or photography class, or any class in which it is helpful to display visual materials, slides can easily be projected onto a wall or a screen. Cameras are inexpensive enough to enable students to photograph and display their own work, as well as keep a record of their achievements in teacher files or student portfolios.

SKILL 15.7 Applying mathematical language to solve problems and communicate understanding

Math is the language of symbols. Math helps us describe both similarities and differences and also helps us think and solve practical problems. The language of math helps us understand the relationship and patterns of numbers and the way they change. Through math language the individual makes sense out of numbers, measurement, and geometrical experiences in the environment.

A popular theory of math learning is *constructivism*. Constructivism argues that prior knowledge greatly influences the learning of math and learning is cumulative and vertically structured. Thus, it is important for teachers to recognize the knowledge and ideas about a subject that students already possess. Instruction must build on the innate knowledge of students and address any common misconceptions. Teachers can gain insight into the prior knowledge of students by beginning each lesson with open questions that allow students to share their thoughts and ideas on the subject or topic.

There are levels of experience with language and concepts. Math learning progresses in a spiral nature, with early learning experiences being merely an introduction and later learning experiences building on earlier ones. As the individual progresses through the spiral, later experiences become more and more abstract and difficult. Exposing the student from an early age to math language in everyday experiences helps them develop expertise in later math concepts.

Mathematical language skills include the abilities to read with comprehension, to express mathematical thoughts clearly, to reason logically, and to recognize and employ common patterns of mathematical thought. Mathematical results are expressed in a foreign language—a language that, like other languages, has its own grammar, syntax, vocabulary, word order, synonyms, negations, conventions, abbreviations, sentence structure, and paragraph structure. Just as one must be proficient in language to understand what is read, so must one be proficient in mathematical language to understand math concepts.

Recognition and understanding of the relationships between concepts and topics is of great value in mathematical problem solving and the explanation of more complex processes.

For instance, multiplication is simply repeated addition. This relationship explains the concept of variable addition. We can show that the expression $4x + 3x = 7x$ is true by rewriting 4 times x and 3 times x as repeated addition, yielding the expression $(x + x + x + x) + (x + x + x)$. Thus, because of the relationship between multiplication and addition, variable addition is accomplished by coefficient addition.

In solving a problem using a new concept, the student may be led to draw pictures representing the problem situation. This will assist the student in visualizing the problem solving process.

Once the concept is grasped the student should be encouraged to move to numeric representation of the concept. At this stage, there is still dependence on graphic representation combined with numeric representation. There should be a gradual move toward using only numbers to describe and solve the problem.

The next step is to represent mathematical concepts using numbers and symbols. The graphic part of the representation should at this time be dropped from the solution process. The concept should become so ingrained that the student will understand symbolic representation.

The highest level of mathematical language is verbal representation. Once the concept is thoroughly internalized, the student should be able to explain the concept and solution verbally. This can be done orally or in written form. Once the student can accurately write the solution, he or she has fully internalized the concept.

Mathematical problem solving can be approached by using graphic representation, numeric solutions, symbols, and verbal explanations.
Each of these methods is important in helping the student understand math concepts.

DOMAIN IV
HEALTH/FITNESS AND FINE ARTS

PERSONALIZED STUDY PLAN

KNOWN MATERIAL/ SKIP IT

PAGE	COMPETENCY AND SKILL	
243	**16: Understand fundamental health and physical education concepts**	☐
	16.1: Demonstrating knowledge of personal and community health promotion, disease prevention and safety, and proper nutritional choices	☐
	16.2: Applying knowledge of strategies for reducing and preventing accidents; tobacco, alcohol, and other drug use; and high-risk situations and relationships	☐
	16.3: Applying knowledge of movement concepts and principles in acquiring and developing motor skills	☐
	16.4: Applying knowledge of developmental learning experiences that help children achieve a health-enhancing level of physical fitness	☐
255	**17: Understand fundamental visual and performing arts concepts**	☐
	17.1: Demonstrating knowledge of the basic structural elements, principles, and vocabulary of the visual and performing arts	☐
	17.2: Demonstrating knowledge of the application of the basic elements of the visual and performing arts to the performance and creation of works of art	☐
	17.3: Applying knowledge of strategies for nurturing artistic modes of expression and the characteristics of children's developmental stages in the visual and performing arts	☐
	17.4: Recognizing the role of visual and performing arts in culture	☐

COMPETENCY 16
UNDERSTAND FUNDAMENTAL HEALTH AND PHYSICAL EDUCATION CONCEPTS

SKILL 16.1 Demonstrating knowledge of personal and community health promotion, disease prevention and safety, and proper nutritional choices

Positive health choices and behavior must be supported by proper education, which includes fitness and health education. Obviously, without an understanding of the various choices available, and the ramifications of each choice, it is difficult to make a wise decision regarding personal and family health choices and behavior. This education should include an introduction to research skills, so that individuals have the freedom to inform themselves of pertinent information when new situations arise that call for them to make health decisions. Good venues for these personal research habits include the Internet, local libraries, and fitness and health-care professionals in the community.

Positive health choices and behavior will also require a layer of economic support, as healthy lifestyle choices will sometimes be more expensive than the less healthy alternative. It is also important for the environment to be conducive to positive choices and behavior regarding health. For example, the availability of resources (both educational and practical) and facilities (medical and fitness) in proximity to the individual can positively impact the decision-making process.

There is an important relationship to consider between physical activity and the development of personal identity and emotional and mental well-being, most notably the impact of positive body image and self-concept. Instructors can help children develop positive body image and self-concept by creating opportunities for the children to experience successes in physical activities and to develop a comfort level with their bodies. This is an important contributor to their personal and physical confidence.

Social Health

For most people, the development of social roles and appropriate social behaviors occurs during childhood. Physical play between parents and children, as well as between siblings and peers, serves as a strong regulator in the developmental process. Chasing games, roughhousing, wrestling, or practicing sport skills such as jumping, throwing, catching, and striking, are some examples of childhood play. These activities may be competitive or noncompetitive and are important for promoting social and moral development of both boys and girls. Unfortunately, fathers will often engage in this sort of activity more with their sons than their daughters. Regardless of the sex of the child, both boys and girls enjoy these types of activities.

Physical play during infancy and early childhood is central to the development of social and emotional competence. Research shows that children who engage in play that is more physical with their parents, particularly with parents who are sensitive and responsive to the child, exhibited greater enjoyment during the play sessions and were more popular with their peers. Likewise, these early interactions with parents, siblings, and peers are important in helping children become more aware of their emotions and to learn to monitor and regulate their own emotional responses. Children learn quickly through watching the responses of their parents which behaviors make their parents smile and laugh and which behaviors cause their parents to frown and disengage from the activity.

If children want the fun to continue, they engage in the behaviors that please others. As children near adolescence, they learn through rough-and-tumble play that there are limits to how far they can go before hurting someone (physically or emotionally), which results in termination of the activity or later rejection of the child by peers. These early interactions with parents and siblings are important in helping children learn appropriate behavior in the social situations of sport and physical activity.

SOCIAL COMPETENCE: ability to get along with and acceptance by peers, family members, teachers, and coaches

Children learn to assess their **SOCIAL COMPETENCE** in sport through the feedback received from parents and coaches. Initially, authority figures teach children, "You can't do that because I said so." As children approach school age, parents begin the process of explaining why a behavior is right or wrong because children continuously ask, "Why?"

Educators have suggested that one of the biggest barriers to success in the classroom today is low self-esteem.

Similarly, when children engage in sports, they learn about taking turns with their teammates, sharing playing time, and valuing rules. They understand that rules are important for everyone and without these regulations, the game would become unfair. The learning of social competence is continuous as we expand our social arena and learn about different cultures. A constant in the learning process is the role of feedback as we assess the responses of others to our behaviors and comments.

SELF-ESTEEM: how we judge our worth and indicates the extent to which an individual believes he or she is capable, significant, successful, and worthy

In addition to the development of social competence, sport participation can help youth develop other forms of self-competence. Most important among these self-competencies is **SELF-ESTEEM.** Educators have suggested that one of the biggest barriers to success in the classroom today is low self-esteem.

Children develop self-esteem by evaluating abilities and by evaluating the responses of others. Children actively observe parents' and coaches' responses to their performances, looking for signs of approval or disapproval of their behavior. Children often interpret feedback and criticism as either a negative or a positive response to the behavior. In sports, research shows that the coach is a critical source of information that influences the self-esteem of children.

Little League baseball players whose coaches use a **POSITIVE APPROACH** to coaching (e.g., more frequent encouragement, positive reinforcement for effort and corrective, instructional feedback), had significantly higher self-esteem ratings over the course of a season than children whose coaches used these techniques less frequently. The most compelling evidence supporting the importance of coaches' feedback was found for those children who started the season with the lowest self-esteem ratings and increased considerably their self-assessment and self-worth. In addition to evaluating themselves more positively, low self-esteem children evaluated their coaches more positively than did children with higher self-esteem who played for coaches who used the positive approach. Moreover, studies show that 95 percent of children who played for coaches trained to use the positive approach signed up to play baseball the next year, compared with 75 percent of the youth who played for untrained adult coaches.

> **POSITIVE APPROACH:** more frequent encouragement, positive reinforcement for effort and corrective, instructional feedback

We cannot overlook the importance of enhanced self-esteem on future participation. A major part of the development of high self-esteem is the pride and joy that children experience as their physical skills improve. Children will feel good about themselves as long as their skills are improving. If children feel that their performance during a game or practice is not as good as that of others, or as good as they think mom and dad would want, they often experience shame and disappointment.

Some children will view mistakes made during a game as a failure and will look for ways to avoid participating in the task if they receive no encouragement to continue. At this point, it is critical that adults (e.g., parents and coaches) intervene to help children to interpret the mistake or "failure." We must teach children that a mistake is not synonymous with failure. Rather, a mistake shows us that we need a new strategy, more practice, and/or greater effort to succeed at the task.

Physical education activities can promote positive social behaviors and traits in a number of different ways. Instructors can foster improved relations with adults and peers by making students active partners in the learning process and delegating responsibilities within the class environment to students. Giving students leadership positions (e.g., team captain) can give them a heightened understanding of the responsibilities and challenges facing educators.

> *Physical education activities can promote positive social behaviors and traits in a number of different ways.*

Team-based physical activities such as team sports promote collaboration and cooperation. In such activities, students learn to work together, both pooling their talents and minimizing the weaknesses of different team members in order to achieve a common goal. The experience of functioning as a team can be very productive for development of loyalty between children, and seeing their peers in stressful situations that they can relate to can promote a more compassionate and considerate attitude among students. Similarly, the need to maximize the strengths of each student on a team (who can complement each other and compensate for weaknesses) is a powerful lesson about valuing and respecting diversity and individual differences. Varying students between leading and following positions in a team hierarchy are good ways to help students gain a comfort level being both followers and leaders.

Fair play, teamwork, and sportsmanship are all values that stem from proper practice of the spirit of physical education classes.

Fairness is another trait that physical activities, especially rules-based sports, can foster and strengthen. Children are by nature very rules-oriented and have a keen sense of what they believe is and isn't fair. Fair play, teamwork, and sportsmanship are all values that stem from proper practice of the spirit of physical education classes. Of course, a pleasurable physical education experience goes a long way toward promoting an understanding of the innate value of physical activity throughout the life cycle.

Finally, communication is another skill that improves enormously through participation in sports and games. Students will come to understand that skillful communication can contribute to a better all-around outcome, whether it be winning the game or successfully completing a team project. They will see that effective communication helps to develop and maintain healthy personal relationships, organize and convey information, and reduce or avoid conflict.

Group Processes and Problem Solving

Physical fitness activities incorporate group processes, group dynamics, and a wide range of cooperation and competition.

Physical fitness activities incorporate group processes, group dynamics, and a wide range of cooperation and competition. Ranging from team sports (which are both competitive and cooperative in nature) to individual competitive sports (like racing), to cooperative team activities without a winner and loser (like a gymnastics team working together to create a human pyramid), there is a great deal of room for the development of mutual respect and support among the students, safe cooperative participation, and analytical, problem solving, teamwork, and leadership skills.

Teamwork situations are beneficial to students because they create opportunities for them to see classmates with whom they might not generally socialize and with whom they may not even get along, in a new light. It also creates opportunities for students to develop reliance on each other and practice interdependence.

Cooperation and competition can also offer opportunities for children to practice group work. These situations provide good opportunities to practice analytical thinking and problem solving in a practical setting.

The social skills and values gained from participation in physical activities are:

- The ability to make adjustments to both self and others by an integration of the individual to society and the environment

- The ability to make judgments in a group situation

- Learning to communicate with others and be cooperative

- The development of the social phases of personality, attitudes, and values in order to become a functioning member of society

- The development of a sense of belonging and acceptance by society

- The development of positive personality traits

- Learning for constructive use of leisure time

- A development of attitude that reflects good moral character

- Respect of school rules and property

The relative levels of pollution in a community can significantly affect family health. For example, proximity to industrial areas, which may be releasing carcinogenic emissions, can be dangerous. Similarly, a smoking habit within the home environment is highly detrimental, as it will negatively affect the respiratory and circulatory systems of all members of the household.

Pollution levels in the community can also affect public health by exposing the community as a whole to toxic and carcinogenic chemicals that negatively affect systems including (but not limited to) the circulatory and respiratory systems.

Healthy environmental conditions involve several areas of concern. These include:

- Drinking water

- Food safety

- Hazardous waste

- Housing

- Indoor air quality

- Land use and community design

- Occupational health

- Outdoor air quality

- Recreational water

- Solid waste and wastewater

- Vector-borne disease

It is the teacher's duty to be aware of these conditions, taking into account their impact on families and children. It is also important for a teacher to do all they can to improve environmental factors as much as is in their power to do so.

Studies have shown that low-income, racial, and ethnic minority individuals are much more likely to be exposed to toxic and hazardous wastes than affluent and white individuals. (Evans G, Kantrowitz E. *Socioeconomic Status and Health: The Potential Role of Environmental Risk Exposure. Annual Review of Public Health*, 2002; 23:303-331)

Though the teacher cannot effectively affect the socioeconomic, racial, or ethnic status of a student, it is important that he or she be aware of the possible impact of such factors on the student's health and the impact that would have on educational opportunities.

National standards relative to overcrowding in housing is considering any home where there is more than one person to a room as being overcrowded. For example, the common three-bedroom home with a living room, kitchen, and dining area, plus two bathrooms, can support only five family members without considered being overcrowded (seven if you count the bathrooms).

Lead is a very dangerous threat to the young school-aged child. The Centers for Disease Control and Prevention estimates that an estimated 4.1 million homes in the United States (25% of U.S. homes with children aged $<$ 6 years) have a lead-based paint hazard and that racial minority and poor children are disproportionately affected. ("Interpreting and Managing Blood Lead Levels $<$ 10 µg/dL in Children and Reducing Childhood Exposures to Lead," Centers for Disease Control and Prevention. Accessed: July, 2002. http://www.cdc.gov/mmwr/preview/mmwrhtml/rr5608a1.htm#top)

SKILL 16.2 Applying knowledge of strategies for reducing and preventing accidents; tobacco, alcohol, and other drug use; and high-risk situations and relationships

Important contemporary health-related issues that significantly affect modern society include HIV, teenage pregnancy, suicide, and substance abuse.

HIV

The human immunodefiency virus (HIV) can devastate both individuals and society. Advances in treatment options, namely pharmaceuticals, have greatly improved the prospects of those who contract the disease. However, due to the expense of treatment, many people, especially those in underdeveloped countries, do not have access to treatment. Thus, prevention is still of utmost importance.

HIV is a retrovirus that attacks the human immune system and causes AIDS (acquired immunodefiency syndrome). AIDS is a failure of the immune system that allows normally benign viruses and bacteria to infect the body, causing life-threatening conditions.

Humans acquire HIV through contact with bodily fluids of infected individuals. For example, transfer of blood, semen, vaginal fluid, and breast milk can cause HIV infection. The best means of prevention of HIV is sexual abstinence outside of marriage, practicing safe sex, and avoiding the use of injected drugs.

Because HIV is a sexually transmitted disease, it disproportionally affects people in the prime of their lives. Infected persons are often heads of households and families and key economic producers. Thus, the impact of HIV on society is particularly damaging. Not only are the costs of treatment great, but families often lose their mothers and fathers and communities lose their best producers and leaders. Society must find ways to fill these gaping voids.

Suicide

Suicide is a particularly troubling problem. Adolescent suicide is always devastating to families and communities. The main cause of adolescent suicide is mental disease, such as depression or anxiety. When untreated, such disorders can cause intense feelings of hopelessness and despair that can lead to suicide attempts. Suicides can tear families apart, often leaving behind feelings of guilt among friends and family members. The best means of suicide prevention is close monitoring of changing behaviors in adolescents. Parents, friends, and family members should watch for and never ignore signs of depression, withdrawal from friends and activities, talk of suicide, and signs of despair and hopelessness. Proper counseling, medication, and care from mental health professionals can often prevent suicide.

Teen Pregnancy

Teen pregnancy hurts the mothers, children, and society, by extension. Pregnancy disrupts the life of adolescent girls, often preventing them from finishing school, completing higher education, and finding quality employment. In addition, teenage girls are not emotionally or financially ready to care for children. Thus, the children of teen pregnancies may have a difficult start in life. Teen pregnancy also affects society because teenage parents often require government assistance and children of teen pregnancies often do not receive appropriate care and parenting. The best means of preventing teenage pregnancy is education about the importance of abstinence and contraception.

Substance Abuse

Substance abuse can lead to adverse behaviors and increased risk of injury and disease. Any substance affecting the normal functions of the body, illegal or not, is potentially dangerous and students and athletes should avoid them completely. Factors contributing to substance abuse include peer pressure, parental substance abuse, physical or psychological abuse, mental illness, and physical disability. Education, vigilance, and parental oversight are the best strategies for the prevention of substance abuse.

FOUR COMMONLY ABUSED SUBSTANCES	
Alcohol	This is a legal substance for adults but is very commonly abused. Moderate to excessive consumption can lead to an increased risk of cardiovascular disease, nutritional deficiencies, and dehydration. Alcohol also causes ill effects on various aspects of performance such as reaction time, coordination, accuracy, balance, and strength.
Nicotine	Another legal but often abused substance that can increase the risk of cardiovascular disease, pulmonary disease, and cancers of the mouth. Nicotine consumption through smoking severely hinders athletic performance by compromising lung function. Smoking especially affects performance in endurance activities.
Marijuana	This is the most commonly abused illegal substance. Adverse effects include a loss of focus and motivation, decreased coordination, and lack of concentration.
Cocaine	Another illegal and somewhat commonly abused substance. Effects include increased alertness and excitability. This drug can give the user a sense of overconfidence and invincibility, leading to a false sense of one's ability to perform certain activities. A high heart rate is associated with the use of cocaine, leading to an increased risk of heart attack, stroke, potentially deadly arrhythmias, and seizures.

Substance abuse—treatment and alternatives

Alternatives to substance use and abuse include regular participation in stress-relieving activities like meditation, exercise, and therapy, all of which can have a relaxing effect (a healthy habit is, for example, to train oneself to substitute exercise for a substance abuse problem). More important, the acquisition of longer-term coping strategies (for example, self-empowerment via practice of problem-solving techniques) is key to maintaining a commitment to alternatives to substance use and abuse.

Aspects of substance abuse treatment that we must consider include:

- the processes of physical and psychological withdrawal from the addictive substance

- acquisition of coping strategies and replacement techniques to fill the void left by the addictive substance

- limiting access to the addictive substance, acquiring self-control strategies

Withdrawal from an addictive substance has both psychological and physical symptoms. The psychological symptoms include depression, anxiety, and strong cravings for the substance. Physical withdrawal symptoms stem from the body, adapted to a steady intake of the addictive substance, adapting to accommodate the no-longer available substance. Depending on the substance, medical intervention may be necessary.

Coping strategies and replacement techniques, as discussed earlier, center around providing the individual with an effective alternative to the addictive substance as a solution to the situations that they would feel necessitate the substance.

Limiting access to the addictive substance (opportunities for use) is important, because the symptoms of withdrawal and the experiences associated with the substance can provide a strong impetus to return to using it. Finally, recovering addicts should learn strategies of self-control and self-discipline to help them stay off of the addictive substance.

SKILL 16.3 Applying knowledge of movement concepts and principles in acquiring and developing motor skills

The development of motor skills in children is a sequential process. We can classify motor skill competency into stages of development by observing children practicing physical skills. The sequence of development begins with simple reflexes and progresses to the learning of postural elements, locomotor skills, and, finally, fine motor skills. The stages of development consider both innate and learned behaviors.

STAGES OF MOTOR LEARNING SKILLS	
Stage 1	Children progress from simple reflexes to basic movements such as sitting, crawling, creeping, standing, and walking.
Stage 2	Children learn more complex motor patterns including running, climbing, jumping, balancing, catching, and throwing.
Stage 3	During late childhood, children learn more specific movement skills. In addition, the basic motor patterns learned in Stage 2 become more fluid and automatic.
Stage 4	During adolescence, children continue to develop general and specific motor skills and master specialized movements. At this point, factors including practice, motivation, and talent begin to affect the level of further development.

Sequential development for locomotor skill acquisition	crawl, creep, walk, run, jump, hop, gallop, slide, leap, skip, step-hop
Sequential development for nonlocomotor skill acquisition	stretch, bend, sit, shake, turn, rock and sway, swing, twist, dodge, fall
Sequential development for manipulative skill acquisition	striking, throwing, kicking, ball rolling, volleying, bouncing, catching, trapping

SKILL 16.4 **Applying knowledge of developmental learning experiences that help children achieve a health-enhancing level of physical fitness**

Instructional Methods for Various Objectives, Situations, and Developmental Levels

The physical educator can select from five basic instructional formats: cognitive structuring, large-group skill instruction, small-group skill instruction, individual skill instruction, and testing.

When utilizing cognitive structuring, the teacher addresses the whole class through lecture, demonstration, or questioning. This method is particularly effective for imparting basic knowledge in a short amount of time. Large-group skill instruction involves all of the students in the class in the related activities. In small-group skill instruction (also called stations), the instructor divides students into groups, each of which works on a different skill or activity. A significant advantage of this format is the ability to maximize instruction in situations where equipment is limited. In addition, small-group activities increase the amount of practice time for each student. In the individual skill instruction format, the instructor asks each student to select a skill to work on. The students decide themselves when they are ready to progress to the next skill. When ready, students simply put away their equipment, gather equipment for the next selected skill, and work at their own pace on the next skill. This self-paced arrangement provides the greatest opportunity for skill mastery. The final instructional format is testing. During testing, the instructor assesses the students utilizing a written or skills test.

Finally, the physical educator may choose to supplement the teaching with the use of instructional devices. Examples of instructional devices include basic physical education equipment such as cones or targets, but may also include various types of technology such as pedometers, DVDs, computer programs, or interactive whiteboards.

Facilitating psychomotor learning

Teaching methods to facilitate psychomotor learning include:

1. Task/reciprocal: The instructor integrates task learning into the learning setting by utilizing stations.

2. Command/direct: Task instruction is teacher-centered. The teacher clearly explains the goals, explains and demonstrates the skills, allocates time for practice, and frequently monitors student progress.

3. Contingency/contract: A task style of instruction that rewards completion of tasks.

Techniques that facilitate psychomotor learning include:

1. Reflex movements: Activities that create an automatic response to stimuli. Responses include flexing, extending, stretching, and postural adjustment.

2. Basic fundamental locomotor movements: Activities that utilize instinctive patterns of movement established by combining reflex movements

3. Perceptual abilities: Activities that involve interpreting auditory, visual, and tactile stimuli in order to coordinate adjustments

4. Physical abilities: Activities to develop physical characteristics of fitness, providing students with the stamina necessary for highly advanced, skilled movement

5. **Skilled movements:** Activities that involve instinctive, effective performance of complex movement, including vertical and horizontal components

6. **Nondiscursive communication:** Activities requiring expression as part of the movement

Facilitating cognitive learning

Teaching methods that facilitate cognitive learning include:

1. **Problem solving:** The instructor presents the initial task and students come to an acceptable solution in unique and divergent ways.

2. **Conceptual theory:** The instructor's focus is on acquisition of knowledge.

3. **Guided inquiry:** Stages of instructions strategically guide students through a sequence of experiences.

> *Initially, performing skills will be variable, inconsistent, error-prone, "off-time," and awkward. Students' focus will be on remembering what to do.*

Initially, performing skills will be variable, inconsistent, error-prone, "off-time," and awkward. Students' focus will be on remembering what to do. Instructors should emphasize clear descriptions of the skill's biomechanics and correct errors in gross movement that affect significant parts of the skill. To make sure students are not overburdened with too much information, they should perform one or two elements at a time. Motivation results from supportive and encouraging comments.

Techniques to facilitate cognitive learning include:

- **Transfer of learning:** Identifying similarities between movements in a skill learned previously and a new skill
- **Planning:** Planning for slightly longer instructions and demonstrations as students memorize cues and skills
- **Using appropriate language:** Using language appropriate for the level of the students
- **Conceptual thinking:** Giving capable students more responsibility for their learning

Aids to facilitate cognitive learning include:

- Frequent assessments of student performance
- Movement activities incorporating principles of biomechanics
- Computers and software
- Recordings of student performance

Facilitating affective development

Teaching methods and techniques that facilitate affective development include:

1. **Fostering a positive learning environment:** Instructors should create a comfortable, positive learning environment by encouraging and praising effort and emphasizing respect for others.

2. **Grouping students appropriately:** Instructors should carefully group students to best achieve equality in ability, age, and personalities.

3. **Ensuring that all students achieve some level of success:** Instructors should design activities that allow students of all ability levels to achieve success and gain confidence.

COMPETENCY 17
UNDERSTAND FUNDAMENTAL VISUAL AND PERFORMING ARTS CONCEPTS

SKILL 17.1 Demonstrating knowledge of the basic structural elements, principles, and vocabulary of the visual and performing arts

Basic Concepts in Visual Arts

Students should have an early introduction to the principles of visual art and should become familiar with the basic level of the following terms:

BASIC ART TERMS	
Abstract	An image that reduces a subject to its essential visual elements, such as lines, shapes, and colors.
Background	Portions or areas of composition that are behind the primary or dominant subject matter or design areas.
Balance	The arrangement of one or more elements in a work of art so that they appear symmetrical or asymmetrical in design and proportion.
Contrast	Juxtaposing one or more elements in opposition, to show their differences.

Continued on next page

Emphasis	Making one or more elements in a work of art stand out in such a way as to appear more important or significant.
Sketch	An image-development strategy; a preliminary drawing.
Texture	The way something feels by representation of the tactile character of surfaces.
Unity	The arrangement of one or more of the elements used to create a coherence of parts and a feeling of completeness or wholeness.

Various Forms of Visual Arts

It is vital that students learn to identify characteristics of visual arts that include materials, techniques, and processes necessary to establish a connection between art and daily life. Early ages should begin to experience art in a variety of forms. It is important to reach many areas at an early age to establish a strong artistic foundation for young students.

Introduction to visual arts

Students should be introduced to the recognition of simple patterns found in the art environment, as well as varied art materials such as clay, paint, crayons, printmaking ink, chalk, and mosaic objects.

Students should be introduced to the recognition of simple patterns found in the art environment, as well as varied art materials such as clay, paint, crayons, printmaking ink, chalk, and mosaic objects. Each of these materials should be introduced and explained for use in daily lessons with young children. More elaborate and involved exposure is appropriate for older elementary students, including the addition of other media such as stone and wood carving, digital photography and video, oil pastels, and stained glass, to name a few.

The major mediums, which are defined by the materials utilized and the activities involved, are:

- Drawing and Painting
- Sculpture
- Printmaking
- Ceramics
- Architecture

- Photography and Filmmaking
- Fiber and Fabric
- Glass
- Jewelry Making and Metal Work

Art Genres by Historical Periods

HISTORICAL PERIODS OF ART AND THEIR DEFINING CHARACTERISTICS	
Ancient Greek Art (circa 800–323 BCE)	Dominant genres from this period were vase paintings, both black-figure and red-figure, and classical sculpture.
Roman Art (circa 480 BCE– 476 CE)	Major genres from the Romans include frescoes (murals done in fresh plaster to affix the paint), classical sculpture, funerary art, state propaganda art, and relief work on cameos.
Middle Ages Art (circa 300–1400 CE)	Significant genres during the Middle Ages include Byzantine mosaics, illuminated manuscripts, ivory relief, altarpieces, cathedral sculpture, and fresco paintings in various styles.
Renaissance Art (1400–1630 CE)	Important genres from the Renaissance included Florentine fresco painting (mostly religious), High Renaissance painting and sculpture, Northern oil painting, Flemish miniature painting, and Northern printmaking.
Baroque Art (1630–1700 CE)	Pivotal genres during the Baroque era include Mannerism, Italian Baroque painting and sculpture, Spanish Baroque, Flemish Baroque, and Dutch portraiture. Genre paintings in still-life and landscape appear prominently in this period.
Eighteenth Century Art (1700–1800 CE)	Predominant genres of the century include Rococo painting, portraiture, social satire, Romantic painting, and Neoclassic painting and sculpture.
Nineteenth Century Art (1800–1900 CE)	Important genres include Romantic painting, academic painting and sculpture, landscape painting of many varieties, realistic painting of many varieties, impressionism, and many varieties of post-impressionism.
Twentieth Century Art (1900–2000 CE)	Major genres of the twentieth century include symbolism, art nouveau, fauvism, expressionism, cubism (both analytical and synthetic), futurism, non-objective art, abstract art, surrealism, social realism, constructivism in sculpture, Pop and Op art, and conceptual art.

Basic Components of Music

Melody, harmony, rhythm, timbre, dynamics and texture are some of the basic components of music.

MELODY is the tune, a specific arrangement of sounds in a pleasing pattern. Melody is often seen as the horizontal aspect of music, because melodic notes on a page travel along horizontally.

> **MELODY:** the tune, a specific arrangement of sounds in a pleasing pattern

HARMONY: refers to the vertical aspect of music, or the musical chords related to a melody

RHYTHM: refers to the duration of musical notes

TIMBRE: the quality of a sound

DYNAMICS: refer to the loudness or softness of music

TEXTURE: in music usually refers to the number of separate components making up the whole of a piece

HARMONY refers to the vertical aspect of music, or the musical chords related to a melody. So, when looking at a piece of music, the harmony notes are the ones lined up below each note of the melody, providing a more complex, fuller sound to a piece of music.

RHYTHM refers to the duration of musical notes. Rhythms are patterns of long and short music note durations. A clear way to describe rhythm to young students is through percussion instruments. A teacher creates a rhythmic pattern of long and short drum beats and asks the students to repeat the rhythm.

TIMBRE is the quality of a sound. If a clarinet and a trumpet play the same exact note, they will still have a different timbre, or unique quality of sound. You can also describe different timbres using the same instrument. You may have two singers, but one has a harsh timbre and the other has a warm or soothing timbre to their voice. Timbre is subjective and lends itself to a number of creative exercises for early childhood students to describe what they hear in terms of the timbre of the sound.

DYNAMICS refer to the loudness or softness of music. Early Childhood students should develop a basic understanding of music vocabulary for dynamics. Piano describes soft music. Forte describes loud music. Pianissimo is very soft music. Double Forte refers to very loud music. Mezzo piano is kind of soft, while mezzo forte is kind of loud. These definitions can be organized on a continuum of soft to loud, with music examples for each.

TEXTURE in music usually refers to the number of separate components making up the whole of a piece. A monophonic texture is a single melody line, such as a voice singing a tune. Polyphonic texture denotes two or more music lines playing at the same time. A single melodic line with harmonic accompaniment is called homophonic texture.

Types of Musical Instruments

Instruments are categorized by the mechanism that creates its sound. Musical instruments can be divided into four basic categories.

- String
- Percussion
- Brass
- Wind

String instruments

STRING INSTRUMENTS all make their sounds through strings. The sound of the instrument depends on the thickness and length of the strings. The slower a string vibrates, the lower the resulting pitch. Also, the way the strings are manipulated varies among string instruments. Some strings are plucked (e.g., guitar) while others use a bow to cause the strings to vibrate (e.g., violin). Some are even connected to keys (e.g., piano). Other common string instruments include the viola, double bass, cello, and piano.

> **STRING INSTRUMENTS:** all make their sounds through strings

Wind instruments

The sound of **WIND INSTRUMENTS** is caused by wind vibrating in a pipe or tube. Air blows into one end of the instrument, and in many wind instruments, air passes over a reed, which causes the air to vibrate. The pitch depends on the air's frequency as it passes through the tube, and the frequency depends on the tube's length or size. Larger tubes create deeper sounds in a wind instrument. The pitch is also controlled by holes or values. As fingers cover the holes or press the valve, the pitch changes for the notes the musician intends. Other common wind instruments include pipe organ, oboe, clarinet and saxophone.

> **WIND INSTRUMENTS:** these instruments make their sounds by wind vibrating in a pipe or tube

Brass instruments

BRASS INSTRUMENTS are similar to wind instruments since music from brass instruments also results from air passing through an air chamber. They are called brass instruments, however, because they are made from metal or brass. Pitch on a brass instrument is controlled by the size or length of the air chamber. Many brass instruments are twisted or coiled which lengthens the air chamber without making the instrument unmanageably long. Like wind instruments, larger air chambers create deeper sounds, and the pitch can be controlled by valves on the instrument. In addition, some brass instruments also control the pitch by the musician's mouth position on the mouthpiece. Common brass instruments include the French horn, trumpet, trombone and tuba.

> **BRASS INSTRUMENTS:** these instruments make their sounds by air passing through an air chamber made from metal or brass

Percussion instruments

To play a **PERCUSSION INSTRUMENT**, the musician hits or shakes the instrument. The sound is created from sound vibrations as a result of shaking or striking the instrument. Many materials, such as metal or wood, are used to create percussion instruments, and different thicknesses or sizes of the material help control the sound. Thicker or heavier materials like drum membranes make deeper sounds, while thinner, metal materials (e.g., triangle) make higher-pitched sounds. Other common percussion instruments include the cymbals, tambourine, bells, xylophone and wood block.

> **PERCUSSION INSTRUMENTS:** these instruments make their sound from vibrations as a result of shaking or striking the instrument

SKILL 17.2 Demonstrating knowledge of the application of the basic elements of the visual and performing arts to the performance and creation of works of art

Principles of design in Western art include unity, balance, center of interest, movement, repetition, variation, rhythm, contrast, space, and tension.

There are different types of visual balance and artists use these various types of balance to create art that conveys a particular message or idea. Balance is a fundamental of design, seen as a visual weight and counterweight. This is apparent in a single image or in the organization of images and objects in a composition.

Examples of balance are:

- **Symmetrical:** The same objects or arrangement are on both sides
- **Asymmetrical:** Objects or arrangements are on different sides
- **Radial:** The axis design or pattern appears to radiate from the center axis
- **Horizontal:** Works that utilize the picture plane from left to right

Lines are the marks left by the painting tools that define the edges of objects in artwork. Their shape and thickness may express movement or tone. Texture in a painting is the "feel" of the canvas, based on the paint used and its method of application. There are two forms of texture in painting: visual and tactile.

Color refers to the hue (e.g., red vs. orange) and intensity or brightness (e.g., neon-green vs. yellow-green) of the colors used. Shapes are formed from the meeting of lines and the enclosing of areas in a two-dimensional space.

SKILL 17.3 Applying knowledge of strategies for nurturing artistic modes of expression and the characteristics of children's developmental stages in the visual and performing arts

Creativity is more than a product—it is also a process. An interesting painting or thought-provoking piece of writing may be examples of creative work, but the decisions people make as they paint, sculpt, write, and think are at the core of the creative process. Children learn in different ways, through visual skills, auditory skills, kinesthetic skills, or a combination of these.

To solve a problem creatively, children need to be able to see a variety of perspectives and to generate several solutions. When working on a problem, teachers should show children how to examine their surroundings for cues that will help them generate a pool of possible solutions.

In addition, adults can encourage creative thought by providing:

- A stimulating, multisensory, learning environment: Collections of objects and reference materials reflecting various cultures will inspire children. These may include books, photographs, paintings, pottery, carvings, sculptures, interactive displays, and displays of work by local and famous artists, craftspeople and musicians, from the present and the past. Give children the opportunity to see and experience other cultures and ways of living to help them learn to respect the choices other people make.

> Give children the opportunity to see and experience other cultures and ways of living to help them learn to respect the choices other people make.

- Carefully chosen pieces of music: Music can be a stimulus for an activity in any area of learning, for example:

  - to introduce a topic and stimulate imagination

  - to inspire drawing, painting, or creative writing

  - to encourage a response through movement or dance

  - background music as children work (encourages whole-brain activity)

  - a calming influence to encourage reflection

- Choices: Children who are given choices show more creativity than children who have all choices made for them.

- Stimulation: Physical environments designed to stimulate the senses can enhance creative problem solving. For example, when shown an object in the shape of a half-moon and asked, "What can we use this for?" children will exhaust their first mental images and begin developing ideas from what they see in their surroundings. Looking around a classroom or playroom for cues is a creative problem-solving method. An environment that provides both novelty and variety will greatly aid creativity.

- Time for play and fantasy: Dramatic play just prior to engaging in problem-solving tasks can lead to more creative thought.

- Independence (with reasonable limits): Parents and teachers should encourage children to think and act freely without adult direction, yet within the limits of rules.

- A time to leave reality behind: Joining together two or more irrelevant elements, called synectics, can lead to creative answers. The process of synectics can take many forms:

  - Hand a child a piece of modeling clay, and ask the child to imagine that he or she is the modeling clay.

– Place a child in a different time and place. For instance, ask a child to describe how he or she would cook a meal without electricity, silverware, or dishes.

– Ask a child to describe a problem or event using pictures instead of words.

– Ask a child to solve a problem using the most fantastic solutions he or she can come up with.

- **An environment where there is no one right answer for every problem:** Teachers who enthusiastically encourage children to develop more than one solution to a problem see greater creativity in problem solving.

> Teachers who enthusiastically encourage children to develop more than one solution to a problem see greater creativity in problem solving.

SKILL 17.4 Recognizing the role of visual and performing arts in culture

Although the elements of design have remained consistent throughout history, the emphasis on specific aesthetic principles has periodically shifted. Aesthetic standards or principles vary from time period to time period and from society to society.

An obvious difference in aesthetic principles occurs between works created by Eastern and Western cultures. Eastern works of art are more often based on spiritual considerations, while much Western art is secular in nature. In attempting to convey reality, Eastern artists generally prefer to use line, local color, and a simplistic view. Western artists tend toward a literal use of line, shape, color, and texture to convey a concise, detailed, complicated view. Eastern artists portray the human figure with symbolic meanings and little regard for muscle structure, resulting in a mystical view of the human experience. Western artists use the "principle of pondering," which requires the knowledge of both human anatomy and an expression of the human spirit.

In attempts to convey the illusion of depth or visual space in a work of art, Eastern and Western artists use different techniques. Eastern artists prefer a diagonal projection of eye movement into the picture plane, and often leave large areas of the surface untouched by detail. The result is the illusion of vast space, an infinite view that coincides with the spiritual philosophies of the East. Western artists rely on several techniques, such as overlapping planes, variation of object size, object position on the picture plane, linear and aerial perspective, color change, and various points of perspective to convey the illusion of depth. The result is space that is limited and closed.

In the application of color, Eastern artists use arbitrary choices of color. Western artists generally rely on literal color usage or emotional choices of color. The result is that Eastern art tends to be more universal in nature, while Western art is more individualized.

An interesting change in aesthetic principles occurred between the Renaissance and Baroque periods in Europe.

The Renaissance period was concerned with the rediscovery of the works of classical Greece and Rome. The art, literature, and architecture was inspired by classical orders, which tended to be formal, simple, and concerned with the ideal human proportions. This means that the painting, sculpture, and architecture was of a Teutonic, or closed nature, composed of forms that were restrained and compact. For example, consider the visual masterpieces of the period: Raphael's painting *The School of Athens*, with its precise use of space; Michelangelo's sculpture *David*, with its compact mass; and the facade of the Palazzo Strozzi, with its defined use of the rectangle, arches, and rustication of the masonry.

Compare the Renaissance characteristics to those of the Baroque period. The word *Baroque* means grotesque, which was the contemporary criticism of the new style. In comparison to the styles of the Renaissance, the Baroque was concerned with the imaginative flights of human fancy. The painting, sculpture, and architecture were of an a-Teutonic, or open, nature, composed of forms that were whimsical and free-flowing. Consider again the masterpieces of the period: Ruben's painting *The Elevation of the Cross*, with its turbulent forms of light and dark tumbling diagonally through space; Puget's sculpture *Milo of Crotona,* with its use of open space and twisted forms; and Borromini's *Chapel of St. Ivo*, with a facade that plays convex forms against concave ones.

Although artists throughout time have used the same elements of design to compose their various artistic works, the emphasis on specific aesthetic principles has periodically shifted. Aesthetic principles vary from time period to time period and from society to society.

In the 1920s and 1930s, the German art historian, Professor Wolfflin outlined these shifts in aesthetic principles in his influential book *Principles of Art History*. He arranged these changes into five categories of "visual analysis," sometimes referred to as the "categories of stylistic development." Wolfflin was careful to point out that no style is inherently superior to any other. They are simply indicators of the phase of development of that particular time or society. However, Wolfflin goes on to state, correctly or not, that once the evolution occurs, it is impossible to regress. These modes of perception apply to drawing, painting, sculpture, and architecture. They are:

WOLFFLIN'S CATEGORIES OF ANALYSIS	
From a Linear Mode to a Painterly Mode	This shift refers to stylistic changes that occur when perception or expression evolves from a linear form that is concerned with the contours and boundaries of objects, to perception or expression that stresses the masses and volumes of objects. From viewing objects in isolation, to seeing the relationships between objects are an important change in perception. Linear mode implies that objects are stationary and unchanging, while the painterly mode implies that objects and their relationships to other objects is always in a state of flux.
From Plane to Recession	This shift refers to perception or expression that evolves from a planar style, when the artist views movement in the work in an "up and down" and "side to side" manner, to a recessional style, when the artist views the balance of a work in an "in and out" manner. The illusion of depth may be achieved through either style, but only the recessional style uses an angular movement forward and backward through the visual plane.
From Closed to Open Form	This shift refers to perception or expression that evolves from a sense of enclosure, or limited space, in "closed form," to a sense of freedom in "open form." The concept is obvious in architecture, as in buildings that clearly differentiate between "outside" and "inside" space, and buildings that open up the space to allow the outside to interact with the inside.
From Multiplicity to Unity	This shift refers to an evolution from expressing unity through the use of balancing many individual parts, to expressing unity by subordinating some individual parts to others. Multiplicity stresses the balance between existing elements, whereas unity stresses emphasis, domination, and accent of some elements over other elements.
From Absolute to Relative Clarity	This shift refers to an evolution from works which clearly and thoroughly express everything there is to know about the object, to works that express only part of what there is to know, and leave the viewer to fill in the rest from his own experiences. Relative clarity, then, is a sophisticated mode, because it requires the viewer to actively participate in the "artistic dialogue." Each of the previous four categories is reflected in this, as linearity is considered to be concise while painting is more subject to interpretation. Planarity is more factual, while recessional movement is an illusion, and so on.

DOMAIN V
SCIENCE

PERSONALIZED STUDY PLAN

PAGE	COMPETENCY AND SKILL	KNOWN MATERIAL/ SKIP IT
269	**18: Understand concepts related to scientific knowledge and inquiry**	☐
	18.1: Recognizing characteristics of scientific knowledge, the historical development of important ideas, and how diverse cultures and individuals have influenced and contributed to developments in science	☐
	18.2: Recognizing questions and concepts that can be explored through scientific inquiry; comparing multiple types of inquiry for answering questions; and evaluating alternative explanations and models based on evidence, current scientific understanding, and logic	☐
	18.3: Demonstrating knowledge of the design of scientific investigations and the use of appropriate scientific instrumentation, equipment, and mathematics as tools in scientific investigations and communication	☐
	18.4: Demonstrating knowledge of connections across the domains of science, between science and technology, and between science and other school subjects and the use of scientific understandings and abilities when making decisions about personal and societal issues	☐
	18.5: Demonstrating knowledge of legal responsibilities and recognized safety guidelines for teaching science and the correct use of required safety equipment for classroom, field, and laboratory settings	☐
	18.6: Demonstrating knowledge of the proper use and care of chemicals, supplies, and equipment used to teach science and of the ethics and restrictions on the use and care of organisms and the collecting of scientific specimens and data	☐
280	**19: Understand the fundamental concepts and principles of physical science**	☐
	19.1: Applying knowledge of the structure and properties of matter and of physical and chemical changes in matter	☐
	19.2: Analyzing the forces that act on objects	☐
	19.3: Demonstrating knowledge of the properties and characteristics of light, heat, electricity, and magnetism	☐
	19.4: Demonstrating knowledge of the properties and characteristics of different forms of energy and of concepts related to the transfer, transformation, and conservation of energy	☐

PERSONALIZED STUDY PLAN

KNOWN MATERIAL/ SKIP IT

PAGE	COMPETENCY AND SKILL	
295	**20: Understand the fundamental concepts and principles of life science**	☐
	20.1: Demonstrating knowledge of the characteristics, structures, functions, and life processes of plants, animals, and other living organisms	☐
	20.2: Demonstrating knowledge of physiological processes that regulate and maintain life processes and behavioral responses to internal or external stimuli	☐
	20.3: Applying knowledge of the life cycles and reproductive processes of common organisms and the principles of heredity in the transmission of traits from one generation to the next	☐
	20.4: Applying knowledge of the interrelationships between organisms and their environment	☐
	20.5: Recognizing characteristics of and interactions among populations of organisms in ecosystems	☐
	20.6: Demonstrating knowledge of the diversity of organisms and the ways in which organisms have adapted to their environments	☐
311	**21: Understand the fundamental concepts and principles of Earth and space science**	☐
	21.1: Recognizing characteristics, properties, and uses of Earth materials	☐
	21.2: Recognizing properties and characteristics of objects in the sky	☐
	21.3: Applying knowledge of Earth's position and movement in the solar system and interactions between Earth, the moon, and the sun	☐
	21.4: Demonstrating knowledge of the properties and processes of Earth's hydrosphere, biosphere, atmosphere, and lithosphere and interactions among them	☐
	21.5: Demonstrating knowledge of the history of Earth, including geologic and atmospheric processes that have changed and shaped the surface of Earth and its environment and evidence of these changes	☐

COMPETENCY 18
UNDERSTAND CONCEPTS RELATED TO SCIENTIFIC KNOWLEDGE AND INQUIRY

SKILL 18.1 **Recognizing characteristics of scientific knowledge** (*e.g., reliance on verifiable data, the use of theoretical models*), **the historical development of important ideas, and how diverse cultures and individuals have influenced and contributed to developments in science**

The History of Science

Science began with the agricultural revolution 10,000 years ago because there was apparently a body of knowledge that enabled humans to increase production. Pythagoras' theorem (circa 490 BCE) was actually recorded on Mesopotamian cuneiform tablets in 1800 BCE. Ancient Greeks discovered the principle behind buoyancy and the approximate radius of Earth. Indians made considerable discoveries in mathematics and astronomy from the 5th to 15th centuries CE. During this period, there were many pure and applied scientific discoveries in China:

- Compasses
- Movable-type printing
- Atlases of stars
- Cast iron
- The iron plough

- The wheelbarrow
- The suspension bridge
- Solid fuel rocket
- Many more

The scientific method began with Muslim scientists in the Middle Ages, not only because of their achievements in optics, mathematics, chemistry, and astronomy, but because philosophers of the Arab Empire explicitly advocated the need for experiments, observations, and measurements.

The rise of science in the West began with the rise of universities in the 12th century. Roger Bacon (1224–1294) is considered one of the early advocates of the scientific method. In the 14th century, there was scientific progress in kinematics, but the Scientific Revolution began in the 16th century with the heliocentric theory of Nicolaus Copernicus. In 1605, Johannes Kepler discovered that planets orbit the sun in elliptical, not circular paths. In 1677, Isaac Newton derived Kepler's laws from the second law of motion.

In the 19th century, science became a profession and an institution in Western nation-states. The economic progress was due in part to the technological advances made possible by science, and scientific progress was made possible by the economic progress. The rise in science in the West was caused by the cultural and institutional circumstances that existed in Western countries. The increase in the number of women scientists and other minority groups in recent years was caused by the changing values of individuals and changes in institutional structures.

Equilibrium

Math, science, and technology have common themes in how they are applied and understood. All three use models, diagrams, and graphs to simplify a concept for analysis and interpretation. Patterns observed in these systems lead to predictions based on these observations. Another common theme among these three systems is equilibrium. EQUILIBRIUM is a state in which forces are balanced, resulting in stability. STATIC EQUILIBRIUM is stability due to a lack of changes and DYNAMIC EQUILIBRIUM is stability due to a balance between opposite forces.

The fundamental relationship between the natural and social sciences is the use of the scientific method and the rigorous standards of proof that both disciplines require. This emphasis on organization and evidence separates the sciences from the arts and humanities. Natural science, particularly biology, is closely related to social science, the study of human behavior. Biological and environmental factors often dictate human behavior; an accurate assessment of behavior requires a sound understanding of biological factors.

Technology, Data, and Science

The combination of science, mathematics, and technology forms the scientific endeavor and makes science a success. It is impossible to study science on its own without the support of other disciplines like mathematics, technology, geology, physics, and other disciplines.

Science is tentative. By definition, it is searching for information by making educated guesses. It must be replicable. Another scientist must be able to achieve the same results under the same conditions at a later time. The term EMPIRICAL means a phenomenon must be assessed through tests and observations. Science changes over time. Science is limited by the available technology. An example of this would be the relationship of the discovery of the cell and the invention of the microscope. As our technology improves, more hypotheses will become theories and possibly laws.

Science is also limited by the data that is able to be collected. Data may be interpreted differently on different occasions. Science limitations cause explanations to be changeable as new technologies emerge. New technologies gather

EQUILIBRIUM: a state in which forces are balanced, resulting in stability

STATIC EQUILIBRIUM: stability due to a lack of changes

DYNAMIC EQUILIBRIUM: stability due to a balance between opposite forces

The fundamental relationship between the natural and social sciences is the use of the scientific method and the rigorous standards of proof that both disciplines require.

EMPIRICAL: a phenomenon must be assessed through tests and observations

The combination of science, mathematics, and technology forms the scientific endeavor and makes science a success.

previously unavailable data and enable us to build upon current theories with new information.

The scientific method is the basic process behind science. It involves several steps beginning with hypothesis formulation and working through to the conclusion.

The scientific method is the basic process behind science.

Posing a Question	Although many discoveries happen by chance, the standard thought process of a scientist begins with forming a question to research. The more limited the question, the easier it is to set up an experiment to answer it.
Form a Hypothesis	Once the question is formulated, take an educated guess about the answer to the problem or question. This "best guess" is your hypothesis.
Doing the Test	To make a test fair, data from an experiment must have a **VARIABLE** such as temperature or mass. A good test will try to manipulate as few variables as possible so as to see which variable is responsible for the result. This requires a second example of a **CONTROL**.
Observe and Record the Data	Reporting of the data should state specifics of how the measurements were calculated. A graduated cylinder needs to be read with proper procedures. As beginning students, technique must be part of the instructional process so as to give validity to the data.
Drawing a Conclusion	After recording data, you compare your data with that of other groups. A conclusion is the judgment derived from the data results.
Graphing Data	Graphing utilizes numbers to demonstrate patterns. The patterns offer a visual representation, making it easier to draw conclusions.

VARIABLE: any condition that can be changed

CONTROL: an extra setup in which all the conditions are the same except for the variable being tested

Apply Knowledge of Designing and Performing Investigations

Normally, knowledge is integrated in the form of a lab report. A report has many sections. It should include a specific title and tell exactly what is being studied.

SCIENCE

ABSTRACT: a summary of the report written at the beginning of the paper

PURPOSE: defines and states the problem

OBSERVATIONS AND RESULTS: the recorded outcomes of the experiment

CONCLUSION: explains why the results proved or disproved the hypothesis

The **ABSTRACT** is a summary of the report written at the beginning of the paper. The **PURPOSE** should always be defined and will state the problem. The purpose should include the **HYPOTHESIS** (educated guess) of what is expected from the outcome of the experiment. The entire experiment should relate to this problem.

It is important to describe exactly what was done to prove or disprove a hypothesis. A control is necessary to prove that the results occurred from the changed conditions and would not have happened normally. Only one variable should be manipulated at a time. **OBSERVATIONS** and **RESULTS** of the experiment should be recorded including all results from data. Drawings, graphs, and illustrations should be included to support information. Observations are objective, whereas analysis and interpretation is subjective. A **CONCLUSION** should explain why the results of the experiment either proved or disproved the hypothesis.

A scientific theory is an explanation of a set of related observations based on a proven hypothesis. A scientific law usually lasts longer than a scientific theory and has more experimental data to support it.

Science uses the metric system, as it is accepted worldwide and allows easier comparison among experiments done by scientists around the world. Learn the following basic units and prefixes:

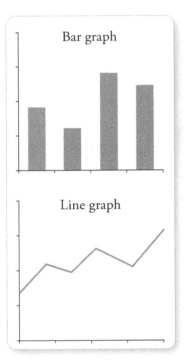

Bar graph

Line graph

UNIT	meter	liter	gram
MEASURE OF	length	volume	mass

UNIT	THE BASE UNIT
deca-(meter, liter, gram)	10X
deci-(meter, liter, gram)	1/10
hecto-(meter, liter, gram)	100X
centi-(meter, liter, gram)	1/100
kilo-(meter, liter, gram)	1000X
milli-(meter, liter, gram)	1/1000

GRAPHING: visually displays collected data for analysis

GRAPHING is an important skill to visually display collected data for analysis. The two types of graphs most commonly used are the line graph and the bar graph (histogram).

Line graphs are set up to show two variables represented by one point on the graph. The *x* axis is the horizontal axis and represents the dependent variable. Dependent variables are those that would be present independent of the experiment. A common example of a dependent variable is time. Time proceeds regardless of anything else occurring. The *y* axis is the vertical axis and represents the independent variable. Independent variables are manipulated by the experiment, such as the amount of light, or the height of a plant. Graphs should be calibrated at equal intervals. If one space represents one day, the next space may not represent ten days. A "best fit" line is drawn to join the points and may not include all the points in the data. Axes must always be labeled, for the graph to be meaningful. A good title will describe both the dependent and the independent variable. Bar graphs are set up similarly in regards to axes, but points are not plotted. Instead, the dependent variable is set up as a bar where the *x* axis intersects with the *y* axis. Each bar is a separate item of data and is not joined by a continuous line.

Indirect Evidence and Models

Some things happen at too fast or too slow a rate or are too small or too large for use to see. In these cases, we have to rely on indirect evidence to develop models of what is intangible. Once data have been collected and analyzed, it is useful to generalize the information by creating a model. A model is a conceptual representation of a phenomenon. Models are useful in that they clarify relationships, helping us to understand the phenomenon and make predictions about future outcomes. The natural sciences and social sciences employ modeling for this purpose.

Many scientific models are mathematical in nature and contain a set of variables linked by logical and quantitative relationships. These mathematical models may include functions, tables, formulas, and graphs. Typically, such mathematical models include assumptions that restrict them to very specific situations. Often this means they can only provide an approximate description of what occurs in the natural world. These assumptions, however, prevent the model from become overly complicated. For a mathematical model to fully explain a natural or social phenomenon, it would have to contain many variables and could become too cumbersome to use. Accordingly, it is critical that assumptions be carefully chosen and thoroughly defined.

Certain models are abstract and simply contain sets of logical principles rather than relying on mathematics. These types of models are generally more vague and are more useful for discovering and understanding new ideas. Abstract models can also include actual physical models built to make concepts more tangible. Abstract models, to an even greater extent than mathematical models, make assumptions and simplify actual phenomena.

> *Proper scientific models must be able to be tested and verified using experimental data.*

Proper scientific models must be able to be tested and verified using experimental data. Often these experimental results are necessary to demonstrate the superiority of a model when two or more conflicting models seek to explain the same phenomenon. Computer simulations are increasingly used in both testing and developing mathematical and even abstract models. These types of simulations are especially useful in situations, such as ecology or manufacturing, where experiments are not feasible or variables are not fully under control.

SKILL 18.3 Demonstrating knowledge of the design of scientific investigations *(e.g., controlled experimentation)* and the use of appropriate scientific instrumentation, equipment, and mathematics as tools in scientific investigations and communication

Common Measurements in a Laboratory

Graduated cylinders and beakers are used for measuring the volume of liquids. There are many sizes and shapes. The surface of the liquid will be curved and this curve is called the meniscus. For water, the meniscus is concaved and for mercury the meniscus is convex. Measurements are made by holding the graduated cylinder at eye-level and reading it from the top or the bottom of the meniscus.

Masses are measured with a triple-beam balance or electronic balance. Temperatures are measured with thermometers, time is measured with a stopwatch, and length is measured with a meter stick. A multimeter is used to measure electric currents and voltages.

Organizing Data

Data from research or experiments is usually obtained in a way that is unrelated to the hypothesis or problem that is being investigated. This is called raw data. The raw data should be organized on a data table with column headings in a way that promotes the purpose of the investigation. There may be more than one column heading depending on the investigation. Also, categories for the data may be selected, and the data is put under the defined categories. The data can also be presented in various kinds of graphs, including line graphs, bar graphs, pie graphs, etc.

See also Skills 13.6 and 18.2

Demonstrating knowledge of connections across the domains of science, between science and technology, and between science and other school subjects and the use of scientific understandings and abilities when making decisions about personal and societal issues

The fields of mathematics, science, and technology are fully integrated and allow us to observe and analyze data from within and between these different fields. An example of one such analysis would be the use of statistical methodologies to examine census data. Data limitations are the greatest factor influencing the outcome of statistical analyses. The consistency and quality of the data pool will have a direct impact on the integrity of the statistical analysis.

When considering census data, there are three basic statistical methods appropriate for the analysis.

1. **Tracking and trend analysis.** Examining time trends in census data is helpful in identifying the growth for a specific area. The changes in population over a specific period of time allow city planners to make appropriate decisions regarding zoning, parks and recreation, and utilities.

2. **Spatial analysis and geographic distribution.** This analysis allows the researcher to find commonalities between population and other factors including health, wealth, education, etc. Such analysis allows for more in-depth understanding of the socioeconomic indicators of a specific area.

3. **Geographic correlation studies.** These studies model the interrelationships of census data between population centers allowing us to compare and contrast different regions, including rates of death and disease.

It is the mathematical field of statistics that allows us to examine scientific data and this is often done using computer technology. Computer programs continue to advance the level of analysis and comparison we may achieve with data such as census data. When used properly statistical analysis or any other research method allows us to link the fields of mathematics and science. Most research in the field of science is completed and analyzed using mathematic principals. They are more interdependent than not, and it is important to recognize the impact they have on one another. Other examples of this interconnectedness include the use of zero as a symbol in keeping track of time using calendars, binary numbers and computers, the mathematic of sound in creating Cochlear implants, and exponential growth when looking at the population and the environment.

See also Skill 23.5 for more information about science and social and environmental issues.

Appropriate Care and Treatment of Laboratory Animals

Dissections

Animals that are not obtained from recognized sources should not be used. Decaying animals or those of unknown origin may harbor pathogens and/or parasites. Specimens should be rinsed before handling. Latex gloves are desirable. If gloves are not available, students with sores or scratches should be excused from the activity. Formaldehyde is a carcinogen and should be avoided or disposed of according to district regulations. Students objecting to dissections for moral reasons should be given an alternative assignment.

Live Specimens

No dissections may be performed on living mammalian vertebrates or birds. Lower-order life and invertebrates may be used.

Biological experiments may be done with all animals except mammalian vertebrates or birds. No physiological harm may result to the animal. All animals housed and cared for in the school must be handled in a safe and humane manner. Animals are not to remain on school premises during extended vacations unless adequate care is provided. Many state laws stipulate that any instructor who intentionally refuses to comply with the laws may be suspended or dismissed.

Microbiology

Pathogenic organisms must never be used for experimentation. Students should adhere to the following rules at all times when working with microorganisms to avoid accidental contamination:

- Treat all microorganisms as if they were pathogenic

- Maintain sterile conditions at all times

If you are taking a national-level exam, you should check the Department of Education for your state for safety procedures. You will want to know what your state expects of you not only for the test but also for performance in the classroom and for the welfare of your students.

Bunsen burner

Outer nonluminous flame
Hottest region
Inner blue cone
Barrel
Gas inlet
Air ports
Base

Appropriate Use and Management of Laboratory Equipment

Bunsen Burners

Hot plates should be used whenever possible to avoid the risk of burns or fire. If Bunsen burners are used, the following precautions should be followed:

- Know the location of fire extinguishers and safety blankets and train students in their use. Long hair and long sleeves should be secured and out of the way.

- Turn the gas all the way on and make a spark with the striker. The preferred method to light burners is to use strikers rather than matches.

- Adjust the air valve at the bottom of the Bunsen burner until the flame shows an inner cone.

- Adjust the flow of gas to the desired flame height by using the adjustment valve.

- Do not touch the barrel of the burner (it is hot).

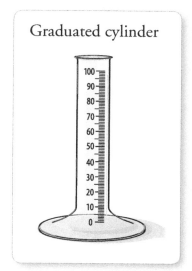

Graduated cylinder

Graduated Cylinder

These are used for precise measurements. They should always be placed on a flat surface. The surface of the liquid will form a meniscus (lens-shaped curve). The measurement is read at the *bottom* of this curve.

Balance

Electronic balances are easier to use, but more expensive. An electronic balance should always be tarred (returned to zero) before measuring and used on a flat surface. Substances should always be placed on a piece of paper to avoid spills and/or damage to the instrument. Triple beam balances must be used on a level surface. There are screws located at the bottom of the balance to make any adjustments. Start with the largest counterweight first and proceed toward the last notch that does not tip the balance. Do the same with the next largest, and so on, until the pointer remains at zero. The total mass is the total of all the readings on the beams. Again, use paper under the substance to protect the equipment.

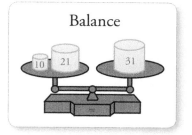

Balance

Buret

A buret is used to dispense precisely measured volumes of liquid. A stopcock is used to control the volume of liquid being dispensed at a time.

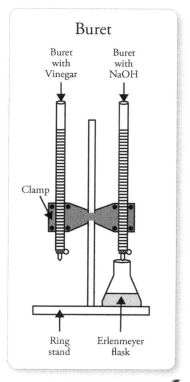

Buret

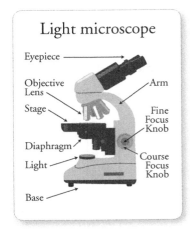

Light microscope

- Eyepiece
- Objective Lens
- Arm
- Stage
- Fine Focus Knob
- Diaphragm
- Light
- Course Focus Knob
- Base

Light Microscopes

These are commonly used in laboratory experiments. Several procedures should be followed to properly care for this equipment:

- Clean all lenses with lens paper only

- Carry microscopes with two hands; one on the arm and one on the base

- Always begin focusing on low power, then switch to high power

- Store microscopes with the low power objective down

- Always use a coverslip when viewing wet mount slides

- Bring the objective down to its lowest position then focus by moving up to avoid breaking the slide or scratching the lens

Wet mount slides should be made by placing a drop of water on the specimen and then putting a glass coverslip on top of the drop of water. Dropping the coverslip at a forty-five degree angle will help avoid air bubbles. Total magnification is determined by multiplying the ocular (usually 10X) and the objective (usually 10X on low, 40X on high).

Appropriate Alternative Sources of and Substitutions for Laboratory Materials

Lab materials are readily available from the many school suppliers that routinely send their catalogues to schools. Often, common materials are available at the local grocery store. The use of locally available flora and fauna both reduces the cost and familiarizes students with the organisms where they live. Innovation and networking with other science teachers will assist in keeping costs of lab materials to a minimum.

Procedures for Safe Preparation, Use, Storage, and Disposal of Chemicals and Other Materials

All science labs should contain safety equipment. The following items are requirements by law.

- Fire blanket which is visible and accessible

- Ground Fault Circuit Interrupters (GFCI) within two feet of water supplies

- Emergency shower capable of providing a continuous flow of water

- Signs designating room exits

- Emergency eye wash station, which can be activated by the foot or forearm

- Eye protection for every student and a means of sanitizing equipment

Ground Fault Circuit Interrupter

RESET

TEST

- Emergency exhaust fans providing ventilation to the outside of the building

- Master cut-off switches for gas, electric, and compressed air. Switches must have permanently attached handles. Cut-off switches must be clearly labeled.

- An ABC fire extinguisher

- Storage cabinets for flammable materials

Also recommended, but not required by law:

- Chemical spill control kit

- Fume hood with a motor which is spark-proof

- Protective laboratory aprons made of flame-retardant material

- Signs that will alert people to potential hazardous conditions

- Containers for broken glassware, flammables, corrosives, and waste

- Labels on all containers

It is the responsibility of teachers to provide a safe environment for their students. Proper supervision greatly reduces the risk of injury and a teacher should never leave a class for any reason without providing alternate supervision. After an accident, two factors are considered: foreseeability and negligence.

FORESEEABILITY is the anticipation that an event may occur under certain circumstances. **NEGLIGENCE** is the failure to exercise ordinary or reasonable care. Safety procedures should be a part of the science curriculum and a well managed classroom is important to avoid potential lawsuits.

The **RIGHT TO KNOW LAW** statutes cover science teachers who work with potentially hazardous chemicals. Briefly, the law states that employees must be informed of potentially toxic chemicals. An inventory must be made available if requested. The inventory must contain information about the hazards and properties of the chemicals. Training must be provided in the safe handling and interpretation of the Material Safety Data Sheet.

These chemicals are potential carcinogens and are not allowed in school facilities:

- Acrylonitriel
- Arsenic compounds
- Asbestos
- Bensidine
- Benzene
- Cadmium compounds

- Chloroform
- Chromium compounds
- Ethylene oxide
- Ortho-toluidine
- Nickel powder
- Mercury

FORESEEABILITY: the anticipation that an event may occur under certain circumstances

NEGLIGENCE: the failure to exercise ordinary or reasonable care

RIGHT TO KNOW LAW: employees must be informed of potentially toxic chemicals

All laboratory solutions should be prepared as directed in the lab manual. Care should be taken to avoid contamination. All glassware should be rinsed thoroughly with distilled water before using and cleaned well after use. Safety goggles should be worn while working with glassware in case of an accident. All solutions should be made with distilled water as tap water contains dissolved particles that may affect the results of an experiment. Chemical storage should be located in a secured, dry area. Chemicals should be stored in accordance with reactability. Acids are to be locked in a separate area. Used solutions should be disposed of according to local disposal procedures. Any questions regarding safe disposal or chemical safety may be directed to the local fire department.

> **SKILL 18.6** Demonstrating knowledge of the proper use and care of chemicals, supplies, and equipment used to teach science and of the ethics and restrictions on the use and care of organisms and the collecting of scientific specimens and data

See also Skill 18.5

COMPETENCY 19
UNDERSTAND THE FUNDAMENTAL CONCEPTS AND PRINCIPLES OF PHYSICAL SCIENCE

> **SKILL 19.1** Applying knowledge of the structure and properties of matter and of physical and chemical changes in matter

Everything in our world is made up of matter, whether it is a rock, a building, an animal, or a person. Matter is defined by two characteristics: It takes up space and it has mass.

MASS: a measure of the amount of matter in an object

MASS is a measure of the amount of matter in an object. Two objects of equal mass will balance each other on a simple balance scale no matter where the scale is located. For instance, two rocks with the same mass that are in balance on Earth will also be in balance on the moon. They will feel heavier on the Earth than on the moon because of the gravitational pull of the Earth. Therefore, although the two rocks have the same mass, they will have a different weight on the moon than on the Earth.

WEIGHT is the measure of the Earth's pull of gravity on an object. It can also be defined as the pull of gravity between other bodies. The units of weight measurement commonly used are the pound (English measure) and the kilogram (metric measure).

WEIGHT: the measure of the Earth's pull of gravity on an object

In addition to mass, matter also has the property of volume. VOLUME is the amount of cubic space that an object occupies. Volume and mass together give a more exact description of an object. Two objects may have the same volume but different mass, or the same mass but different volumes.

VOLUME: the amount of cubic space that an object occupies

For instance, consider two cubes that are each one cubic centimeter, one made from plastic and one from lead. They have the same volume, but the lead cube has more mass. The measure that we use to describe the cubes takes into consideration both the mass and the volume. DENSITY is the mass of a substance contained per unit of volume. If the density of an object is less than the density of a liquid, the object will float in the liquid. If the object is denser than the liquid, then the object will sink.

DENSITY: the mass of a substance contained per unit of volume

Density is stated in grams per cubic centimeter (g/cm^3), where the gram is the standard unit of mass. To find an object's density, you must measure its mass and its volume. Then divide the mass by the volume ($D = m/V$).

To discover an object's density, first use a balance scale to find its mass. Then calculate its volume. If the object is a regular shape, you can find the volume by multiplying the length, width, and height together. However, if it is an irregular shape, you can find the volume by seeing how much water it displaces. Measure the water in the container before and after the object is submerged. The difference is the volume of the object.

SPECIFIC GRAVITY is the ratio of the density of a substance to the density of water. For instance, the specific density of one liter of alcohol is calculated by comparing its mass (0.81 kg) to the mass of one liter of water (1 kg):

SPECIFIC GRAVITY: the ratio of the density of a substance to the density of water

$$\frac{\text{mass of 1 L alcohol}}{\text{mass of 1 L water}} = \frac{0.81 \text{ kg}}{1.00 \text{ kg}} = 0.81$$

Physical and Chemical Characteristics and Changes

Physical and chemical properties of matter describe the appearance or behavior of substances. A physical property can be observed without changing the identity of a substance. For instance, you can describe the color, mass, shape, and volume of a book. A chemical property describes the ability of a substance to be changed into new substances. Baking powder goes through a chemical change as it changes into carbon dioxide gas during the baking process.

Matter constantly changes. A physical change is a change that does not produce a new substance. The freezing and melting of water is an example of a physical change. Cutting a length of rope in half or into small pieces is also an example of a physical change. Only the length of the rope changes; the properties of the rope have not been changed in any way.

> Rusting and burning are examples of chemical changes.

A chemical change (or chemical reaction) is any change of a substance into one or more other substances. Burning materials turn into smoke; a seltzer tablet fizzes into gas bubbles. When steel rusts, the composition of the material has undergone a change. Rusting and burning are examples of chemical changes.

> **ELEMENT:** a substance that cannot be broken down into other substances

An **ELEMENT** is a substance that cannot be broken down into other substances. To date, scientists have identified 109 elements: 89 are found in nature and 20 are synthetic.

> **ATOM:** the smallest particle of an element that retains the properties of that element

An **ATOM** is the smallest particle of an element that retains the properties of that element. All of the atoms of a particular element are the same. The atoms of each element are different from the atoms of other elements. Elements are assigned an identifying symbol of one or two letters. The symbol for oxygen is O; it stands for one atom of oxygen. However, because oxygen atoms in nature are joined together in pairs, the symbol O_2 represents oxygen.

> **MOLECULE:** the smallest particle of a substance that can exist independently and still have all of the properties of that substance

This pair of oxygen atoms is a molecule. A **MOLECULE** is the smallest particle of a substance that can exist independently and still have all of the properties of that substance. A molecule of most elements is made up of one atom. However, oxygen, hydrogen, nitrogen, and chlorine molecules are made of two atoms each.

> **COMPOUND:** two or more elements that have been chemically combined

A **COMPOUND** is made of two or more elements that have been chemically combined. Atoms join together when elements are chemically combined. The result is that the elements lose their individual identities; the compound that they become has different properties.

We use a formula to show the elements of a chemical compound. A chemical formula is a shorthand way of showing what is in a compound through symbols and subscripts. The letter symbols let us know what elements are involved and the number subscript indicates how many atoms of each element are involved. No subscript is used if there is only one atom of a given element involved. For example, carbon dioxide is made up of one atom of carbon (C) and two atoms of oxygen (O_2), so the formula is represented as CO_2.

Substances can combine without a chemical change. A mixture is any combination of two or more substances in which the substances keep their own properties. A fruit salad is a mixture (so is an ice cream sundae, although you might not recognize each part if it is stirred together). Colognes and perfumes are other examples. You may not readily recognize the individual elements; however, they can be separated.

Compounds and mixtures are similar in that they are made up of two or more substances. However, they have the opposite characteristics, as shown in the table:

Compounds	• Made up of one kind of particle
	• Formed during a chemical change
	• Broken down only by chemical changes
	• Properties are different from their parts
	• Have a specific amount of each ingredient
Mixtures	• Made up of two or more particles
	• Not formed by a chemical change
	• Can be separated by physical changes
	• Properties are the same as their parts
	• Do not necessarily have a definite amount of each ingredient.

Common compounds are acids, bases, salts, and oxides. These are classified according to their characteristics.

An acid contains the element hydrogen (H). It is never wise to taste a substance to identify it; however, acids have a sour taste. Vinegar and lemon juice are both acids, and acids occur in many foods in a weak state. Strong acids can burn skin and destroy materials.

Common compounds are acids, bases, salts, and oxides. These are classified according to their characteristics.

ACIDS AND THEIR USES	
Acid	**Used In**
Sulfuric acid (H_2SO_4)	Medicines, alcohol, dyes, car batteries
Nitric acid (HNO_3)	Fertilizers, explosives, cleaning materials
Carbonic acid (H_2CO_3)	Soft drinks
Acetic acid ($HC_2H_3O_2$)	Making plastics, rubber, photographic film, and as a solvent

Bases have a bitter taste, and the stronger ones feel slippery. Like acids, strong bases can be dangerous and should be handled carefully. All bases contain the elements oxygen and hydrogen (OH). Many household cleaning products contain bases.

COMMON BASES AND THEIR USES	
Base	**Used In**
Sodium hydroxide (NaOH)	Making soap, paper, vegetable oils and refining petroleum
Ammonium hydroxide (NH_4OH)	Making deodorants, bleaching and cleaning compounds
Potassium hydroxide (KOH)	Making soaps, drugs, dyes, alkaline batteries, and purifying industrial gases
Calcium hydroxide ($Ca(OH)_2$)	Making cement and plaster

Blue litmus paper turns red in an acid. Red litmus paper turns blue in a base.

An indicator is a substance that changes color when it comes in contact with an acid or a base. Litmus paper is an indicator. Blue litmus paper turns red in an acid. Red litmus paper turns blue in a base.

A substance that is neither acid nor base is neutral. Neutral substances do not change the color of litmus paper.

Salt is formed when an acid and a base combine chemically in a process called neutralization. Water is also formed. Table salt (NaCl) is an example of this process. Salts are also used in toothpaste. Other examples of salts include Epsom salts, cream of tartar, and calcium chloride ($CaCl_2$), which is used on frozen streets and walkways to melt ice.

Oxides are compounds that are formed when oxygen combines with another element. Rust is an oxide formed when oxygen combines with iron.

States of Matter

There are three states of matter: solid, liquid, and gas. While all three are made up of atoms and molecules, they are different in their characteristics.

Solids

- Have a definite shape that can be changed in some way
- Have a definite volume that cannot be changed

- Mass can be changed when the physical shape is diminished, such as sawing a board into two pieces

- Can be any color and temperature

- Some will melt under high temperatures, in which case they become liquid

- Are very hard

Liquids

- Take the shape of the container into which they are poured

- When a liquid results from melting a solid, it has the same color as the solid

- Flow

- Cannot be compressed and keep the same volume

- Weight may be lighter than that of a solid weight because of evaporation

- Are soft

Gases

- Do not keep their shape and fill a container

- Flow very quickly

- Are colorless

- Can be compressed and take on a different volume than that of a solid or liquid

- Are of high temperature

- Are extremely light and do not have weight

SKILL **Analyzing the forces that act on objects** *(e.g., using graphs to analyze the*
19.2 *motion of objects in terms of speed and direction)*

A force is described as a push or a pull. It provides the energy needed for an object to start moving, change direction, or stop moving. Forces occur in pairs—balanced and unbalanced.

A balanced force does not cause movement or change in movement that is occurring. The two objects are equally balanced because they are of the same size and are opposite in direction. Competing in an arm wrestling competition against

A force is described as a push or a pull. It provides the energy needed for an object to start moving, change direction, or stop moving.

a person who has the same strength as you will result in no movements of the arms. Even though you are both pushing in opposite directions, the amount of force is the same and both competitors' arms remain straight up and down. One force cancels out the other, and there will be no change in the motion.

An unbalanced force always causes a change in motion. When there are two unbalanced forces acting against each other, the larger object has the greatest force and will cause the other object to move. In the case of an arm wrestling competition, the person with the greatest force will bend the arm of the other competitor to the table.

Unbalanced forces can also act on objects moving in the same direction. An object at rest can be pushed to move in a guided direction, such as a car with people pushing from the front or the rear.

> **DYNAMICS:** the study of the relationship between motion and the forces affecting motion

DYNAMICS is the study of the relationship between motion and the forces affecting motion. Force causes motion.

Mass and weight are not equivalent quantities. An object's mass gives it a reluctance to change its state of motion. It is also the measure of an object's resistance to acceleration. The force that the Earth's gravity exerts on an object with a specific mass is called the object's weight on Earth. Weight is a force that is measured in newtons. Weight (W) = mass times acceleration due to gravity ($W = mg$). To understand the difference between mass and weight, picture two rocks of equal mass on a balance scale. If the scale is balanced in one place, it will be balanced everywhere, regardless of the gravitational field; however, the weight of the stones would vary on a spring scale, depending on the gravitational field. In other words, the stones would be balanced both on Earth and on the moon; however, the weight of the stones would be greater on Earth than on the moon.

Surfaces that touch each other have a certain resistance to motion. This resistance is friction. Some principles of friction include:

- The materials that make up the surfaces will determine the magnitude of the frictional force.

- The frictional force is independent of the area of contact between the two surfaces.

- The direction of the frictional force is opposite to the direction of motion.

- The frictional force is proportional to the normal force between the two surfaces in contact.

Static friction is the force of friction of two surfaces that are in contact but do not have any motion relative to each other, such as a block sitting on an inclined plane. Kinetic friction is the force of friction of two surfaces in contact with each other when there is relative motion between the surfaces.

When an object moves in a circular path, a force must be directed toward the center of the circle in order to keep the motion going. This constraining force is called centripetal force. Gravity is the centripetal force that keeps a satellite circling the Earth.

ELECTRICAL FORCE is the influential power resulting from electricity as an attractive or repulsive interaction between two charged objects. The electrical force is determined using Coulomb's law. As shown below, the appropriate unit for charge is the Coulomb (C), and the appropriate unit for distance is the meter (m). Use of these units will result in a force expressed in newtons. The demand for these units emerges from the units on Coulomb's constant.

$$F_{elect} = k \times Q_1 \times \frac{Q_2}{d^2}$$

> **ELECTRICAL FORCE:** the influential power resulting from electricity as an attractive or repulsive interaction between two charged objects

How objects affect each other when they are not in mechanical contact remains something of a mystery. Newton wrestled with the concept of "action-at-a-distance" (as electrical force is now classified) and eventually concluded that it was necessary for there to be some form of ether, or intermediate medium, which made it possible for one object to transfer force to another. We now know that no ether exists. It is possible for objects to exert forces on one another without any medium to transfer the force. From our fluid notion of electrical forces, we still associate forces as being due to the exchange of something between two objects. The electrical field force acts between two charges in the same way that the gravitational field force acts between two masses.

> *The appropriate unit for charge is the Coulomb (C).*

Magnetic force occurs when magnetized items interact with other items in specific ways. If a magnet is brought close enough to a ferromagnetic material (that is not magnetized itself), the magnet will strongly attract the ferromagnetic material regardless of orientation. Both the north and south pole of the magnet will attract the other item with equal strength. Paramagnetic materials are weakly attracted to a magnetic field. This occurs regardless of the north-south orientation of the field. Calculating the attractive or repulsive magnetic force between two magnets is, generally, an extremely complex operation, as it depends on the shape, magnetization, orientation, and separation of the magnets.

In nuclear force, the protons in the nucleus of an atom are positively charged. If protons interact, they are usually pushed apart by electromagnetic force; however, when two or more nuclei come very close together, nuclear force comes into play. Nuclear force is a hundred times stronger than electromagnetic force so the nuclear force may be able to "glue" the nuclei together to allow fusion. The nuclear force is also known as the strong force. The nuclear force keeps together the most basic of elementary particles, the quarks. Quarks combine to form the protons and neutrons in the atomic nucleus.

FORCE OF GRAVITY: the force at which the Earth, Moon, or other massively large object attracts another object toward itself

The FORCE OF GRAVITY is the force at which the Earth, Moon, or other massively large object attracts another object toward itself. By definition, this is the weight of the object. All objects on Earth experience a force of gravity that is directed "downward" toward the center of the Earth. The force of gravity on Earth is always equal to the weight of the object as found by the equation:

$$F_{grav} = m \times g$$

where $g = 9.8 \frac{m}{s^2}$ (on Earth)

and m = mass (in kg)

Forces on Objects at Rest and Moving Objects

Overcoming inertia is the tendency of any object to oppose a change in motion. An object at rest tends to stay at rest. An object that is moving tends to keep moving.

The formula $F = \frac{m}{a}$ is shorthand for force equals mass over acceleration. An object will not move unless the force is strong enough to move the mass. Also, there can be opposing forces holding the object in place. For instance, a strong current might be forcing a boat to drift away but an equal and opposite force might be a rope holding it to a dock.

CENTRIPETAL FORCE: inward force that keeps an object moving in a circle

Centripetal force is provided, for example, by the high banking of a curved road and by friction between the wheels and the road. This inward force that keeps an object moving in a circle is called CENTRIPETAL FORCE.

Work is done on an object when an applied force moves through a distance.

Power is the work done divided by the amount of time that it took to do it (power = $\frac{work}{time}$).

Machines

Examples of simple machines include an inclined plane, a lever, a wheel and axle, and a pulley.

MECHANICAL ADVANTAGE: the amount of effort saved when one uses simple or complex machines

Compound machines are two or more simple machines working together. A wheelbarrow is an example of a complex machine. It uses a lever, a wheel, and an axle. Machines of all types ease one's workload by changing the size or direction of an applied force. The amount of effort saved when one uses simple or complex machines is called MECHANICAL ADVANTAGE.

SKILL 19.3 Demonstrating knowledge of the properties and characteristics of light, heat, electricity, and magnetism

All heat transfer is the movement of thermal energy from hot to cold matter. This movement down a thermal gradient is a consequence of the second law of thermodynamics. The three methods of heat transfer are:

- **Conduction:** Electron diffusion or photo vibration is responsible for this mode of heat transfer. The bodies of matter themselves do not move; the heat is transferred because adjacent atoms vibrate against each other or electrons flow between atoms. This type of heat transfer is most common when two solids come in direct contact with each other, because molecules in a solid are in close contact with one another. Metals are good conductors of thermal energy because their metallic bonds allow the freest movement of electrons. Similarly, conduction is better in denser solids. Examples of conduction can be seen in the use of copper to quickly convey heat in cookware, the flow of heat from a hot-water bottle to a person's body, or the cooling of a warm drink with ice.

- **Convection:** Convection involves some conduction but involves the movement of warm particles to cooler areas. Convection can be either natural or forced, depending on how the current of warm particles develops. Natural convection occurs when molecules near a heat source absorb thermal energy (typically via conduction), become less dense, and rise. Cooler molecules then take their place and a natural current is formed. Forced convection, as the name suggests, occurs when liquids or gases are moved by pumps, fans, or other means to come into contact with warmer or cooler masses. Because the free motion of particles with different thermal energy is key to this mode of heat transfer, convection is most common in liquid and gases. Convection can, however, transfer heat between a liquid or gas and a solid.

  Forced convection is used in "forced hot air" home heating systems and is common in industrial manufacturing processes. Additionally, natural convection is responsible for ocean currents and many atmospheric events. Finally, natural convection often arises in association with conduction, for example, in the air near a radiator or the water in a pot on the stove.

- **Radiation:** This method of heat transfer occurs via electromagnetic radiation. All matter warmer than absolute zero (that is, all known matter) radiates heat. This radiation occurs regardless of the presence of any medium. Thus, it occurs even in a vacuum. Since light and radiant heat are both part of the electromagnetic spectrum, we can easily visualize how heat is transferred via radiation. For instance, like light, radiant heat is reflected by shiny materials and absorbed by dark materials. Common examples of radiant heat include the sunlight traveling from the Sun to warm the Earth, the use of radiators in homes, and the warmth of incandescent lightbulbs.

Light and Optics

Shadows illustrate one of the basic properties of light: Light travels in a straight line.

Shadows illustrate one of the basic properties of light: Light travels in a straight line. If you put your hand between a light source and a wall, you will interrupt the light and produce a shadow.

When light hits a surface, it is reflected. The angle of the incoming light (angle of incidence) is the same as the angle of the reflected light (angle of reflection). It is this reflected light that allows you to see objects. You see the objects when the reflected light reaches your eyes.

Different surfaces reflect light differently. Rough surfaces scatter light in many different directions. Smooth surfaces reflect light in one direction. If a surface is smooth and shiny (like a mirror), you see your image in the surface.

When light enters a different medium, it bends. This bending, or change of speed, is called refraction.

Light can be diffracted, or bent, around the edges of an object. Diffraction occurs when light goes through a narrow slit. As it passes through the slit, the light bends slightly around the edges of the slit. You can demonstrate this by pressing your thumb and forefinger together, making a very thin slit between them. Hold them about three inches from your eye and look at a distant source of light. The pattern you observe is caused by the diffraction of light.

Electricity

Electrostatics is the study of stationary electric charges. A plastic rod that is rubbed with fur or a glass rod that is rubbed with silk will become electrically charged and will attract small pieces of paper. The charge on the plastic rod rubbed with fur is negative, and the charge on glass rod rubbed with silk is positive.

Electrically charged objects share these characteristics:

1. Like charges repel one another

2. Opposite charges attract each other

3. Charge is conserved

A neutral object has no net charge. If the plastic rod and fur are initially neutral, when the rod becomes charged by the fur, a negative charge is transferred from the fur to the rod. The net negative charge on the rod is equal to the net positive charge on the fur.

Materials through which electric charges can easily flow are called **CONDUCTORS**. Metals that are good conductors include silicon and boron. On the other hand, an **INSULATOR** is a material through which electric charges do not move easily, if at all. Examples of insulators are the nonmetal elements of the periodic table. A simple device used to indicate the existence of a positive or negative charge is called an electroscope. An electroscope is made up of a conducting knob with very lightweight conducting leaves usually made of foil (gold or aluminum) attached to it. When a charged object touches the knob, the leaves push away from each other because like charges repel. It is not possible to tell whether the charge is positive or negative.

Touch the knob with a finger while a charged rod is nearby. The electrons will be repulsed and flow out of the electroscope through the hand. If you remove your hand while the charged rod remains close, the electroscope will retain the charge.

When an object is rubbed with a charged rod, the object will take on the same charge as the rod; however, charging by induction gives the object the opposite charge as that of the charged rod.

Charge can be removed from an object by connecting it to the earth through a conductor. The removal of static electricity by conduction is called **GROUNDING**.

Electricity can be used to change the chemical composition of a material. For instance, when electricity is passed through water, it breaks the water down into hydrogen gas and oxygen gas.

Circuit breakers in a home monitor the electric current. If there is an overload, the circuit breaker will create an open circuit, stopping the flow of electricity.

Computers can be made small enough to fit inside a plastic credit card by creating what is known as a solid-state device. In this device, electrons flow through solid material such as silicon.

Resistors are used to regulate volume on a television or radio or for a dimmer switch for lights.

A bird can sit on an uninsulated electrical wire without being electrocuted because the bird and the wire have about the same potential; however, if the bird touches two wires at the same time, it would not have to worry about flying south next year.

In an electrical storm, a car is relatively safe from lightning because of the resistance of the rubber tires. A metal building would not be a safe place unless it had a lightning rod to attract the lightning and conduct it into the ground.

CONDUCTORS: materials through which electric charges can easily flow

INSULATORS: materials through which electric charges do not move easily, if at all

GROUNDING: the removal of static electricity by conduction

In an electrical storm, a car is relatively safe from lightning because of the resistance of the rubber tires.

Heat and Temperature

Heat and temperature are different physical quantities. Heat is a measure of energy. Temperature is the measure of how hot (or cold) a body is with respect to a standard object.

Two concepts are important in the discussion of temperature changes. Objects are in thermal contact if they can affect each other's temperature. Set a hot cup of coffee on a desktop. The two objects are in thermal contact with each other and will begin affecting each other's temperature. The coffee will become cooler and the desktop warmer. Eventually, they will have the same temperature. When this happens, they are in thermal equilibrium.

We cannot rely on our sense of touch to determine temperature because the heat from a hand may be conducted more efficiently by certain objects than others, making them feel colder. Thermometers are used to measure temperature. In thermometers, a small amount of mercury in a capillary tube will expand when heated. The thermometer and the object whose temperature it is measuring are put in contact long enough for them to reach thermal equilibrium. The temperature can then be read from the thermometer scale.

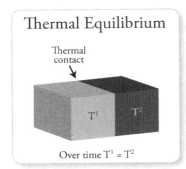

Thermal Equilibrium

Thermal contact

T^1 T^2

Over time $T^1 = T^2$

Three temperature scales are used:

- Celsius: The freezing point of water is set at 0 degrees and the steam (boiling) point is 100 degrees. The interval between the two is divided into 100 equal parts called degrees Celsius.

- Fahrenheit: The freezing point of water is 32 degrees and the boiling point is 212 degrees. The interval between is divided into 180 equal parts called degrees Fahrenheit.

Temperature readings can be converted from one to the other as follows:

Fahrenheit to Celsius	Celsius to Fahrenheit
$C = \frac{5}{9}(F - 32)$	$F = \left(\frac{9}{5}\right)C + 32$

- Kelvin: The Kelvin scale has degrees that are the same size as those of the Celsius scale, but the zero point is moved to the triple point of water. Water inside a closed vessel is in thermal equilibrium in all three states (ice, water, and vapor) at 273.15 degrees Kelvin. This temperature is equivalent to .01 degrees Celsius. Because the degrees are the same in the two scales, temperature changes are the same in Celsius and Kelvin.

Temperature readings can be converted from Celsius to Kelvin:

Celsius to Kelvin	Kelvin to Celsius
K = C + 273.15	C = K − 273.15

The heat capacity of an object is the amount of heat energy it takes to raise the temperature of the object by one degree.

Heat capacity (C) per unit mass (m) is called specific heat (c):

$$c = \frac{C}{m} = \frac{Q}{m}$$

There are a number of ways that heat is measured. In each case, the measurement is dependent upon raising the temperature of a specific amount of water by a specific amount. These conversions of heat energy and work are called the mechanical equivalent of heat.

A **CALORIE** is the amount of energy it takes to raise one gram of water one degree Celsius.

A **KILOCALORIE** is the amount of energy it takes to raise one kilogram of water by one degree Celsius. Food calories are kilocalories.

In the International System of Units (SI), the calorie is equal to 4.184 joules.

A British thermal unit (BTU) = 252 calories = 1.054 kilojoules(kJ).

> **CALORIE:** the amount of energy it takes to raise one gram of water one degree Celsius

> **KILOCALORIE:** the amount of energy it takes to raise one kilogram of water by one degree Celsius

FORMS OF ENERGY	
Thermal Energy	The total internal energy of objects created by the vibration and movement of atoms and molecules. Heat is thermal energy that is transferred due to a difference in temperature between two objects or between an object and its environment.
Acoustic Energy	Also called sound energy; energy in the form of mechanical waves that are able to propagate through materials. The brain interprets these waves as they enter through the ears.
Radiant Energy	The energy that propagates by way of electromagnetic waves. Visible light, which is interpreted by the brain as colors, is an example of radiant energy. Energy propagated through forms of "invisible light," such as radio waves, infrared waves, and X-rays, is also radiant energy.
Electrical Energy	Energy stored in electrical fields, which result from the presence of electrical charges. Electrical fields are the source of such phenomena as electricity, which is a common application of electrical energy, and lightning, which is a natural result of a buildup of electrical energy in the atmosphere.

Continued on next page

Magnetic Energy	Energy stored in magnetic fields, which are produced by moving electrical charges. For instance, a current-carrying wire is able to deflect the needle of a compass. Magnetic energy transfers from the fields produced by electrical current to mechanical energy in the needle as the needle seeks to align itself with the prevailing magnetic field.
Solar Energy	Energy emitted by the sun, which can be in the form of electromagnetic waves (light) or a flux (flow) of particles of matter. The most obvious result of solar energy is daylight. Other phenomena, such as the aurora borealis, or northern lights, result from ionized particles emitted from the sun.
Chemical Energy	The energy stored in the chemical bonds of molecules. For example, the combustion, or burning, of gasoline results in a release of chemical energy, as the hydrocarbon molecules are broken to produce heat and light. This process powers automobiles and other machinery.
Mechanical Energy	The sum of the potential and kinetic energies of a mechanical system. Kinetic energy is energy of motion, and potential energy is stored energy that may result from the presence of some force. Thus, an object held stationary at some distance above the ground has a certain amount of potential gravitational energy, since its release would result in the object falling freely. On the other hand, once in motion, the object would also display kinetic energy. While the object falls, if factors such as friction are ignored, potential energy is continually converted to kinetic energy.
Nuclear Energy	The energy present in the nucleus of atoms. Division, combination, or collision of nuclei can release nuclear energy, depending on the particular characteristics of the nuclei involved in the process. Nuclear energy has been harnessed for peaceful means to produce electricity, and it is also the basis of weapons such as the hydrogen bomb.

Because energy is generally conserved, it can continuously transition from one form to another. For instance, an engine burns gasoline, thus converting the chemical energy of the gasoline into mechanical (specifically, kinetic) energy. Also, plants convert the radiant energy of the sun into chemical energy, which is found in glucose; and a battery converts chemical energy into electrical energy.

Potential energy is stored energy. Examples include:

- Chemical energy stored in atoms
- Mechanical energy stored in objects by the application of force; for example, an elastic band
- Nuclear energy
- Gravitational energy

Kinetic energy is energy in motion. Examples include:

- Electrical energy
- Radiant energy

- Thermal energy

- Motion energy

- Sound

COMPETENCY 20
UNDERSTAND THE FUNDAMENTAL CONCEPTS AND PRINCIPLES OF LIFE SCIENCE

SKILL **Demonstrating knowledge of the characteristics, structures,**
20.1 **functions, and life processes of plants, animals, and other living**
organisms

Living things are called organisms, a term that describes complex, adaptive systems that function as a whole. Several characteristics have traditionally been used to describe organisms and differentiate them from nonliving things:

- **Living things are made of one or more cells**: The cells grow, reproduce, and die.

- **Living things must adapt to environmental changes**: Living things respond to external stimuli.

- **Living things carry on metabolic processes**: They use and make energy.

characteristics of orgnisms

Living things also have a similar chemical makeup. First, all organisms are carbon based, that is, they are made primarily of organic molecules with carbon backbones. Even more specifically, they all use the same twenty amino acids as protein building blocks. Finally, they all use nucleic acids to carry genetic information that ultimately codes for proteins and determines the organism's makeup.

While the distinction between living and nonliving things may seem obvious when we compare, for instance, a rock and a dog, there are some gray areas. For example, viruses are not usually considered organisms because they are acellular and must rely on host cells to metabolize and reproduce. However, it can be argued that some obligate parasites and endosymbionts are similarly incapable of "independent" reproduction, but are still considered living things. Additionally, viruses are similar to organisms in that they are carbon based and carry genetic information in the form of nucleic acids.

Some have suggested a broader definition of organisms, such as "any living structure, such as a plant, animal, fungus, or bacterium, capable of growth and reproduction." Such a definition would encompass both cellular and acellular life and also leave room for synthetic and possibly extraterrestrial life forms. At present, however, it is not likely that viruses will be recharacterized as living things.

The structure of a cell is often related to the cell's function. Root hair cells differ from flower stamens or leaf epidermal cells.

The nucleus of an animal cell is a round body inside the cell. It controls the cell's activities. The nuclear membrane contains threadlike structures called chromosomes. The genes are units that control cell activities found in the nucleus. The cytoplasm has many structures in it. Vacuoles contain the food for the cell. Other vacuoles contain waste materials. Animal cells differ from plant cells because they have cell membranes.

Plant cells have cell walls. A cell wall differs from a cell membrane. A cell membrane is very thin and is a part of the cell, but a cell wall is thick and is a nonliving part of the cell.

Differences Between Plant and Animal Cells

Because they are both eukaryotic cells, the general structure of plant and animal cells is similar. That is, they both have a nucleus and various membrane-bound organelles. However, plant cells possess two unique features not seen in animal cells: cell walls and chloroplasts. Cell walls are composed of cellulose, hemicellulose, and a variety of other materials, and are found just outside the cell membrane. Chloroplasts are large, double-membrane-bound organelles that contain the light-absorbing substance chlorophyll.

There are a few more subtle differences between plant and animal cells:

- Lysosomes are common in animal cells but rarely seen in plant cells.

- Vacuoles are uncommon in animal cells, and when they appear, are small and often temporary; nearly all plant cells have large vacuoles.

- Centrioles are seen only in the lowest forms of plant life; all animal cells possess centrioles.

- Plastids are seen in the cytoplasm of most plant cells, but never in animal cells.

In both plants and animals, cells combine to make tissues that serve specific functions. Further, as is seen in all types of organisms, the structure of a cell is uniquely related to its function. For example, most plant cells perform two unique functions that are associated with the special features detailed above. The first is photosynthesis, the process by which plants transform sunlight into usable energy. Chlorophyll within the chloroplasts absorbs sunlight and photosynthesis takes place across the membranes. Animal cells do not photosynthesize and so do not contain chloroplasts.

The second special function of plant cells relates to the manner in which non-woody plants maintain structural integrity. The necessary structure is created using turgor pressure (hydrostatic pressure) and both vacuoles and cell walls are important in this phenomenon. In a plant cell, the large central vacuole fills with water, which exerts pressure on the cell wall. The cell wall prevents the cell from bursting and creates a turgid cell. The pressure of each cell wall against its neighbors creates stiff tissue that allows the plant to stay upright. This also explains why plants that do not have enough water wilt; their vacuoles lose water and can no longer exert pressure, which causes the plant to droop. Such a mechanism is not necessary in animal cells because most animals have specialized tissues (bones, muscles, exoskeletons, etc.) to perform this function. Accordingly, cell walls and large vacuoles are not seen in animal cells.

Human Body

Skeletal system

The function of the skeletal system is support. Vertebrates have an endoskeleton, with muscles attached to bones. Skeletal proportions are controlled by area-to-volume relationships. Body size and shape are limited due to the forces of gravity. Surface area is increased to improve efficiency in all organ systems.

The axial skeleton consists of the bones of the skull and vertebrae. The appendicular skeleton consists of the bones of the legs, arms, tailbone, and shoulder girdle. Bone is a connective tissue. Parts of the bone include compact bone, which gives strength; spongy bone, which contains red marrow to make blood cells; yellow marrow in the center of long bones to store fat cells; and the periostenum, which is the protective covering on the outside of the bone.

A joint is defined as a place where two bones meet. Joints enable movement. Ligaments attach bone to bone. Tendons attach bones to muscles.

Muscular system

The function of the muscular system is movement. There are three types of muscle tissue. Skeletal muscle is voluntary. These muscles are attached to bones. Smooth muscle is involuntary. It is found in organs and enables functions such as digestion and respiration. Cardiac muscle is a specialized type of smooth muscle and is found in the heart. Muscles can only contract; therefore they work in antagonistic pairs to allow back-and-forward movement. Muscle fibers are made of groups of myofibrils, which are made of groups of sarcomeres. Actin and myosin are proteins, which make up the sarcomere.

Nervous system

The neuron is the basic unit of the nervous system. It consists of an axon, which carries impulses away from the cell body; the dendrite, which carries impulses toward the cell body; and the cell body, which contains the nucleus. Synapses are spaces between neurons. Chemicals called neurotransmitters are found close to the synapse. The myelin sheath, composed of Schwann cells, covers the neurons and provides insulation.

The reflex arc is the simplest nerve response. The brain is bypassed. When a stimulus (like touching a hot stove) occurs, sensors in the hand send the message directly to the spinal cord. This stimulates motor neurons that contract the muscles to move the hand. Voluntary nerve responses involve the brain. Receptor cells send the message to sensory neurons that lead to association neurons. The message is taken to the brain. Motor neurons are stimulated and the message is transmitted to effector cells that cause the end effect.

Organization of the nervous system

The somatic nervous system is controlled consciously. It consists of the central nervous system (brain and spinal cord) and the peripheral nervous system (nerves that extend from the spinal cord to the muscles). The autonomic nervous system is unconsciously controlled by the hypothalamus in the brain. Smooth muscles, the heart, and digestion are all controlled by the autonomic nervous system. The sympathetic nervous system works in opposition to the parasympathetic nervous system. For example, if the sympathetic nervous system stimulates an action, the parasympathetic nervous system would terminate that action.

The somatic nervous system is controlled consciously. The autonomic nervous system is unconsciously controlled by the hypothalamus in the brain.

Digestive system

The function of the digestive system is to break food down and absorb it into the bloodstream, where it can be delivered to all cells of the body for use in cellular respiration. The teeth and saliva begin digestion by breaking food down into smaller pieces and lubricating it so it can be swallowed. The lips, cheeks, and tongue form a bolus (ball) of food. The food is carried down the pharynx by the process of peristalsis (wave-like contractions) and enters the stomach through the cardiac sphincter, which closes to keep food from going back up.

In the stomach, pepsinogen and hydrochloric acid form pepsin, the enzyme that breaks down proteins. The food is broken down further by this chemical action and turned into chyme. The pyloric sphincter muscle opens to allow the food to enter the small intestine, where most nutrient absorption occurs. Any food left after the trip through the small intestine enters the large intestine. The large intestine functions to reabsorb water and produce vitamin K. The feces, or remaining waste, are passed out through the anus.

Respiratory system

The respiratory system functions in the exchange of oxygen (needed) and carbon dioxide (waste). It delivers oxygen to the bloodstream and picks up carbon dioxide for release out of the body. Air enters the mouth and nose, where it is warmed, moistened, and filtered of dust and particles. Cilia in the trachea trap unwanted material in mucus, which can be expelled. The trachea splits into two bronchial tubes, which divide into smaller and smaller bronchioles in the lungs. The internal surface of the lungs is composed of alveoli, which are thin-walled air sacs. These provide a large surface area for gas exchange. The alveoli are lined with capillaries. Oxygen diffuses into the bloodstream and carbon dioxide diffuses out to be exhaled. The oxygenated blood is carried to the heart and delivered to all parts of the body.

The thoracic cavity holds the lungs. The diaphragm, a muscle below the lungs, makes inhalation possible. As the volume of the thoracic cavity increases, the diaphragm muscle flattens out and inhalation occurs. When the diaphragm relaxes, exhalation occurs.

Circulatory system

The function of the circulatory system is to carry oxygenated blood and nutrients to all cells of the body and return carbon dioxide waste to be expelled from the lungs. Unoxygenated blood enters the heart through the inferior and superior vena cava. The first chamber it encounters is the right atrium. It goes through the tricuspid valve to the right ventricle, on to the pulmonary arteries, and then to the lungs, where it is oxygenated. It returns to the heart through the pulmonary vein, into the left atrium. It travels through the bicuspid valve to the left ventricle, where it is pumped to all parts of the body through the aorta.

Heart

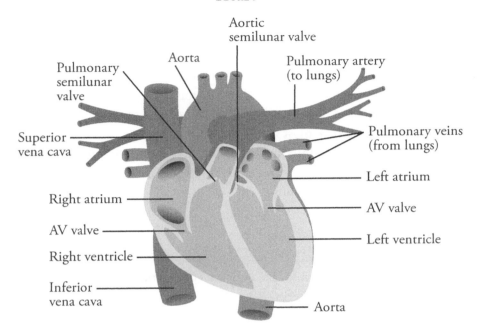

Blood vessels include:

- **Arteries:** Lead away from the heart. All arteries carry oxygenated blood except the pulmonary artery.

- **Arterioles:** Arteries branch off to form these smaller passages.

- **Capillaries:** Arterioles branch off to form tiny capillaries that reach every cell. Blood moves very slowly in capillaries due to their small size.

- **Venules:** Capillaries combine to form larger venules. The vessels are now carrying waste products from the cells.

- **Veins:** Venules combine to form larger veins, leading back to the heart. Veins and venules have thinner walls than arteries, because they are not under as much pressure. Veins contain valves to prevent the backward flow of blood due to gravity.

Components of the blood include:

- **Plasma:** 60 percent of the blood is plasma, the liquid part of blood. Plasma contains salts called electrolytes, nutrients, and waste.

- **Erythrocytes:** Also called red blood cells; Erthrocytes contain hemoglobin, which carries oxygen molecules.

- **Leukocytes:** Also called white blood cells, which are larger than red blood cells. Leukocytes are phagocytic and can engulf invaders. White blood cells are not confined to the blood vessels and can enter the interstitial fluid between cells.

- **Platelets:** Assist in blood clotting. Platelets are made in the bone marrow.

Lymphatic system (Immune system)

Nonspecific defense mechanisms do not target specific pathogens, but are a whole-body response. Results of nonspecific mechanisms are seen as symptoms of an infection. These mechanisms include the skin, mucous membranes, and cells of the blood and lymph (i.e., white blood cells, macrophages). Fever is a result of an increase in the member of white blood cells. Pyrogens are released by white blood cells, which set the body's thermostat to a higher temperature. This inhibits the growth of microorganisms. It also increases metabolism to increase phagocytosis and body repair.

Specific defense mechanisms (antibodies) recognize foreign material (antigens) and respond by destroying the invader. These mechanisms are specific in purpose and diverse in type. They are able to recognize individual pathogens. Memory of the invaders provides immunity upon further exposure.

IMMUNITY is the body's ability to recognize and destroy an antigen before it causes harm. Active immunity develops after recovery from an infectious disease such as chicken pox or after a vaccination (e.g., for measles, mumps, and rubella). Passive immunity can be passed from one individual to another; it is not permanent. A good example is the immunities passed from mother to nursing child.

> **IMMUNITY:** the body's ability to recognize and destroy an antigen before it causes harm

Excretory system

The function of the excretory system is to rid the body of nitrogenous wastes in the form of urea. The functional units of excretion are the nephrons, which make up the kidneys. Antidiuretic hormone (ADH), which is made in the hypothalamus and stored in the pituitary, is released when differences in osmotic balance occur. This will cause more water to be reabsorbed. As the blood becomes more dilute, ADH release ceases.

The Bowman's capsule contains the glomerulus, a tightly packed group of capillaries. The glomerulus is under high pressure. Waste and fluids leak out due to pressure. Filtration is not selective in this area. Selective secretion by active and passive transport occur in the proximal convoluted tubule. Unwanted molecules are secreted into the filtrate. Selective secretion also occurs in the loop of Henle. Salt is actively pumped out of the tube and much water is lost due to the hyperosmosity of the inner part (medulla) of the kidney. As the fluid enters the distal convoluted tubule, more water is reabsorbed. Urine forms in the collecting duct, which leads to the ureter, then to the bladder where it is stored. Urine is passed from the bladder through the urethra. The amount of water reabsorbed into the body depends on how much water or fluids an individual has consumed. Urine can be very dilute or very concentrated if dehydration is present.

Endocrine system

The function of the endocrine system is to manufacture proteins called hormones. Hormones are released into the bloodstream and carried to a target tissue where they stimulate an action. Hormones may build up over time to cause their effect, as in puberty or the menstrual cycle.

Hormones are specific and fit receptors on the target tissue cell surface. The receptor activates an enzyme, which converts ATP to cyclic AMP. Cyclic AMP (cAMP) is a second messenger from the cell membrane to the nucleus. The genes found in the nucleus turn on or off to cause a specific response.

There are two classes of hormones. Steroid hormones come from cholesterol and cause sexual characteristics and mating behavior. These hormones include estrogen and progesterone in females and testosterone in males. Peptide hormones are made in the pituitary, adrenal glands (kidneys), and the pancreas. They include:

- Follicle-stimulating hormone (FSH): Production of sperm or egg cells
- Luteinizing hormone (LH): Functions in ovulation
- Luteotropic hormone (LTH): Assists in production of progesterone
- Growth hormone (GH): Stimulates growth
- Antidiuretic hormone (ADH): Assists in retention of water
- Oxytocin: Stimulates labor contractions at birth and let-down of milk
- Melatonin: Regulates circadian rhythms and seasonal changes
- Epinephrine (adrenaline): Causes fight-or-flight reaction of the nervous system

Hormones work on a feedback system. The increase or decrease in one hormone may cause the increase or decrease in another. Release of hormones causes a specific response.

Reproductive system

Sexual reproduction greatly increases diversity due to the many combinations possible through meiosis and fertilization. Spermatogenesis begins at puberty in the male. The sperm mature in the seminiferous tubules located in the testes. Oogenesis, the production of egg cells, is usually complete by the birth of a female. Egg cells are not released until menstruation begins at puberty. Meiosis forms one ovum with all the cytoplasm and three polar bodies, which are reabsorbed by the body. The ovum are stored in the ovaries and released each month from puberty to menopause.

Sperm are stored in the seminiferous tubules in the testes, where they mature. Mature sperm are found in the epididymis located on top of the testes. After ejaculation, the sperm travels up the vas deferens, where they mix with semen made in the prostate and seminal vesicles and travel out the urethra.

Eggs are stored in the ovaries. Ovulation releases an egg into the fallopian tube, which is ciliated to move the egg along. Fertilization normally occurs in the fallopian tube. If pregnancy does not occur, the egg passes through the uterus and is expelled through the vagina. Levels of progesterone and estrogen stimulate menstruation. In the event of pregnancy, hormonal levels are affected by the implantation of a fertilized egg, so menstruation does not occur.

Pregnancy

If fertilization occurs, the zygote implants in about two to three days in the uterus. Implantation promotes secretion of human chorionic gonadotropin (HCG). This is what is detected in pregnancy tests. The HCG keeps the level of progesterone elevated to maintain the uterine lining in order to feed the developing embryo until the umbilical cord forms. Labor is initiated by oxytocin, which causes labor contractions and dilation of the cervix. Prolactin and oxytocin cause the production of milk.

Animal Respiration

Animals take in oxygen and give off waste gases. For instance, a fish uses its gills to extract oxygen from the water. Bubbles are evidence that waste gases are expelled. Respiration without oxygen is called anaerobic respiration. Anaerobic respiration in animal cells is also called lactic acid fermentation. The end product is lactic acid.

Animal Reproduction

Animal reproduction can be asexual or sexual. Geese lay eggs. Animals such as bear cubs, deer, and rabbits are born alive. Some animals reproduce frequently while others do not. Some species of animals only produce one baby while others produce many (clutch size).

Animal Digestion

Some animals only eat meat (carnivores) while others only eat plants (herbivores). Many animals eat both (omnivores). The purpose of digestion is to break down carbohydrates, fats, and proteins. Many organs are needed to digest food. The process begins with the mouth. Certain animals, such as birds, have beaks to puncture wood or allow for the consumption of large fish. The tooth structure of a beaver is designed to cut down trees. Tigers are known for their sharp teeth, used to rip through the hides of their prey.

Enzymes are catalysts that help speed up chemical reactions by lowering effective activation energy. Enzyme rate is affected by temperature, pH, and the amount of substrate. Saliva is an enzyme that changes starches into sugars.

Animal Circulation

Mammals are warm-blooded; their blood temperature stays constant regardless of outside temperature. Amphibians are cold-blooded; their blood temperature varies with the outside temperature.

SKILL 20.2 **Demonstrating knowledge of physiological processes that regulate and maintain life processes and behavioral responses to internal or external stimuli**

> **PHOTOSYNTHESIS:** the process by which plants make carbohydrates from the energy of the Sun, carbon dioxide, and water

PHOTOSYNTHESIS is the process by which plants make carbohydrates from the energy of the Sun, carbon dioxide, and water. Oxygen is a waste product. Photosynthesis occurs in the chloroplast where the pigment chlorophyll traps energy from the Sun. It has two major steps:

- Light reactions: Sunlight is trapped, water is split, and oxygen is given off. ATP is made and hydrogens reduce NADP to $NADPH_2$. The light reactions occur in light. The products of the light reactions enter into the dark reactions (Calvin cycle).

- Dark reactions: Carbon dioxide enters during the dark reactions. This can occur with or without the presence of light. The energy transferred from $NADPH_2$ and ATP allow for the fixation of carbon into glucose.

During times of decreased light, plants break down the products of photosynthesis through cellular respiration. Glucose, with the help of oxygen, breaks down and produces carbon dioxide and water as waste. The plants use approximately fifty percent of the products of photosynthesis for energy.

Water travels up the xylem of the plant through the process of transpiration. Water sticks to itself (cohesion) and to the walls of the xylem (adhesion). As it evaporates through the stomata of the leaves, the water is pulled up the column from the roots. Environmental factors such as heat and wind increase the rate of transpiration. High humidity decreases the rate of transpiration.

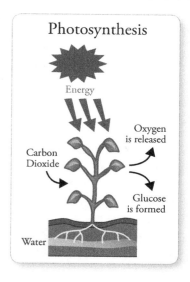

Photosynthesis

Angiosperms are the largest group in the plant kingdom. They are the flowering plants that produce seeds for reproduction. They first appeared about seventy million years ago when the dinosaurs were disappearing. The land was drying up and their ability to produce seeds that could remain dormant until conditions became acceptable allowed for their success. Compared to other plants, they also had more advanced vascular tissue and larger leaves for increased photosynthesis. Angiosperms reproduce through a method of double fertilization in which an ovum is fertilized by two sperm. One sperm produces the new plant; the other forms the food supply for the developing plant.

The success of plant reproduction involves the seeds moving away from the parent plant to decrease competition for space, water, and minerals. Seeds can be carried by wind (maple trees), water (palm trees), or animals (burrs), or ingested by animals and released in their feces in another area.

Gravity keeps plants rooted in the ground. Water allows the roots to take nourishment from the soil and extend down into the soil. The fertility of the soil also acts as a stimulus; if the nourishment the plants need does not exist in the ground, they will die.

> Plants do not possess a nervous system, but, like animals, they do respond to stimuli in their environment.

Plants need sunlight to grow and will grow toward the sun. Too much heat causes them to wither and die, but cold weather can have the same result. Plants start to bud in spring as the atmosphere and the ground start to warm up. They die when the weather turns cold and remain dormant in the soil, if they are perennial, until spring.

TROPISM is the term given to the response of plants to grow toward or away from a stimulus in the environment. In phototropism, light sends the hormone auxin to the portion of the plant receiving the most shade so that it starts to grow toward the light. Plants also respond to touch. Some curl up when touched and others tend to flatten, trying to get away from the touch.

> **TROPISM:** the response of plants to grow toward or away from a stimulus in the environment

Applying knowledge of the life cycles and reproductive processes of common organisms and the principles of heredity in the transmission of traits from one generation to the next

Theories of Evolution

Charles Darwin proposed a mechanism for his theory of evolution, termed natural selection. **NATURAL SELECTION** describes the process by which favorable traits accumulate in a population, changing the population's genetic makeup over time. Darwin theorized that all individual organisms, even those of the same species, are different, and those individuals that happen to possess traits favorable for survival would produce more offspring. Thus, in the next generation, the number of individuals with the favorable trait increases, and the process continues.

Darwin, in contrast to other evolutionary scientists, did not believe that traits acquired during an organism's lifetime (e.g., increased musculature), or the desires and needs of the organism, affected the evolution of populations. For example, Darwin argued that the evolution of long trunks in elephants resulted from environmental conditions that favored those elephants that had longer trunks. The individual elephants did not stretch their trunks to reach food or water and pass on the new, longer trunks to their offspring.

Jean Baptiste Lamarck proposed an alternative mechanism of evolution. Lamarck believed that individual organisms develop traits in response to changing environmental conditions and pass on these new traits to their offspring. For example, Lamarck argued that the trunks of individual elephants lengthen as a result of stretching for scarce food and water, and elephants pass on the longer trunks to their offspring.

Mutations, random changes in nucleotide sequence, are a basic mechanism of evolution. Mutations in DNA result from copying errors during cell division, exposure to radiation and chemicals, and interaction with viruses. Simple point mutations, deletions, or insertions can alter the function or expression of existing genes, but do not contribute greatly to evolution. On the other hand, gene duplication—the duplication of an entire gene—often leads to the creation of new genes that may contribute to the evolution of a species. Because gene duplication results in two copies of the same gene, the extra copy is free to mutate and develop without the selective pressure experienced by mutated single-copy genes. Gene duplication and subsequent mutation often leads to the creation of new genes. When new genes resulting from mutations lend the mutated organism a reproductive advantage relative to environmental conditions, natural selection and evolution can occur.

Recombination is the exchange of DNA between a pair of chromosomes during meiosis. Recombination does not introduce new genes into a population,

NATURAL SELECTION: the process by which favorable traits accumulate in a population, changing the population's genetic makeup over time

Different molecular and environmental processes and conditions drive the evolution of populations. The various mechanisms of evolution either introduce new genetic variation or alter the frequency of existing variation.

but does affect the expression of genes and the combination of traits expressed by individuals. Thus, recombination increases the genetic diversity of populations and contributes to evolution by creating new combinations of genes.

Isolation is the separation of members of a species by environmental barriers that the organisms cannot cross. Environmental change, either gradual or sudden, often results in isolation. An example of gradual isolation is the formation of a mountain range or desert between members of a species. An example of sudden isolation is the separation of members of a species by a flood or earthquake. Isolation leads to evolution because the separated groups cannot reproduce together and differences arise. In addition, because the environment of each group is different, the groups adapt and evolve differently. Extended isolation can lead to SPECIATION, the development of new species.

Sexual reproduction and selection contributes to evolution by consolidating genetic mutations and creating new combinations of genes. Genetic recombination during sexual reproduction introduces new combinations of traits and patterns of gene expression. Consolidation of favorable mutations through sexual reproduction speeds the processes of evolution and natural selection. On the other hand, consolidation of deleterious mutations creates individuals with severe defects or abnormalities.

Genetic drift is, along with natural selection, one of the two main mechanisms of evolution. Genetic drift refers to the chance deviation in the frequency of alleles (traits) resulting from the randomness of zygote formation and selection. Because only a small percentage of all possible zygotes become mature adults, parents do not necessarily pass all of their alleles on to their offspring. Genetic drift is particularly important in small populations because chance deviations in allelic frequency can quickly alter the genotypic makeup of the population. In extreme cases, certain alleles may completely disappear from the gene pool. Genetic drift is particularly influential when environmental events and conditions produce small, isolated populations.

> **SPECIATION:** the development of new species

SKILL 20.4 Applying knowledge of the interrelationships between organisms and their environment

Essential elements are recycled through an ecosystem. At times, the element needs to be "fixed" in a useable form. Cycles are dependent on plants, algae, and bacteria to fix nutrients for use by animals.

Water Cycle	Two percent of all the available water is fixed and held in ice or the bodies of organisms. Available water includes surface water (lakes, ocean, and rivers) and ground water (aquifers, wells). Ninety-six percent of all available water is from ground water. Water is recycled through the processes of evaporation and precipitation. The water present now is the water that has been here since our atmosphere formed.
Carbon Cycle	Ten percent of all available carbon in the air (from carbon dioxide gas) is fixed by photosynthesis. Plants fix carbon in the form of glucose, animals eat the plants and are able to obtain their source of carbon. When animals release carbon dioxide through respiration, the plants again have a source of carbon to fix.
Nitrogen Cycle	Eighty percent of the atmosphere is in the form of nitrogen gas. Nitrogen must be fixed and taken out of the gaseous form to be incorporated into an organism. Only a few genera of bacteria have the correct enzymes to break the triple bond between nitrogen atoms. These bacteria live within the roots of legumes (peas, beans, alfalfa) and add bacteria to the soil so it may be taken up by the plant. Nitrogen is necessary to make amino acids and the nitrogenous bases of DNA.
Phosphorus Cycle	Phosphorus exists as a mineral and is not found in the atmosphere. Fungi and plant roots have structures called mycorrhizae that are able to fix insoluble phosphates into useable phosphorus. Urine and decayed matter returns phosphorus to the earth where it can be fixed in the plant. Phosphorus is needed for the backbone of DNA and for the manufacture of ATP.

SKILL 20.5 Recognizing characteristics of and interactions among populations of organisms in ecosystems

POPULATION: a group of the same species in a specific area

COMMUNITY: a group of populations residing in the same area

BIOMES: communities that are ecologically similar in regard to temperature, rainfall, and the species that live there

Ecology is the study of organisms, where they live and their interactions with the environment. A POPULATION is a group of the same species in a specific area. A COMMUNITY is a group of populations residing in the same area. Communities that are ecologically similar in regard to temperature, rainfall, and the species that live there are called BIOMES.

Specific biomes include:

Marine	Covers seventy-five of the earth. This biome is organized by the depth of the water. The intertidal zone is from the tide line to the edge of the water. The littoral zone is from the water's edge to the open sea. It includes coral reef habitats and is the most densely populated area of the marine biome. The open sea zone is divided into the epipelagic zone and the pelagic zone. The epipelagic zone receives more sunlight and has a larger number of species. The ocean floor is called the benthic zone and is populated with bottom feeders.
Tropical Rain Forest	Temperature is constant (25 degrees C), rainfall exceeds 200 cm per year. Located around the area of the equator, the rain forest has abundant, diverse species of plants and animals.
Savanna	Temperatures range from 0-25 degrees C depending on the location. Rainfall is from 90 to 150 cm per year. Plants include shrubs and grasses. The savanna is a transitional biome between the rain forest and the desert.
Desert	Temperatures range from 10 to 38 degrees C. Rainfall is under 25 cm per year. Plant species include xerophytes and succulents. Lizards, snakes, and small mammals are common animals.
Temperate Deciduous Forest	Temperature ranges from -24 to 38 degrees C. Rainfall is between 65 to 150 cm per year. Deciduous trees are common, as well as deer, bear, and squirrels.
Taiga	Temperatures range from -24 to 22 degrees C. Rainfall is between 35 to 40 cm per year. Taiga is located very north and very south of the equator, getting close to the poles. Plant life includes conifers and plants that can withstand harsh winters. Animals include weasels, mink, and moose.
Tundra	Temperatures range from -28 to 15 degrees C. Rainfall is limited, ranging from 10 to 15 cm per year. The tundra is located even further north and south than the taiga. Common plants include lichens and mosses. Animals include polar bears and musk ox.
Polar or Permafrost	Temperature ranges from -40 to 0 degrees C. It rarely gets above freezing. Rainfall is below 10 cm per year. Most water is bound up as ice. Life is limited.

Succession

SUCCESSION is an orderly process of replacing a community that has been damaged or beginning one where no life previously existed.

- Primary succession occurs after a community has been totally wiped out by a natural disaster or where life never existed before, as in a flooded area.

- Secondary succession takes place in communities that were once flourishing but were disturbed by some source, either man or nature, yet were not totally stripped.

> **SUCCESSION:** an orderly process of replacing a community that has been damaged or beginning one where no life previously existed

A climax community is a community that is established and flourishing.

FEEDING RELATIONSHIPS	
Parasitism	Two species that occupy a similar place; the parasite benefits from the relationship, the host is harmed.
Commensalism	Two species that occupy a similar place; neither species is harmed or benefits from the relationship.
Mutualism (symbiosis)	Two species that occupy a similar place; both species benefit from the relationship.
Competition	Two species that occupy the same habitat or eat the same food are said to be in competition with each other.
Predation	Animals that eat other animals are called predators. The animals they feed on are called the prey. Population growth depends upon competition for food, water, shelter, and space. The amount of predators determines the amount of prey, which in turn affects the number of predators.
Carrying Capacity	This is the total amount of life a habitat can support. Once the habitat runs out of food, water, shelter, or space, the carrying capacity decreases, and then stabilizes.

ECOLOGICAL PROBLEMS CAUSED BY MAN	
Biological Magnification	Chemicals and pesticides accumulate along the food chain. Tertiary consumers have more accumulated toxins than animals at the bottom of the food chain.
Simplification of the Food Web	Three major crops feed the world (rice, corn, wheat). The planting of these foods wipe out habitats and push animals residing there into other habitats causing overpopulation or extinction.
Fuel Sources	Strip mining and the overuse of oil reserves have depleted these resources. At the current rate of consumption, conservation or alternate fuel sources will guarantee our future fuel sources.
Pollution	Although technology gives us many advances, pollution is a side effect of production. Waste disposal and the burning of fossil fuels have polluted our land, water and air. Global warming and acid rain are two results of the burning of hydrocarbons and sulfur.
Global Warming	Rainforest depletion and the use of fossil fuels and aerosols have caused an increase in carbon dioxide production. This leads to a decrease in the amount of oxygen which is directly proportional to the amount of ozone. As the ozone layer depletes, more heat enters our atmosphere and is trapped. This causes an overall warming effect which may eventually melt polar ice caps, causing a rise in water levels and changes in climate that will affect weather systems worldwide.

Table continued on next page

Endangered Species	Construction of homes to house people in our overpopulated world has caused the destruction of habitat for other animals leading to their extinction.
Overpopulation	The human race is still growing at an exponential rate. Carrying capacity has not been met due to our ability to use technology to produce more food and housing. Space and water cannot be manufactured and eventually our nonrenewable resources will reach a crisis state. Our overuse affects every living thing on this planet.

SKILL 20.6 Demonstrating knowledge of the diversity of organisms and the ways in which organisms have adapted to their environments

See also Skills 20.3, 20.4, and 20.5

COMPETENCY 21
UNDERSTAND THE FUNDAMENTAL CONCEPTS AND PRINCIPLES OF EARTH AND SPACE SCIENCE

SKILL 21.1 Recognizing characteristics, properties, and uses of Earth materials

Soils are composed of particles of sand, clay, various minerals, tiny living organisms, and humus, as well as the decayed remains of plants and animals. Soils are divided into three classes according to their texture:

Humus = dark, organic material in soils

- Sandy soils: Gritty, and their particles do not bind together firmly. Sandy soils are porous, and water passes through them rapidly. As a result, they have poor absorption.

- Clay soils: Smooth and greasy, and their particles bind together firmly. Clay soils are moist and usually do not allow water to easily pass through them. This type of soil has the lowest potential for runoff.

- Loamy soils: Feel somewhat like velvet, and their particles clump together. Loamy soils are composed of sand, clay, and silt, and they may be able to hold water. Some loamy soils allow for the flow of water. Percolation, or the filtering and movement of water through porous materials, is best in this type of soil.

The formation of soil is a process that occurs over millions of years. Various factors come into play that make the soil different in different regions of the world.

There are five important factors involved in the development of soil:

1. Parent material: This can be both mineral and organic materials of the Earth. It can be the ash left behind by the eruption of a volcano, material that is carried to and deposited in an area by wind or water, or formed from the decomposition of organisms. It can also be the result of material left behind by glaciers as they melt.

2. Climate: Weathering depends on the climate of the area and determines the fineness of the soil that results. Temperature and water are two major forces that affect the amount of weathering that takes place.

3. Living organisms: As plants and animals die, they add material to the parent material that has been affected by weathering. These organisms are usually found in the subsoil and the topsoil. As the live animals dig into the soil, they provide more spaces for water to seep through, and in this way more air gets deeper into the soil as well.

4. Topography: The flatness or hilliness of an area contributes to the amount of weathering and runoff that takes place.

5. Time: Since it takes several centuries to form only one inch of soil, the soils of the Earth are millions of years old.

The three major sub-divisions of rocks are igneous, sedimentary, and metamorphic; however, it is common for one type of rock to transform into another type, which is known as the rock cycle.

Rocks are aggregates of minerals. They are classified by the differences in their chemical composition and the way that they are formed. The three major subdivisions of rocks are igneous, sedimentary, and metamorphic; however, it is common for one type of rock to transform into another type, which is known as the rock cycle.

Igneous Rocks

IGNEOUS ROCKS:
formed from molten rock called magma

IGNEOUS ROCKS are formed from molten rock called magma. There are two types of igneous rock: volcanic and plutonic. As the name suggests, volcanic rock is formed when magma reaches the Earth's surface as lava. Plutonic rock is also derived from magma, but it is formed when magma cools and crystallizes beneath the surface of the Earth.

Igneous rocks can be classified according to their texture, their composition, and the way that they formed. As magma cools, the elements and compounds begin to form crystals. The more slowly the magma cools, the larger the crystals grow. Rocks with large crystals are said to have a coarse-grained texture. Granite is an example of a coarse-grained rock. Rocks that cool rapidly before any crystals can form have a glassy texture, such as obsidian, also commonly known as volcanic glass.

Sedimentary Rocks

SEDIMENTARY ROCKS are formed by layered deposits of inorganic and/or organic matter. Layers, or strata, of rock are laid down horizontally to form sedimentary rocks. Sedimentary rocks that form as mineral solutions (i.e., seawater) evaporate are called precipitate. Those that contain the remains of living organisms are termed biogenic. Finally, those that form from the freed fragments of other rocks are called clastic. Because the layers of sedimentary rocks reveal chronology and often contain fossils, these types of rock have been key in helping scientists understand the history of the Earth. Chalk, limestone, sandstone, and shale are all examples of sedimentary rock.

> **SEDIMENTARY ROCKS:** formed by layered deposits of inorganic and/or organic matter

Lithification of sedimentary rocks

When fluid sediments are transformed into solid sedimentary rocks, the process is known as lithification. A common process affecting sediments is compaction, when the weights of overlying materials compress and compact the deeper sediments. The compaction process leads to cementation, when sediments are converted to sedimentary rock.

Metamorphic Rocks

METAMORPHIC ROCKS are created when rocks are subjected to high temperatures and pressures. The original rock, or protolith, may have been igneous, sedimentary, or even an older metamorphic rock. The temperatures and pressures necessary to achieve transformation are higher than those observed on the Earth's surface and are high enough to alter the minerals in the protolith. Because these rocks are formed within the Earth's crust, studying metamorphic rocks gives us clues to conditions in the Earth's mantle. In some metamorphic rocks, different-colored bands are apparent. These bands, called foliation, result from strong pressures being applied from specific directions. Examples of metamorphic rock include slate and marble.

> **METAMORPHIC ROCKS:** created when rocks are subjected to high temperatures and pressures

Metamorphic rocks are classified into two groups: foliated (leaflike) and unfoliated. Foliated rocks consist of compressed, parallel bands of minerals, which give the rocks a striped appearance. Examples of such rocks include slate, schist, and gneiss. Unfoliated rocks are not banded. Examples include quartzite, marble, and anthracite.

SKILL 21.2 Recognizing properties and characteristics of objects in the sky (e.g., sun, planets, comets)

Solar System

Montage of planetary images taken by spacecraft managed by the Jet Propulsion Laboratory. Courtesy of NASA Jet Propulsion Laboratory, Pasadena, CA.

The Sun is the largest star in the Earth's solar system and all life on Earth depends on it. It is always changing, and its magnetic fields cause activity on the Sun itself as well as on the Earth.

Galileo, the first scientist to study the Sun, discovered that its surface is often covered by dark and irregularly shaped regions, called sunspots. This led him to the correct conclusion that the Sun rotates. There are groups of sunspots that can last for weeks or months, and all but the smallest of these have two regions.

The Sun provides the heat and light needed for life to flourish. All living organisms need heat and the energy from the Sun in order to survive. The huge stream of radiation produced by the Sun is the cause of solar wind. Solar wind does not have the effect on Earth that it does on other planets because Earth's gravity keeps the wind blowing through the solar system from reaching the Earth. However, weather in space caused by the Sun does have an effect on Earth. For example:

- High levels of radiation affect space satellites, often causing them to fail.

- Solar energy can cause the Earth to become warmer than usual, resulting in power failures when there is too much demand on air-conditioning systems to cool people's homes and offices.

- Space weather can disrupt communication by interfering with radio signals and distorting GPS signals.

Planets

There are eight established planets in our solar system: Mercury, Venus, Earth, Mars, Jupiter, Saturn, Uranus and Neptune. Pluto was an established planet in our solar system, but, as of summer 2006, its status is being reconsidered. The planets are divided into two groups based on distance from the sun. The inner planets include Mercury, Venus, Earth and Mars. The outer planets include Jupiter, Saturn, Uranus and Neptune.

PLANETS IN THE SOLAR SYSTEM	
Mercury	The closest planet to the Sun. Its surface has craters and rocks. The atmosphere is composed of hydrogen, helium, and sodium. Mercury was named after the Roman messenger god.
Venus	Has a slow rotation when compared to Earth. Venus and Uranus rotate in opposite directions from the other planets. This opposite rotation is called retrograde rotation. The surface of Venus is not visible due to the extensive cloud cover. The atmosphere is composed mostly of carbon dioxide, while sulfuric acid droplets in the dense cloud cover give Venus a yellow appearance. Venus has a greater greenhouse effect than that observed on Earth, and the dense clouds combined with carbon dioxide trap heat. Venus was named after the Roman goddess of love.
Earth	Considered a water planet, with 70 percent of its surface covered by water. Gravity holds the masses of water in place. The different temperatures observed on Earth allow for the different states of water (solid, liquid, gas) to exist. The atmosphere is composed mainly of oxygen and nitrogen. Earth is the only planet known to support life.
Mars	Surface contains numerous craters, active and extinct volcanoes, ridges, and valleys with extremely deep fractures. Iron oxide found in the dusty soil makes the surface seem rust-colored and the skies seem pink in color. The atmosphere is composed of carbon dioxide, nitrogen, argon, oxygen, and water vapor. Mars has polar regions with ice caps composed of water as well as two satellites (moons). Mars was named after the Roman war god.
Jupiter	The largest planet in the solar system. Jupiter has sixteen satellites. The atmosphere is composed of hydrogen, helium, methane, and ammonia. There are white-colored bands of clouds indicating rising gases and dark-colored bands of clouds indicating descending gases. The gas movement is caused by heat resulting from the energy of Jupiter's core. Jupiter has a strong magnetic field and a great red spot that is thought to be a hurricane-like cloud.
Saturn	The second largest planet in the solar system. Saturn has rings of ice, rock, and dust particles circling it. Its atmosphere is composed of hydrogen, helium, methane, and ammonia. It has more than twenty satellites. Saturn was named after the Roman god of agriculture.
Uranus	The third largest planet in the solar system and has retrograde revolution. Uranus is a gaseous planet. It has ten dark rings and fifteen satellites. Its atmosphere is composed of hydrogen, helium, and methane. Uranus was named after the Greek god of the heavens.
Neptune	Another gaseous planet with an atmosphere consisting of hydrogen, helium, and methane. Neptune has three rings and two satellites. It was named after the Roman sea god because its atmosphere is the same color as the seas.
Pluto	Once considered the smallest planet in the solar system, it is no longer considered a planet, but, rather, a dwarf planet. Pluto's atmosphere probably contains methane, ammonia, and frozen water. Pluto has one satellite. It revolves around the Sun once every 250 years. Pluto was named after the Roman god of the underworld.

Comets, Asteroids, and Meteors

Astronomers believe that rocky fragments may be the remains of the birth of the solar system that never formed into a planet. These asteroids are found in the region between Mars and Jupiter.

COMETS are masses of frozen gases, cosmic dust, and small rocky particles. Astronomers think that most comets originate in a dense comet cloud beyond Pluto. A comet consists of a nucleus, a coma, and a tail. A comet's tail always points away from the Sun. The most famous comet, Halley's comet, is named after the person who first discovered it in 240 BCE. It returns to the skies near Earth every seventy-five to seventy-six years.

METEOROIDS are composed of particles of rock and metal of various sizes. When a meteoroid travels through the Earth's atmosphere, friction causes its surface to heat up and it begins to burn. A burning meteoroid falling through the Earth's atmosphere is called a METEOR (also known as a "shooting star").

METEORITES are meteors that strike the Earth's surface. A physical example of a meteorite's impact on the Earth's surface can be seen in Arizona; the Barringer Crater is a huge meteor crater. There are many other meteor craters throughout the world.

Oort Cloud and Kuiper Belt

The OORT CLOUD is a hypothetical spherical cloud surrounding our solar system. It extends approximately three light years or 30 trillion kilometers from the Sun. The cloud is believed to be made up of materials that were ejected from the inner solar system because of interaction with Uranus and Neptune, but are gravitationally bound to the Sun. It is named the Oort cloud after Jan Oort, who suggested its existence in 1950. Comets from the Oort cloud exhibit a wide range of sizes, inclinations, and eccentricities; they are often referred to as long-period comets because they have a period of greater than 200 years.

The KUIPER BELT is the name given to a vast population of small bodies orbiting the Sun beyond Neptune. There are more than 70,000 of these small bodies, some with diameters larger than 100 kilometers extending outwards from the orbit of Neptune to 50AU. They exist mostly within a ring or belt surrounding the Sun. It is believed that the objects in the Kuiper Belt are primitive remnants of the earliest phases of the solar system. It is also believed that the Kuiper Belt is the source of many short-period comets (comets with periods of less than 200 years). It is a reservoir for the comets in the same way that the Oort cloud is a reservoir for long-period comets.

Sidebar notes:

Astronomers think that most comets originate in a dense comet cloud beyond Pluto.

COMETS: masses of frozen gases, cosmic dust, and small rocky particles

METEOROIDS: composed of particles of rock and metal of various sizes

METEOR: a burning meteoroid falling through the Earth's atmosphere also known as a "shooting star"

METEORITES: meteors that strike the Earth's surface

OORT CLOUD: a hypothetical spherical cloud surrounding our solar system extending approximately three light years or 30 trillion kilometers from the Sun

KUIPER BELT: a vast population of small bodies orbiting the Sun beyond Neptune

Occasionally, the orbit of a Kuiper Belt object will be disturbed by the interactions of the giant planets in such a way as to cause the object to cross the orbit of Neptune. It will then very likely have a close encounter with Neptune, sending it out of the solar system, into an orbit crossing those of the other giant planets, or even into the inner solar system. Prevailing theory states that scattered disk objects began as Kuiper Belt objects, which were scattered by gravitational interactions with the giant planets.

> ### SKILL 21.3 Applying knowledge of Earth's position and movement in the solar system and interactions between Earth, the moon, and the sun
> (e.g., seasons, tides)

Earth is the third planet away from the Sun in our solar system. Earth's numerous types of motion and states of orientation greatly affect global conditions, such as seasons, tides, and lunar phases. The Earth orbits the Sun with a period of 365 days. During this orbit, the average distance between the Earth and Sun is 93 million miles. The shape of the Earth's orbit around the Sun deviates from the shape of a circle only slightly. This deviation, known as the Earth's eccentricity, has a very small affect on the Earth's climate. The Earth is closest to the Sun at perihelion, occurring around January 2 of each year, and is farthest from the Sun at aphelion, occurring around July 2. Because the Earth is closest to the sun in January, the northern winter is slightly warmer than the southern winter.

Seasons

The rotation axis of the Earth is not perpendicular to the orbital (ecliptic) plane. The axis of the Earth is tilted 23.45° from the perpendicular. The tilt of the Earth's axis is known as the obliquity of the ecliptic and is mainly responsible for the four seasons of the year by influencing the intensity of solar rays received by the Northern and Southern Hemispheres.

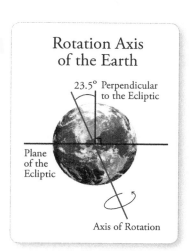

Rotation Axis of the Earth

23.5° Perpendicular to the Ecliptic

Plane of the Ecliptic

Axis of Rotation

The four seasons—spring, summer, fall, and winter—are extended periods of characteristic average temperature, rainfall, storm frequency, and vegetation growth or dormancy. The effect of the Earth's tilt on climate is best demonstrated at the solstices, the two days of the year when the Sun is farthest from the Earth's equatorial plane. At the Summer Solstice (June Solstice), the Earth's tilt on its axis causes the Northern Hemisphere to the lean toward the Sun, while the Southern Hemisphere leans away. Consequently, the Northern Hemisphere receives more intense rays from the Sun and experiences summer during this time, while the Southern Hemisphere experiences winter. At the Winter Solstice (December

Solstice), it is the Southern Hemisphere that leans toward the Sun and thus experiences summer. Spring and fall are produced by varying degrees of the same leaning toward or away from the Sun.

Tides

TIDE: the cyclic rise and fall of large bodies of water

The orientation of and gravitational interaction between the Earth and the Moon are responsible for the ocean tides that occur on Earth. The term **TIDE** refers to the cyclic rise and fall of large bodies of water. Gravitational attraction is defined as the force of attraction between all bodies in the universe. At the location on Earth closest to the Moon, the gravitational attraction of the Moon draws seawater toward the Moon in the form of a tidal bulge. On the opposite side of the Earth, another tidal bulge forms in the direction away from the Moon because at this point, the Moon's gravitational pull is the weakest. "Spring tides" are especially strong tides that occur when the Earth, Sun, and Moon are in line, allowing both the Sun and the Moon to exert gravitational force on the Earth and increase tidal bulge height. These tides occur during the full moon and the new moon. "Neap tides" are especially weak tides occurring when the gravitational forces of the Moon and the Sun are perpendicular to one another. These tides occur during quarter moons.

Lunar Phases

Teaching lunar phases:

www.moonconnection .com/moon_phases.phtml

The Earth's orientation in respect to the solar system is also responsible for our perception of the phases of the Moon. As the Earth orbits the Sun with a period of 365 days, the Moon orbits the Earth every 27 days. As the Moon circles the Earth, its shape in the night sky appears to change. The changes in the appearance of the Moon from Earth are known as "lunar phases." These phases vary cyclically according to the relative positions of the Moon, the Earth, and the Sun. At all times, half of the Moon is facing the Sun and is thus illuminated by reflecting the Sun's light. As the Moon orbits the Earth and the Earth orbits the Sun, the half of the Moon that faces the Sun changes. However, the Moon is in synchronous rotation around the Earth, meaning that nearly the same side of the Moon faces the Earth at all times. This side is referred to as the near side of the Moon. Lunar phases occur as the Earth and Moon orbit the Sun and the fractional illumination of the Moon's near side changes.

When the Sun and Moon are on opposite sides of the Earth, observers on Earth perceive a full Moon, meaning the Moon appears circular because the entire illuminated half of the Moon is visible. As the Moon orbits the Earth, the Moon "wanes" as the amount of the illuminated half of the Moon that is visible from Earth decreases. A gibbous Moon is between a full Moon and a half Moon, or between a half Moon and a full Moon. When the Sun and the Moon are on the same side of Earth, the illuminated half of the Moon is facing away from Earth, and the Moon appears invisible. This lunar phase is known as the new Moon. The time between each full Moon is approximately 29.53 days.

LUNAR PHASES		
New Moon		The moon is invisible or the first signs of a crescent appear
Waxing Crescent		The right crescent of the moon is visible
First Quarter		The right quarter of the moon is visible
Waxing Gibbous		Only the left crescent is not illuminated
Full Moon		The entire illuminated half of the moon is visible
Waning Gibbous		Only the right crescent of the moon is not illuminated
Last Quarter		The left quarter of the moon is illuminated
Waning Crescent		Only the left crescent of the moon is illuminated

Viewing the moon from the Southern Hemisphere would cause these phases to occur in the opposite order.

SKILL 21.4 Demonstrating knowledge of the properties and processes of Earth's hydrosphere, biosphere, atmosphere, and lithosphere and interactions among them

Features, Functions, and Characteristics of the Atmospheric Layers

Dry air is composed of three basic components; dry gas, water vapor, and solid particles (dust from soil, etc.).

MOST ABUNDANT DRY GASES IN THE ATMOSPHERE		
Chemical Symbol	Gas	% in atmosphere
N_2	Nitrogen	78.09
O_2	Oxygen	20.95
AR	Argon	0.93
CO_2	Carbon Dioxide	0.03

FOUR MAIN LAYERS OF ATMOSPHERE (BASED ON TEMPERATURE)	
Troposphere	Closest to the Earth's surface, all weather phenomena occur here as it is the layer with the most water vapor and dust. Air temperature decreases with increasing altitude. The average thickness of the troposphere is 7 miles (11 km).
Stratosphere	Containing very little water, clouds within this layer are extremely rare. The ozone layer is located in the upper portions of the stratosphere. Air temperature is fairly constant but does increase somewhat with height due to the absorption of solar energy and ultraviolet rays from the ozone layer.
Mesosphere	Air temperature again decreases with height in this layer. It is the coldest layer with temperatures in the range of -1000° C at the top.
Thermosphere	Extends upward into space. Oxygen molecules in this layer absorb energy from the Sun, causing temperatures to increase with height. The lower part of the thermosphere is called the ionosphere. Here charged particles or ions and free electrons can be found. When gases in the ionosphere are excited by solar radiation, the gases give off light and glow in the sky. These glowing lights are called the Aurora Borealis in the Northern Hemisphere and Aurora Australis in Southern Hemisphere. The upper portion of the thermosphere is called the exosphere. Gas molecules are very far apart in this layer. Layers of exosphere are also known as the Van Allen Belts and are held together by Earth's magnetic field.

CLOUD TYPES	
Cirrus	White and feathery; high in the sky
Cumulus	Thick, white, fluffy
Stratus	Layers of clouds cover most of the sky
Nimbus	Heavy, dark clouds that represent thunderstorm clouds

Variations on the clouds mentioned above include Cumulo-nimbus and Strato-nimbus.

Atmospheric Conditions and Weather

El Niño refers to a sequence of changes in the ocean and atmospheric circulation across the Pacific Ocean. The water around the equator is unusually hot every two to seven years. Trade winds normally blow east to west across the equatorial latitudes, piling warm water into the western Pacific. A huge mass of heavy thunderstorms usually forms in the area and produces vast currents of rising air that displace heat poleward. This helps create the strong midlatitude jet streams. The world's climate patterns are disrupted by this change in location of thunderstorm activity.

Air masses moving toward or away from the Earth's surface are called air currents. Air moving parallel to Earth's surface is called wind. Weather conditions are generated by winds and air currents carrying large amounts of heat and moisture from one part of the atmosphere to another. Wind speeds are measured by instruments called anemometers.

The wind belts in each hemisphere consist of convection cells that encircle Earth like belts. There are three major wind belts on Earth:

1. Trade winds

2. Prevailing westerlies

3. Polar easterlies

Wind belt formation depends on the differences in air pressures that develop in the doldrums, the horse latitudes, and the polar regions. The doldrums surround the equator. Within this belt, heated air usually rises straight up into Earth's atmosphere. The horse latitudes are regions of high barometric pressure with calm and light winds, and the Polar regions contain cold dense air that sinks to the Earth's surface.

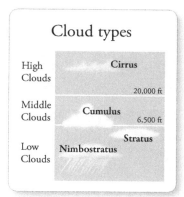

Cloud types

High Clouds — Cirrus — 20,000 ft

Middle Clouds — Cumulus — 6,500 ft

Low Clouds — Nimbostratus — Stratus

Teaching cloud formations:

www.summitpost.org /article/171461 /cloud-formations.html

Winds caused by local temperature changes include sea breezes and land breezes.

SEA BREEZES are caused by the unequal heating of the land and an adjacent, large body of water. Land heats up faster than water. The movement of cool ocean air toward the land is called a sea breeze. Sea breezes usually begin blowing about midmorning; ending about sunset.

SEA BREEZE: caused by the unequal heating of the land and an adjacent, large body of water

A breeze that blows from the land to the ocean or a large lake is called a **LAND BREEZE.**

LAND BREEZE: a breeze that blows from the land to the ocean or a large lake

MONSOONS are huge wind systems that cover large geographic areas and that reverse direction seasonally. The monsoons of India and Asia are examples of these seasonal winds. They alternate wet and dry seasons. As denser cooler air over the ocean moves inland, a steady seasonal wind called a summer or wet monsoon is produced.

MONSOONS: huge wind systems that cover large geographic areas and that reverse direction seasonally

The air temperature at which water vapor begins to condense is called the **DEW POINT.**

DEW POINT: the air temperature at which water vapor begins to condense

RELATIVE HUMIDITY is the actual amount of water vapor in a certain volume of air compared to the maximum amount of water vapor this air could hold at a given temperature.

RELATIVE HUMIDITY: the actual amount of water vapor in a certain volume of air compared to the maximum amount of water vapor this air could hold at a given temperature

Knowledge of Types of Storms

A **THUNDERSTORM** is a brief, local storm produced by the rapid upward movement of warm, moist air within a cumulo-nimbus cloud. Thunderstorms always produce lightning and thunder and are accompanied by strong wind gusts and heavy rain or hail.

THUNDERSTORM: a brief, local storm produced by the rapid upward movement of warm, moist air within a cumulo-nimbus cloud

A severe storm with swirling winds that may reach speeds of hundreds of km per hour is called a **TORNADO.** Such a storm is also referred to as a "twister." The sky is covered by large cumulo-nimbus clouds and violent thunderstorms; a funnel-shaped swirling cloud may extend downward from a cumulo-nimbus cloud and reach the ground. Tornadoes are storms that leave a narrow path of destruction on the ground.

TORNADO: a severe storm with swirling winds that may reach speeds of hundreds of km per hour

A swirling, funnel-shaped cloud that extends downward and touches a body of water is called a **WATERSPOUT.**

HURRICANES are storms that develop when warm, moist air carried by trade winds rotate around a low-pressure "eye." A large, rotating, low-pressure system accompanied by heavy precipitation and strong winds is called a tropical cyclone (better known as a hurricane). In the Pacific region, a hurricane is called a typhoon.

Storms that occur only in the winter are known as blizzards or ice storms. A blizzard is a storm with strong winds, blowing snow, and frigid temperatures. An ice storm consists of falling rain that freezes when it strikes the ground, covering everything with a layer of ice.

The Water Cycle

Water that falls to Earth is called precipitation. Precipitation can be in the form of a liquid (rain) or a solid (snow and hail), or it can freeze during the process of precipitating (sleet). Precipitation is part of a continuous process, called the WATER CYCLE, in which water at the Earth's surface evaporates, condenses into clouds, and returns to Earth. Water located below the surface is called groundwater.

> **HURRICANES:** storms that develop when warm, moist air carried by trade winds rotate around a low-pressure "eye"

> **WATERSPOUT:** a swirling, funnel-shaped cloud that extends downward and touches a body of water

> **WATER CYCLE:** a continuous process, in which water at the Earth's surface evaporates, condenses into clouds, and returns to Earth

The Water Cycle

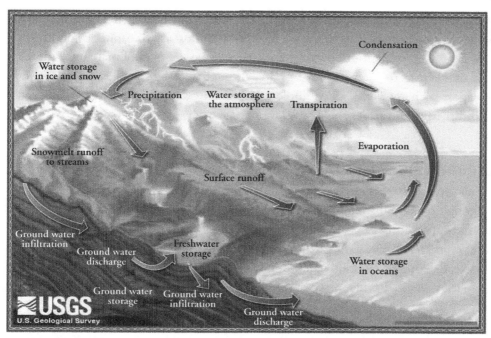

By John M. Evans USGS, Colorado District.

Precipitation can result from a number of atmospheric factors. Air, like any gas, has a limited capacity to hold another dissolved gas (in this case, water vapor). Changes in conditions, such as a decrease in temperature or an increase in water vapor content, can result in condensation of water vapor into liquid water. When this occurs in the atmosphere, clouds begin to form. As the droplets of water, which result from condensation around small particles (condensation nuclei) suspended in the air, grow in size and weight, they eventually reach a point beyond which they can no longer remain suspended in the cloud. The droplets then fall to the ground as precipitation.

Liquid water becomes water vapor through the process of evaporation. This tends to occur more readily in warmer conditions, since more thermal energy is available to allow the water to change from the liquid phase to the gas phase. Evaporation occurs readily when large bodies of water, such as oceans, are present, and it is balanced by the amount of water vapor already contained in the surrounding air. Air can eventually reach saturation, beyond which point no more water vapor can be contained. Addition of further water vapor to saturated air, or reduction of the temperature, results in condensation. In addition to evaporation, water can be transformed directly from the solid phase to the gas phase through sublimation. Sublimation can occur in the presence of snow or ice, especially when the air has low water vapor content.

Water that has evaporated or sublimated into the atmosphere, largely from sizable bodies of water or ice, can later turn into precipitation as atmospheric conditions change. This precipitation, in turn, can either evaporate or sublimate once more, or it may return to a larger body of water through above-ground or below-ground transport such as a river. This completes the water cycle, as precipitated water can be returned to the atmosphere as a gas once again.

Groundwater

Groundwater provides drinking water for fifty-three percent of the population in the United States.

Much groundwater is clean enough to drink without any type of treatment. Although rocks and soil filter impurities from water as it flows over them, many groundwater sources are becoming contaminated. Septic tanks, broken pipes, agricultural fertilizers, garbage dumps, rainwater runoff and leaky underground tanks can all pollute groundwater. Removal of large volumes of groundwater can cause the collapse of soil and rock underground, causing the ground to sink.

Along shorelines, excessive depletion of underground water supplies allows the intrusion of saltwater into the freshwater field, making the groundwater supply undrinkable.

Runoff

Surface runoff is water that flows over land before reaching a river, lake, or ocean. Runoff occurs when precipitation falls at a rate that exceeds the ability of the soil to absorb it or when the soil becomes saturated. Certain human activities have increased runoff by making surfaces increasingly impervious to precipitation. Water is prevented from being absorbed into the ground due to pavement and buildings in urban areas and due to heavily tilled farmland in rural areas. Instead of renewing the groundwater supplies, the precipitation is channeled directly to streams and other bodies of water. Not only does this reduce groundwater supplies, but it can also trigger increased erosion, siltation, and flooding. Increased rates of erosion are particularly damaging to agricultural endeavors, since fertile topsoil is carried away at a higher rate.

Another important environmental effect of human activity on runoff is additional contribution to water pollution. As the runoff flows across land, it picks up and carries particulates and soil contaminants. The pollutants, including agricultural pesticides and fertilizers, can accumulate in lakes and other bodies of water.

Leaching

LEACHING is the liquid extraction of substances contained in a solid. Leaching includes the natural processes by which water removes soluble nutrients from soil and minerals from rocks. Agriculturally, the process of leaching is often exploited to lower high salt concentrations in soil. The nutrient loss caused by leaching can be mitigated by special crop planting and fertilizer application techniques.

> **LEACHING:** the liquid extraction of substances contained in a solid

Leaching may have negative environmental consequences because it can lead to contamination of soil when water liberates contaminants in buried waste (such as nuclear waste or materials in landfills). Water can also dissolve agricultural chemicals and carry them to both above-ground and underground water sources.

Aquifers and reservoirs

An **AQUIFER** is an underground region of porous material that contains water. The material can be porous rock or another substance such as sand or gravel. Aquifers may or may not be surrounded by nonporous materials, and thus may or may not be relatively isolated. The water contained in an aquifer, if it is sufficiently close to the surface, can be tapped by a well to serve residential or other purposes. Since water can flow within an aquifer, contamination and overuse is a danger, thus posing problems in cases of extensive dependence on a particular aquifer for supplying water.

> **AQUIFER:** an underground region of porous material that contains water

Reservoirs are man-made lakes designed for storing water. They may either be the result of a lake bed that is specifically constructed to be filled with water later, or the result of damming a river or other body of water. Reservoirs can serve a number of uses, ranging from water treatment to hydroelectric power generation.

Mountains

OROGENY is the term given to natural mountain building. A mountain is terrain that has been raised high above the surrounding landscape by volcanic action or some form of tectonic plate collisions. The plate collisions could either be intercontinental collisions or ocean floor collisions with a continental crust (subduction).

> **OROGENY:** natural mountain building

The physical composition of mountains includes igneous, metamorphic, and sedimentary rocks; some may have rock layers that are tilted or distorted by plate collision forces.

> *The physical composition of mountains includes igneous, metamorphic, and sedimentary rocks.*

There are many different types of mountains. The physical attributes of a mountain range depend upon the angle at which plate movement thrusts layers of rock to the surface. Many mountains (the Adirondacks, the Southern Rockies) were formed along high-angle faults.

Folded mountains (the Alps, the Himalayas) are produced by the folding of rock layers during their formation. The Himalayas are the highest mountains in the world; they contain Mount Everest, which rises almost nine kilometers above sea level. The Himalayas were formed when India collided with Asia. The movement that created this collision is still in process at the rate of a few centimeters per year.

Fault-block mountains (in Utah, Arizona, and New Mexico) are created when plate movement produces tension forces instead of compression forces. The area under tension produces normal faults, and rock along these faults is displaced upward.

Dome mountains are formed as magma tries to push up through the crust but fails to break the surface. Dome mountains resemble a huge blister on the Earth's surface.

Upwarped mountains (the Black Hills of South Dakota) are created in association with a broad arching of the crust. They can also be formed by rock thrust upward along high angle faults.

The formation of mountains

Mountains are produced by different types of processes. Most major mountain ranges are formed by the processes of folding and faulting.

In folding, mountains are produced by the folding of rock layers. Crustal movements may press horizontal layers of sedimentary rock together from the sides, squeezing them into wavelike folds. Up-folded sections of rock are called anticlines; down-folded sections of rock are called synclines. The Appalachian Mountains are an example of folded mountains, with long ridges and valleys in a series of anticlines, and synclines formed by folded rock layers.

FAULTS are fractures in the Earth's crust that have been created by either tension or compression forces transmitted through the crust. These forces are produced by the movement of separate blocks of crust. Faultings are categorized on the basis of the relative movement between the blocks on both sides of the fault plane. The movement can be horizontal, vertical, or oblique.

A dip-slip fault occurs when the movement of the plates is vertical and opposite. The displacement is in the direction of the inclination, or dip, of the fault. Dip-slip faults are classified as normal faults when the rock above the fault plane moves down relative to the rock below.

Reverse faults are created when the rock above the fault plane moves up relative to the rock below. Reverse faults with a very low angle to the horizontal are also referred to as thrust faults.

Faults in which the dominant displacement is horizontal movement along the trend or strike (length) of the fault are called strike-slip faults. When a large strike-slip fault is associated with plate boundaries it is called a transform fault. The San Andreas fault in California is a well-known transform fault.

Faults that have both vertical and horizontal movement are called oblique-slip faults.

Volcanoes

VOLCANISM is the term given to the movement of magma through the crust and its emergence as lava onto the Earth's surface. Volcanic mountains are built up by successive deposits of volcanic materials.

An ACTIVE VOLCANO is one that is currently erupting or building to an eruption. A DORMANT VOLCANO is one that is between eruptions but still shows signs of internal activity that might lead to an eruption in the future. An EXTINCT VOLCANO is said to be no longer capable of erupting. Most of the world's active volcanoes are found along the rim of the Pacific Ocean, which is also a major earthquake zone. This curving belt of active faults and volcanoes is often called the Ring of Fire. The world's best known volcanic mountains include Mount Etna in Italy and Mount Kilimanjaro in Africa. The Hawaiian Islands are actually the tops of a chain of volcanic mountains that rise from the ocean floor.

The Appalachian Mountains are an example of folded mountains.

FAULTS: fractures in the Earth's crust that have been created by either tension or compression forces transmitted through the crust

VOLCANISM: the movement of magma through the crust and its emergence as lava onto the Earth's surface

ACTIVE VOLCANO: a volcano that is currently erupting or building to an eruption

DORMANT VOLCANO: a volcano that is between eruptions but still shows signs of internal activity that might lead to an eruption in the future

EXTINCT VOLCANO: a volcano no longer capable of erupting

There are three types of volcanic mountains:

- Shield volcanoes are associated with quiet eruptions. Lava emerges from the vent or opening in the crater and flows freely out over the Earth's surface until it cools and hardens into a layer of igneous rock. A repeated lava flow builds this type of volcano into the largest type of volcanic mountain. Mauna Loa in Hawaii is the largest shield volcano on Earth.

- Cinder-cone volcanoes are associated with explosive eruptions as lava is hurled high into the air in a spray of droplets of various sizes. These droplets cool and harden into cinders and particles of ash before falling to the ground. The ash and cinder pile up around the vent to form a steep, cone-shaped hill called the cinder cone. Cinder-cone volcanoes are relatively small but may form quite rapidly.

- Composite volcanoes are those built by both lava flows and layers of ash and cinders. Mount Fuji in Japan, Mount St. Helens in the United States (Washington), and Mount Vesuvius in Italy are all famous composite volcanoes.

When lava cools, igneous rock is formed. This formation can occur either above or below ground.

INTRUSIVE ROCK: any igneous rock that was formed below the Earth's surface

EXTRUSIVE ROCK: any igneous rock that was formed at the Earth's surface

DIKES: old lava tubes formed when magma entered a vertical fracture and hardened

CALDERA: normally formed by the collapse of the top of a volcano

INTRUSIVE ROCK includes any igneous rock that was formed below the Earth's surface. Batholiths are the largest structures of intrusive rock and are composed of near-granite materials; they are the core of the Sierra Nevada Mountains. **EXTRUSIVE ROCK** includes any igneous rock that was formed at the Earth's surface.

DIKES are old lava tubes formed when magma entered a vertical fracture and hardened. Sometimes magma squeezes between two rock layers and hardens into a thin horizontal sheet called a sill. A laccolith is formed in much the same way as a sill, but the magma that creates a laccolith is very thick and does not flow easily. It pools and forces the overlying strata outward, creating an obvious surface dome.

A **CALDERA** is normally formed by the collapse of the top of a volcano. This collapse can be caused by a massive explosion that destroys the cone and empties most, if not all, of the magma chamber below the volcano. The cone collapses into the empty magma chamber, forming a caldera.

An inactive volcano may have magma solidified in its pipe. This structure, called a volcanic neck, is resistant to erosion and today may be the only visible evidence of the past presence of an active volcano.

Glaciations

About twelve thousand years ago, a vast sheet of ice covered a large part of the northern United States. This huge, frozen mass had moved southward from the northern regions of Canada as several large bodies of slow-moving ice, or glaciers. A glacier is a large mass of ice that moves or flows over the land in response to gravity. Glaciers form among high mountains and in other cold regions. The term **ICE AGE** is used to describe a time period in which glaciers advance over a large portion of a continent.

Evidence of glacial coverage remains as abrasive grooves, large boulders from northern environments dropped in southern locations, glacial troughs created by the rounding out of steep valleys by glacial scouring, and the remains of glacial sources called cirques that were created by frost wedging the rock at the bottom of the glacier. Remains of plants and animals found in warm climates that have been discovered in the moraines and outwash plains help support the theory of periods of warmth during past ice ages.

The major ice age began about two to three million years ago. This age saw the advancement and retreat of glacial ice over millions of years. Theories relating to the origin of glacial activity include plate tectonics, through which it can be demonstrated that some continental masses, now in temperate climates, were at one time blanketed by ice and snow. Another theory involves changes in the Earth's orbit around the sun, changes in the angle of the Earth's axis, and the wobbling of the Earth's axis. Support for the validity of this theory has come from deep-ocean research that indicates a correlation between climatic sensitive microorganisms and the changes in the Earth's orbital status.

There are two main types of glaciers: valley glaciers and continental glaciers. Erosion by valley glaciers is characteristic of U-shaped erosion. Valley glaciers produce sharp-peaked mountains such as the Matterhorn in Switzerland. Erosion by continental glaciers is characteristic of the movement of glaciers over mountains, leaving smoothed, rounded mountains and ridges in their paths.

Plate tectonics

Data obtained from many sources led scientists to develop the theory of **PLATE TECTONICS**. This theory is the most current model that explains not only the movement of the continents, but also the changes in the Earth's crust caused by internal forces.

Plates are rigid blocks of the Earth's crust and upper mantle. These blocks make up the lithosphere. The Earth's lithosphere is broken into nine large moving sections, or slabs, and several small ones, called plates. The major plates are named after the continents they are "transporting."

> About twelve thousand years ago, a vast sheet of ice covered a large part of the northern United States.

> **ICE AGE:** a time period in which glaciers advance over a large portion of a continent

> **PLATE TECTONICS:** the model that explains not only the movement of the continents, but also the changes in the Earth's crust caused by internal forces

crust & upper mantle = lithosphere ✗

The plates float on and move with a layer of hot, plastic-like rock in the upper mantle. Geologists believe that the heat currents circulating within the mantle cause this plastic zone of rock to slowly flow, carrying along the overlying crustal plates.

Movement of these crustal plates creates areas where the plates diverge as well as areas where they converge. A major area of divergence is located in the mid-Atlantic. Currents of hot mantle rock rise and separate in this area, creating new oceanic crust at the rate of two to ten centimeters per year.

Convergence is when the oceanic crust collides with either another oceanic plate or a continental plate. The oceanic crust sinks, forming an enormous trench and generating volcanic activity. Convergence also includes continent-to-continent plate collisions. When two plates slide past one another, a transform fault is created.

These movements produce many major features of the Earth's surface, such as mountain ranges, volcanoes, and earthquake zones. Most of these features are located at plate boundaries, where the plates interact by spreading apart, pressing together, or sliding past each other. These movements are very slow, averaging only a few centimeters a year.

Boundaries form between spreading plates where the crust is forced apart in a process called rifting. Rifting generally occurs at midocean ridges. Rifting can also take place within a continent, splitting the continent into smaller landmasses that drift away from each other, thereby forming an ocean basin between them. The Red Sea is a product of rifting. As the seafloor spreading takes place, new material is added to the inner edges of the separating plates. In this way the plates grow larger, and the ocean basin widens. This is the process that broke up the supercontinent Pangaea and created the Atlantic Ocean.

Boundaries between plates that are colliding are zones of intense crustal activity. When a plate of ocean crust collides with a plate of continental crust, the more dense oceanic plate slides under the lighter continental plate and plunges into the mantle. This process is called subduction, and the site where it takes place is called a subduction zone. A subduction zone is usually seen on the seafloor as a deep depression called a trench.

The crustal movement, which is identified by plates sliding sideways past each other, produces a plate boundary characterized by major faults that are capable of unleashing powerful earthquakes. The San Andreas fault forms such a boundary between the Pacific plate and the North American plate.

DOMAIN VI
SOCIAL STUDIES

PERSONALIZED STUDY PLAN

PERSONALIZED STUDY PLAN

KNOWN MATERIAL/ SKIP IT

PAGE	COMPETENCY AND SKILL	
372	**24:** **Understand characteristics of and interactions among individuals, groups, and institutions**	☐
	24.1: Demonstrating knowledge of the characteristics of different forms of government, including the government of Minnesota-based American Indian tribes, and the reasons people create and change governments	☐
	24.2: Demonstrating knowledge of the origins, core democratic values, and principles of constitutional democracy in the United States	☐
	24.3: Demonstrating knowledge of the structure and functions of government in the United States	☐
	24.4: Recognizing the rights and responsibilities of individuals in society and of the ideals, principles, and practices that promote productive community involvement	☐
	24.5: Demonstrating knowledge of interactions among individuals, groups, and institutions in a society	☐
	24.6: Demonstrating knowledge of the concepts of global connection and independence, including needs and wants and how people organize for the production, distribution, and consumption of goods and services	☐
	24.7: Demonstrating knowledge of the relationships among science, technology, and society	☐

COMPETENCY 22

UNDERSTAND THE PROCESSES AND TOOLS OF INQUIRY AND PROBLEM SOLVING IN SOCIAL STUDIES

SKILL 22.1 **Demonstrating knowledge of sources of information used in social studies and their ethical use** *(e.g., primary sources, Internet, copyright, source citations)*

The resources used in the study of history can be divided into two major groups: primary sources and secondary sources.

Primary Sources

PRIMARY SOURCES are works, records, etc., that were created during the period being studied or immediately after it. SECONDARY SOURCES are works written significantly after the period being studied and are based on primary sources.

Primary sources include the following kinds of materials:

- Documents that reflect the immediate, everyday concerns of people: memoranda, bills, deeds, charters, newspaper reports, pamphlets, graffiti, popular writings, journals or diaries, records of decision-making bodies, letters, receipts, and snapshots

- Theoretical writings, which reflect care and consideration in composition and an attempt to convince or persuade. The topic is generally deeper and more concerned with pervasive values than is the case with "immediate" documents. These may include newspaper or magazine editorials, sermons, political speeches, or philosophical writings.

- Narrative accounts of events, ideas, or trends, written with intentionality by someone contemporary with the events described

- Statistical data, although statistics can be misleading

- Literature—novels, stories, poetry, and essays from the period—as well as coins, archaeological artifacts, and art produced during the period

PRIMARY SOURCES: works, records, etc., that were created during the period being studied or immediately after it

SECONDARY SOURCES: works written significantly after the period being studied and based on primary sources

Guidelines for use of primary sources

1. Be certain that you understand how language was used at the time of writing and that you understand the context in which it was produced.

2. Do not read history blindly; be certain that you understand both explicit and implicit references in the material.

3. Read the entire text you are reviewing; do not simply extract a few sentences to read.

4. Although anthologies of materials may help you identify primary source materials, the full original text should be consulted.

SKILL 22.2 **Recognizing stages in the inquiry process** *(e.g., developing the essential question; forming a hypothesis; finding, collecting, and organizing historical research)*

Research topics are selected by seeking out that which is not yet understood and studying it to see what can be learned. Begin by asking a question. What is it that you want to know? Knowing this question defines the purpose of the research. Next, construct a theory, or hypothesis. Then do thorough research. Locate sources, collect historical data, and organize the information. Then, analyze the data and draw a conclusion. Finally, communicate the results—for example, in the form of a research paper or slide show.

See also Skill 22.1

SKILL 22.3 **Applying knowledge of the use of tools of inquiry and problem solving** *(e.g., graphs, maps, time lines)*

Illustrations often make it easier to demonstrate an idea visually rather than through text or speech. Among the more common illustrations used in social science are various types of maps, graphs and charts.

Although maps have advantages over globes and photographs, they do have a major disadvantage: most maps are flat and the Earth is a sphere. It is impossible to reproduce an object shaped like a sphere accurately on a flat surface. In order to put the Earth's features on a map they must be stretched in some way. This stretching is called distortion. Distortion does not mean that maps are wrong; it simply means that they are not perfect representations of the Earth or its parts. Cartographers, or mapmakers, understand the problems of distortion. They try to design maps so there is as little distortion as possible.

The process of putting the features of the Earth onto a flat surface is called projection. All maps are really map projections. There are many different types. Each one deals in a different way with the problem of distortion. Map projections are made in a number of ways. Some are done using complicated mathematics. However, the basic ideas behind map projections can be understood by looking at the three most common types:

Cylindrical Projections	These are done by taking a cylinder of paper and wrapping it around a globe. A light is used to project the globe's features onto the paper. Distortion is least where the paper touches the globe. For example, if the paper was wrapped so that it touched the globe at the equator, the map from this projection would have just a little distortion near the equator.
	However, the distortion would increase as you moved further away from the equator. The best known and most widely used cylindrical projection is the Mercator Projection. It was first developed in 1569 by Gerardus Mercator, a Flemish mapmaker.
Conical Projections	The name for these maps come from the fact that the projection is made onto a paper cone that touches a globe at the base of the cone only. It can also be made so that it cuts through part of the globe in two different places. The distortion is least where the paper touches the globe. If the cone touches at two different points, there is some distortion at both of them. Conical projections are most often used to map areas in the middle latitudes. Maps of the United States are most often conical projections. This is because most of the country lies within these latitudes.
Flat-Plane Projections	These are made with a flat piece of paper. It touches the globe at one point only. Areas near this point show little distortion. Flat-plane projections are often used to show the areas of the north and south poles. One such flat projection is called a Gnomonic Projection. On this kind of map all meridians appear as straight lines. Gnomonic projections are useful because any straight line drawn between points on it forms a Great-Circle Route.

Great-Circle Routes can best be described by thinking of a globe and, when using the globe, the shortest route between two points on it can be found by simply stretching a string from one point to the other. However, if the string was extended in reality, so that it took into effect the globe's curvature, it would then make a great-circle. A GREAT CIRCLE is any circle that cuts a sphere, such as the globe, into two equal parts. Because of distortion, most maps do not show great-circle routes as straight lines. Gnomonic projections, however, do show the shortest distance between the two places as a straight line, which is why they are valuable for navigation. They are called Great-Circle Sailing Maps.

GREAT CIRCLE: any circle that cuts a sphere, such as the globe, into two equal parts

To properly analyze a given map one must be familiar with the various parts and symbols that most modern maps use. For the most part, these are standardized, with different maps using similar parts and symbols. These can include:

The Title	All maps should have a title, just like all books should. The title tells you what information is found on the map.
The Legend	Most maps have a legend. A legend tells the reader about the various symbols that are used on that particular map and what the symbols represent (also called a map key).
The Grid	A grid is a series of lines that are used to find exact places and locations on the map. There are several different kinds of grid systems in use; however, most maps use the longitude and latitude system, known as the Geographic Grid System.
Directions	Most maps have some directional system to show which way the map is being presented. Often on a map, a small compass will be present, with arrows showing the four basic directions: north, south, east, and west.
The Scale	This is used to show the relationship between a unit of measurement on the map versus the real world measure on the Earth. Maps are drawn to many different scales. Some maps show a lot of detail for a small area. Others show a greater span of distance. One should always be aware of what scale is being used. For instance, the scale might be something like 1 inch = 10 miles for a map of a small area. A map showing the whole world might have a scale in which 1 inch = 1,000 miles. One must look at the map key in order to see what units of measurements the map is using.

Maps have four main properties. They are:

1. The size of the areas shown on the map

2. The shapes of the areas

3. Consistent scales

4. Straight line directions

A map can be drawn so that it is correct in one or more of these properties. No map can be correct in all of them.

Equal Areas	One property that maps can have is that of equal areas. In an equal area map, the meridians and parallels are drawn so that the areas shown have the same proportions as they do on the Earth. For example, Greenland is about 118th the size of South America, thus it will be shown as 118th the size on an equal area map. The Mercator projection is an example of a map that does not have equal areas. In it, Greenland appears to be about the same size of South America. This is because the distortion is very bad at the poles and Greenland lies near the North Pole.
Conformal Map	A second map property is conformal, or correct shapes. There are no maps that can show very large areas of the Earth in their exact shapes. Only globes can do that; however, conformal maps are as close as possible to true shapes. The United States is often shown by a Lambert Conformal Conic Projection Map.
Consistent Scales	Many maps attempt to use the same scale on all parts of the map. Generally, this is easier when a map shows a relatively small part of the Earth's surface. For example, a map of Florida might be a consistent scale map. Generally maps showing large areas are not consistent scale maps. This is so because of distortion. Often such maps will have two scales noted in the key. One scale, for example, might be accurate to measure distances between points along the Equator. Another might be accurate to measure distances between the North Pole and the South Pole. Maps showing physical features often try to show information about the elevation or relief of the land. Elevation is the distance above or below the sea level. The elevation is usually shown with colors, for instance, all areas on a map which are at a certain level will be shown in the same color.
Relief Maps	These show the shape of the land surface: flat, rugged, or steep. Relief maps usually give more detail than simply showing the overall elevation of the land's surface. Relief is sometimes shown with colors, but another way to show relief is by using contour lines. These lines connect all points of a land surface that are the same height surrounding the particular area of land.
Thematic Maps	These are used to show specific information, often on a single theme, or topic. Thematic maps show the distribution or amount of something over a certain given area—things such as population density, climate, economic information, cultural, political information, etc.

Graphs

There are two major reasons that graphs are used:

1. To present a model or theory visually in order to show how two or more variables interrelate

2. To present real-world data visually in order to show how two or more variables interrelate

The most-often used graphs are known as bar graphs and line graphs. Graphs themselves are most useful when one wishes to demonstrate the sequential increase or decrease of a variable or to show specific correlations between two or more variables in a given circumstance.

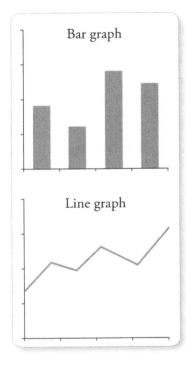

Bar graph

Line graph

Bar graphs are commonly used because they visually show the difference in a given set of variables, which is easy to see and understand. However, a bar graph is limited in that it cannot show the actual proportional increase, or decrease, of each given variable. In order to show a decrease, a bar graph must show the "bar" under the starting line, which is impossible in this format.

Thus, in order to accomplish this, one must use a **line graph**. Line graphs can be of two types:

1. **Linear graph:** Uses a series of straight lines

2. **Nonlinear graph:** Uses a curved line

Though the lines can be either straight or curved, all of the lines are called curves.

A line graph uses a number line or **axis**. The numbers on the axis are generally placed in order, equal distances from one another. The number line is used to represent a number, degree, or some such other variable at an appropriate point on the line. Two lines are used, intersecting at a specific point. They are referred to as the *x*-axis and the *y*-axis. The *y*-axis is a vertical line the *x*-axis is a horizontal line. Together they form a **coordinate system**. The difference between two points on the line of the *x*-axis and the *y*-axis is called the **slope** of the line, or the change in the value on the vertical axis divided by the change in the value on the horizontal axis. The *y*-axis number is called the rise and the *x*-axis number is called the run; thus, the equation for slope is:

$$\text{SLOPE} = \frac{\textbf{RISE (change in value on the vertical axis)}}{\textbf{RUN (change in value on the horizontal axis)}}$$

The slope tells the amount of increase or decrease of a given variable.

To use charts correctly, one should remember the reasons one uses graphs. It is usually a question as to which, a graph or chart, is more capable of accurately portraying the information one wants to illustrate. One of the most common types of chart, because it is easiest to read and understand, is the **pie chart**.

Piecharts are used often, especially when illustrating the differences in percentages among various items, or demonstrating the divisions of a whole.

Spatial organization is a description of how things are grouped in a given space. In geographical terms, this can describe people, places, and environments anywhere on Earth.

The most basic form of spatial organization for people is where they live. The vast majority of people live near other people—in villages, towns, cities, and settlements. People live near others in order to take advantage of the goods and services that naturally arise from cooperation. Villages, towns, cities, and settlements are, to varying degrees, near bodies of water. Water is a staple of survival for every person on the planet and is also a good source of energy for factories and other industries, as well as a form of transportation for people and goods.

SKILL 22.4 **Applying knowledge of a variety of social studies processes** *(e.g., differentiating facts from opinions, recognizing cause-and-effect relationships, assessing credibility of source information)*

Approaches to Studying History

History is filled with wonderful facts, intriguing stories, and innumerous combinations of perspectives and interpretations on just about every major event in its history. These problems and issues encountered in the past have affected history in immeasurable ways. It is nearly impossible to consider all of the thoughts, values, ideas and perspectives involved.

When studying a time period of United States history, students and teachers should decide on broad key questions that relate to major impacts, nature of social change, urbanization, cultural effects and so on when entering into an historical analysis. These questions can serve as a foundation to the study, providing a focus for students as they explore the related perspectives.

> *When studying a time period of United States history, students and teachers should decide on broad key questions that relate to major impacts, nature of social change, urbanization, cultural effects, and so on when entering into an historical analysis.*

Using primary sources

From here, students can explore one or more of these key questions by creating subtopics beneath them as they consider the major elements such as time period, cultural impacts, various viewpoints, previous and concurrent events and so on. This is a great place in which to introduce **PRIMARY RESOURCES** in the field of social science.

> **PRIMARY RESOURCE:** a source that is first-hand evidence about a certain period in history

Diaries, field trips, field trips to historic sites and museums, historical documents, photos, artifacts, and other records of the past provide students with an alternative voices and accounts of events. It is within primary resources, first-hand accounts of events that provide the richest and least "processed" information. For example, a letter from a freed slave would provide more valuable information about attitudes toward African Americans in the North in 1860 than a textbook entry.

THINGS TO CONSIDER WHEN ANALYZING HISTORICAL RESOURCES	
The Author	Who is the author? What motivated this author? Why did they create this resource? Is he or she representing a group?
The Time Frame	When was this resource produced? How has it reached us? Was it contemporary at the time of production?
The Location	Where was this document produced?
The Type of Document	Is it a letter, a poem, a report, a song, a study?
The Audience	Who was intended to see this piece?

Judging thinking skills

When engaging in higher-ordered thinking skills, students should develop their skills through enthusiastic experiences where they can:

- Examine a situation

- Raise questions

- Compare differing ideas, interests, perspectives, actions, and institutions represented in these sources

- Elaborate upon what they read and see to develop interpretations, explanations, or solutions to the questions they have raised

- Analyze historical fiction, nonfiction, and historical illustrations

- Distinguish between fact and fiction

- Consider multiple perspectives

- Explain causes in analyzing historical actions

- Challenge arguments of historical inevitability

- Hypothesize the influence of the past

Teachers must also create an open and engaging learning environment rich where students can examine data. Use of libraries, historical collections, museums, newspapers, collections, students' families and artifacts, professional and community resources, historians, local colleges, and more allow students to see history for themselves—the first step in truly teaching them how to analyze history.

Methods in Teaching Geography and Other Social Sciences

Interdisciplinary approaches are very useful and appropriate in teaching social studies. Making a map of an area of study, doing a play that depicts the culture of the region, tallying information about the population of the area, and linking historical events to current sociological and political aspects all offer good strategies for teaching social studies content. Project-based approaches that incorporate the following can be quite effective:

- Cooperative learning

- Research methods

- Discovery- and inquiry-based lessons

- Audio-visual resources

Immersion in the culture and geography of an area can take many forms; this method is most productive when the students are part of the process of determining what the activities will be in the unit of study, particularly in the intermediate grades.

> Interdisciplinary approaches are very useful and appropriate in teaching social studies.

Using literature to support learning in the social sciences

Native American literature

The foundation of Native American writing is found in storytelling, oratory, and autobiographical and historical accounts of tribal village life; reverence for the environment; and the postulation that the Earth with all of its beauty was given in trust, to be cared for and passed on to future generations.

Early Native American writings that would interest young adults are:

- *Geronimo: His Own Story*—Apache edited by S.M. Barrett

- *Native American Myths and Legends* by C.F. Taylor

- *When Legends Die* by Hal Barland

African-American literature

African-American literature covers three distinct periods: pre–Civil War, post–Civil War and Reconstruction, and post–Civil War through the present. Some featured resources include:

- Harriet Beecher Stowe's *Uncle Tom's Cabin*

- Ernest Gaines' *The Autobiography of Miss Jane Pittman*

- Maya Angelou's *I Know Why the Caged Bird Sings*

- Alex Haley's *Roots*

The Colonial period

Some good examples of works from the colonial period include *The Mayflower Compact* and Thomas Paine's *Common Sense*. Benjamin Franklin's essays from *Poor Richard's Almanac* were popular during his day and are good as well.

American folklore

Folktales with characters such as Washington Irving's Ichabod Crane and Rip Van Winkle create a unique American folklore, with characters marked by their environment and the superstitions of the New Englander. The poetry of Fireside Poets such as James Russell Lowell, Oliver Wendell Holmes, Henry Wadsworth Longfellow, and John Greenleaf Whittier was recited by American families and read in the long New England winters.

COMPETENCY 23
UNDERSTAND CHARACTERISTICS OF AND INTERACTIONS AMONG PEOPLE, PLACES, AND ENVIRONMENTS

> **SKILL 23.1** Applying knowledge of the major themes of geography *(i.e., location, place, region, movement, and human-environment interactions)*

GEOGRAPHY: the study of location and how living things and Earth's features are distributed throughout the Earth

GEOGRAPHY involves studying location and how living things and Earth's features are distributed throughout the Earth. It includes where animals, people, and plants live and the effects of their relationship with Earth's physical features. Geographers also explore the locations of Earth's features, how they got there, and why it is so important.

AREAS OF GEOGRAPHICAL STUDY	
Regional	Elements and characteristics of a place or region.
Topical	One Earth feature or one human activity occurring throughout the entire world.

Continued on next page

Physical	Earth's physical features, what creates and changes them, their relationships to each other, as well as human activities.
Human	Human activity patterns and how they relate to the environment including political, cultural, historical, urban, and social geographical fields of study.

Two of the most important terms in the study of geography are absolute and relative location. First, what is **location**? We want to know this in order to determine where something is and where we can find it. We want to point to a spot on a map and say, "That is where we are" or "That is where we want to be." In another way, we want to know where something is as compared to other things. It is very difficult for many people to describe something without referring to something else. Associative reasoning is a powerful way to think.

- Absolute location is the exact whereabouts of a person, place, or thing, according to any kind of geographical indicators you want to name. You could be talking about latitude and longitude or GPS or any kind of indicators at all. For example, Paris is at 48 degrees North longitude and 2 degrees East latitude. You can't get much more exact than that. If you had a map that showed every degree of latitude and longitude, you could pinpoint exactly where Paris was and have absolutely no doubt that your geographical depiction was accurate.

- Relative location, on the other hand, is always a description that involves more than one thing. When you describe a relative location, you tell where something is by describing what is around it. The same description of where the nearest post office is in terms of absolute location might be this: "It's down the street from the supermarket, on the right side of the street, next to the dentist's office."

SIX THEMES OF GEOGRAPHY	
Location	Including relative and absolute location. A relative location refers to the surrounding geography, e.g., "on the banks of the Mississippi River." Absolute location refers to a specific point, such as 41 degrees North latitude, 90 degrees West longitude, or 123 Main Street.

Continued on next page

Spatial Organization	A description of how things are grouped in a given space. In geographical terms, this can describe people, places, and environments anywhere and everywhere on Earth. The most basic form of spatial organization for people is where they live. The vast majority of people live near other people, in villages and towns and cities and settlements. These people live near others in order to take advantage of the goods and services that naturally arise from cooperation. These villages and towns and cities and settlements are, to varying degrees, near bodies of water. Water is a staple of survival for every person on the planet and is also a good source of energy for factories and other industries, as well as a form of transportation for people and goods. For example, in a city, where are the factories and heavy industry buildings? Are they near airports or train stations? Are they on the edge of town, near major roads? What about housing developments? Are they near these industries, or are they far away? Where are the other industry buildings? Where are the schools and hospitals and parks? What about the police and fire stations? How close are homes to each of these things? Towns and especially cities are routinely organized into neighborhoods, so that each house or home is near to most things that its residents might need on a regular basis. This means that large cities have multiple schools, hospitals, grocery stores, fire stations, etc.
Place	A place has both human and physical characteristics. Physical characteristics include features such as mountains, rivers, and deserts. Human characteristics are the features created by human interaction with their environment such as canals and roads.
Human-Environmental Interaction	The theme of human-environmental interaction has three main concepts: humans adapt to the environment (wearing warm clothing in a cold climate); humans modify the environment (planting trees to block a prevailing wind); and humans depend on the environment (for food, water, and raw materials).
Movement	The theme of movement covers how humans interact with one another through trade, communications, immigration, and other forms of interaction.
Regions	A region is an area that has some kind of unifying characteristic, such as a common language or a common government. There are three main types of regions. Formal regions are areas defined by actual political boundaries, such as a city, county, or state. Functional regions are defined by a common function, such as the area covered by a telephone service. Vernacular regions are less formally defined areas that are formed by people's perception, e.g., the Middle East, and the South.

Geography involves studying location and how living things and Earth's features are distributed throughout the Earth. It includes where animals, people, and plants live and the effects of their relationship with Earth's physical features.

Geographers also explore the locations of Earth's features, how they got there, and why it is so important. Another way to describe where people live is by the geography and topography around them. The vast majority of people on the planet live in areas that are very hospitable. Yes, people live in the Himalayas and in the Sahara, but the populations in those areas are small indeed when compared to the plains of China, India, Europe, and the United States. People naturally want to live where they won't have to work really hard just to survive, and world population patterns reflect this.

Human communities subsisted initially as gatherers—gathering berries, leaves, etc. With the invention of tools it became possible to dig for roots, hunt small animals, and catch fish from rivers and oceans. Humans observed their environments and soon learned to plant seeds and harvest crops. As people migrated to areas in which game and fertile soil were abundant, communities began to develop. When people had the knowledge to grow crops and the skills to hunt game, they began to understand division of labor. Some of the people in the community tended to agricultural needs while others hunted game.

As habitats attracted larger numbers of people, environments became crowded and there was competition. The concept of division of labor and sharing of food soon followed. Groups of people focused on growing crops while others concentrated on hunting. Experience led to the development of skills and of knowledge that make the work easier. Farmers began to develop new plant species and hunters began to protect animal species from other predators for their own use. This ability to manage the environment led people to settle down, to guard their resources, and to manage them.

Camps soon became villages. Villages became year-round settlements. Animals were domesticated and gathered into herds that met the needs of the village. With the settled life it was no longer necessary to "travel light." Pottery was developed for storing and cooking food.

By 8000 BCE, culture was beginning to evolve in these villages. Agriculture was developed for the production of grain crops, which led to a decreased reliance on wild plants. Domesticating animals for various purposes decreased the need to hunt wild game. Life became more settled. It was then possible to turn attention to such matters as managing water supplies, producing tools, and making cloth. There was both the social interaction and the opportunity to reflect upon existence. Mythologies arose and various kinds of belief systems. Rituals arose that reenacted the mythologies that gave meaning to life.

As farming and animal husbandry skills increased, the dependence upon wild game and food gathering declined. With this change came the realization that a larger number of people could be supported on the produce of farming and animal husbandry.

Two things seem to have come together to produce CULTURES and CIVILIZATIONS: a society and culture based on agriculture and the development of centers of the community with literate social and religious structures.

> **CULTURE:** the set of values, conventions, or social practices associated with a particular group

> **CIVILIZATION:** a high level of cultural and technological development

The members of these hierarchies then managed water supplies and irrigation and ritual and religious life and exerted their own right to use a portion of the goods produced by the community for their own subsistence in return for their management.

Sharpened skills, development of more sophisticated tools, commerce with other communities, and increasing knowledge of their environment, the resources available to them, and responses to the needs to share good, order community life, and protect their possessions from outsiders led to further division of labor and community development.

As trade routes developed and travel between cities became easier, trade led to specialization. Trade enables a people to obtain the goods they desire in exchange for the goods they are able to produce. This, in turn, leads to increased attention to refinements of technique and the sharing of ideas. The knowledge of a new discovery or invention provides knowledge and technology that increases the ability to produce goods for trade. As each community learns the value of the goods it produces and improves its ability to produce the goods in greater quantity, industry is born.

SKILL 23.2 **Demonstrating knowledge of characteristics of ancient and modern cultures and their historical contributions, including the culture of Minnesota-based American Indian tribes**

PREHISTORY: the period of man's achievements before the development of writing

PREHISTORY is defined as the period of man's achievements before the development of writing. In the Stone Age cultures, there were three different periods:

- Lower Paleolithic Period, with the use of crude tools
- Upper Paleolithic Period, exhibiting a greater variety of better-made tools and implements, the wearing of clothing, highly organized group life, and skills in art
- Neolithic Period, which showed domesticated animals, food production, the arts of knitting, spinning and weaving cloth, starting fires through friction, building houses rather than living in caves, the development of institutions including the family, religion, and a form of government or the origin of the state

Ancient civilizations were those cultures which developed to a greater degree and were considered advanced. These included the following eleven with their major accomplishments.

Egypt

Egypt made numerous significant contributions including construction of the great pyramids; development of hieroglyphic writing; preservation of bodies after death; making paper from papyrus; contributing to developments in arithmetic and geometry; the invention of the method of counting in groups of 1–10 (the decimal system); completion of a solar calendar; and laying the foundation for science and astronomy.

The ancient civilization of the **Sumerians** invented the wheel; developed irrigation through use of canals, dikes, and devices for raising water; devised the system of cuneiform writing; learned to divide time; and built large boats for trade. The Babylonians devised the famous CODE OF HAMMURABI, a code of laws.

The ancient **Assyrians** were warlike and aggressive due to a highly organized military and used horse drawn chariots.

The **Hebrews**, also known as the ancient Israelites, instituted MONOTHEISM, which is the worship of one God, Yahweh, and combined the thirty-nine books of the Hebrew and Bible, or Christian Old Testament, we have today.

The **Minoans** had a system of writing using symbols to represent syllables in words. They built palaces with multiple levels containing many rooms, water, and sewage systems with flush toilets, bathtubs, hot and cold running water, and bright paintings on the walls.

The **Mycenaeans** changed the Minoan writing system to aid their own language and used symbols to represent syllables.

The **Phoenicians** were sea traders well known for their manufacturing skills in glass and metals and the development of their famous purple dye. They became so very proficient in the skill of navigation that they were able to sail by the stars at night. Further, they devised an alphabet using symbols to represent single sounds, which was an improved extension of the Egyptian writing system.

> **CODE OF HAMMURABI:**
> a Babylonian code of laws

> **MONOTHEISM:** the worship of one God

India

In India, the caste system was developed, the principle of zero in mathematics was discovered, and the major religion of Hinduism was begun. In India, Hinduism was a continuing influence along with the rise of Buddhism. Industry and commerce developed along with extensive trading with the Near East. Outstanding advances in the fields of science and medicine were made along with being one of the first to be active in navigation and maritime enterprises during this time.

China

China began building the Great Wall, practiced crop rotation and terrace farming, increased the importance of the silk industry, and developed caravan routes across Central Asia for extensive trade. Also, the Chinese increased proficiency in rice cultivation and developed a written language based on drawings or pictographs (no alphabet symbolizing sounds as each word or character had a form different from all others). China is considered by some historians to be the oldest uninterrupted civilization in the world and was in existence around the same time as the ancient civilizations founded in **Egypt**, **Mesopotamia**, and the **Indus Valley**. The Chinese studied nature and weather; stressed the importance of education, family, and a strong central government; followed the religions of Buddhism, Confucianism, and Taoism; and invented such things as gunpowder, paper, printing, and the magnetic compass.

The **Tang Dynasty** extended from 618 to 907 CE. Its capital was the most heavily populated of any city in the world at the time. Buddhism was adopted by the imperial family (Li) and became an integral part of Chinese culture. The emperor, however, feared the monasteries and began to take action against them in the tenth century. Confucianism experienced a rebirth during the time of this dynasty as an instrument of state administration.

Following a civil war, the central government lost control of local areas. Warlords arose in 907, and China was divided into north and south. These areas came to be ruled by short-lived minor dynasties. A major political accomplishment of this period was the creation of a class of career government officials, who functioned between the populace and the government. This class of "SCHOLAR-OFFICIALS" continued to fulfill this function in government and society until 1911.

> **SCHOLAR-OFFICIALS:** a class of career government officials, who functioned between the populace and the government

The period of the Tang Dynasty is generally considered a pinnacle of Chinese civilization. Through contact with the Middle East and India, the period of the Tang Dynasty was marked by great creativity in many areas. Block printing was invented, and made much information and literature available to wide audiences.

In science, astronomers calculated the paths of the sun and the moon and the movements of the constellations. This facilitated the development of the calendar. In agriculture, such technologies as cultivating the land by setting it on fire, the curved-shaft plow, separate cultivation of seedlings, and sophisticated irrigation system increased productivity. Hybrid breeds of horses and mules were created to strengthen the labor supply. In medicine, there were achievements like the understanding of the circulatory system and the digestive system and great advances in pharmacology. Ceramics was another area in which great advances were made. A new type of glazing was invented that gave Tang Dynasty porcelain and earthenware its unique appearance through three-colored glazing.

In literature, the poetry of the period is generally considered the best in the entire history of Chinese literature. The rebirth of Confucianism led to the publication of many commentaries on the classical writings. Encyclopedias on several subjects were produced, as well as histories and philosophical works.

Persia

The ancient Persians developed an alphabet; contributed the religions/philoso-phies of **Zoroastrianism**, **Mithraism**, and **Gnosticism**; and allowed conquered peoples to retain their own customs, laws, and religions.

Greece

The classical civilization of Greece reached the highest levels in man's achieve-ments based on the foundations already laid by such ancient groups as the Egyptians, Phoenicians, Minoans, and Mycenaeans.

Among the more important contributions of Greece were the Greek alphabet derived from the Phoenician letters that formed the basis for the Roman alphabet and our present-day alphabet. Extensive trading and colonization resulted in the spread of the Greek civilization. The love of sports, with emphasis on a sound body, led to the tradition of the Olympic Games. Greece was responsible for the rise of independent, strong city-states. Note the complete contrast between inde-pendent, freedom-loving Athens with its practice of pure democracy (i.e., direct, personal, active participation in government by qualified citizens) and the rigid, totalitarian, militaristic Sparta. Other important areas that the Greeks are credited with influencing include drama, epic and lyric poetry, fables, myths centered on the many gods and goddesses, science, astronomy, medicine, mathematics, philosophy, art, architecture, and recording historical events. The conquests of Alexander the Great spread Greek ideas to the areas he conquered and brought to the Greek world many ideas from Asia including the value of ideas, wisdom, curiosity, and the desire to learn as much about the world as possible.

A most interesting and significant characteristic of the Greek, Hellenic, and Roman civilizations was SECULARISM where emphasis shifted away from religion to the state. Men were not absorbed in or dominated by religion as had been the case in Egypt and the nations located in Mesopotamia. Religion and its leaders did not dominate the state and its authority was greatly diminished.

> **SECULARISM:** when emphasis shifts away from religion to the state

Japan

Civilization in Japan appeared during this time, having borrowed much of their culture from China. It was the last of these classical civilizations to develop.

Although they used, accepted, and copied Chinese art, law, architecture, dress, and writing, the Japanese refined these into their own unique way of life, including incorporating the religion of Buddhism into their culture.

Africa

The civilizations in Africa south of the Sahara were developing the refining and use of iron, especially for farm implements and later for weapons. Trading was overland using camels and at important seaports. The Arab influence was extremely important, as was their later contact with Indians, Christian Nubians, and Persians. In fact, their trading activities were probably the most important factor in the spread of and assimilation of different ideas and stimulation of cultural growth.

Vikings

The Vikings had a lot of influence at this time, spreading their ideas and knowledge of trade routes and sailing, accomplished first through their conquests and later through trade.

Byzantium and the Saracens

In other parts of the world were the Byzantine and Saracenic (or Islamic) civilizations, both dominated by religion. The major contributions of the Saracens were in the areas of science and philosophy. Included were accomplishments in astronomy, mathematics, physics, chemistry, medicine, literature, art, trade, manufacturing, agriculture, and a marked influence on the Renaissance period of history. The Byzantines (Christians) made important contributions in art and the preservation of Greek and Roman achievements including architecture (especially in Eastern Europe and Russia), the Code of Justinian and Roman law.

Ghana

The ancient empire of Ghana occupied an area that is now known as Northern Senegal and Southern Mauritania. There is no absolute certainty regarding the origin of this empire. Oral history dates the rise of the empire to the seventh century BCE. Most believe, however, that the date should be placed much later. Many believe the nomads who were herding animals on the fringes of the desert posed a threat to the early Soninke people, who were an agricultural community. In times of drought, it is believed the nomads raided the agricultural villages for water and places to pasture their herds. To protect themselves, it is believed that these farming communities formed a loose confederation that eventually became the empire of ancient Ghana.

The empire's economic vitality was determined by geographical location. It was situated midway between the desert, which was the major source of salt, and the gold fields. This location along the trade routes of the camel caravans provided exceptional opportunity for economic development. The caravans brought copper, salt, dried fruit, clothing, manufactured goods, etc. For these goods, the people of Ghana traded kola nuts, leather goods, gold, hides, ivory, and slaves. In addition, the empire collected taxes on every trade item that entered the boundaries of the empire. With the revenue from the trade goods tax, the empire supported a government, an army that protected the trade routes and the borders, the maintenance of the capital, and primary market centers. But it was control of the gold fields that gave the empire political power and economic prosperity. The location of the gold fields was a carefully guarded secret. By the tenth century, Ghana was very rich and controlled an area about the size of the state of Texas. Demand for this gold sharply increased in the ninth and tenth centuries as the Islamic states of Northern Africa began to mint coins. As the gold trade expanded, so did the empire. The availability of local iron ore enabled the early people of the Ghana kingdom to make more efficient farm implements and effective weapons.

Major Developments in Human History

The **SCIENTIFIC REVOLUTION** was characterized by a shift in scientific approach and ideas. Near the end of the sixteenth century, Galileo Galilei introduced a radical approach to the study of motion. He moved from attempts to explain why objects move the way they do and began to use experiments to describe precisely how they move. He also used experimentation to describe how forces affect nonmoving objects. Other scientists continued in the same approach. This was the period when experiments dominated scientific study. This method was particularly applied to the study of physics.

The **AGRICULTURAL REVOLUTION** occurred first in England. It was marked by experimentation that resulted in increased production of crops from the land and a new and more technical approach to the management of agriculture. The revolution in agricultural management and production was hugely enhanced by the industrial revolution and the invention of the steam engine. The introduction of steam-powered tractors greatly increased crop production and significantly decreased labor costs. Developments in agriculture were also enhanced by the scientific revolution and the learning from experimentation that led to philosophies of crop rotation and soil enrichment. Improved system of irrigation and harvesting also contributed to the growth of agricultural production.

The **INDUSTRIAL REVOLUTION**, which began in Great Britain and spread elsewhere, was the development of power-driven machinery (fueled by coal and steam) leading to the accelerated growth of industry with large factories replacing homes

SCIENTIFIC REVOLUTION: characterized by a shift in scientific approach and ideas

Outstanding scientists of the period included:
- *Johannes Kepler*
- *Evangelista Torricelli*
- *Blaise Pascal*
- *Isaac Newton*
- *Gottfried Leibniz*

AGRICULTURAL REVOLUTION: marked by experimentation that resulted in increased production of crops from the land and a new and more technical approach to the management of agriculture

INDUSTRIAL REVOLUTION: the development of power-driven machinery leading to the accelerated growth of industry with large factories replacing homes and small workshops as work centers

and small workshops as work centers. The lives of people changed drastically and a largely agricultural society changed to an industrial one. In Western Europe, the period of empire and colonialism began. The industrialized nations seized and claimed parts of Africa and Asia in an effort to control and provide the raw materials needed to feed the industries and machines in the "mother country." Later developments included power based on electricity and internal combustion, replacing coal and steam.

The **INFORMATION REVOLUTION** refers to the sweeping changes during the latter half of the twentieth century as a result of technological advances and a new respect for the knowledge or information provided by trained, skilled, and experienced professionals in a variety of fields. This approach to understanding a number of social and economic changes in global society arose from the ability to make computer technology both accessible and affordable. In particular, the development of the computer chip has led to such technological advances as the Internet, the cell phone, cybernetics, wireless communication, and the related ability to disseminate and access a massive amount of information quite readily.

> **INFORMATION REVO-LUTION:** the sweeping changes during the latter half of the twentieth century as a result of technological advances and a new respect for the knowledge or information provided by trained, skilled and experienced professionals in a variety of fields

In terms of economic theory and segmentation, it is now very much the norm to think of three basic economic sectors: agriculture and mining, manufacturing, and "services." Indeed, labor is now often divided between manual labor and informational labor. The fact that businesses are involved in the production and distribution, processing and transmission of information has, according to some, created a new business sector.

The Information Revolution has clearly changed modern life in many ways, such as the creation of devices and processes that actually control much of the world as it is experienced by the average person. It has most certainly revolutionized the entertainment industry, as well as influencing the way people spend their time. In education, new technology has made information on virtually any subject instantly accessible. It has also thoroughly altered the minute-to-minute knowledge people have of world events. Sixty years ago, news from the war front became available by radio for the first time. Visual images, however, were primarily available through the weekly newsreels shown in motion picture theaters. Today, live pictures from the battlefield are instantly available to people, no matter where they are. This technology has also made it possible for "smart wars" to be fought, reducing the number of civilian casualties.

Cultural History of Minnesota

> The name "Minnesota" is Siouan, meaning "land of cloudy waters."

Various cultures have contributed to Minnesota's history since before it was a part of the United States, starting with the American Indian tribes who have lived across the northern United States for many generations. In particular, the Ojibwe (or Anishinaabe) and Sioux (or Dakota) nations are a significant presence today, with 11 reservations across the state.

The Dakota nation is divided into three groups: the Dakota, Lakota and Nakota. These groups spread to different parts of the area. They lived in the northern forests and along the Mississippi River banks, and farmed extensively. The Anishinaabe are the third largest tribe in the U.S. (second only to the Cherokee and the Navajo). They originated around Lake Superior and are known for their canoes and the cultivation of wild rice. Ojibwe is the Canadian name for this tribe; Chippewa is thought to be a mispronunciation by French speakers of the name "Ojibwe" and is not the preferred name by most Native Americans.

Significant European ethnic groups that contributed to the development of Minnesota, especially in the years between 1850 and 1900, were from Sweden, Germany, and Norway. Their descendants remain a large portion of the population today, retaining their religious and cultural traditions.

> This site provides links to the various American Indian tribes in Minnesota:
>
> www.state.mn.us /portal/mn/jsp /content.do?subchannel =-536888182&programid =536906700&id =-8494&agency =NorthStar&sp2=y
>
> Minnesota State University at Mankato has a comprehensive website with detailed information Minnesota history:
>
> www.mnsu.edu/emuseum /history/mnstatehistory/

SKILL 23.3 Demonstrating knowledge of historical and modern perspectives of significant eras, themes, individuals, and chronological relationships in U.S. and Minnesota history

During the colonial period, political parties, as the term is now understood, did not exist. The issues, which divided the people, were centered on the relations of the colonies to the mother country. There was initially little difference of opinion on these issues. About the middle of the eighteenth century, after England began to develop a harsher colonial policy, two factions arose in America. One favored the attitude of home government and the other declined to obey and demanded a constantly increasing level of self-government. The former came to be known as TORIES, the latter as WHIGS. During the course of the American Revolution a large number of Tories left the country either to return to England or move to Canada.

TORIES: favored the attitude of home government

WHIGS: declined to obey and demanded a constantly increasing level of self-government

From the beginning of the Confederation, there were differences of opinion about the new government. One faction favored a loose confederacy in which the individual state would retain all powers of sovereignty except the absolute minimum required for the limited cooperation of all the states. The other faction, which steadily gained influence, demanded that the central government be granted all the essential powers of sovereignty and the what should be left to the states was only the powers of local self-government. The inadequacy of the Confederation demonstrated that the latter were promoting a more effective point of view.

Revolutionary War
1775- 1783

1789

Runner up= VP
John Adams

The first real party organization developed soon after the inauguration of George Washington as president. His cabinet included people of both factions. Hamilton was the leader of the Nationalists—the Federalist Party—and Jefferson was the spokesman for the Anti-Federalists, later known as Republicans, Democratic-Republicans, and finally Democrats. Several other parties formed over the years including the Anti-Masonic Party and the Free Soil Party, which existed for the 1848 and 1852 elections only. They opposed slavery in the lands acquired from Mexico. The Liberty Party of this period was abolitionist.

The American Party was called the "Know Nothings." It lasted from 1854 to 1858 and was opposed to Irish-Catholic immigration. The Constitution Union Party was formed in 1860. It was made up of entities from other extinguished political powers. It claimed to support the Constitution above all and thought this would do away with the slavery issue. The National Union Party of 1864 was formed only for the purpose of the Lincoln election. That was the only reason for its existence.

Coming up:
- *Westward Expansion*
- *Social Reform Movement*
- *Religious Revival*
- *Cultural Growth*

Westward Expansion

The Industrial Revolution had spread from Great Britain to the United States. Before 1800, most manufacturing activities were done in small shops or in homes. However, starting in the early 1800s, factories with modern machines were built making it easier to produce goods faster. The eastern part of the country became a major industrial area although some developed in the West. At about the same time, improvements began to be made in building roads, railroads, canals, and steamboats. The increased ease of travel facilitated the westward movement and boosted the economy with faster and cheaper shipment of goods and products, covering larger areas. Some of the innovations include the Erie Canal connecting the interior and Great Lakes with the Hudson River and the coastal port of New York.

Westward expansion occurred for a number of reasons, most important being economic. Cotton had become most important to most of the people who lived in the southern states. The effects of the Industrial Revolution, which began in England, were now being felt in the United States. With the invention of power-driven machines, the demand for cotton fiber greatly increased for the yarn needed in spinning and weaving. Eli Whitney's cotton gin made the separation of the seeds from the cotton much more efficient and faster. This, in turn, increased the demand and more and more farmers became involved in the raising and selling of cotton.

The innovations and developments of better methods of long-distance transportation moved the cotton in greater quantities to textile mills in England as well as the areas of New England and Middle Atlantic states in the United States. As prices increased along with increased demand, southern farmers began expanding by clearing increasingly more land to grow more cotton. Movement, settlement, and farming headed west to utilize the fertile soils. This, in turn, demanded increased need for a large supply of cheap labor. The system of slavery expanded, both in numbers and in the movement to lands "west" of the South.

Cotton farmers and slave owners were not the only ones heading west. Many, in other fields of economic endeavor, began the migration: trappers, miners, merchants, ranchers, and others were all seeking their fortunes. The Lewis and Clark expedition stimulated the westward push. Fur companies hired men, known as Mountain Men, to go westward, searching for the animal pelts to supply the market and meet the demands of the East and Europe. These men in their own way explored and discovered the many passes and trails that would eventually be used by settlers in their trek to the west. The California gold rush also had a very large influence on the movement west.

In the American Southwest, the results were exactly the opposite. Spain had claimed this area since the 1540s, had spread northward from Mexico City and, in the 1700s, had established missions, forts, villages, towns, and very large ranches. After the purchase of the Louisiana Territory in 1803, Americans began moving into Spanish territory. A few hundred American families in what is now Texas were allowed to live there but had to agree to become loyal subjects to Spain. In 1821, Mexico successfully revolted against Spanish rule, won independence, and chose to be more tolerant toward the American settlers and traders. The Mexican government encouraged and allowed extensive trade and settlement, especially in Texas. Many of the new settlers were Southerners and brought with them their slaves. Slavery was outlawed in Mexico and technically illegal in Texas, although the Mexican government looked the other way.

The Red River Cession was the next acquisition of land and came about as part of a treaty with Great Britain in 1818:

- It included parts of **North** and **South Dakota** and **Minnesota**.

- In 1819, **Florida**, both east and west, was ceded to the United States by Spain along with parts of **Alabama**, **Mississippi**, and **Louisiana**.

- **Texas** was annexed in 1845.

- After the war with Mexico in 1848 the government paid $15 million for what would become the states of **California**, **Utah**, **Nevada**, and parts of four other states.

- In 1846, the **Oregon Country** was ceded to the United States, which extended the western border to the Pacific Ocean. The northern U.S. boundary was established at the 49th parallel. The states of **Idaho**, **Oregon**, and **Washington** were formed from this territory.

- In 1853, the **Gadsden Purchase** rounded out the present boundary of the 48 conterminous states with payment to Mexico of $10 million for land that makes up the present states of New **Mexico** and **Arizona**.

The election of Andrew Jackson as president signaled a swing of the political pendulum from government influence of the wealthy, aristocratic Easterners to the interests of the Western farmers and pioneers and the era of the "common man." Jacksonian democracy was a policy of equal political power for all. After the War of 1812, Henry Clay and supporters favored economic measures that came to be known as the American System. This involved tariffs protecting American farmers and manufacturers from having to compete with foreign products, stimulating industrial growth and employment. With more people working, more farm products would be consumed, prosperous farmers would be able to buy more manufactured goods, and the additional monies from tariffs would make it possible for the government to make needed internal improvements. To get this going, in 1816, Congress not only passed a high tariff, but also chartered a second Bank of the United States. Upon becoming President, Jackson fought to get rid of the bank.

Many social reform movements began during this period, including:

- Education
- Women's rights
- Labor and working conditions
- Temperance
- Prisons and insane asylums

But the most intense and controversial was the abolitionists' efforts to end slavery, an effort alienating and splitting the country, hardening Southern defense of slavery, and leading to four years of bloody war. The abolitionist movement had political fallout, affecting admittance of states into the Union and the government's continued efforts to keep a balance between total numbers of free and slave states. Congressional legislation after 1820 reflected this.

Robert Fulton's *Clermont*, the first commercially successful steamboat, led the way in the fastest way to ship goods, making it the most important way to do so. Later, steam-powered railroads soon became the biggest rival of the steamboat as a means of shipping, eventually being the most important transportation method opening the West. With expansion into the interior of the country, the United States became the leading agricultural nation in the world. The hardy pioneer farmers produced a vast surplus and emphasis went to producing products with a high-sale value. These implements, such as the cotton gin and reaper, improved production. Travel and shipping were greatly assisted in areas not yet touched by railroad or, by improved or new roads, such as the National Road in the East and in the West the Oregon and Santa Fe Trails.

People were exposed to works of literature, art, newspapers, drama, live entertainment, and political rallies. With better communication and travel, more information was desired about previously unknown areas of the country, especially the West. The discovery of gold and other mineral wealth resulted in a literal surge of settlers and even more interest.

Public schools were established in many of the states with more and more children being educated. With more literacy and more participation in literature and the arts, the young nation was developing its own unique culture becoming less and less influenced by and dependent on that of Europe.

More industries and factories required more and more labor. Women, children, and, at times, entire families worked the long hours and days, until the 1830s. By that time, the factories were getting even larger and employers began hiring immigrants who were coming to America in huge numbers. Before then, efforts were made to organize a labor movement to improve working conditions and increase wages. It never really caught on until after the Civil War, but the seed had been sown.

In between the growing economy, expansion westward of the population, and improvements in travel and mass communication, the federal government did face periodic financial depressions. Contributing to these downward spirals were land speculations, availability and soundness of money and currency, failed banks, failing businesses, and unemployment. Sometimes conditions outside the nation would help trigger it; at other times, domestic politics and presidential elections affected it. The growing strength and influence of two major political parties with opposing philosophies and methods of conducting government did not ease matters at times.

As 1860 began, the nation had extended its borders north, south, and west. Industry and agriculture were flourishing. Although the United States did not involve itself actively in European affairs, the relationship with Great Britain was much improved and it and other nations that dealt with the young nation accorded it more respect and admiration. Nevertheless, war was on the horizon. The country was deeply divided along political lines concerning slavery and the election of Abraham Lincoln.

Religion has always been a factor in American life. Many early settlers came to America in search of religious freedom. Religion, particularly Christianity, was an essential element of the value and belief structure shared by the Founding Fathers. Yet the Constitution prescribes a separation of Church and State.

- The First Great Awakening was a religious movement within American Protestantism in the 1730s and 1740s. This was primarily a movement among Puritans seeking a return to strict interpretation of morality and values as well as emphasizing the importance and power of personal religious or spiritual experience. Many historians believe the First Great Awakening unified the people of the original colonies and supported the independence of the colonists.

- The Second Great Awakening (the Great Revival) was a broad movement within American Protestantism that led to several kinds of activities that were distinguished by region and denominational tradition. In general terms, the Second Great Awakening, which began in the 1820s, was a time of recognition that "awakened religion" must weed out sin on both a personal and a social level. It inspired a wave of social activism. In New England, the Congregationalists established missionary societies to evangelize the West. Publication and education societies arose, most notably the American Bible Society. This social activism gave rise to the temperance movement, prison reform efforts, and help for the handicapped and mentally ill. This period was particularly notable for the abolition movement. In the Appalachian region, the camp meeting was used to revive religion. The camp meeting became a primary method of evangelizing new territory.

- The Third Great Awakening (the Missionary Awakening) gave rise to the Social Gospel Movement. This period (1858 to 1908) resulted in a massive growth in membership of all major Protestant denominations through their missionary activities. This movement was partly a response to claims that the Bible was fallible. Many churches attempted to reconcile or change biblical teaching to fit scientific theories and discoveries. Colleges associated with Protestant churches began to appear rapidly throughout the nation. In terms of social and political movements, the Third Great Awakening was the most expansive and profound. Coinciding with many changes in production and labor, it won battles against child labor and stopped the exploitation of women in factories. Compulsory elementary education for children came from this movement, as did the establishment of a set work day. Much was also done to protect and rescue children from abandonment and abuse, to improve the care of the sick, to prohibit the use of alcohol and tobacco, as well as numerous other "social ills."

Numerous conflicts, often called the Indian Wars, broke out between the U.S. army and many different native tribes. Many treaties were signed with the various tribes, but most were broken by the government for a variety of reasons. Two of the most notable battles were the Battle of Little Bighorn in 1876, in which native people defeated General Custer and his forces, and the massacre of Native

Americans in 1890 at Wounded Knee. In 1876, the U.S. government ordered all surviving Native Americans to move to reservations.

As African Americans left the rural South and migrated to the North in search of opportunity, many settled in Harlem in New York City. By the 1920s Harlem had become a center of life and activity for people of color. The music, art, and literature of this community gave birth to a cultural movement known as the Harlem Renaissance. The artistic expressions that emerged from this community in the 1920s and 1930s celebrated the black experience, black traditions, and the voices of black America.

Many refer to the decade of the 1920s as The Jazz Age. The decade was a time of optimism and exploration of new boundaries. It was a clear movement in many ways away from conventionalism. Jazz music, uniquely American, was the country's popular music at the time. The jazz musical style perfectly typified the mood of society. Jazz is essentially free-flowing improvisation on a simple theme with a four-beat rhythm. Jazz originated in the poor districts of New Orleans as an outgrowth of the Blues.

As jazz grew in popularity and in the intricacy of the music, it gave birth to Swing and the era of Big Band Jazz by the mid 1920s.

NINETEENTH CENTURY CULTURAL CONTRIBUTORS	
AMERICAN	**CONTRIBUTION**
Lucretia Mott and Elizabeth Cady Stanton	Women's rights
Emma Hart Willard, Catharine Esther Beecher, and Mary Lyon	Education for women
Dr. Elizabeth Blackwell	The first woman doctor
Antoinette Louisa Blackwell	The first female minister
Dorothea Lynde Dix	Reforms in prisons and insane asylums
Elihu Burritt and William Ladd	Peace movements
Robert Owen	A Utopian society
Horace Mann, Henry Barmard, Calvin E. Stowe, Caleb Mills, and John Swett	Public education

Continued on next page

Major writers and works of the Harlem Renaissance:
- *Langston Hughes (The Weary Blues)*
- *Nella Larsen (Passing)*
- *Zora Neale Hurston (Their Eyes Were Watching God)*
- *Claude McKay*
- *Countee Cullen*
- *Jean Toomer*

The leading jazz musicians of the time included:
- *Buddy Bolden,*
- *Joseph "King" Oliver*
- *Duke Ellington*
- *Louis Armstrong*
- *Jelly Roll Morton*

Notable musicians of the Big Band era:
- *Bing Crosby*
- *Frank Sinatra*
- *Don Redman*
- *Fletcher Henderson*
- *Count Basie*
- *Benny Goodman*
- *Billie Holiday*
- *Ella Fitzgerald*
- *The Dorsey Brothers*

AMERICAN	CONTRIBUTION
Benjamin Lundy, David Walker, William Lloyd Garrison, Isaac Hooper, Arthur and Lewis Tappan, Theodore Weld, Frederick Douglass, Harriet Tubman, James G. Birney, Henry Highland Garnet, James Forten, Robert Purvis, Harriet Beecher Stowe, Wendell Phillips, and John Brown	Abolition of slavery and the Underground Railroad
Louisa Mae Alcott, James Fenimore Cooper, Washington Irving, Walt Whitman, Henry David Thoreau, Ralph Waldo Emerson, Herman Melville, Richard Henry Dana, Nathaniel Hawthorne, Henry Wadsworth Longfellow, John Greenleaf Whittier, Edgar Allan Poe, Oliver Wendell Holmes	Famous writers
John C. Fremont, Zebulon Pike, Kit Carson	Explorers
Henry Clay, Daniel Webster, Stephen Douglas, John C. Calhoun	Statesmen
Robert Fulton, Cyrus McCormick, Eli Whitney	Inventors
Noah Webster	American dictionary and spellers

Hispanic Americans have contributed to American life and culture since before the Civil War. Hispanics have distinguished themselves in every area of society and culture. Mexicans taught Californians to pan for gold and introduced the technique of using mercury to separate silver from worthless ores. Six state names are of Hispanic origin.

Native Americans have made major contributions to the development of the nation and have been contributors, either directly or indirectly in every area of political and cultural life. In the early years of European settlement, Native Americans were both teachers and neighbors. Even during periods of extermination and relocation, their influence was profound.

Asian Americans, particularly in the West and in large cities, have made significant contributions despite immigration bans, mistreatment, and confinement. Asians were particularly important in the construction of the transcontinental railroad, mining metals, and providing other kinds of labor and service.

Minnesota History

Early European exploration of the land that was to become Minnesota began in the 1600s by fur traders, primarily French. By the mid 1700s, Minnesota was the center of British fur trading. The land changed hands among major European nations and the fledging U.S., and was eventually won by the U.S. in 1783 after the American Revolution. Minnesota became a territory in 1849, and achieved statehood in 1858.

By 1858, much of the land had been taken or purchased for small sums from the Ojibwe and Sioux tribes, and was made available to European immigrants. Many of these future Minnesotans were from Germany, Sweden, and Norway. Farming was a primary industry, as were timbering and iron mining, and suited the newcomers well. The advance of the railroad across the U.S. also brought in many immigrants. The railroad companies actively recruited workers from across Europe.

By 1862, this influx of immigrants prompted the U.S. government to redraw the boundaries of previous treaties establishing reservations for the Dakota Sioux Indians. These treaty violations, along with crop blight and other factors, led to the U.S. – Dakota War. Ultimately, the Sioux surrendered. Many fled the area, and others were punished for war crimes, including the mass execution of 38 Sioux and the imprisonment of many others. It took decades for some degree of reconciliation between the native and non-native peoples of Minnesota to begin.

By 1862, this influx of immigrants prompted the U.S. government to redraw the boundaries of previous treaties establishing reservations for the Dakota Sioux Indians. These treaty violations, along with crop blight and other factors, led to the U.S. – Dakota War.

In 1851, the University of Minnesota became the first college-level school in the state. Henry Silbey was elected as the first governor in 1859, and the well-known medical center The Mayo Clinic was founded in 1883. Minnesota's growth continued, as did the growth of many middle and western states, throughout the later 1800s and into the 1900s, with a mix of industries and settlers. Recent immigration patterns have included the Hmong people, originally from China, Vietnam, Laos, and Thailand, who were displaced to various countries in Southeast Asia before coming to the U.S. Minnesota now has the largest population of Hmong people anywhere in this country.

Here is a link to the Minnesota Historical Society's webpage of educational resources for teachers and students:

www.mnhs.org/school/

See also Skill 23.2 for more information.

SKILL 23.4 **Demonstrating knowledge of historical and modern perspectives of significant eras, themes, individuals, and chronological relationships in world history**

Studying war has been one approach to describing events across human history. This is one theme that can be used to organize and understand previous eras, individuals, and timelines. Examples of other themes are culture, social movements, political structures, and the arts.

1861–1865

Civil War

Coming up:
• The Second World War
• The Korean War
• The Vietnam War
• The Cold War

In 1833, Congress lowered tariffs, this time at a level acceptable to South Carolina. Although President Jackson believed in states' rights, he also firmly believed in and determined to keep the preservation of the Union. A constitutional crisis had been averted but sectional divisions were getting deeper and more pronounced. The abolition movement was growing rapidly, becoming an important issue in the North. The slavery issue was at the root of every problem, crisis, event, decision, and struggle from then on. The next crisis involved the issue concerning Texas. By 1836, Texas was an independent republic with its own constitution. During its fight for independence, Americans were sympathetic to and supportive of the Texans and some recruited volunteers who crossed into Texas to help the struggle. Problems arose when the state petitioned Congress for statehood. Texas wanted to allow slavery but Northerners in Congress opposed admission to the Union because it would disrupt the balance between free and slave states and give Southerners in Congress increased influence.

A few years later, Congress took up consideration of new territories between Missouri and present-day Idaho. Again, heated debate over permitting slavery in these areas flared up. Those opposed to slavery used the **MISSOURI COMPROMISE** to prove their point showing that the land being considered for territories was part of the area the Compromise had been designated as banned to slavery. On May 25, 1854, Congress passed the infamous **KANSAS-NEBRASKA ACT** which nullified the provision creating the territories of Kansas and Nebraska. This provided for the people of these two territories to decide for themselves whether or not to permit slavery to exist there. Feelings were so deep and divided that any further attempts to compromise would meet with little, if any, success. Political and social turmoil swirled everywhere. Kansas was called "Bleeding Kansas" because of the extreme violence and bloodshed throughout the territory because two governments existed there, one pro-slavery and the other anti-slavery.

MISSOURI COMPROMISE: Congressional solution to the addition of slave states to the union; it forbade slavery to areas north of latitude 36° 30′N

KANSAS-NEBRASKA ACT: Congressional act that allowed the territories of Kansas and Nebraska to decide for themselves whether to allow slavery; it repealed the Missouri Compromise

The Supreme Court, in 1857, handed down a decision guaranteed to cause explosions throughout the country. Dred Scott was a slave whose owner had taken him from slave state Missouri, then to free state Illinois, into Minnesota Territory, free under the provisions of the Missouri Compromise, then finally back to slave state Missouri. Abolitionists pursued the dilemma by presenting a court case, stating that since Scott had lived in a free state and free territory, he was in actuality a free man. Two lower courts had ruled before the Supreme Court became involved, one ruling in favor and one against. The Supreme Court decided that residing in a free state and free territory did not make Scott a free man because Scott (and all other slaves) was not a U.S. citizen or a state citizen of Missouri. Therefore, he did not have the right to sue in state or federal courts.

The Court went a step further and ruled that the old Missouri Compromise was now unconstitutional because Congress did not have the power to prohibit slavery in the Territories.

In 1858, Abraham Lincoln and Stephen A. Douglas were running for the office of U.S. Senator from Illinois and participated in a series of debates, which directly affected the outcome of the 1860 Presidential election. Douglas, a Democrat, was up for reelection and knew that if he won this race, he had a good chance of becoming President in 1860. Lincoln, a Republican, was not an abolitionist but he believed that slavery was morally wrong and he supported the Republican Party principle that slavery must not be allowed to extend any further.

The final straw came with the election of Lincoln to the presidency the next year. Due to a split in the Democratic Party, there were four candidates from four political parties. With Lincoln receiving a minority of the popular vote and a majority of electoral votes, the Southern states, one by one, voted to secede from the Union, as they had promised they would do if Lincoln and the Republicans were victorious. The die was cast.

It is ironic that South Carolina was the first state to secede from the Union and the first shots of the war were fired on Fort Sumter in Charleston Harbor. Both sides quickly prepared for war. The North had more in its favor: a larger population; superiority in finances and transportation facilities; manufacturing, agricultural, and natural resources. The North possessed most of the nation's gold, had about ninety-two percent of all industries, and almost all known supplies of copper, coal, iron, and various other minerals. Most of the nation's railroads were in the North and Midwest, men and supplies could be moved wherever needed; food could be transported from the farms of the Midwest to workers in the East and to soldiers on the battlefields. Trade with nations overseas could go on as usual due to control of the navy and the merchant fleet. The Northern states numbered twenty-four and included western states (California and Oregon) and border states (Maryland, Delaware, Kentucky, Missouri, and West Virginia).

The eleven states of the Southern Confederacy were:

- South Carolina
- Mississippi
- North Carolina
- Georgia
- Louisiana
- Tennessee
- Florida
- Texas
- Arkansas
- Alabama
- Virginia

Although outnumbered in population, the South was completely confident of victory. They knew that all they had to do was fight a defensive war and protect their own territory.

The North had to invade and defeat an area almost the size of Western Europe. Another advantage of the South was that a number of its best officers had graduated from the U.S. Military Academy at West Point and had had long years of army experience. Many had exercised varying degrees of command in the Indian Wars and the war with Mexico. Men from the South were conditioned to living outdoors and were more familiar with horses and firearms than men from northeastern cities. Since cotton was such an important crop, Southerners felt that British and French textile mills were so dependent on raw cotton that they would be forced to help the Confederacy in the war.

Jefferson Davis president of the Confederate states

The South won decisively until the Battle of Gettysburg, July 1 through 3, 1863. Until Gettysburg, Lincoln's commanders, McDowell and McClellan, were less than desirable, Burnside and Hooker, not what was needed. Lee, on the other hand, had many able officers: Jackson and Stuart were depended on heavily by him. Jackson died at Chancellorsville and was replaced by Longstreet. Lee decided to invade the North and depended on J.E.B. Stuart and his cavalry to keep him informed of the location of Union troops and their strengths.

Robert E. Lee Confederate general

The day after Gettysburg, on July 4, Vicksburg, Mississippi, surrendered to Union General Ulysses Grant, thus severing the western Confederacy from the eastern part. In September 1863, the Confederacy won its last important victory at Chickamauga. In November, the Union victory at Chattanooga made it possible for Union troops to go into Alabama and Georgia, splitting the eastern Confederacy in two. Lincoln gave Grant command of all Northern armies in March of 1864. Grant led his armies into battles in Virginia while Phil Sheridan and his cavalry did as much damage as possible. In a skirmish at a place called Yellow Tavern, Virginia, Sheridan's and Stuart's forces met. Stuart was fatally wounded.

620,000 of 2.4 million soldiers killed

The Civil War took more American lives than any other war in history, the South losing one-third of its soldiers in battle compared to about one-sixth for the North. More than half of the total deaths were caused by disease and the horrendous conditions of field hospitals. Both sides paid a tremendous economic price but the South suffered more severely from direct damages. Destruction was pervasive with towns, farms, trade, industry, lives, and homes of men, women, children all destroyed and an entire Southern way of life was lost. The South had no voice in the political, social, and cultural affairs of the nation, lessening to a great degree the influence of the more traditional Southern ideals. The Northern Yankee Protestant ideals of hard work, education, and economic freedom became the standard of the United States and helped influence the development of the nation into a modem, industrial power.

The effects of the Civil War were tremendous. It changed the methods of waging war and has been called the first modern war. It introduced weapons and tactics

that, when improved later, were used extensively in wars of the late 1800s and
1900s.

- Civil War soldiers were the first to fight in trenches, first to fight under a
  unified command, and first to wage a defense called "major cordon defense," a
  strategy of advance on all fronts.

- They were also the first to use repeating and breech loading weapons.

- Observation balloons were first used during the war along with submarines,
  ironclad ships, and mines.

- Telegraphy and railroads were put to use first in the Civil War.

It was considered a modern war because of the vast destruction, and was "total
war," involving the use of all resources of the opposing sides. There was no way it
could have ended other than total defeat and unconditional surrender of one side
or the other.

By executive proclamation and constitutional amendment, slavery was officially
ended, although there remained deep prejudice and racism, still raising its ugly
head today. Also, the Union was preserved and the states were finally truly united.
Sectionalism, especially in the area of politics, remained strong for another hundred years but not to the degree and with the violence as existed before 1861. It
has been noted that the Civil War may have been American democracy's greatest
failure because from 1861 to 1865, calm reason—basic to democracy—fell to
human passion. Yet, democracy did survive.

The victory of the North established that no state has the right to end or leave the
Union. Because of unity, the United States became a major global power. Lincoln
never proposed to punish the South. He was most concerned with restoring the
South to the Union in a program that was flexible and practical rather than rigid
and unbending. In fact he never really felt that the states had succeeded in leaving
the Union but that they had left the "family circle" for a short time.

World Wars

The American isolationist mood was given a shocking and lasting blow in 1941
with the Japanese attack on Pearl Harbor. The nation arose and forcefully entered
the international arena as never before. Declaring itself "the arsenal of democracy,"
it entered the Second World War and emerged not only victorious, but also
as the strongest power on the Earth. It would now, like it or not, have a permanent and leading place in world affairs.

In the aftermath of the Second World War, with the Soviet Union emerging as
the second strongest power on Earth, the United States embarked on a policy

MARSHALL PLAN: U.S. program for rebuilding the economic foundation of Western Europe following WWII

TRUMAN DOCTRINE: President Harry S. Truman's foreign policy declaring the United States "leader of the free world"

COLD WAR: the state of political tension and military rivalry between the Soviet Union and the West from the end of WWII to the 1980s

UNITED NATIONS: an international organization composed of most countries of the world and dedicated to promoting peace, security, and economic development

DÉTENTE: the easing of tensions or strained relations between rivals

known as "containment" of the Communist menace. This involved what came to be known as the Marshall Plan and the Truman Doctrine. The MARSHALL PLAN involved the economic aid that was sent to Europe in the aftermath of the Second World War aimed at preventing the spread of communism. To that end, the United States has devoted a larger and larger share of its foreign policy, diplomacy, and both economic and military might to combating it.

The TRUMAN DOCTRINE offered military aid to those countries that were in danger of communist upheaval. This led to the era known as the COLD WAR in which the United States took the lead along with the Western European nations against the Soviet Union and the Eastern Bloc countries. It was also at this time that the United States finally gave up on George Washington's advice against "European entanglements" and joined the North Atlantic Treaty Organization (NATO). This was formed in 1949 and was composed of the United States and several Western European nations for the purposes of opposing communist aggression.

The UNITED NATIONS was formed in 1945 to replace the defunct League of Nations for the purposes of ensuring world peace. Even with American involvement, it would prove largely ineffective in its goals. In the 1950s, the United States embarked on what was called the "Eisenhower Doctrine," after the then-President Eisenhower. This aimed at trying to maintain peace in a troubled area of the world, the Middle East. However, unlike the Truman Doctrine in Europe, it would have little success.

The United States also became involved in a number of world conflicts in the ensuing years. Each had at the core the struggle against communist expansion. Among these were the **Korean War** (1950–1953), the **Vietnam War** (1965–1975), and various continuing entanglements in Central and South America and the Middle East. By the early 1970s under the leadership of then-Secretary of State Henry Kissinger, the United States and its allies embarked on the policy that came to be known as DÉTENTE. This was aimed at the easing of tensions between the United States and its allies and the Soviet Union and its allies.

By the 1980s, the United States embarked on what some saw as a renewal of the Cold War. This owed to the fact that the United States was becoming more involved in trying to prevent communist insurgency in Central America. A massive expansion of its armed forces and the development of space-based weapons systems were undertaken at this time. As this occurred, the Soviet Union, with a failing economic system and a foolhardy adventure in Afghanistan, found itself unable to compete. By 1989, events had come to a head. This ended with the breakdown of the Communist Bloc, the virtual end of the monolithic Soviet Union, and the collapse of the communist system by the early 1990s.

Now the United States remains active in world affairs in trying to promote peace and reconciliation, with a new specter rising to challenge it and the world—the specter of nationalism.

See also Skills 23.2 and 23.3

SKILL 23.5 Demonstrating knowledge of natural resources and how their management and use affects the environment

NATURAL RESOURCES are naturally occurring materials that are critically important or necessary to human life and civilization. A major source of contention in our modern society is the proper use and conservation of our natural resources. Although most people think of coal, oil, iron, and other minerals when they think of natural resources, the definition also includes other often overlooked resources such as forests, soil, water, air, and land.

NATURAL RESOURCES: naturally occurring materials that are critically important or necessary to human life and civilization

Renewable and Nonrenewable Resources

Our natural resources are classified into two broad categories: renewable resources and nonrenewable resources. A RENEWABLE RESOURCE is a resource that is capable of replenishment or regeneration on a human timescale. Examples of renewable resources include forests and water.

A NONRENEWABLE RESOURCE is a resource that, once exhausted, is not capable of replenishment or regeneration on a human timescale. Examples of nonrenewable resources include petroleum and minerals.

RENEWABLE RESOURCE: a resource that is capable of replenishment or regeneration on a human timescale

As the world's population has increased and civilization has advanced, becoming increasingly dependent on technology, the demand on our natural resources has soared. More important, the per capita consumption of resources has dramatically increased.

NONRENEWABLE RESOURCE: a resource that, once exhausted, is not capable of replenishment or regeneration on a human timescale

The key focus in nonrenewable resources is the every-increasing demand for energy.

Despite a finite supply of fossil fuels and radioactive fuels such as uranium, the demand for energy continues to increase at a high rate. At our present rate of consumption, there are only twenty-eight years of petroleum reserves left, and uranium reserves are estimated to be exhausted in forty years.

To alleviate this predictable energy gap, scientists are exploring new methods of recovering additional fuels from once economically unfeasible sites and researching alternative energy sources.

Alternative Energy Resources

Research efforts into alternative energy sources are directed at producing viable renewable energy sources.

ALTERNATIVE ENERGY SOURCE	
Hydroelectric Power	Power produced from falling water. Waterwheels have been in use for centuries. The drawback to this energy source lies in the availability of suitable locations for dams and the expense of construction.
Wind Power	Windmills are another ancient technology being revisited by engineers. However, wind generators produce very little electricity for the expense involved, and suitable locations with steady, high winds (windfields) are limited.
Tidal Power	The generation of electricity by deflecting and diverting strong tidal currents through offshore turbines that drive electric generators. Again, the presence of proper conditions is necessary (strong tidal power) and suitable locations are limited.
Geothermal Energy	In some areas of the world, such as New Zealand, Iceland, and Italy, energy is produced from hot igneous rocks within the Earth. Rainwater percolates porous strata near an active magma chamber and turns into steam. Some of the steam returns to the surface through natural fissures or is extracted through drilled vents. The steam is captured and routed to turbine-powered electrical generators to produce geothermal power. The steam can also be used to directly heat buildings. The limitations of this alternative energy source are obvious: Most metropolitan locations are not situated near active magma chambers. However, New Zealand does manage to gather enough power to meet approximately 5 percent of its overall electrical needs.
Solar Energy	Solar power can be utilized directly as a source of heat or to produce electricity. The most common use of solar power is to heat water. An array of dark-colored piping is placed on the roof of a structure. As water circulates through the piping, it is heated. Solar cells produce electricity from the solar radiation. Photons striking the junction between two semiconductors (usually selenium) induce an electrical current that is stored in batteries. Although this source of power is pollution-free, there are two main limitations. First, the production of power is limited by the distribution and periods of insulation. In addition, atmospheric conditions can interfere with collection efforts (e.g., cloud cover, pollution, and storms). Second, the solar cells individually produce very small amounts of electricity (called trickle changes) and must be arrayed in large banks.
Biomass	Plant and animal wastes (decaying or decayed) can be burned to produce heat for steam turbine electrical generators. In most highly developed countries the biomass is first converted to either methane gas (given off by decaying biomass) or alcohol, but in some underdeveloped countries, the biomass is still burned directly as a fuel source. For centuries, peat bogs were used as a traditional source of home-heating and cooking fuel.

Continued on next page

Fusion Power	Although the technology does not currently exist, researchers are actively pursuing the means to make fusion power a reality. Unlike fission, the other form of nuclear energy currently in use, fusion does not rely on splitting the atoms of uranium or other potentially deadly radioactive elements. Instead, fusion power mimics the process that produces the energy of the Sun.
	Fusion energy is produced when small atomic nuclei fuse together to form new atoms. In a fusion reaction, two isotopes of hydrogen, deuterium, and tritium combine to make helium.
	The most significant advantage offered by fusion power as compared to fission power is that no dangerous radioactive isotopes are produced. The reaction produces only harmless helium that easily diffuses into the atmosphere and escapes into outer space. Additionally, the elements required for a fusion reaction are abundant on Earth (i.e., deuterium and tritium are extracted from seawater) and readily renew themselves through natural processes.

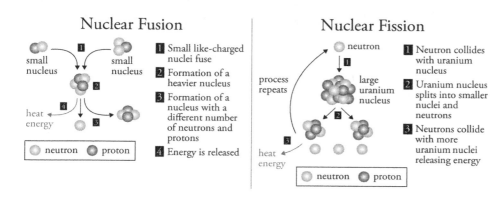

Addressing the Issues

Our increasing population, urbanization, and dependence on technology are the key factors that drive the rapid consumption of our resources. How long our natural resources will last depends on future demand and willingness on the part of governments to efficiently manage their energy needs and resources.

As grim as the projected shortfalls may seem, there is some hope. Better agricultural techniques to prevent soil depletion, reclamation of waterways, banning the use of chemicals damaging to the atmosphere, recycling plastics and metals, and seeking alternative energy sources are all examples of ongoing initiatives to ensure resources for future generations.

SKILL 23.6 Demonstrating knowledge of the environment as an integrating concept across academic disciplines

See also Skills 20.5 and 23.5

COMPETENCY 24

UNDERSTAND CHARACTERISTICS OF AND INTERACTIONS AMONG INDIVIDUALS, GROUPS, AND INSTITUTIONS

> **SKILL 24.1** Demonstrating knowledge of the characteristics of different forms of government, including the government of Minnesota-based American Indian tribes, and the reasons people create and change governments

Historically, the functions of government, or people's concepts of government and its purpose and function, have varied considerably. In the theory of political science, the function of government is to secure the common welfare of the members of the given society over which it exercises control. In different historical eras, governments have attempted to achieve the common welfare by various means in accordance with the traditions and ideology of the given society.

Among primitive peoples, systems of control were rudimentary at best. They arose directly from the ideas of right and wrong that had been established in the group and were common in that particular society. Control was exercised most often by means of group pressure, most often in the forms of taboos and superstitions and in many cases by ostracism, or banishment from the group. Thus, in most cases, because of the extreme tribal nature of society in those early times, this lead to very unpleasant circumstances for the individual so treated. Without the protection of the group, a lone individual was most often in for a sad, and very short, fate (no other group would accept such an individual into their midst and survival alone was extremely difficult if not impossible).

Among more civilized peoples, governments began to assume more institutional forms. They rested on a well-defined legal basis. They imposed penalties on violators of the social order. They used force, which was supported and sanctioned by their people. The government was charged with establishing the social order and was supposed to do so in order to be able to discharge its functions.

Ideas about government—who should govern and how—have been considered by various thinkers and philosophers. The most influential of them, and those who have had the most influence on our present society, were the ancient Greek philosophers such as Plato and Aristotle.

Aristotle's conception of government was based on a simple idea: The function of government was to provide for the general welfare of its people. A good government, and one that should be supported, was one that did so in the best way possible, with the least pressure on the people. Bad governments were those that subordinated the general welfare to that of the individuals who ruled. At no time should any function of any government be in the personal interest of any one individual, no matter who that individual was.

This does not mean that Aristotle had no sympathy for the individual or for individual happiness (an accusation that has been leveled at Plato by readers of *The Republic*, which was the first important philosophical text to explore these issues). Rather, Aristotle believed that a society is greater than the sum of its parts, or that "the good of the many outweighs the good of the few and also of the one."

However, a good government will always weigh the relative merits of what is good for a given individual in society against what is good for the society as a whole. This basic concept has continued to our own time and has found its fullest expression in the idea of representative democracy and political and personal freedom. In addition, a good government maintains social order while allowing the greatest possible exercise of individual autonomy.

> *Aristotle's conception of government was based on a simple idea: The function of government was to provide for the general welfare of its people.*

Common Forms of Government

The most familiar form of government throughout history was the monarchy. Dictatorships or **AUTHORITARIAN GOVERNMENTS** are included in this description, because the basic idea—that one person was in charge of the government—applies to all of them. In this kind of government, the head of state was responsible for governing his or her subjects. Written laws have increasingly been the standard as the centuries have progressed. Monarchies and one-person governments still exist today, although they are rare. In these states, the emphasis is on keeping the monarch in power, and many laws of the country have been written with that purpose in mind.

Authoritarian governments still exist today, mostly in the form of **COMMUNIST GOVERNMENTS**, like China. In this form of government, all the members of the government belong to one political party; in China's case, it is the Communist Party. Not all members of the government hold identical beliefs about small issues, but significant issues require party unity. Organization of alternative political parties is widely and strongly discouraged. This was the case in the Soviet Union, the best-known communist state, which disappeared in 1991. Also, in many authoritarian governments, industries exist to produce revenue for the state. The flip side of this is that the government is responsible for the upkeep and outlays for these industries. This was more the case in the Soviet Union than it is in China, but certain elements of authoritarianism pervade Chinese society.

> **AUTHORITARIAN GOVERNMENTS:** governments in which the head of state is responsible for governing his or her subjects

> **COMMUNIST GOVERNMENTS:** governments in which all members of government belong to one political party, and in which industries are owned by the state

REPRESENTATIVE GOVERNMENT: government in which the people are ultimately responsible for the government's actions and the laws it passes because members of government are chosen in public elections

CONSTITUTIONAL MONARCHY: a form of government in which a monarch functions as the head of state, but an elected body, such as a parliament, has the most input in determining the government's actions

In Minnesota, as in other states in the U.S., Native American tribes on reservations are sovereign nations, and, as such, are self-governing.

See the Native American Rights Fund website for more information about tribal government, American Indian citizenship, treaty issues, and related matters at:

www.narf.org/pubs/misc /faqs.html

The most familiar form of government to Westerners is REPRESENTATIVE GOVERNMENT, commonly called a republic or democracy. The idea behind this form of government is that the people in a society are ultimately responsible for their government and the laws that it passes, enforces, and interprets, because they, the people, elect many of the members of that government. The members of a representative government are much more aware of public opinion than their authoritarian-government counterparts. A blended form of government called a CONSTITUTIONAL MONARCHY has evolved in some countries. In this form, a monarch retains a role as head of state but an elected governing body, such as a parliament, has the most significant input in the actual functioning of the government. Examples include the United Kingdom, Sweden, Malaysia, the Netherlands, Japan, and Spain.

The Western tradition of representative government began, in Greece, with direct democracy, then progressed to the republic in Rome, and on into other democracies and republics, most famously the United States and many other countries around the world. These governments are termed democracies by many, but they are more properly called republics. A democracy involves everyone in a society having a say in who is elected to that society's government. This is certainly not the case in the U.S., because not all U.S. citizens vote, and, indeed, not all citizens are allowed to vote. Another main difference between a true democracy and the kind of democracy practiced in the U.S. and other countries today is that in a true democracy, a vote on anything can be called at any time.

Native Americans in Minnesota

In Minnesota, as in other states in the U.S., Native American tribes on reservations are sovereign nations, and, as such, are self-governing. Although Native Americans are also U.S. citizens and retain, for example, the right to vote and the duty of military service, they also have autonomy with regard to the functioning of reservations. Each band (a group within a tribe or nation) has the right to establish its own internal form of government. These bodies of elected representatives are called, variously, tribal councils, boards of trustees, assemblies, and other names; their leaders are elected in varying ways according to tribal law.

Some groups, such as the Mille Lacs Band of Ojibwe, have a governmental structure similar to that of the U.S., with a separation of powers to provide checks and balances within their government. They have a legislative branch, a judicial branch, and an executive branch. The Indian Affairs Council of Minnesota, established in 1962, serves as a liaison between the Indian nations and the United States government.

SKILL 24.2 Demonstrating knowledge of the origins, core democratic values, and principles of constitutional democracy in the United States

The American nation was founded very much with the idea that the people would have a large degree of autonomy and liberty. The famous maxim no taxation without representation was a rallying cry for the Revolution, not only because the people didn't want to suffer the increasingly oppressive series of taxes imposed on them by the British Parliament, but also because the people could not in any way influence the lawmakers in Parliament in regard to those taxes. No American colonist had a seat in Parliament and no American colonist could vote for members of Parliament.

One of the most famous words in the Declaration of Independence is "liberty," the pursuit of which all people should be free to attempt. That idea, that a people should be free to pursue their own course, even to the extent of making their own mistakes, has dominated political thought in the 200-plus years of the American republic.

REPRESENTATION, the idea that a people can vote—or even replace—their law-makers was not a new idea, except in America. Residents of other British colonies did not have these rights, of course, and America was only a colony, according to the conventional wisdom of the British government at the time. What the Sons of Liberty and other revolutionaries were asking for was to stand on an equal footing with the Mother Country. Along with the idea of representation comes the notion that key ideas and concepts can be deliberated and discussed, with theoretically everyone having a chance to voice their views. This applied to both lawmakers and the people who elected them. Lawmakers wouldn't just pass bills that became laws; rather, they would debate the particulars and go back and forth on the strengths and weaknesses of proposed laws before voting on them. Members of both houses of Congress had the opportunity to speak out on the issues, as did the people at large, who could contact their lawmakers and express their views. This idea ran very much counter to the experience that the Founding Fathers had before the Revolution—that of taxation without representation. The different branches of government were designed to serve as a mechanism of checks and balances on each other so that no one branch could become too powerful. They each have their own specific powers.

> **REPRESENTATION:** the idea that a people can vote

Another key concept in the American ideal is equality, the idea that every person has the same rights and responsibilities under the law. The Great Britain that the American colonists knew was one of a stratified society, with social classes firmly in place. Not everyone was equal under the law or in the coffers; and it was clear for all to see that the more money and power a person had, the easier it was for that person to avoid things like serving in the army and being charged with a crime. The goal of the Declaration of Independence and the Constitution was to provide equality for all who read those documents. The reality, though, was vastly different for large sectors of society, including women and nonwhite Americans.

Due process under law was also a big concern of the founders. Various amendments protect the rights of people. Amendments five through eight protect citizens who are accused of crimes and are brought to trial. Every citizen has the right to due process of law (due process as defined earlier being that the government must follow the same fair rules for everyone brought to trial). These rules include the right to a trial by an impartial jury, the right to be defended by a lawyer, and the right to a speedy trial. The last two amendments limit the powers of the federal government to those that are expressly granted in the Constitution; any rights not expressly mentioned in the Constitution, thus, belong to the states or to the people.

This feeds into the idea of basic opportunity. The "American Dream" is that every individual has an equal chance to make his or her fortune in a new land and that the United States welcomes and even encourages that initiative. The history of the country is filled with stories of people who ventured to America and made their fortunes in the Land of Opportunity. Unfortunately for anyone who wasn't a white male, that basic opportunity was sometimes a difficult thing to achieve.

The three most basic rights guaranteed by the Declaration of Independence are "life, liberty, and the pursuit of happiness."

1. Life. The first one is self-explanatory: Americans are guaranteed the right to live their lives in America.

2. Liberty. The second one is basic as well: Americans are guaranteed the right to live their lives free in America. (Although this principle has been violated for many people throughout our history; for example, Native Americans and slaves.)

3. The Pursuit of Happiness. The last basic right is more esoteric but no less important: Americans are guaranteed the right to pursue a happy life. First and foremost, they are allowed the ability to make a life for themselves in America, "the Land of Opportunity." That happiness also extends to the pursuit of life free from oppression or discrimination, two things that, again, some Americans have been deprived of throughout our history.

DECLARATION OF IN-DEPENDENCE: founding document of the United States

The **DECLARATION OF INDEPENDENCE** is an outgrowth of both ancient Greek ideas of democracy and individual rights and the ideas of the European Enlightenment and the Renaissance, especially the ideology of the political thinker John Locke. Thomas Jefferson (1743–1826) the principle author of the Declaration borrowed much from Locke's theories and writings. John Locke was one of the most influential political writers of the seventeenth century; he put great emphasis on human rights and put forth the belief that when governments violate those rights people should rebel. He wrote the book *Two Treatises of Government* in 1690, which had tremendous influence on political thought in the American colonies and helped to shape the U.S. Constitution and Declaration of Independence.

The Declaration of Independence was the founding document of the United States of America. The **ARTICLES OF CONFEDERATION** were the first attempt of the newly independent states to reach a new understanding amongst their selves. The Declaration was intended to demonstrate the reasons that the colonies were seeking separation from Great Britain. Conceived by and written for the most part by Thomas Jefferson, it is not only important for what it says, but also for how it says it. The Declaration is in many respects a poetic document. Instead of a simple recitation of the colonists' grievances, it set out clearly the reasons why the colonists were seeking their freedom from Great Britain. They had tried all means to resolve the dispute peacefully.

> **ARTICLES OF CON-FEDERATION:** the first constitution of the United States credited during the Revolutionary War

It was the right of a people, when all other methods of addressing their grievances have been tried and failed, to separate themselves from that power that was keeping them from fully expressing their rights to life, liberty, and the pursuit of happiness.

A convention met under the presidency of George Washington, with fifty-five of the sixty-five appointed members present. A constitution was written in four months. The **CONSTITUTION OF THE UNITED STATES** is the fundamental law of the republic. It is a precise, formal, written document of the extraordinary, or supreme, type of constitution. The founders of the Union established it as the highest governmental authority. There is no national power superior to it. The foundations were so broadly laid as to provide for the expansion of national life and to make it an instrument which would last for all time. To maintain its stability, the framers created a difficult process for making any changes to it. No amendment can become valid until it is ratified by three fourths of all of the states. The British system of government was part of the basis of the final document. But significant changes were necessary to meet the needs of a partnership of states that were tied together as a single federation, yet sovereign in their own local affairs. This constitution established a system of government that was unique and advanced far beyond other systems of its day.

> **CONSTITUTION OF THE UNITED STATES:** the fundamental law of the republic

The constitution binds the states in a governmental unity in everything that affects the welfare of all. At the same time, it recognizes the right of the people of each state to independence of action in matters that relate only to them. Since the Federal Constitution is the law of the land, all other laws must conform to it.

The debates conducted during the Constitutional Congress represent the issues and the arguments that led to the compromises in the final document. The debates also reflect the concerns of the Founding Fathers that the rights of the people be protected from abrogation by the government itself and the determination that no branch of government should have enough power to continually dominate the others. There is, therefore, a SYSTEM OF CHECKS AND BALANCES.

> **SYSTEM OF CHECKS AND BALANCES:** the determination that no branch of government should have enough power to continually dominate the others

The System of Checks and Balances

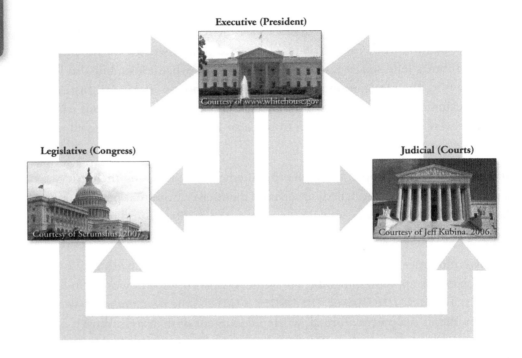

Executive (President)
Courtesy of www.whitehouse.gov

Legislative (Congress)
Courtesy of Scrumshus, 2007.

Judicial (Courts)
Courtesy of Jeff Kubina, 2006.

Bill of Rights

The first ten amendments to the United States Constitution dealing with civil liberties and civil rights are collectively referred to as the Bill of Rights. James Madison was credited with writing most of them. They are, in brief:

1. Freedom of religion

2. Right to bear arms

3. Security from the quartering of troops in homes

4. Right against unreasonable search and seizures

5. Right against self-incrimination

6. Right to trial by jury, right to legal council

7. Right to jury trial for civil actions

8. No cruel or unusual punishment allowed

9. These rights shall not deny other rights the people enjoy

10. Powers not mentioned in the Constitution shall be retained by the states or the people

---

SKILL 24.3 **Demonstrating knowledge of the structure and functions of government in the United States**

In the United States, the three branches of the federal government are the executive, the legislative, and the judicial. They divide their powers in the following manner:

Legislative Branch

Article I of the Constitution established the legislative, or law-making branch of the government, called the Congress. It is made up of two houses: the House of Representatives and the Senate. Voters in all states elect the members who serve in each respective house of Congress. The legislative branch is responsible for making laws, raising and printing money, regulating trade, establishing the postal service and federal courts, approving the president's appointments, and declaring war and supporting the armed forces. The Congress has the power to change the Constitution and to impeach, or bring charges against, the president. Charges for impeachment are brought by the House of Representatives and tried in the Senate.

Executive Branch

Article II of the Constitution created the executive branch of the government, headed by the president, who leads the country, recommends new laws, and can veto bills passed by the legislative branch. As the chief of state, the president is responsible for carrying out the laws of the country and the treaties and declarations of war passed by the legislative branch. The president appoints federal judges and is commander-in-chief of the military. Other members of the executive branch include the vice-president, who is also elected, various cabinet members he might appoint, and ambassadors, presidential advisers, members of the armed forces, and other appointed officers and civil servants of government agencies, departments, and bureaus. Though the president appoints them, the legislative branch must then approve them.

Judicial Branch

Article III of the Constitution established the judicial branch of government headed by the Supreme Court. The Supreme Court has the power to rule that a law passed by Congress or an act of the executive branch is illegal and unconstitutional. In an appeal capacity, citizens, businesses, and government officials can also ask the Supreme Court to review a decision made in a lower court if they believe that the ruling by a judge is unconstitutional. The judicial branch includes lower federal courts known as federal district courts that have been established by Congress.

Checks and balances is a system established by the Constitution in which each branch of the federal government has the power to check or limit the actions of other branches.

Separation of powers is a system of U.S. government in which each branch of government has its own specifically designated powers and cannot interfere with the powers of another.

U.S. citizens have to register in order to vote and, at that time, they can declare their membership in a political party. The Democratic and Republican parties are the two with the most money and power, but other political parties abound.

Candidates affiliate themselves with political parties. Candidates then go about the business of campaigning, which includes publicizing their candidacy, what they believe in, and what they will do if elected. Candidates sometimes get together for debates, to showcase their views on important issues of the day and how those views differ from those of their opponents. Candidates give public speeches, attend public functions, and express their views to reporters, for coverage in newspapers and magazines and on radio and television. On Election Day, candidates hope that what they've done is enough.

Elections take place regularly, so voters know just how long it will be before the next election. Presidential elections are held every four years. Voters technically have the option to recall elected candidates. Such a measure, however, is drastic and requires a large number of signatures to get the motion on the ballot and then a large number of votes to have the measure approved. As such, recalls of elected candidates are relatively rare.

Another method of removing public officials from office is impeachment. This, too, is rare, but does happen. Both houses of the state or federal government have to approve the impeachment measure by a large margin. In the case of the federal government, the House of Representatives votes to impeach a federal official and the Senate votes to convict or acquit.

Electoral College

The College of Electors—or the Electoral College, as it is more commonly known—has a long and distinguished history of mirroring the political will of the American voters. On some occasions, however, Electoral College results have not been entirely in sync with that political will.

Article II of the Constitution lists the specifics of the Electoral College. The Founding Fathers included the Electoral College as one of the famous "checks and balances" for two reasons:

1. They wanted states with small populations to have more of an equal weight in the presidential election.

2. They didn't trust the common people to be able to make an informed decision about which candidate would make the best president.

The same thinking that came up with the idea of two senators for each state created the Electoral College. The large-population states had their populations reflected in the House of Representatives. New York and Pennsylvania, two of the states with the largest populations, had the greatest number of members in the House of Representatives. But these two states still had only two senators—the same number that small-population states like Rhode Island and Delaware had. The same principle applied in the Electoral College. Each state had just one vote, regardless of how many members of the House represented that state.

Technically, the electors do not have to vote for a particular candidate. The Constitution does not require them to do so. However, tradition holds that the electors vote for the candidate chosen by their state and so the vast majority of electors do just that. The Electoral College meets a few weeks after the presidential election. This meeting is generally a formality. When all the electoral votes are counted, the candidate with the most votes wins. In most cases, the candidate who wins the popular vote also wins in the Electoral College, but this has not always been the case.

Election of 2000

In 2000 in Florida, the Supreme Court decided the election. The Democratic Party's candidate was Vice President Al Gore. The Republican Party's candidate was George W. Bush, governor of Texas and son of former president George Bush. The election was hotly contested, and many states went down to the wire, decided by only a handful of votes. The one state that seemed to be flip-flopping as election day turned into election night was Florida. In the end, Gore won the popular vote by nearly 540,000 votes. But he didn't win the electoral vote. The vote was so close in Florida that a recount was necessary under federal law. Eventually, the Supreme

Court weighed in and stopped all the recounts. The last count had Bush winning by less than a thousand votes. That gave him Florida and the White House.

Powers of the Federal Government

1. To tax

2. To borrow and coin money

3. To establish postal service

4. To grant patents and copyrights

5. To regulate interstate and foreign commerce

6. To establish courts

7. To declare war

8. To raise and support the armed forces

9. To govern territories

10. To define and punish felonies and piracy on the high seas

11. To fix standards of weights and measures

12. To conduct foreign affairs

Powers of the States

1. To regulate intrastate trade

2. To establish local governments

3. To protect general welfare

4. To protect life and property

5. To ratify amendments

6. To conduct elections

7. To make state and local laws

Concurrent Powers of the Federal Government and States

1. Both Congress and the states may tax

2. Both may borrow money

3. Both may charter banks and corporations

4. Both may establish courts

5. Both may make and enforce laws

6. Both may take property for public purposes

7. Both may spend money to provide for the public welfare

Implied Powers of the Federal Government

1. To establish banks or other corporations, implied from delegated powers to tax, borrow, and to regulate commerce

2. To spend money for roads, schools, health, insurance, etc., implied from powers to establish post roads, to tax to provide for general welfare and defense, and to regulate commerce

3. To create military academies, implied from powers to raise and support an armed force

4. To locate and generate sources of power and sell surplus, implied from powers to dispose of government property, commerce, and war powers

5. To assist and regulate agriculture, implied from power to tax and spend for general welfare and regulate commerce

SKILL 24.4 **Recognizing the rights and responsibilities of individuals in society and of the ideals, principles, and practices that promote productive community involvement**

Humans are social animals who naturally form groups based on familial, cultural, national, and other lines. Conflicts and differences of opinion are just as natural between these groups.

ETHNOCENTRISM:
the belief that one's own culture is the central and usually superior culture

One source of differing views among groups is ethnocentrism. ETHNOCENTRISM, as the word suggests, is the belief that one's own culture is the central and usually superior culture. An ethnocentric view usually considers different practices in other cultures as inferior or even "savage."

Psychologists have suggested that ethnocentrism is a naturally occurring attitude. For the large part, people are most comfortable among other people who share their same upbringing, language, and cultural background, and are likely to judge other cultural behaviors as alien or foreign.

Historical developments are likely to affect different groups in different ways, some positively and some negatively. These effects can strengthen the ties an individual feels to the group he or she belongs to and solidify differences between groups.

Processes of Social and Cultural Change

- Innovation is the introduction of new ways of performing work or organizing societies, and can spur drastic changes in a culture. Prior to the innovation of agriculture, for instance, human cultures were largely nomadic and survived by hunting and gathering their food. Agriculture led directly to the development of permanent settlements and a radical change in social organization. Likewise, technological innovations in the Industrial Revolution of the nineteenth century changed the way work was performed and transformed the economic institutions of western cultures. Recent innovations in communications are changing the way cultures interact today.

- Cultural diffusion is the movement of cultural ideas or materials between populations independent of the movement of those populations. Cultural diffusion can take place when two populations are close to one another, through direct interaction, or across great distances, through mass media and via other routes. American movies are popular all over the world, for instance. Within the United States, hockey, traditionally a Canadian pastime, has become a popular sport. These are both examples of cultural diffusion.

- Adaptation is the process that individuals and societies go through in changing their behavior and organization to cope with social, economic and environmental pressures.

- Acculturation is an exchange or adoption of cultural features when two cultures come into regular direct contact. An example of acculturation is the adoption of Christianity and western dress by many Native Americans in the United States.

- **Assimilation** is the process of a minority ethnic group largely adopting the culture of the larger group it exists within. These groups are typically immigrants moving to a new country, as with the European immigrants who traveled to the United States at the beginning of the twentieth century who assimilated to American culture.

- **Extinction** is the complete disappearance of a culture. Extinction can occur suddenly, from disease, famine, or war when the people of a culture are completely destroyed, or slowly over time as a culture adapts, acculturates, or assimilates to the point where its original features are lost.

Teaching human development and interactions:

www.mrdonn.org /sociology.html

http://db.education-world .com/perl/browse?cat _id=2255

www.studysphere.com /Site/Sphere_6155.html

SKILL 24.5 Demonstrating knowledge of interactions among individuals, groups, and institutions in a society

Social scientists use the term **CULTURE** to describe the way of life of a group of people. Culture not only includes art, music, and literature, but also beliefs, customs, languages, traditions, and inventions. The term **GEOGRAPHY** is defined as the study of Earth's features and living things with regard to their location, relationship with each other, how they came to be there, and why they are so important.

PHYSICAL GEOGRAPHY is concerned with the locations of such features as climate, water, and land; how these relate to and affect each other and human activities; and what forces shaped and changed them. All three of these features affect the lives of all humans and have a direct influence on what is made and produced, where it occurs, how it occurs, and what makes it possible. The combination of the different climate conditions and types of landforms as well as other surface features work together all around the Earth to give the many varied cultures unique characteristics and distinctions.

CULTURAL GEOGRAPHY studies the location, characteristics, and influence of the physical environment on different cultures around the world. Also included in these studies are the comparisons among and influences of the many varied cultures. Ease of travel and state-of-the-art communication techniques ease the difficulties of understanding cultural differences.

A **POPULATION** is a group of people living within a certain geographic area. Populations are usually measured on a regular basis by census, which also measures age, economic status, ethnicity, and other data.

CULTURE: the way of life of a group of people

GEOGRAPHY: the study of Earth's features and living things with regard to their location, relationship with each other, how they came to be there, and why they are so important

PHYSICAL GEOGRAPHY: concerned with the locations of such features as climate, water, and land; how these relate to and affect each other and human activities; and the forces that shaped and changed them

CULTURAL GEOGRAPHY: studies the location, characteristics, and influence of the physical environment on different cultures around the world

POPULATION: a group of people living within a certain geographic area

When a population grows, it must either expand its geographic boundaries to make room for new people or increase its density. Population density is simply the number of people in a population divided by the geographic area in which they live. Cultures with a high population density are likely to have different ways of interacting with one another than those with low density, as people live in closer proximity to one another.

As a population grows, its economic needs change. There are more people with more basic needs, and more workers are needed to produce the goods to meet those needs. If a population's production or purchasing power does not keep pace with its growth, its economy can be adversely affected. The age distribution of a population can affect the economy as well, if the number of young and old people who are not working is disproportionate to those who are.

Growth in some areas may spur migration to other parts of a population's geographic region that are less densely populated. This redistribution of population also places demands on the economy, as infrastructure is needed to connect new areas to older population centers, and land is put to new use.

Populations can grow naturally, when the rate of birth is higher than the rate of death, or by adding new people from other populations through immigration. Immigration is often a source of societal change as people from other cultures bring their institutions and language to a new area. Immigration has an impact on a population's educational and economic institutions as immigrants enter the workforce and enroll their children in schools.

Populations can decline in number, when the death rate exceeds the birth rate, or when people migrate to another area. War, famine, disease, and natural disasters can dramatically reduce a population. The economic problems caused by population decline can be similar to those from overpopulation. In extreme cases, a population may decline to the point where it can no longer perpetuate itself and its members and their culture either disappear or are absorbed into another population. When changes in human and other populations and migration, climate change, or natural disasters disrupt the delicate balance of a habitat or an ecosystem, species either adapt or become extinct.

The study of social phenomena can draw on the methods and theories of several disciplines.

QUALITATIVE RESEARCH: such as researching the types of rituals a culture has

QUANTITATIVE RESEARCH: such as measuring the relative sizes of ethnic groups

- Anthropology is largely concerned with the institutions of a society and intercultural comparisons. Anthropologists observe people of a particular culture acting within their culture and interacting with people of other cultures, and interpret social phenomena. Anthropology relies on **QUALITATIVE RESEARCH**, such as researching the types of rituals a culture has, as well as **QUANTITATIVE RESEARCH**, such as measuring the relative sizes of ethnic groups.

- **Psychology** is mainly centered on the study of the individual and his behavior. As humans are social animals, the methods of psychology can be used to study society and culture by asking questions about how individuals behave within these groups, what motivates them, and the ways they find to express themselves.

- **Sociology** covers how humans act as a society and within a society, and examines the rules and mechanisms they follow as a society. Sociology also looks at groups within a society and how they interact. The field relies on research methods from several disciplines, including anthropology and psychology.

THEORIES OF SOCIAL PHENOMENA	
Causality	The reason something happens, its cause, is a basic category of human thinking. We want to know the causes of some major event in our lives. Within the study of history, causality is the analysis of the reasons for change. The question we are asking is why and how a particular society or event developed in the particular way it did given the context in which it occurred.
Conflict	Conflict within history is opposition of ideas, principles, values or claims. Conflict may take the form of internal clashes of principles or ideas or claims within a society or group or it may take the form of opposition between groups or societies.
Bias	A prejudice or a predisposition either toward or against something. In the study of history, bias can refer to the persons or groups studied, in terms of a society's bias toward a particular political system, or it can refer to the historian's predisposition to evaluate events in a particular way.
Interdependence	A condition in which two things or groups rely upon one another, as opposed to independence, in which each thing or group relies only upon itself.
Identity	The state or perception of being a particular thing or person. Identity can also refer to the understanding or self-understanding of groups, nations, etc.
Nation–state	A particular type of political entity that provides a sovereign territory for a specific nation in which other factors also unites the citizens (e.g., language, race, ancestry, etc.).
Culture	The civilization, achievements, and customs of the people of a particular time and place.

Sociologists have identified five different types of institutions around which societies are structured: family, education, government, religion, and economy. These institutions provide a framework for members of a society to learn about and participate in a society, and allow for a society to perpetuate its beliefs and values to succeeding generations.

The five different types of institutions around which societies are structured are family, education, government, religion, and economy.

1. The family is the primary social unit in most societies. It is through the family that children learn the most essential skills for functioning in their society such as language and appropriate forms of interaction. The family is connected to ethnicity, which is partly defined by a person's heritage.

2. Education is an important institution in a society, as it allows for the formal passing on of a culture's collected knowledge. The institution of education is connected to the family, as that is where a child's earliest education takes place. The United States has a public school system administered by the states that ensures a basic education and provides a common experience for most children.

3. A society's governmental institutions often embody its beliefs and values. Laws, for instance, reflect a society's values by enforcing its ideas of right and wrong. The structure of a society's government can reflect a society's ideals about the role of an individual in his society. The American form of democracy emphasizes the rights of the individual, but in return expects individuals to respect the rights of others, including those of ethnic or political minorities.

4. Religion is frequently the institution from which springs a society's primary beliefs and values and can be closely related to other social institutions. Many religions have definite teachings on the structure and importance of the family, for instance. The U.S. Constitution guarantees the free practice of religion, which has led to a large number of denominations practicing in the United States today.

5. A society's economic institutions define how an individual can contribute and receive economic reward from his society. The United States has a capitalist economy motivated by free enterprise. While this system allows for economic advancement for the individual, it can also produce areas of poverty and economic depression.

SKILL 24.6 **Demonstrating knowledge of the concepts of global connection and independence, including needs and wants and how people organize for the production, distribution, and consumption of goods and services**

Economics is the study of how a society allocates its scarce resources to satisfy what are basically unlimited and competing wants. Economics can also be defined as a study of the production, consumption, and distribution of goods and services.

A fundamental fact of economics is that resources are scarce and that wants are infinite. The fact that scarce resources have to satisfy unlimited wants means that choices have to be made. If society uses its resources to produce good A, then it doesn't have those resources to produce good B. This tradeoff is referred to as the opportunity cost, or the value of the sacrificed alternative.

On the consumption side of the market, consumers buy the goods and services that give them satisfaction, or utility. They want to obtain the most utility they can for their dollar. The quantity of goods and services that consumers are willing and able to purchase at different prices during a given period of time is referred to as demand. Since consumers buy the goods and services that give them satisfaction, this means that, for the most part, they don't buy the goods and services that don't give them satisfaction. Consumers are, in effect, voting for the goods and services that they want with dollars, or what is called dollar voting. A good that society wants acquires enough dollar votes for the producer to make a profit.

This process in which consumers vote with their dollars is called consumer sovereignty. Consumers are basically directing the allocation of scarce resources in the economy with their dollar spending. Firms, which are in business to earn profits, hire resources or inputs in accordance with consumer preferences. This is the way resources are allocated in a market economy.

Price plays an important role in a market economy. Demand was defined above. Supply is based on production costs. The supply of a good or service is defined as the quantity of a good or service that a producer is willing and able to sell at different prices during a given period of time. Market equilibrium occurs when the buying decisions of buyers are equal to the selling decisions of sellers, or when the demand and supply curves intersect. At this point, the quantity that sellers want to sell at a particular price is equal to the quantity the buyers want to buy at that price. This is the market equilibrium price.

A **TRADITIONAL ECONOMY** is one based on custom. This usually describes the situation that exists in many less-developed countries. The people do things the way their ancestors did so they are not too technologically advanced. Since their whole mindset is directed toward tradition, they are not very interested in technology, equipment, and new ways of doing things. Technology and equipment are viewed as a threat to the old way of doing things and to their tradition. There is very little upward mobility for the same reason.

The model of **CAPITALISM** is based on private ownership of the means of production and operates on the basis of free markets, on both the input and output side. The free markets function to coordinate market activity and to achieve an efficient allocation of resources. Laissez-faire capitalism is based on the premise of no government intervention in the economy. The market will eliminate any

> Economics is the study of how a society allocates its scarce resources to satisfy what are basically unlimited and competing wants

> The supply of a good or service is defined as the quantity of a good or service that a producer is willing and able to sell at different prices during a given period of time.

TRADITIONAL ECONOMY: an economy based on tradition and old ways of doing things

CAPITALISM: an economic system based on private ownership of capital

unemployment or inflation that occurs. Government needs only to provide the framework for the functioning of the economy and to protect private property. The role of financial incentives is crucial for it results in risk-taking and research and development. Capitalist economies tend to have democratic forms of government because the system is based on competition and individual freedoms.

A **COMMAND ECONOMY** is almost the exact opposite of a market economy. A command economy is based on government ownership of the means of production and the use of planning to take the place of the market. Instead of the market determining the output mix and the allocation of resources, the bureaucracy fulfills this role by determining the output mix and establishing production target for the enterprises, which are publicly owned. The result is inefficiency. There is little interest in innovation and research because there is no financial reward for the innovator. A command economy tends to have an authoritarian form of government because a planning mechanism that replaces the market requires a planning authority to make decisions supplementing the freedom of choice of consumers and workers.

> **COMMAND ECONOMY:** an economy in which decisions about production and allocation are made by the governement

A **MIXED ECONOMY** uses a combination of markets and planning, with the degree of each varying according to country. The real world can be described as mixed economies, each with varying degrees of planning. The use of markets results in the greatest efficiency since markets direct resources in and out of industries according to changing profit conditions. However, government is needed to perform various functions. The degree of government involvement in the economy can vary in mixed economies. Government is needed to keep the economy stable during periods of inflation and unemployment.

> **MIXED ECONOMY:** an economy in which certain sectors are left to private ownership and the free market, while others are regulated by the government

All of the major economies of the world are mixed economies. They use markets but have different degrees of government involvement in the functioning of the markets and in the provision of public goods. For example, in some countries health care and education are provided by government and are not a part of the private sector. In the United States, most health care and higher education is private and at the expense of the consumer.

Trade

The theory of comparative advantage says that trade should be based on the comparative opportunity costs between two nations. The nation that can produce a good more cheaply should specialize in the production of that good and trade for the good in which it has the comparative disadvantage. In this way, both nations will experience gains from trade. A basis for trade exists if there are differing comparative costs in each country.

> *The nation that can produce a good more cheaply should specialize in the production of that good and trade for the good in which it has the comparative disadvantage.*

Suppose country A can produce ten units of good x or ten units of good y with its resources. Country B can produce thirty units of x or ten units of y with its resources. What are the relative costs in each country? In country A, one x costs one unit of y, and in country B, one x costs three units of y. Good y is cheaper in country B than it is in country A, $\frac{1}{3}x = 1y$ in country B versus $1y = 1x$ in country A. Country B has the comparative advantage in the production of y and country A has the comparative advantage in the production of good x. According to trade theory, each country should specialize in the production of the good in which it has the comparative advantage. Country B will devote all of its resources to the production of good y, and country A will devote all of its resources to the production of good x. Each country will trade for the good in which it has the comparative disadvantage.

In today's world, markets are international. Nations are all part of a global economy. No nation exists in isolation or is totally independent of other nations. Isolationism is referred to as autarky or a closed economy. Membership in a global economy means that what one nation does affects other nations because economies are linked through international trade, commerce, and finance. International transactions affect the levels of income, employment, and prices in each of the trading economies.

The relative importance of trade is based on what percentage of gross domestic product (GDP) trade constitutes. In a country like the United States, trade represents only a small percentage of GDP. In other nations, trade may represent over 50 percent of GDP. For those countries, changes in international transactions can cause many economic fluctuations and problems.

In a country like the United States, trade represents only a small percentage of GDP. In other nations, trade may represent over 50 percent of GDP.

Trade barriers

Trade barriers are one way economic problems are caused in other countries. Suppose a domestic government is confronted with rising unemployment in a domestic industry due to cheaper foreign imports. Consumers are buying the cheaper foreign import instead of the higher-priced domestic good. In order to protect domestic labor, the government imposes a tariff, thus raising the price of the more efficiently produced foreign good. The result of the tariff is that consumers buy more of the domestic good and less of the foreign good. The problem is that the foreign good is the product of the foreign nation's labor. A decrease in the demand for the foreign good means foreign producers don't need as much labor, so they lay off workers in the foreign country.

The result of the trade barrier is that unemployment has been exported from the domestic country to the foreign country. Treaties like the North American Free Trade Agreement (NAFTA) are a way of lowering or eliminating trade barriers on a regional basis. As trade barriers are lowered or eliminated, labor and output markets change. Some grow; some shrink. These adjustments are taking place now for Canada, the United States, and Mexico.

Capital Markets

The same thing can happen through the exchange rate and other capital markets. Capital goes where it receives the highest rate of return, regardless of national borders. Nations can affect their exchange rate values by buying and selling foreign exchange in the currency markets. Suppose the United States decides that a lower-valued dollar will stimulate its exports, leading to higher employment levels in the United States. The United States, in effect, sells dollars on the open market, thus increasing the supply of dollars on the world market. The effect is a depreciation of the dollar. The lower-valued dollar makes U.S. exports more attractive to foreigners, who buy the relatively cheaper U.S. exports instead of the now relatively higher priced domestic goods. The increased demand for U.S. exports leads to higher employment levels in the export industries in the United States. The lower demand for domestic products in the foreign country leads to unemployment in its domestic industries.

Labor Costs

The existence of multinational corporations means that plants also go where the costs are lowest because it leads to higher levels of profits for them.

> **SKILL 24.7** Demonstrating knowledge of the relationships among science, technology, and society

TECHNOLOGICAL SYSTEM: a system that consists of different parts and uses scientific knowledge to solve problems

A **TECHNOLOGICAL SYSTEM** is a system that consists of different parts and uses scientific knowledge to solve problems. It means that a system designed to solve a problem or helping people. We often use the word system in many different ways—fuel system, digestive system, communication system, to name a few.

Systems are made up of subsystems or components. All systems have some basic parts that include:

- Inputs: The resources used by the system
- Processes: The actions taken to use the inputs
- Outputs: The result of the system

- Feedback: Adjustments made to the processes to improve the outputs

- Goals: Reason for the system

All technological systems have these five parts.

CASE STUDY

As an example of a technological system, let's discuss transportation system: Transportation is the movement of people and goods from one place to another. Transportation technology is built around the vehicle. The vehicle in use must be designed to serve the purpose.

Every vehicle must have:

- A structure
- A guidance system
- A means of propulsion

- Control systems
- A means of transmission
- Measurement devices

Most technological systems have two major goals:

1. The first goal is to meet human needs, such as moving people and goods used by people from place to place. In a city like New York City, the transport system is crucial for people because of the long distances they have to travel and the cost of driving a car and the time involved in reaching the destination.

2. The second goal is to profit. It is the reward earned by owners of the transportation system for taking financial risks. But one thing is very important—the best technological system will be useless unless it helps people live better.

SUBCOMPONENTS OF THE TRANSPORTATION SYSTEM	
Modern Forms of Transport	These include road, rail, water, air, etc. These are very important because each has its own use to people using them. Each has its merits and demerits.
Intermodal Transport	Today, passengers move from one mode of transport (e.g., subway) to another (bus). There are facilities called intermodal facilities to help people and to make them comfortable during transit. An intermodal station may serve air, rail, and highway transportation.
Nodes and Stops	Stations are an important component of any public transportation system. Airport, heliport, airport terminal, bus stop, metro station, park and ride, ship terminal, ferry slip, pier or wharf are examples of Nodes and stops.
Ticket Systems	This is a very important component because it generates income. There are various types of tickets (passes, one-time tickets, multiuse tickets, discount cards, city cards, etc.). Depending on their use, passengers buy these cards or tickets.

When we analyze transportation systems, we become aware of various components and their uses. Ultimately, the single most important use of transportation systems is to move people and goods from one place to another and, while doing this, the owners make money.

A **TECHNOLOGICAL SERVICE** can be defined as a service that is provided to the society using scientific knowledge. Any service that is provided to the society is for the benefit of that society. Here we are going to discuss one of the most important services for the society—education. Education is absolutely important to any society because it breaks down the barriers that divide us on the basis of gender, race, socioeconomic status, etc. Education has the capacity to even out these differences to a significant level. It is not possible to have a society without any differences and tiers. If we had an ideal society, we would be bored to death, since there would be no controversy, competition, etc.

> **TECHNOLOGICAL SERVICE:** a service that is provided to the society using scientific knowledge

In a typical society, education is very valuable. It is the single most important thing that can bring changes in the clients who are pursuing it. Education is a very effective technological service.

But the technology used must also be human-centered, although the nonliving resources—the buildings, the transport system—are also important. Finances are crucial because this service is money hungry. Wise spending of money on this product will influence generations to come in a positive manner.

A **TECHNOLOGICAL SOLUTION** is a solution using the knowledge of science to solve a problem. This problem could be human-related or non-human-related.

> **TECHNOLOGICAL SOLUTION:** a solution using the knowledge of science to solve a problem

CASE STUDY

As an example, let us discuss the technological solution for patients whose kidneys are not functioning. A machine that is used for daily haemodialysis by individuals is called a Personal Haemodialysis System (PHD). Daily haemodialysis has been tried with excellent clinical results for more than three decades, but the attempts were short-lived for two reasons—lack of suitable equipment and adequate reimbursement.

The benefits of daily haemodialysis are:

- Improved blood pressure control
- Cardiac morphology and function
- Endocrine function
- Energy
- Physical activity
- Vitality
- Haematocrit
- Mental health
- Mineral metabolism
- Nutrition
- Social functioning
- Sexual function
- Patient survival
- Use of drugs, mortality, and hospitalization decreased

Although haemodialysis technology has improved in recent decades; it was not specifically prepared for frequent home haemodialysis. With this background

information on daily haemodialysis, we will discuss here the appropriate tests for
this technological solution called PHD.

TESTS FOR PHD	
Simplicity of the Design	The design of the system must be relatively simple because all patients may not be well-acquainted or comfortable with the use of modern technology. It must be user-friendly.
Efficiency	As a machine, it has to perform with high efficiency rate and do all the functions for which it is made.
Cost Effective	This machine must be relatively cheap, making it affordable to majority of the patients who use it. Ideally, it should be affordable to all sections of the society. Realistically, some members of the society will definitely need federal/charitable organizations' support to buy it.
Time	The treatment time it takes must be reasonably short. Some people may not dialyze themselves properly and completely if it takes too long.
Size	The size of the machine is critical, because it may neet to be carried along by patients when they travel.
Power Supply/ Battery Operated	It is absolutely essential that this machine can be operated even when there is no power, for example, while in transit.

SAMPLE TEST

SAMPLE TEST

I. Reading

(Rigorous) (Skill 1.1)

1. **Which of the following is NOT one of the metalinguistic abilities acquired by children from early involvement in reading activities?**

    A. Conventions of print

    B. Word consciousness

    C. Spelling fluency

    D. Functions of print

(Average) (Skill 1.2)

2. **Phonological awareness skills include all of the following EXCEPT:**

    A. Segmenting words into sounds

    B. Blending sounds into words

    C. Visually identifying letters

    D. Recognizing rhyming words

(Average) (Skill 1.3)

3. **Effective instructional methods for teaching phonemic awareness include all of the following EXCEPT:**

    A. Distinguishing between a sound and a word

    B. Singing familiar songs and replacing key words

    C. Sounding out words for pictures

    D. Encouraging independent reading

(Rigorous) (Skill 1.4)

4. **Awareness of the relationship between spoken and written language can be developed by all of the following EXCEPT:**

    A. Using labels in the classroom on everyday objects

    B. Clapping syllables in words

    C. Using letter cards to create messages

    D. Writing down the things children say

(Rigorous) (Skill 1.5)

5. **All of the following are true EXCEPT:**

    A. Assessing phonics skills almost always involves having students write down letters related to sounds

    B. Assessment of phonemic awareness is almost always an individual oral task

    C. Both formal and informal assessment methods can be used to assess phonics skills

    D. A test with multiple choice questions is a good choice for formally assessing phonics skills

(Rigorous) (Skill 2.1)

6. **In promoting literacy, storybook reading matters because:**

    A. It familiarizes children with classic children's storybooks

    B. Children learn about the range of topics available to them

    C. It is invariably a positive early reading experience

    D. It gives children knowledge about, strategies for, and attitudes toward reading

(Average) (Skill 2.1)

7. Instructional strategies that help children develop concepts about print includes all of the following EXCEPT:

   A. Reading books aloud to students

   B. Having students recreate sounds the teacher has demonstrated

   C. Making a Word Wall

   D. Using big books and song charts

(Average) (Skill 2.3)

8. Another name for graphophonemic awareness is:

   A. Phonological awareness

   B. Directionality of print

   C. Alphabetic principle

   D. Phonology

(Easy) (Skill 2.4)

9. The "What's in a Name?" game has which of the following benefits?

   A. Letter recognition

   B. Counting practice

   C. Learning classmates' names

   D. All of the above

(Average) (Skill 2.6)

10. Which of the following is true with regard to English Language Learners (ELL)?

    A. ELL students should learn to read initially in their first language.

    B. ELL students should learn to read initially in English, regardless of their first language.

    C. Learning to speak English before being taught to read English is helpful.

    D. Both A and C

(Average) (Skill 3.1)

11. To decode is to:

    A. Use a special code to decipher a message

    B. Sound out a printed sequence of letters

    C. Change communication signals into messages

    D. Change a message into symbols

(Average) (Skill 3.1)

12. To encode means to:

    A. Change a message into symbols

    B. Construct meaning from a code

    C. Change communication signals into messages

    D. Sound out a printed sequence of letters

(Average) (Skill 3.3)

13. When students understand how sentences are built and the words needed for the sentences to "sound" right, they have developed a sense of:

A. Morphology

B. Syntax

C. Semantics

D. Fluency

(Average) (Skill 3.5)

14. The four basic word types are:

A. Regular for reading and spelling, Regular for reading but not spelling, Irregular for reading and spelling, Irregular for reading but not spelling

B. Regular for reading and spelling, Regular for spelling but not Reading, Irregular for reading and spelling, Irregular for spelling but not reading

C. Regular for reading and spelling, Regular for reading but not spelling, Rule-based, Irregular

D. Regular for reading and spelling, Regular for reading but not spelling, Irregular, Complex

(Average) (Skill 3.5)

15. Which of the following indicates that a student is a fluent reader?

A. Reads texts with expression or prosody

B. Reads word-to-word and haltingly

C. Must intentionally decode a majority of the words

D. In a writing assignment, sentences are poorly organized structurally

(Average) (Skill 4.1)

16. If a student has a poor vocabulary, the teacher should recommend first that:

A. The student read newspapers, magazines and books on a regular basis

B. The student enroll in a Latin class

C. The student write the words repetitively after looking them up in the dictionary

D. The student use a thesaurus to locate synonyms and incorporate them into his/her vocabulary

(Rigorous) (Skill 4.2)

17. Which word in the following sentence is a bound morpheme?

The quick brown fox jumped over the lazy dog

A. The

B. Fox

C. Lazy

D. Jumped

(Average) (Skill 4.2)

18. Contextual redefinition is:

A. An example of using context clues to aid vocabulary development

B. Useful to teachers working with ELLs

C. A process of absorbing a new curriculum into an existing format

D. Not especially relevant to most elementary students

(Average) (Skill 4.4)

19. **All of the following are true about the Fortune Cookie Strategy EXCEPT:**

    A. It facilitates multiculturalism

    B. It engages multiple senses

    C. It helps children learn about the roots of words and idioms

    D. It encourages competitive learning

(Average) (Skill 4.7)

20. **Having children write out a step-by-step description of a vocabulary activity is referred to as a:**

    A. Personal narrative

    B. Procedural narrative

    C. Procedural detail

    D. Personal detail

(Average) (Skill 5.1)

21. **Which of the following is NOT true about topic sentences?**

    A. They are more general than the other sentences in the paragraph.

    B. They contain the main idea.

    C. They are the first sentence in the paragraph.

    D. They can be framed as a question, with the other sentences providing the "answers."

(Rigorous) (Skill 5.2)

22. **At what point does exposition occur within a story?**

    A. After the rising action

    B. After the denouement

    C. Before the rising action

    D. Before the setting

(Average) (Skill 5.2)

23. **Which is an untrue statement about a theme in literature?**

    A. The theme is always stated directly somewhere in the text.

    B. The theme is the central idea in a literary work.

    C. All parts of the work (plot, setting, mood, etc.) should contribute to the theme in some way.

    D. By analyzing the various elements of the work, the reader should be able to arrive at an indirectly stated theme.

(Average) (Skill 5.3)

24. **A K-W-L chart is which of the following?**

    A. Graphic organizer

    B. Abbreviations chart

    C. Word list

    D. Venn diagram

(Average) (Skill 5.3)

25. **K-W-L charts are useful for which of the following?**

    A. Comprehension of expository text

    B. Format for note taking

    C. Report writing

    D. All of the above

(Rigorous) (Skill 5.4)

26. All of the following are true about self-questioning strategies EXCEPT:

    A. They tend to make readers less curious

    B. They cause readers to be less lazy as they read

    C. They help develop comprehension skills

    D. They involve self-predicting and asking "why"

(Rigorous) (Skill 5.5)

27. Which of the following is inaccurate about word mapping?

    A. It is a teaching strategy

    B. It is an assessment strategy

    C. It helps children visually represent the elements of a given concept

    D. It helps children focus specifically on the root word

(Rigorous) (Skill 6.1)

28. Which of the following is a ballad?

    A. "The Knight's Tale"

    B. *Julius Caesar*

    C. *Paradise Lost*

    D. "The Rime of the Ancient Mariner"

(Easy) (Skill 6.1)

29. Which of the following is NOT a characteristic of a fable?

    A. Animals that feel and talk like humans

    B. Happy solutions to human dilemmas

    C. Teaches a moral or standard for behavior

    D. Illustrates specific people or groups without directly naming them

(Easy) (Skill 6.1)

30. When selecting multicultural literature it is most important that the culture be portrayed:

    A. Accurately

    B. In a fun manner

    C. In all genres

    D. With regards to music and the arts

(Easy) (Skill 6.2)

31. A simile is:

    A. A direct comparison between two things

    B. An indirect comparison between two things

    C. When human characteristics are applied to things that are not human, such as animals

    D. Deliberate exaggeration for comic effect

(Average) (Skill 6.2)

32. Which of the following is an example of alliteration?

    A. "The City's voice itself is soft like Solitude."

    B. "Both in one faith unanimous; though sad"

    C. "By all their country's wishes blest!"

    D. "In earliest Greece to these with partial choice."

(Rigorous) (Skill 6.6)

33. Which of the following reading strategies is NOT associated with fluent reading abilities?

    A. Pronouncing unfamiliar words by finding similarities with familiar words

    B. Establishing a purpose for reading

    C. Formulating questions about the text while reading

    D. Reading sentences word by word

(Easy) (Skill 6.6)

34. Which of the following is a formal reading level assessment?

    A. A standardized reading test

    B. A teacher-made reading test

    C. An interview

    D. A reading diary

(Easy) (Skill 7.1)

35. What is the plural of the word *rose*?

    A. Rosis

    B. Rosses

    C. Roses

    D. Rose's

(Rigorous) (Skill 7.1)

36. Which word needs to be corrected in the sentence below?

    The presents on the table is wrapped in beautiful wrapping paper.

    A. Presents

    B. Is

    C. Wrapped

    D. Beautiful

(Easy) (Skill 7.2)

37. Which of the following is an opinion?

    A. The sky is blue.

    B. Albany is the capital of New York State.

    C. A dog is the best pet to have.

    D. Humans breathe.

(Easy) (Skill 7.2)

38. Which of the following is a fact?

    A. It's going to rain.

    B. John is a liar.

    C. Joe said he believes John is a liar.

    D. The world is going to the dogs.

(Rigorous) (Skill 7.5)

39. All of the following are examples of ongoing informal assessment techniques used to observe student progress EXCEPT:

    A. Analyses of student work product

    B. Collection of data from assessment tests

    C. Effective questioning

    D. Observation of students

II. Communication Arts

(Rigorous) (Skill 8.1)

40. Instructions for assembling a bicycle are an example of which type of writing?

    A. Narrative

    B. Descriptive

    C. Expository

    D. Persuasive

(Easy) (Skill 8.1)

41. Texts that present information to readers in a quick and efficient manner are called:

    A. Essays

    B. Memoirs

    C. Journals

    D. Newspaper articles

(Easy) (Skill 8.2)

42. Which of the following is NOT a technique of prewriting?

    A. Clustering

    B. Listing

    C. Brainstorming

    D. Proofreading

(Easy) (Skill 8.3)

43. Which of the following addresses mostly grammatical and technical errors?

    A. Revising

    B. Editing

    C. Proofreading

    D. Rough draft writing

(Rigorous) (Skill 8.4)

44. Which of the following should NOT be included in the opening paragraph of an informative essay?

    A. Thesis sentence

    B. Details and examples supporting the main idea

    C. A broad, general introduction to the topic

    D. A style and tone that grabs the reader's attention

(Average) (Skill 8.5)

45. Which is NOT a true statement concerning an author's literary tone?

    A. Tone is partly revealed through the selection of details.

    B. Tone is the expression of the author's attitude toward his/her subject.

    C. Tone in literature is usually satiric or angry.

    D. Tone in literature corresponds to the tone of voice a speaker uses.

(Average) (Skill 8.6)

46. Which of the following is NOT true about literacy portfolios?

    A. Literacy portfolios are a good example of formal assessment of student writing.

    B. Literacy portfolios may include work samples, checklists, and records of independent reading.

    C. Literacy portfolios provide an opportunity to review student progress, set goals, and share information with parent/guardians.

    D. Literacy portfolios often contain self-assessment forms.

(Average) (Skill 9.1)

47. In preparing students for their oral presentations, the instructor provided all of these guidelines EXCEPT one. Which is NOT an effective guideline?

    A. Even if you are using a lectern, feel free to move about. This will connect you to the audience.

    B. Your posture should be natural, not stiff. Keep your shoulders toward the audience.

    C. Gestures can help communicate as long as you don't overuse them or make them distracting.

    D. You can avoid eye contact if you focus on your notes. This will make you appear more knowledgeable.

(Average) (Skill 9.2)

48. Which of the following is NOT an advisable strategy for making sense of oral language?

    A. Observe body language and other nonverbal cues

    B. Take notes to outline major points

    C. Critique, question, and evaluate others' as well as students' own oral presentations

    D. Ignore prior knowledge of the topic because it does not help understand what is being presented

(Rigorous) (Skill 9.2)

49. Processes that can enhance one's ability to remember information include which of the following?

    A. Repetition, association, visualization, and description

    B. Repetition, association, visualization, and concentration

    C. Description, association, visualization, and concentration

    D. Association, alliteration, visualization, and concentration

(Rigorous) (Skill 9.3)

50. Evaluating media may involve all of the following EXCEPT:

    A. Getting background information on the source of the information

    B. Comparing information from different sources

    C. Ignoring the tone or attitude of the author and focusing on the content only

    D. Assessing the author's purpose in writing the piece

III. Mathematics

(Easy) (Skill 10.1)

51. State the number modeled below.

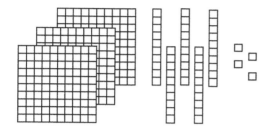

   A. 354

   B. 345

   C. 453

   D. 543

(Average) (Skill 10.1)

52. Which of the numbers is an example of an irrational number?

   A. 3

   B. $\sqrt{7}$

   C. 0.5

   D. $\frac{3}{4}$

(Rigorous) (Skill 10.1)

53. Which of the following is an irrational number?

   A. .362626262...

   B. $4^{\frac{1}{3}}$

   C. $\sqrt{5}$

   D. $-\sqrt{16}$

(Average) (Skill 10.2)

54. In similar polygons, if the perimeters are in a ratio of $x{:}y$, the sides are in a ratio of:

   A. $x{:}y$

   B. $x^2{:}y^2$

   C. $2x{:}y$

   D. $\frac{1}{2}x{:}y$

(Average) (Skill 10.3)

55. Mathematical operations are done in the following order:

   A. Simplify inside grouping characters such as parentheses, brackets, square root, fraction bar, etc.; multiply out expressions with exponents; do multiplication or division, from left to right; do addition or subtraction, from left to right.

   B. Do multiplication or division, from left to right; simplify inside grouping characters such as parentheses, brackets, square root, fraction bar, etc.; multiply out expressions with exponents; do addition or subtraction, from left to right.

   C. Simplify inside grouping characters such as parentheses, brackets, square root, fraction bar, etc.; do addition or subtraction, from left to right; multiply out expressions with exponents; do multiplication or division, from left to right.

   D. None of the above

(Rigorous) (Skill 10.3)

56. Solve for x: $|2x + 3| > 4$

   A. $-\frac{7}{2} > x > \frac{1}{2}$

   B. $-\frac{1}{2} > x > \frac{7}{2}$

   C. $x < \frac{7}{2}$ or $x < -\frac{1}{2}$

   D. $x < -\frac{7}{2}$ or $x > \frac{1}{2}$

(Rigorous) (Skill 10.5)

57. Which property is demonstrated by the equation below?

$$60 + 24 = 12(5 + 2)$$

A. Commutative

B. Associative

C. Additive identity

D. Distributive

(Average) (Skill 11.1)

58. The relationship between two variables can be analyzed by using which of the following?

A. Symbolic rule

B. Table

C. Written description

D. All of the above

(Average) (Skill 11.2)

59. What is this table intended to demonstrate?

Number of Sunglasses Sold	1	5	10	15
Total Dollars Earned	9	45	90	135

A. Number of sunglasses sold

B. Relationship between two quantities

C. Amount of money made

D. Amount of money made on 15 pairs of sunglasses

(Easy) (Skill 11.3)

60. Look at this number: 4,087,361

What number represents the ten-thousands place?

A. 4

B. 6

C. 0

D. 8

Answer: D. 8

The ten-thousands place is the fifth place to the left of the decimal.

(Easy) (Skill 11.3)

61. This graph shows which kind of relationship?

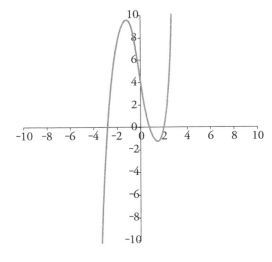

A. Non-linear

B. Linear

C. Profit

D. Algebraic

(Average) (Skill 11.5)

62. This sequence of numbers represents which of the following?

    1, 1, 2, 3, 5, 8, 13, 21, 34…

    A. An exponential pattern of growth

    B. A quadratic function

    C. A recursive function

    D. A linear function

(Easy) (Skill 12.1)

63. _____ lines do NOT intersect.

    A. Perpendicular

    B. Parallel

    C. Intersecting

    D. Skew

(Average) (Skill 12.1)

64. All of the following are examples of obtuse angles EXCEPT:

    A. 110 degrees

    B. 90 degrees

    C. 135 degrees

    D. 91 degrees

(Average) (Skill 12.1)

65. Kindergarten students are doing a butterfly art project. They fold paper in half. On one half, they paint a design. Then they fold the paper closed and reopen it. The resulting picture is a butterfly with matching sides. What math principle does this demonstrate?

    A. Slide

    B. Rotation

    C. Symmetry

    D. Transformation

(Rigorous) (Skill 12.4)

66. Find the area of the figure below.

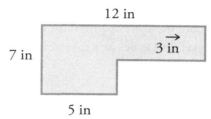

    A. 56 in²

    B. 27 in²

    C. 71 in²

    D. 170 in²

(Average) (Skill 12.4)

67. What is the area of a square with a side length of 13 feet?

    A. 169 feet

    B. 169 square feet

    C. 52 feet

    D. 52 square feet

(Rigorous) (Skill 12.5)

68. 3 km is equivalent to:

    A. 300 cm

    B. 300 m

    C. 3000 cm

    D. 3000 m

(Rigorous) (Skill 12.5)

69. Given the formula $d = rt$, (where d = distance, r = rate, and t = time), calculate the time required for a vehicle to travel 585 miles at a rate of 65 miles per hour.

    A. 8.5 hours

    B. 6.5 hours

    C. 9.5 hours

    D. 9 hours

(Average) (Skill 13.2)

70. Consider this set of test scores from a math test. Find the mean, median, and the mode.

    90, 92, 83, 83, 83, 90, 90, 83, 90, 93, 90, 97, 80, 67, 90, 85, 63, 60

    A. Mean: 83.72, mode: 90, median: 86.5

    B. Mean: 86.5, mode: 83, 90, median: 83.72

    C. Mean: 1507, mode: 90, median 83

    D. Mean 90, mode 83.72, median 90

(Average) (Skill 13.2)

71. Corporate salaries are listed for several employees. Which would be the best measure of central tendency?

$24,000	$24,000
$26,000	$28,000
$30,000	$120,000

    A. Mean

    B. Median

    C. Mode

    D. No difference

(Easy) (Skill 13.3)

72. Emma did a presentation to the class of the data she collected. She organized her data in the following chart.

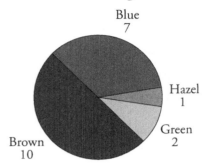

    Which display type did she use to organize her data?

    A. Line graph

    B. Pictograph

    C. Circle graph

    D. Bar graph

(Average) (Skill 13.3)

73. Which type of graph uses symbols to represent quantities?

    A. Bar graph

    B. Line graph

    C. Pictograph

    D. Circle graph

(Rigorous) (Skill 13.5)

74. What is the probability of drawing 2 consecutive aces from a standard deck of cards?

    A. $\frac{5}{31}$

    B. $\frac{1}{221}$

    C. $\frac{2}{104}$

    D. $\frac{2}{52}$

(Average) (Skill 13.6)

75. SnowGlow pulls every fifth snow globe from their manufacturing line to check for leaks. This is an example of which type of sampling?

   A. Convenience

   B. Quota

   C. Cluster

   D. Systematic

(Rigorous) (Skill 14.1)

76. Which of the following conclusion(s) can be made by using this Venn diagram?

   A. All Newfoundlands are in the working group

   B. All dogs are in the working group

   C. All working group dogs are Newfoundlands

   D. None of the above

(Average) (Skill 14.1)

77. Based on the previous question, which of the following is a correct "if-then" statement?

   A. If a dog is in the working group, then it is a Newfoundland

   B. If a dog is a Newfoundland, then it is in the working group

   C. Neither A nor B

   D. Both A and B

(Rigorous) (Skill 14.2)

78. Which of the following is true about permutations and combinations?

   A. There are more steps involved in permutations than in combinations

   B. The steps in combinations must be done in a certain order

   C. The steps in permutations must be done in a certain order

   D. There are more steps involved in combinations than in permutations

(Rigorous) (Skill 14.5)

79. Sequences of numbers vary in the way in which the term of the sequence is set. Which of the following is true?

   A. Geometric sequences are based on a variable difference between the terms

   B. Geometric sequences are based on a common ratio between the terms

   C. Arithmetic sequences are based on a common ratio between the terms

   D. Arithmetic sequences are based on a variable difference between the terms

(Average) (Skill 15.1)

80. Sammy knows that Yee Lin has made dinner five nights in a row, so he concludes that she will make dinner again on the sixth night. The approach to his conclusion is known as:

   A. Deductive reasoning

   B. Conditional thinking

   C. Conclusive reasoning

   D. Inductive reasoning

(Average) (Skill 15.1)

81. **Which of the following is true?**

    A. In conditional statements, an "if-then" format is used

    B. The hypothesis in a conditional statement is the "if" clause

    C. Another form used to show the hypothesis-conclusion relationship is "If p, then q"

    D. All of the above

(Easy) (Skill 15.3)

82. **Scientific notation can be best described as:**

    A. A research language used by mathematicians and scientists

    B. A method for writing very large or very small numbers

    C. A method of describing data

    D. The results of statistical analysis

(Easy) (Skill 15.4)

83. **When students are checking for the reasonableness of an answer, which problem-solving strategy can be used?**

    A. Draw a diagram

    B. Work backwards

    C. Guess and check

    D. Estimation and approximation

(Easy) (Skill 15.4)

84. **You are teaching your students how to solve problems using measurement. Fluid ounces, cups, pints, and quarts, gallons are all units for what type of measurement?**

    A. Length

    B. Capacity

    C. Weight

    D. Mass

(Average) (Skill 15.4)

85. **The four steps of problem-solving are:**

    A. Understand the problem, devise a plan, carry out the plan, write down the solution

    B. Understand the problem, devise a plan, carry out the plan, look back

    C. Devise a plan, carry out the plan, look back, and revise future plans

    D. Understand and carry out the plan, look back, write it up, and revise future plans

(Average) (Skill 15.5)

86. **Which of the following is NOT true about the history of mathematics?**

    A. The source of using decimals instead of fractions is attributed to Islamic mathematician Al-Kashi.

    B. Mathematicians in India and from the Mayan civilization were the first to invent the idea of zero.

    C. Calculus and analytical geometry emerged in the 17th century.

    D. Most of the concepts in mathematics occurred in the last 500 years.

(Rigorous) (Skill 15.6)

87. **Why are manipulatives, models, and technology used by math teachers?**

    A. To promote interest

    B. To address diverse learning needs

    C. To give hands-on math experience

    D. All of the above

IV. Health/Fitness and Fine Arts

(Average) (Skill 16.1)

88. **Social skills and values developed by physical activity include all of the following EXCEPT:**

    A. Winning at all costs

    B. Making judgments in groups

    C. Communicating and cooperating

    D. Respecting rules and property

(Average) (Skill 16.1)

89. **Which type of physical education activities would be most likely to help students develop a sense of belonging?**

    A. Solitary activities

    B. Teamwork activities

    C. Competitive activities

    D. Creative activities

(Average) (Skill 16.1)

90. **A positive approach to coaching includes all of the following EXCEPT:**

    A. Instructive, corrective feedback

    B. Repeated demonstration of how to do a task

    C. Frequent encouragement

    D. Positive reinforcement for effort

(Average) (Skill 16.2)

91. **Which of the following is NOT a basic aspect of routine substance abuse treatment?**

    A. Physically and psychologically withdrawing from the addictive substance

    B. Acquiring coping strategies and replacement techniques to fill the void left by the addictive substance

    C. Limiting access to the addictive substance and acquiring self-control strategies

    D. Being placed in an alternative living situation

(Average) (Skill 16.3)

92. **What is the proper sequential order of development for the acquisition of nonlocomotor skills?**

    A. Stretch, sit, bend, turn, swing, twist, shake, rock and sway, dodge, fall

    B. Bend, stretch, turn, twist, swing, sit, rock and sway, shake, dodge, fall

    C. Stretch, bend, sit, shake, turn, rock and sway, swing, twist, dodge, fall

    D. Bend, stretch, sit, turn, twist, swing, sway, rock and sway, dodge, fall

(Easy) (Skill 16.4)

93. Which of the following is the best definition of "transfer of learning?"

    A. How teachers teach students basic facts

    B. Relating learning in physical education to other subjects

    C. Identifying similarities between movements in a skill learned previously and a new skill

    D. The way learning occurs from one year to the next

(Rigorous) (Skill 16.4)

94. Which of the following are basic instructional methods for physical educators?

    A. Cognitive structuring, small-group skill instruction, individual skill instruction, and guided inquiry

    B. Cognitive structuring, small-group skill instruction, individual skill instruction, and testing

    C. Large-group skill instruction, small-group skill instruction, and guided inquiry

    D. Cognitive structuring, problem-solving, individual skill instruction, and testing

(Easy) (Skill 17.1)

95. The French horn, trumpet, trombone, and tuba are a part of which musical instrument category?

    A. Stringed Instruments

    B. Brass Instruments

    C. Percussion Instruments

    D. Wind Instruments

(Average) (Skill 17.1)

96. The quality of sound is the definition of:

    A. Timbre

    B. Rhythm

    C. Harmony

    D. Melody

(Rigorous) (Skill 17.2)

97. In the visual arts, works that project a design from the center axis are said to have:

    A. Horizontal balance

    B. Radial balance

    C. Symmetrical balance

    D. Asymmetrical balance

(Average) (Skill 17.3)

98. The process of creativity involves all of the following EXCEPT:

    A. Independence and choice

    B. A stimulating environment

    C. Clearly defined product outcomes

    D. A playful attitude

(Rigorous) (Skill 17.4)

99. Aesthetic principles vary from culture to culture. Which of the following is NOT an element of Eastern art?

    A. Universal in nature

    B. Portrays the human figure with symbolic meanings

    C. Conveys a concise, detailed and complicated view

    D. Uses arbitrary choices of color

(Rigorous) (Skill 17.4)

100. **Which time period of arts do the themes of "Roman mythology, Humanism, and Ancient legends" reflect?**

    A. Renaissance arts

    B. Baroque arts

    C. Mesopotamian arts

    D. Middle Ages arts

V. Science

(Average) (Skill 18.1)

101. **The best definition of "empirical" is:**

    A. Assessment through observations and tests

    B. Something that has been scientifically proven

    C. Something created by a scientist's hypothesis

    D. Observed information

(Rigorous) (Skill 18.2)

102. **Which of the following is an example of scientific evolution?**

    A. Giraffes need to reach higher for leaves to eat, so their necks stretch. The giraffe babies are then born with longer necks. Eventually, there are more long-necked giraffes in the population.

    B. Giraffes with longer necks are able to reach more leaves, so they eat more and have more babies than other giraffes. Eventually, there are more long-necked giraffes in the population.

    C. Giraffes want to reach higher for leaves to eat, so they release enzymes into their bloodstream, which in turn causes fetal development of longer-necked giraffes. Eventually, there are more long-necked giraffes in the population.

    D. Giraffes with long necks are more attractive to other giraffes, so they get the best mating partners and have more babies. Eventually, there are more long-necked giraffes in the population.

(Average) (Skill 18.2)

103. **Which of the following is NOT considered ethical behavior for a scientist?**

    A. Using unpublished data and citing the source

    B. Publishing data before other scientists have had a chance to replicate the results

    C. Collaborating with other scientists from different laboratories

    D. Publishing work with an incomplete list of citations

(Rigorous) (Skill 18.2)

104. In an experiment measuring the growth of bacteria at different temperatures, what is the independent variable?

    A. Number of bacteria

    B. Growth rate of bacteria

    C. Temperature

    D. Size of bacteria.

(Average) (Skill 18.3)

105. Which of the following sampling techniques is least likely to be biased?

    A. Stratified

    B. Quota

    C. Random

    D. Cluster

(Rigorous) (Skill 18.4)

106. Which of the following statistical methods would be most appropriate for analyzing census data to determine the rate of population growth?

    A. Geographic correlation studies

    B. Spatial analysis

    C. Tracking and trend analysis

    D. None of the above

(Average) (Skill 18.5)

107. Which of the following data sets is properly represented by a bar graph?

    A. Number of people choosing to buy cars vs. color of car bought

    B. Number of people choosing to buy cars vs. age of car customer

    C. Number of people choosing to buy cars vs. distance from car lot to customer home

    D. Number of people choosing to buy cars vs. time since last car purchase

(Easy) (Skill 18.5)

108. Chemicals should be stored:

    A. In the principal's office

    B. In a dark room

    C. According to their reactivity with other substances

    D. In a double-locked room

(Easy) (Skill 19.1)

109. A student's motor development is influenced by:

    A. Culture

    B. Environment

    C. Family

    D. All of the above

(Easy) (Skill 19.1)

110. Volume is:

    A. Area of the faces, excluding the bases

    B. Total area of all the faces, including the bases

    C. The number of cubic units in a solid

    D. The measurement around the object

(Rigorous) (Skill 19.1)

111. **Which statement best explains why a balance scale is used to measure both weight and mass?**

    A. The weight and mass of an object are identical concepts

    B. The force of gravity between two objects depends on the mass of the two objects

    C. Inertial mass and gravitational mass are identical

    D. A balance scale compares the weight of two objects

(Average) (Skill 19.2)

112. **The following are examples of chemical reactions EXCEPT:**

    A. Melting ice into water

    B. Dissolving a seltzer tablet in water

    C. Using a fire-cracker

    D. Burning a piece of plastic

(Rigorous) (Skill 19.3)

113. **Which of the following devices is used to regulate the flow of electrical current to achieve a certain output?**

    A. Conductor

    B. Resistor

    C. Fuse

    D. Circuit breaker

(Easy) (Skill 19.4)

114. **Which statement is true about temperature?**

    A. Temperature is a measurement of heat

    B. Temperature is how hot or cold an object is

    C. The coldest temperature ever measured is zero degrees Kelvin

    D. The temperature of a molecule is its kinetic energy

(Rigorous) (Skill 20.1)

115. **Which kingdom is comprised of organisms made of one cell with no nuclear membrane?**

    A. Monera

    B. Protista

    C. Fungi

    D. Algae

(Average) (Skill 20.1)

116. **What cell organelle contains the cell's stored food?**

    A. Vacuoles

    B. Golgi Apparatus

    C. Ribosomes

    D. Lysosomes

(Rigorous) (Skill 20.1)

117. **Enzymes speed up reactions by:**

    A. Utilizing ATP

    B. Lowering pH, allowing reaction speed to increase

    C. Increasing volume of substrate

    D. Lowering energy of activation

(Rigorous) (Skill 20.2)

118. Angiosperms, the largest group in the plant kingdom, have which of the following characteristics?

   A. The ability to remain dormant for a period of time and still produce plants

   B. Have decreased photosynthesis due to their leaf size

   C. Rely on single fertilization to reproduce

   D. All of the above

(Rigorous) (Skill 20.3)

119. Identify the correct sequence of organization of living things from lower to higher order:

   A. Cell, Organelle, Organ, Tissue, System, Organism

   B. Cell, Tissue, Organ, Organelle, System, Organism

   C. Organelle, Cell, Tissue, Organ, System, Organism

   D. Organelle, Tissue, Cell, Organ, System, Organism

(Rigorous) (Skill 20.4)

120. Which of the following types of rock are made from magma?

   A. Fossils

   B. Sedimentary

   C. Metamorphic

   D. Igneous

(Easy) (Skill 20.4)

121. An ecosystem can be described as:

   A. The connection between plants, plant eaters, and animal eaters

   B. Relationships between a community and its physical environment

   C. The specific environment or place where an animal or plant lives

   D. Organisms that live and reproduce there in an environment

(Easy) (Skill 20.5)

122. Which of the following describes the interaction between community members when one species feeds off another species but does not kill it immediately?

   A. Parasitism

   B. Predation

   C. Commensalism

   D. Mutualism

(Rigorous) (Skill 21.1)

123. The theory of "sea floor spreading" explains:

   A. The shapes of the continents

   B. How continents were named

   C. How continents move apart

   D. How continents sink to become part of the ocean floor

(Rigorous) (Skill 21.2)

124. Which of the following is the best definition for "meteorite?"

   A. A mineral composed of mica and feldspar

   B. Material from outer space that has struck the earth's surface

   C. An element that has properties of both metals and nonmetals

   D. A very small unit of length measurement

(Average) (Skill 21.3)

125. Why is the winter in the Southern Hemisphere colder than winter in the Northern Hemisphere?

   A. Earth's axis of 24-hour rotation tilts at an angle of 23°

   B. The elliptical orbit of Earth around the Sun changes the distance of the Sun from Earth

   C. The Southern Hemisphere has more water than the Northern Hemisphere

   D. The greenhouse effect is greater in the Northern Hemisphere

(Rigorous) (Skill 21.4)

126. The most abundant gas in the atmosphere is:

   A. Oxygen

   B. Nitrogen

   C. Carbon dioxide

   D. Methane

(Average) (Skill 21.5)

127. The Himalayas are an example of which type of mountain formation?

   A. Dome

   B. Fault-block

   C. Upwarped

   D. Folded

(Rigorous) (Skill 21.5)

128. In the following equation, what does G represent?

$$F_{\text{gravity}} = G\frac{m_1 m_2}{d^2}$$

   A. The distance between the two masses

   B. The universal gravitational constant

   C. Coulomb's constant

   D. The speed of the object

VI. Social Studies

(Easy) (Skill 22.1)

129. Which civilization invented the wheel?

   A. Egyptians

   B. Romans

   C. Assyrians

   D. Sumerians

(Average) (Skill 22.2)

130. Which of the following is a weakness of "periodization?"

   A. It is arbitrary

   B. It facilitates understanding

   C. It identifies similarities

   D. It categorizes knowledge

(Easy) (Skill 22.2)

131. **Archaeology is the study of which of the following?**

   A. Norms, values, and standards

   B. Material remains of humans

   C. Genetic characteristics

   D. The historical development of language

(Average) (Skill 22.2)

132. **The term *spatial organization* refers to:**

   A. Latitude and longitude lines

   B. The alignment of the stars

   C. How things are grouped in a given space

   D. The space between point A and point B

(Rigorous) (Skill 22.3)

133. **The process of putting the features of the Earth onto a flat surface is called:**

   A. Distortion

   B. Projection

   C. Cartography

   D. Illustration

(Average) (Skill 22.3)

134. **Which shows the relationship between a unit of measure on a map and the real world?**

   A. The scale

   B. The legend

   C. The grid

   D. The compass rose

(Average) (Skill 23.1)

135. **Which of the following is NOT one of the six major themes in geography?**

   A. Regions

   B. Religion

   C. Place

   D. Movement

(Average) (Skill 23.1)

136. **The Northern Hemisphere contains which of the following?**

   A. Europe

   B. South America

   C. Africa

   D. Australia

(Average) (Skill 23.2)

137. **Which country is considered by some historians to be the oldest uninterrupted civilization in the world?**

   A. Japan

   B. China

   C. Canada

   D. Mexico

(Rigorous) (Skill 23.2)

138. **What is the "Pax Romana"?**

   A. A long period of peace enabling free travel and trade, spreading people, cultures, goods, and ideas all over the world

   B. A period of war where the Romans expanded their empire

   C. The Roman government

   D. A time where the government was overruled

(Easy) (Skill 23.3)

139. What was the name of the cultural revival after the Civil War that took place in New York?

A. The Revolutionary War

B. The Second Great Awakening

C. The Harlem Renaissance

D. The Gilded Age

(Easy) (Skill 23.3)

140. The Westward Expansion occurred for a number of reasons; however, the most important reason was:

A. Colonization

B. Slavery

C. Independence

D. Economics

(Easy) (Skill 23.4)

141. The Cold War involved which two countries?

A. China and Japan

B. The United States and the Soviet Union

C. England and Brazil

D. Afghanistan and the United States

(Average) (Skill 23.4)

142. The year 1619 was a memorable one for the colony of Virginia. Three important events occurred, resulting in lasting effects on U.S. history. Which one of the following is NOT one of the events?

A. Twenty African slaves arrived.

B. The London Company granted the colony a charter, making it independent.

C. The colonists were given the right by the London Company to govern themselves through representative government in the Virginia House of Burgesses.

D. The London Company sent to the colony 60 women who were quickly married, establishing families and stability in the colony.

(Average) (Skill 23.5)

143. Which of the following is the most accurate definition of a nonrenewable resource?

A. A nonrenewable resource is never replaced once used.

B. A nonrenewable resource is replaced on a timescale that is very long relative to human life spans.

C. A nonrenewable resource is a resource that can only be manufactured by humans.

D. A nonrenewable resource is a species that has already become extinct.

(Average) (Skill 24.1)

144. **Native American tribes based in Minnesota are governed by:**

    A. Tribal councils

    B. Assemblies

    C. Boards of trustees

    D. All of the above

(Easy) (Skill 24.2)

145. **The Bill of Rights consists of which Amendments?**

    A. Amendments 1–5

    B. Amendments 1–10

    C. Amendments 1 and 2

    D. Amendments 1–22

(Average) (Skill 24.3)

146. **The ability of the president to veto an act of congress is an example of:**

    A. Separation of powers

    B. Checks and balances

    C. Judicial review

    D. Presidential prerogative

(Easy) (Skill 24.3)

147. **What are the three branches of the United States government?**

    A. Legislative, judicial, international affairs

    B. Legislative, executive, foreign trade

    C. Legislative, executive, judicial

    D. Executive, judicial, state governments

(Average) (Skill 24.4)

148. _____ is the belief that one's own culture is the central and the superior culture.

    A. Ethnocentrism

    B. Egocentric

    C. Prejudice

    D. Superiority

(Rigorous) (Skill 24.6)

149. **Economics is defined as a study of:**

    A. How scarce resources are allocated to satisfy unlimited wants

    B. Anything that is manufactured to be used in the production process

    C. Anyone who sells his ability to produce goods and services

    D. Decisions of buyers equal to the selling decision of seller

(Rigorous) (Skill 24.6)

150. **Laissez-faire capitalism is based on:**

    A. Government ownership of the means of production

    B. Custom, and usually exists in less developed countries

    C. The premise of no government intervention in the economy

    D. None of the above

Answer Key

ANSWER KEY								
1. C	18. A	35. C	52. B	69. D	86. D	103. D	120. D	137. B
2. C	19. D	36. B	53. C	70. A	87. D	104. C	121. B	138. A
3. D	20. B	37. C	54. A	71. B	88. A	105. C	122. A	139. C
4. B	21. C	38. C	55. A	72. C	89. B	106. C	123. C	140. D
5. A	22. C	39. B	56. D	73. C	90. B	107. A	124. B	141. B
6. D	23. A	40. C	57. D	74. B	91. D	108. C	125. B	142. B
7. B	24. A	41. D	58. D	75. D	92. C	109. D	126. B	143. B
8. C	25. D	42. D	59. B	76. A	93. C	110. C	127. D	144. D
9. D	26. A	43. C	60. D	77. B	94. B	111. C	128. B	145. B
10. D	27. D	44. B	61. A	78. C	95. B	112. A	129. D	146. B
11. C	28. D	45. C	62. C	79. B	96. A	113. B	130. A	147. C
12. A	29. D	46. A	63. B	80. D	97. B	114. B	131. B	148. A
13. B	30. A	47. D	64. B	81. D	98. C	115. A	132. C	149. A
14. C	31. A	48. D	65. C	82. B	99. C	116. A	133. B	150. C
15. A	32. A	49. B	66. A	83. D	100. A	117. D	134. A	
16. A	33. D	50. C	67. B	84. B	101. A	118. A	135. B	
17. D	34. A	51. A	68. D	85. B	102. B	119. C	136. A	

Rigor Table

RIGOR TABLE	
Rigor level	**Questions**
Easy 25%	9, 29, 30, 31, 34, 35, 37, 38, 41, 42, 43, 51, 60, 61, 63, 72, 82, 83, 84, 93, 95, 108, 109, 110, 114, 121, 122, 129, 131, 139, 140, 141, 145, 147
Average 45%	2, 3, 7, 8, 10, 11, 12, 13, 14, 15, 16, 18, 19, 20, 21, 23, 24, 25, 32, 45, 46, 47, 48, 52, 54, 55, 58, 59, 62, 64, 65, 67, 70, 71, 73, 75, 77, 80, 81, 85, 86, 88, 89, 90, 91, 92, 96, 98, 101, 103, 105, 107, 112, 116, 125, 127, 130, 132, 134, 135, 136, 137, 142, 143, 144, 146, 148
Rigorous 30%	1, 4, 5, 6, 17, 22, 26, 27, 28, 33, 36, 39, 40, 44, 49, 50, 53, 57, 66, 68, 69, 74, 76, 78, 79, 87, 94, 97, 99, 100, 102, 104, 106, 111, 113, 115, 117, 118, 119, 120, 123, 124, 126, 128, 133, 138, 149, 150

Sample Test with Rationales:

I. Reading

(Rigorous) (Skill 1.1)

1. **Which of the following is NOT one of the metalinguistic abilities acquired by children from early involvement in reading activities?**

    A. Conventions of print

    B. Word consciousness

    C. Spelling fluency

    D. Functions of print

    Answer: C. Spelling fluency

    Conventions of print, word consciousness, and functions of print are all learned from children's early involvement with reading. Spelling fluency is learned a little later on in reading and a fluent speller is often good at reading comprehension.

(Average) (Skill 1.2)

2. **Phonological awareness skills include all of the following EXCEPT:**

    A. Segmenting words into sounds

    B. Blending sounds into words

    C. Visually identifying letters

    D. Recognizing rhyming words

    Answer: C. Visually identify letters

    Phonological awareness refers to the ability to recognize the sounds of spoken language.

(Average) (Skill 1.3)

3. **Effective instructional methods for teaching phonemic awareness include all of the following EXCEPT:**

    A. Distinguishing between a sound and a word

    B. Singing familiar songs and replacing key words

    C. Sounding out words for pictures

    D. Encouraging independent reading

    Answer: D. Encouraging independent reading

    Although encouraging independent reading is a good teaching method for many aspects of literacy and reading, it is not specifically related to developing phonemic awareness, which focuses solely on understanding that language is made up of sounds that become words.

(Rigorous) (Skill 1.4)

4. **Awareness of the relationship between spoken and written language can be developed by all of the following EXCEPT:**

    A. Using labels in the classroom on everyday objects

    B. Clapping syllables in words

    C. Using letter cards to create messages

    D. Writing down the things children say

    Answer: B. Clapping syllables in words

    Clapping syllables and other sound-only activities do not aid students in making the link between spoken and written language, though they are good strategies for other aspects of phonological awareness skills.

(Rigorous) (Skill 1.5)

5.　All of the following are true EXCEPT:

A. Assessing phonics skills almost always involves having students write down letters related to sounds

B. Assessment of phonemic awareness is almost always an individual oral task

C. Both formal and informal assessment methods can be used to assess phonics skills

D. A test with multiple choice questions is a good choice for formally assessing phonics skills

Answer: A. Assessing phonics skills almost always involves having students write down letters related to sounds.

While many assessment methods related to phonics involve having the student write the letter that corresponds with a sound, there are other methods that are also effective. One example is listening to students read aloud and making notes about appropriate or inappropriate usage of phonics skills.

(Rigorous) (Skill 2.1)

6.　In promoting literacy, storybook reading matters because:

A. It familiarizes children with classic children's storybooks

B. Children learn about the range of topics available to them

C. It is invariably a positive early reading experience

D. It gives children knowledge about, strategies for, and attitudes toward reading

Answer: D. It gives children knowledge about, strategies for, and attitudes toward reading

Storybook reading is the most strongly supported strategy in the literacy literature, and also the most common, though some groups of children have fewer experiences with it than others. Although storybook reading does familiarizes children with the books and topics available, the importance of the experience is more about attitudes toward reading, especially the incorporation of reading as a regular part of life. For most children, having a book read aloud to them is a positive experience, though in families where anger, abuse, or control is an issue, storytime might be fraught with more complicated and sometimes negative feelings.

(Average) (Skill 2.1)

7.　Instructional strategies that help children develop concepts about print includes all of the following EXCEPT:

A. Reading books aloud to students

B. Having students recreate sounds the teacher has demonstrated

C. Making a Word Wall

D. Using big books and song charts

Answer: B. Having students recreate sounds the teacher has demonstrated

Recreating sounds does not have any direct connection to print. Therefore, this is not a good approach to use in helping children understand concepts of print.

(Average) (Skill 2.3)

8. Another name for graphophonemic awareness is:

    A. Phonological awareness

    B. Directionality of print

    C. Alphabetic principle

    D. Phonology

    Answer: C. Alphabetic principle

    The alphabetic principle details the theory that written words are composed of patterns of letters that represent the sounds of spoken words.

(Easy) (Skill 2.4)

9. The "What's in a Name?" game has which of the following benefits?

    A. Letter recognition

    B. Counting practice

    C. Learning classmates' names

    D. All of the above

    Answer: D. All of the above

    The "What's in a Name?" game offers multiple learning experiences for individual students and can help the class develop a sense of cohesiveness.

(Average) (Skill 2.6)

10. Which of the following is true with regard to English Language Learners (ELL)?

    A. ELL students should learn to read initially in their first language.

    B. ELL students should learn to read initially in English, regardless of their first language.

    C. Learning to speak English before being taught to read English is helpful.

    D. Both A and C

    Answer: D. Both A and C

    Researchers have found that children do better when they develop a good foundation for phonological awareness by learning oral language before learning to read. They have also learned that students do better if they initially learn to read in their first or native tongue.

(Average) (Skill 3.1)

11. To decode is to:

    A. Use a special code to decipher a message

    B. Sound out a printed sequence of letters

    C. Change communication signals into messages

    D. Change a message into symbols

Answer: C. Change communication signals into messages

To decode means to change communication signals into messages. Reading comprehension requires that the reader learn the code within which a message is written and be able to decode it to get the message.

(Average) (Skill 3.1)

12. **To encode means to:**

    A. Change a message into symbols

    B. Construct meaning from a code

    C. Change communication signals into messages

    D. Sound out a printed sequence of letters

Answer: A. Change a message into symbols

Encoding involves changing a message into symbols. For example, to encode oral language into writing (spelling), to encode an idea into words, or to encode a mathematical or physical idea into appropriate mathematical symbols.

(Average) (Skill 3.3)

13. **When students understand how sentences are built and the words needed for the sentences to "sound" right, they have developed a sense of:**

    A. Morphology

    B. Syntax

    C. Semantics

    D. Fluency

Answer: B. Syntax

Syntax refers to the rules or patterned relationships that correctly create phrases and sentences from words. When readers develop an understanding of syntax, they begin to understand the structure of how sentences are built.

(Average) (Skill 3.5)

14. **The four basic word types are:**

    A. Regular for reading and spelling, Regular for reading but not spelling, Irregular for reading and spelling, Irregular for reading but not spelling

    B. Regular for reading and spelling, Regular for spelling but not Reading, Irregular for reading and spelling, Irregular for spelling but not reading

    C. Regular for reading and spelling, Regular for reading but not spelling, Rule-based, Irregular

    D. Regular for reading and spelling, Regular for reading but not spelling, Irregular, Complex

Answer: C. Regular for reading and spelling, Regular for reading but not spelling, Rule-based, Irregular

English orthography is made up of four basic word types:

- Regular for reading and spelling (e.g., *cat, print*)
- Regular for reading but not for spelling (e.g., *float, brain*—could be spelled *flote* or *brane*, respectively)
- Rule-based (e.g., *canning*—doubling rule, *faking*—drop *e* rule)
- Irregular (e.g., *beauty*)

(Average) (Skill 3.5)

15. **Which of the following indicates that a student is a fluent reader?**

    A. Reads texts with expression or prosody

    B. Reads word-to-word and haltingly

    C. Must intentionally decode a majority of the words

    D. In a writing assignment, sentences are poorly organized structurally

    Answer: A. Reads texts with expression or prosody

    A fluent reader reads texts with expression or prosody. The teacher should listen to the children read aloud, but there are also clues to reading levels in their writing.

(Average) (Skill 4.1)

16. **If a student has a poor vocabulary, the teacher should recommend first that:**

    A. The student read newspapers, magazines and books on a regular basis

    B. The student enroll in a Latin class

    C. The student write the words repetitively after looking them up in the dictionary

    D. The student use a thesaurus to locate synonyms and incorporate them into his/her vocabulary

    Answer: A. The student read newspapers, magazines and books on a regular basis

    The teacher can personally influence what the student chooses as reading material, but the student must be able to choose independently where to search for the reading pleasure indispensable for enriching vocabulary.

(Rigorous) (Skill 4.2)

17. **Which word in the following sentence is a bound morpheme?**

    The quick brown fox jumped over the lazy dog

    A. The

    B. Fox

    C. Lazy

    D. Jumped

    Answer: D. Jumped

    The suffix "-ed" is an affix that cannot stand alone as a unit of meaning. Thus, it is bound to the free morpheme "jump." "The" is always an unbound morpheme since no suffix or prefix can alter its meaning. As written, "fox" and "lazy" are unbound, but their meaning can be changed with affixes, such as "foxes" or "laziness."

(Average) (Skill 4.2)

18. **Contextual redefinition is:**

    A. An example of using context clues to aid vocabulary development

    B. Useful to teachers working with ELLs

    C. A process of absorbing a new curriculum into an existing format

    D. Not especially relevant to most elementary students

    Answer: A. An example of using context clues to aid vocabulary development

    Context clues are bits of information students cull from a text that help them use their background information to understand an unfamiliar word. Contextual redefinition is a strategy that helps children use context more effectively.

(Average) (Skill 4.4)

19. **All of the following are true about the Fortune Cookie Strategy EXCEPT:**

    A. It facilitates multiculturalism

    B. It engages multiple senses

    C. It helps children learn about the roots of words and idioms

    D. It encourages competitive learning

    Answer: D. It encourages competitive learning

    This learning activity is designed to expose children to a diversity of proverbs and sayings that can facilitate vocabulary development. It offers a good experience of collaborative learning at various levels, involving other students, cultures, and family members.

(Average) (Skill 4.7)

20. **Having children write out a step-by-step description of a vocabulary activity is referred to as a:**

    A. Personal narrative

    B. Procedural narrative

    C. Procedural detail

    D. Personal detail

    Answer: B. Procedural narrative

    Children get an increased sense of word ownership (and therefore greater knowledge) when they write out a procedural narrative of one of their word searches. Young students can dictate their procedural narratives and then have them posted in the classroom.

(Average) (Skill 5.1)

21. **Which of the following is NOT true about topic sentences?**

    A. They are more general than the other sentences in the paragraph.

    B. They contain the main idea.

    C. They are the first sentence in the paragraph.

    D. They can be framed as a question, with the other sentences providing the "answers."

    Answer: C. They are the first sentence in the paragraph.

    Though they are generally the opening sentence in a paragraph, topic sentences are not always in the first position.

(Rigorous) (Skill 5.2)

22. **At what point does exposition occur within a story?**

    A. After the rising action

    B. After the denouement

    C. Before the rising action

    D. Before the setting

    Answer: C. Before the rising action

    Exposition is where characters and their situations are introduced. *Rising action* is the point at which conflict starts to occur. *Climax* is the highest point of conflict, often a turning point. *Falling action* is the result of the climax. *Denouement* is the final resolution of the plot.

(Average) (Skill 5.2)

23. **Which is an untrue statement about a theme in literature?**

    A. The theme is always stated directly somewhere in the text.

    B. The theme is the central idea in a literary work.

    C. All parts of the work (plot, setting, mood, etc.) should contribute to the theme in some way.

    D. By analyzing the various elements of the work, the reader should be able to arrive at an indirectly stated theme.

    Answer: A. The theme is always stated directly somewhere in the text.

    The theme is not always stated directly somewhere in the text. The theme may be stated directly, but it can also be implicit in various aspects of the work, such as the interaction between characters, symbolism, or description.

(Average) (Skill 5.3)

24. **A K-W-L chart is which of the following?**

    A. Graphic organizer

    B. Abbreviations chart

    C. Word list

    D. Venn diagram

Answer: A. Graphic organizer

K-W-L is a graphic organizer strategy which activates children's prior knowledge and also helps them to target their reading of expository texts. This focus is achieved through having the children reflect on key questions.

Before the child reads the expository passage:

"What do I know?" and "What do I want to find out?"

After the child has read the expository passage:

"What have I learned from the passage?" and "What do I still want to learn?"

(Average) (Skill 5.3)

25. **K-W-L charts are useful for which of the following?**

    A. Comprehension of expository text

    B. Format for note taking

    C. Report writing

    D. All of the above

Answer: D. All of the above

K-W-L is useful and can even be introduced as early as grade 2 with extensive teacher discussion support. It not only serves to support the child's comprehension of a particular expository text, but also models for children a format for note taking. Beyond note taking, when the teacher wants to introduce report writing, the K-W-L format provides excellent outlines and question introductions for at least three paragraphs of a report.

(Rigorous) (Skill 5.4)

26. **All of the following are true about self-questioning strategies EXCEPT:**

    A. They tend to make readers less curious

    B. They cause readers to be less lazy as they read

    C. They help develop comprehension skills

    D. They involve self-predicting and asking "why"

    Answer: A. They tend to make readers less curious

    In fact, self-questioning strategies tend to make readers more curious, because they involve having students actively asking questions throughout the reading process.

(Rigorous) (Skill 5.5)

27. **Which of the following is inaccurate about word mapping?**

    A. It is a teaching strategy

    B. It is an assessment strategy

    C. It helps children visually represent the elements of a given concept

    D. It helps children focus specifically on the root word

    Answer: D. It helps children focus specifically on the root word

    Although there may be occasions when the root of a word is included in word mapping, it is not a particular focus of word mapping.

(Rigorous) (Skill 6.1)

28. **Which of the following is a ballad?**

    A. "The Knight's Tale"

    B. *Julius Caesar*

    C. *Paradise Lost*

    D. "The Rime of the Ancient Mariner"

    Answer: D. "The Rime of the Ancient Mariner"

    "The Knight's Tale" is a Romantic poem from the longer *Canterbury Tales* by Chaucer. *Julius Caesar* is a Shakespearian play. *Paradise Lost* is an epic poem in blank verse. A ballad is an *in medias res* story told or sung, usually in verse and accompanied by music, and usually with a refrain—a repeated section. Typically, ballads are based on folk stories.

(Easy) (Skill 6.1)

29. **Which of the following is NOT a characteristic of a fable?**

    A. Animals that feel and talk like humans

    B. Happy solutions to human dilemmas

    C. Teaches a moral or standard for behavior

    D. Illustrates specific people or groups without directly naming them

Answer: D. Illustrates specific people or groups without directly naming them

A fable is a short tale with animals, humans, gods, or even inanimate objects as characters. Fables often conclude with a moral, delivered in the form of an epigram (a short, witty, and ingenious statement in verse). Fables are among the oldest forms of writing in human history: they appear in Egyptian papyri of 1500 BCE. The most famous fables are those of Aesop, a Greek slave living in about 600 BCE. In India, the Pantchatantra appeared in the third century. The most famous modern fables are those of seventeenth century French poet Jean de La Fontaine.

(Easy) (Skill 6.1)

30. **When selecting multicultural literature it is most important that the culture be portrayed:**

    A. Accurately

    B. In a fun manner

    C. In all genres

    D. With regards to music and the arts

    Answer: A. Accurately

    The most important aspect of multicultural literature is that it is an accurate representation of the culture.

(Easy) (Skill 6.2)

31. **A simile is:**

    A. A direct comparison between two things

    B. An indirect comparison between two things

    C. When human characteristics are applied to things that are not human, such as animals

    D. Deliberate exaggeration for comic effect

    Answer: A. A direct comparison between two things

    A simile commonly uses the words "like" or "as" to make the comparison. For example: "The boy was as red as a lobster." A metaphor is an indirect comparison, as in "The boy was lobster-faced." Personification is when human characteristics are applied to things that are not human, as in "The lobster laughed when he skedaddled away." A hyperbole is a deliberate exaggeration, as in "We laughed our heads off at that sight."

(Average) (Skill 6.2)

32. **Which of the following is an example of alliteration?**

    A. "The City's voice itself is soft like Solitude."

    B. "Both in one faith unanimous; though sad"

    C. "By all their country's wishes blest!"

    D. "In earliest Greece to these with partial choice."

Answer: A. "The City's voice itself is soft like Solitude."

Alliteration is the repetition of consonant sounds in two or more neighboring words or syllables, usually the beginning sound. This line from Shelley's "Stanzas Written in Dejection Near Naples" is an especially effective use of alliteration using the sibilant *s* not only at the beginning of words but also within words. Alliteration usually appears in prosody; however, effective use of alliteration can be found in other genres.

(Rigorous) (Skill 6.6)

33. **Which of the following reading strategies is NOT associated with fluent reading abilities?**

   A. Pronouncing unfamiliar words by finding similarities with familiar words

   B. Establishing a purpose for reading

   C. Formulating questions about the text while reading

   D. Reading sentences word by word

Answer: D. Reading sentences word by word

Pronouncing unfamiliar words by finding similarities with familiar words, establishing a purpose for reading, and formulating questions about the text while reading are all excellent strategies fluent readers use to enhance their comprehension of a text. Reading sentences word by word is a trait of a non-fluent reader because it inhibits comprehension. The reader is focused on each word by itself rather than the meaning of the whole sentence and how it fits into the text.

(Easy) (Skill 6.6)

34. **Which of the following is a formal reading level assessment?**

   A. A standardized reading test

   B. A teacher-made reading test

   C. An interview

   D. A reading diary

Answer: A. A standardized reading test

If an assessment is standardized, it has to be objective. B, C and D are all subjective assessments.

(Easy) (Skill 7.1)

35. **What is the plural of the word *rose*?**

   A. Rosis

   B. Rosses

   C. Roses

   D. Rose's

Answer: C. Roses

When making a word that ends in *e* plural, add an *s*.

(Rigorous) (Skill 7.1)

36. **Which word needs to be corrected in the sentence below?**

   The presents on the table is wrapped in beautiful wrapping paper.

   A. Presents

   B. Is

   C. Wrapped

   D. Beautiful

Answer: B. Is

Is needs to be replaced with the word *are*. *Is* should be used in the singular form. *Are* is used in the plural form, and there is more than one present. Therefore, the sentence should read, "The presents on the table *are* wrapped in beautiful wrapping paper."

(Easy) (Skill 7.2)

37. **Which of the following is an opinion?**

    A. The sky is blue.

    B. Albany is the capital of New York State.

    C. A dog is the best pet to have.

    D. Humans breathe.

    Answer: C. A dog is the best pet to have.

    An opinion is a subjective evaluation based upon personal beliefs.

(Easy) (Skill 7.2)

38. **Which of the following is a fact?**

    A. It's going to rain.

    B. John is a liar.

    C. Joe said he believes John is a liar.

    D. The world is going to the dogs.

    Answer: C. Joe said he believes John is a liar.

    It's a fact that Joe said this, even though what he said may not be a fact.

(Rigorous) (Skill 7.5)

39. **All of the following are examples of ongoing informal assessment techniques used to observe student progress EXCEPT:**

    A. Analyses of student work product

    B. Collection of data from assessment tests

    C. Effective questioning

    D. Observation of students

    Answer: B. Collection of data from assessment tests

    Assessment tests are formal progress-monitoring measures.

II. Communication Arts

(Rigorous) (Skill 8.1)

40. **Instructions for assembling a bicycle are an example of which type of writing?**

    A. Narrative

    B. Descriptive

    C. Expository

    D. Persuasive

    Answer: C. Expository

    The purpose of expository writing is to inform or provide information. Some examples include directions to a particular place or the instructions for putting together a toy that arrives unassembled.

(Easy) (Skill 8.1)

41. Texts that present information to readers in a quick and efficient manner are called:

   A. Essays

   B. Memoirs

   C. Journals

   D. Newspaper articles

Answer: D. Newspaper articles

Nonfiction comes in a variety of styles and can include opinion and perspective. Newspaper articles are short texts which rely completely on factual information and are presented in a very straightforward, sometimes choppy manner. The purpose of these texts is simply to present information to readers in a quick and efficient manner. The key in teaching students about nonfiction is to expose them to a variety of types of nonfiction and discuss how those types are similar to and different from one another.

(Easy) (Skill 8.2)

42. Which of the following is NOT a technique of prewriting?

   A. Clustering

   B. Listing

   C. Brainstorming

   D. Proofreading

Answer: D. Proofreading

Proofreading cannot be a method of prewriting, since it is done on already-written texts.

(Easy) (Skill 8.3)

43. Which of the following addresses mostly grammatical and technical errors?

   A. Revising

   B. Editing

   C. Proofreading

   D. Rough draft writing

Answer: C. Proofreading

During the proofreading process, grammatical and technical errors are addressed. The other choices indicate times when writing or rewriting is taking place.

(Rigorous) (Skill 8.4)

44. Which of the following should NOT be included in the opening paragraph of an informative essay?

   A. Thesis sentence

   B. Details and examples supporting the main idea

   C. A broad, general introduction to the topic

   D. A style and tone that grabs the reader's attention

Answer: B. Details and examples supporting the main idea

The introductory paragraph should introduce the topic, capture the reader's interest, state the thesis, and prepare the reader for the main points in the essay. Details and examples, however, should be given in the second part of the essay, so as to help develop the thesis presented at the end of the introductory paragraph. This follows the inverted triangle method, consisting of a broad, general statement followed by some information, and then the thesis at the end of the paragraph.

(Average) (Skill 8.5)

45. **Which is NOT a true statement concerning an author's literary tone?**

   A. Tone is partly revealed through the selection of details.

   B. Tone is the expression of the author's attitude toward his/her subject.

   C. Tone in literature is usually satiric or angry.

   D. Tone in literature corresponds to the tone of voice a speaker uses.

Answer: C. Tone in literature is usually satiric or angry.

Tone in literature conveys a mood and can be as varied as the tone of voice of a speaker (e.g., sad, nostalgic, whimsical, angry, formal, intimate, satirical, sentimental, etc.).

(Average) (Skill 8.6)

46. **Which of the following is NOT true about literacy portfolios?**

   A. Literacy portfolios are a good example of formal assessment of student writing.

   B. Literacy portfolios may include work samples, checklists, and records of independent reading.

   C. Literacy portfolios provide an opportunity to review student progress, set goals, and share information with parent/guardians.

   D. Literacy portfolios often contain self-assessment forms.

Answer: A. Literacy portfolios are a good example of formal assessment of student writing.

A literacy portfolio is an informal assessment tool. An example of a formal assessment tool for writing would be a standardized test with a writing component.

(Average) (Skill 9.1)

47. **In preparing students for their oral presentations, the instructor provided all of these guidelines EXCEPT one. Which is NOT an effective guideline?**

   A. Even if you are using a lectern, feel free to move about. This will connect you to the audience.

   B. Your posture should be natural, not stiff. Keep your shoulders toward the audience.

   C. Gestures can help communicate as long as you don't overuse them or make them distracting.

   D. You can avoid eye contact if you focus on your notes. This will make you appear more knowledgeable.

Answer: D. You can avoid eye contact if you focus on your notes. This will make you appear more knowledgeable.

Although many people are nervous about making eye contact, they should focus on two or three people at a time. Body language, such as movement, posture, and gestures, helps the speaker connect to the audience.

(Average) (Skill 9.2)

48. Which of the following is NOT an advisable strategy for making sense of oral language?

A. Observe body language and other nonverbal cues

B. Take notes to outline major points

C. Critique, question, and evaluate others' as well as students' own oral presentations

D. Ignore prior knowledge of the topic because it does not help understand what is being presented

Answer: D. Ignore prior knowledge of the topic because it does not help understand what is being presented

Observing body language and other nonverbal cues, taking notes to outline major points, and critiquing, questioning, and evaluating others' as well as students' own oral presentations are all good strategies when listening to an oral presentation. Ignoring prior knowledge of the topic does not help make sense of oral language. Utilizing one's own prior knowledge of a topic allows the listener to bring his or her own set of information to help understand what is being presented.

(Rigorous) (Skill 9.2)

49. Processes that can enhance one's ability to remember information include which of the following?

A. Repetition, association, visualization, and description

B. Repetition, association, visualization, and concentration

C. Description, association, visualization, and concentration

D. Association, alliteration, visualization, and concentration

Answer: B. Repetition, association, visualization, and concentration

Association relates information, visualization makes it vivid, concentration focuses it, and repetition helps store it. Description may be involved any of these processes. Alliteration, a literary device, is the repetition of consonant sounds, and may be utilized in any of the processes.

(Rigorous) (Skill 9.3)

50. Evaluating media may involve all of the following EXCEPT:

A. Getting background information on the source of the information

B. Comparing information from different sources

C. Ignoring the tone or attitude of the author and focusing on the content only

D. Assessing the author's purpose in writing the piece

Answer: C. Ignoring the tone or attitude of the author and focusing on the content only.

The author's tone or attitude can be useful in assessing any type of information, whether a newspaper, website page, or journal article. Gathering as much data as possible about the author and the publisher can be very useful in determining the reliability of information.

III. Mathematics

(Easy) (Skill 10.1)

51. State the number modeled below.

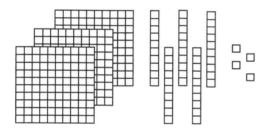

A. 354

B. 345

C. 453

D. 543

Answer: A. 354

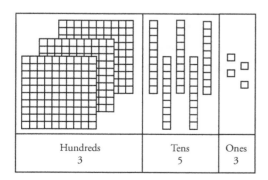

Hundreds 3	Tens 5	Ones 3

(Average) (Skill 10.1)

52. Which of the numbers is an example of an irrational number?

A. 3

B. $\sqrt{7}$

C. 0.5

D. $\frac{3}{4}$

Answer: B. $\sqrt{7}$

An irrational number is a real number that cannot be written as the ratio of two integers. There are infinite, non-repeating decimals. $\sqrt{7} = 2.64575\ldots$

(Rigorous) (Skill 10.1)

53. Which of the following is an irrational number?

A. .362626262...

B. $4^{\frac{1}{3}}$

C. $\sqrt{5}$

D. $-\sqrt{16}$

Answer: C. $\sqrt{5}$

Irrational numbers are real numbers that cannot be written as the ratio of two integers, such as infinite, non-repeating decimals. $\sqrt{5}$ fits this description; the others do not.

(Average) (Skill 10.2)

54. In similar polygons, if the perimeters are in a ratio of *x:y*, the sides are in a ratio of:

A. $x{:}y$

B. $x^2{:}y^2$

C. $2x{:}y$

D. $\frac{1}{2}x{:}y$

Answer: A. $x{:}y$

In similar polygons, the sides are in the same ratio as the perimeters.

(Average) (Skill 10.3)

55. **Mathematical operations are done in the following order:**

    A. Simplify inside grouping characters such as parentheses, brackets, square root, fraction bar, etc.; multiply out expressions with exponents; do multiplication or division, from left to right; do addition or subtraction, from left to right.

    B. Do multiplication or division, from left to right; simplify inside grouping characters such as parentheses, brackets, square root, fraction bar, etc.; multiply out expressions with exponents; do addition or subtraction, from left to right.

    C. Simplify inside grouping characters such as parentheses, brackets, square root, fraction bar, etc.; do addition or subtraction, from left to right; multiply out expressions with exponents; do multiplication or division, from left to right.

    D. None of the above

Answer: A. Simplify inside grouping characters such as parentheses, brackets, square root, fraction bar, etc.; multiply out expressions with exponents; do multiplication or division, from left to right; do addition or subtraction, from left to right.

When facing a mathematical problem that requires all mathematical properties to be performed first, you do the math within the parentheses, brackets, square roots, or fraction bars. Then you multiply out expressions with exponents. Next, you do multiplication or division. Finally, you do addition or subtraction.

(Rigorous) (Skill 10.3)

56. **Solve for x:** $|2x + 3| > 4$

    A. $-\frac{7}{2} > x > \frac{1}{2}$

    B. $-\frac{1}{2} > x > \frac{7}{2}$

    C. $x < \frac{7}{2}$ or $x < -\frac{1}{2}$

    D. $x < -\frac{7}{2}$ or $x > \frac{1}{2}$

Answer: D. $x < -\frac{7}{2}$ or $x > \frac{1}{2}$

The quantity within the absolute value symbols must be either > 4 or $< {-4}$. Solve the two inequalities $2x + 3 > 4$ or $2x + 3 < {-4}$.

(Rigorous) (Skill 10.5)

57. **Which property is demonstrated by the equation below?**

    $60 + 24 = 12(5 + 2)$

    A. Commutative

    B. Associative

    C. Additive identity

    D. Distributive

Answer: D. Distributive

The distributive property states that $a(b + c) = ab + ac$. In this example, $a = 12$, $b = 5$, and $c = 2$.

(Average) (Skill 11.1)

58. The relationship between two variables can be analyzed by using which of the following?

   A. Symbolic rule

   B. Table

   C. Written description

   D. All of the above

Answer: D. All of the above

Relationship, between variables can be understood by using all of the methods listed, as well as points on a graph. The function $y = 2x + 1$ is written as a symbolic rule. The same relationship can be shown in a table or graph. This relationship could be written in words by saying that the value of y is equal to two times the value of x, plus one.

(Average) (Skill 11.2)

59. What is this table intended to demonstrate?

Number of Sunglasses Sold	1	5	10	15
Total Dollars Earned	9	45	90	135

   A. Number of sunglasses sold

   B. Relationship between two quantities

   C. Amount of money made

   D. Amount of money made on 15 pairs of sunglasses

Answer: B. Relationship between two quantities

A relationship between two quantities can be shown using a table, graph, or rule. In this example, the rule $y = 9x$ describes the relationship between the total amount earned, y, and the total number of $9.00 sunglasses sold, x.

(Easy) (Skill 11.3)

60. Look at this number: 4,087,361

   What number represents the ten-thousands place?

   A. 4

   B. 6

   C. 0

   D. 8

Answer: D. 8

The ten-thousands place is the fifth place to the left of the decimal.

(Easy) (Skill 11.3)

61. This graph shows which kind of relationship?

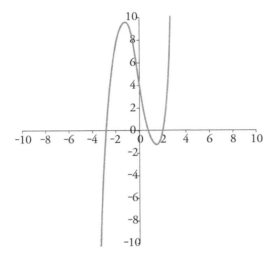

A. Non-linear

B. Linear

C. Profit

D. Algebraic

Answer: A. Non-linear

The plotted coordinates do not make a straight line when linked. Therefore the *x*, *y* relationship is non-linear.

(Average) (Skill 11.5)

62. This sequence of numbers represents which of the following?

1, 1, 2, 3, 5, 8, 13, 21, 34…

A. An exponential pattern of growth

B. A quadratic function

C. A recursive function

D. A linear function

Answer: C. A recursive function

A recursive function is an example of an iterative process, which is the repeated use of the same steps. This number sequence is a famous recursive functioned called the Fibonacci sequence, in which the next term is found by adding the two previous terms.

(Easy) (Skill 12.1)

63. _____ lines do NOT intersect.

A. Perpendicular

B. Parallel

C. Intersecting

D. Skew

Answer: B. Parallel

Parallel lines continue at equal distance apart indefinitely. The other choices all intersect at some point.

(Average) (Skill 12.1)

64. All of the following are examples of obtuse angles EXCEPT:

A. 110 degrees

B. 90 degrees

C. 135 degrees

D. 91 degrees

Answer: B. 90 degrees

An obtuse angle is greater than 90 degrees. A 90 degree angle is a right angle.

(Average) (Skill 12.1)

65. Kindergarten students are doing a butterfly art project. They fold paper in half. On one half, they paint a design. Then they fold the paper closed and reopen it. The resulting picture is a butterfly with matching sides. What math principle does this demonstrate?

    A. Slide

    B. Rotation

    C. Symmetry

    D. Transformation

    Answer: C. Symmetry

    By folding the painted paper in half, the design is mirrored on the other side, creating symmetry and reflection. The butterfly design is symmetrical about the center.

(Rigorous) (Skill 12.4)

66. **Find the area of the figure below.**

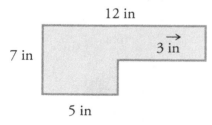

    A. 56 in²

    B. 27 in²

    C. 71 in²

    D. 170 in²

Answer: A. 56 in²

Divide the figure into two rectangles with a horizontal line. Then find the area of each rectangle. The area of the top rectangle is 36 in², and the area of the bottom rectangle is 20 in².

(Average) (Skill 12.4)

67. **What is the area of a square with a side length of 13 feet?**

    A. 169 feet

    B. 169 square feet

    C. 52 feet

    D. 52 square feet

Answer: B. 169 square feet

Area = length times width (*lw*)
Length = 13 feet
Width = 13 feet (It is a square, so the length and width are the same.)
Area = 169 square feet

Area is measured in square feet, so the correct answer is B.

(Rigorous) (Skill 12.5)

68. **3 km is equivalent to:**

    A. 300 cm

    B. 300 m

    C. 3000 cm

    D. 3000 m

Answer: D. 3000 m

To change kilometers to meters, move the decimal 3 places to the right.

(Rigorous) (Skill 12.5)

69. Given the formula $d = rt$, (where d = distance, r = rate, and t = time), calculate the time required for a vehicle to travel 585 miles at a rate of 65 miles per hour.

    A. 8.5 hours

    B. 6.5 hours

    C. 9.5 hours

    D. 9 hours

    Answer: D. 9 hours

    We are given $d = 585$ miles and $r = 65$ miles per hour and $d = rt$. Solve for t. $585 = 65t \rightarrow = 9$ hours.

(Average) (Skill 13.2)

70. Consider this set of test scores from a math test. Find the mean, median, and the mode.

    90, 92, 83, 83, 83, 90, 90, 83, 90, 93, 90, 97, 80, 67, 90, 85, 63, 60

    A. Mean: 83.72, mode: 90, median: 86.5

    B. Mean: 86.5, mode: 83, 90, median: 83.72

    C. Mean: 1507, mode: 90, median 83

    D. Mean 90, mode 83.72, median 90

    Answer: A. Mean: 83.72, mode: 90, median: 86.5

    The mean is the sum of the data items divided by the number of items. The mode is the item that appears the most times. The median is found by putting the data items in order from smallest to largest and selecting the item in the middle (or the average of the two items in the middle).

(Average) (Skill 13.2)

71. Corporate salaries are listed for several employees. Which would be the best measure of central tendency?

    $24,000 $24,000
    $26,000 $28,000
    $30,000 $120,000

    A. Mean

    B. Median

    C. Mode

    D. No difference

    Answer: B. Median

    The median provides the best measure of central tendency in this case where the mode is the lowest number and the mean would be disproportionately skewed by the outlier $120,000.

(Easy) (Skill 13.3)

72. Emma did a presentation to the class of the data she collected. She organized her data in the following chart.

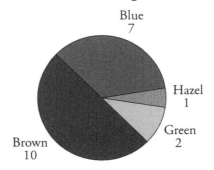

    Which display type did she use to organize her data?

    A. Line graph

    B. Pictograph

    C. Circle graph

    D. Bar graph

Answer: C. Circle graph

A circle graph is a way of displaying data as areas of a circle.

(Average) (Skill 13.3)

73. **Which type of graph uses symbols to represent quantities?**

A. Bar graph

B. Line graph

C. Pictograph

D. Circle graph

Answer: C. Pictograph

A pictograph shows comparison of quantities using symbols. Each symbol represents a number of items.

(Rigorous) (Skill 13.5)

74. **What is the probability of drawing 2 consecutive aces from a standard deck of cards?**

A. $\frac{5}{31}$

B. $\frac{1}{221}$

C. $\frac{2}{104}$

D. $\frac{2}{52}$

Answer: B. $\frac{1}{221}$

$P(\text{first ace}) = \frac{4}{52}$. $P(\text{second ace}) = \frac{3}{51}$.

$P(\text{first ace and second ace}) = P(\text{one ace}) \times P(\text{second ace}|\text{first ace}) = \frac{4}{52} \times \frac{3}{51} = \frac{1}{221}$. This is answer B.

(Average) (Skill 13.6)

75. **SnowGlow pulls every fifth snow globe from their manufacturing line to check for leaks. This is an example of which type of sampling?**

A. Convenience

B. Quota

C. Cluster

D. Systematic

Answer: D. Systematic

Systematic sampling involves collecting data from samples determined by a defined interval.

(Rigorous) (Skill 14.1)

76. **Which of the following conclusion(s) can be made by using this Venn diagram?**

A. All Newfoundlands are in the working group

B. All dogs are in the working group

C. All working group dogs are Newfoundlands

D. None of the above

Answer: A. All Newfoundlands are in the working group

Conditional statements can be illustrated using a Venn diagram. A diagram can be drawn with one figure inside another figure. The inner figure represents the hypothesis. The outer figure represents the conclusion. If the hypothesis is taken to be true, then you are located inside the inner figure. If you are located in the inner figure you are also inside the outer figure, so that proves the conclusion is true. Sometimes that conclusion can then be used as the hypothesis for another conditional, which can result in a second conclusion.

(Average) (Skill 14.1)

77. **Based on the previous question, which of the following is a correct "if-then" statement?**

   A. If a dog is in the working group, then it is a Newfoundland

   B. If a dog is a Newfoundland, then it is in the working group

   C. Neither A nor B

   D. Both A and B

Answer: B. If a dog is a Newfoundland, then it is in the working group

Conclusions can be iterated as "if-then" statements. Determine the statements that are true based on the diagram, and then find the conclusion.

(Rigorous) (Skill 14.2)

78. **Which of the following is true about permutations and combinations?**

   A. There are more steps involved in permutations than in combinations

   B. The steps in combinations must be done in a certain order

   C. The steps in permutations must be done in a certain order

   D. There are more steps involved in combinations than in permutations

Answer: C. The steps in permutations must be done in a certain order

In permutations, factorials must be considered. Therefore, the possible outcomes or elements must be arranged in a specific order. In combinations, the elements can be compiled in any order.

(Rigorous) (Skill 14.5)

79. **Sequences of numbers vary in the way in which the term of the sequence is set. Which of the following is true?**

   A. Geometric sequences are based on a variable difference between the terms

   B. Geometric sequences are based on a common ratio between the terms

   C. Arithmetic sequences are based on a common ratio between the terms

   D. Arithmetic sequences are based on a variable difference between the terms

Answer: B. Geometric sequences are based on a common ratio between the terms

Number sequences are understood by comparing consecutive numbers. The ratio or the difference between any two numbers in the sequence will be the same, thus "common." Geometric sequences have common ratios and arithmetic sequences have common differences.

(Average) (Skill 15.1)

80. **Sammy knows that Yee Lin has made dinner five nights in a row, so he concludes that she will make dinner again on the sixth night. The approach to his conclusion is known as:**

    A. Deductive reasoning

    B. Conditional thinking

    C. Conclusive reasoning

    D. Inductive reasoning

    Answer: D. Inductive reasoning

    Sammy's conclusion is based on inductive reasoning. On the basis of several days' observations, it can be concluded that Yee Lin will make dinner the next day as well. This may or may not be true, but it is a conclusion developed by inductive reasoning.

(Average) (Skill 15.1)

81. **Which of the following is true?**

    A. In conditional statements, an "if-then" format is used

    B. The hypothesis in a conditional statement is the "if" clause

    C. Another form used to show the hypothesis-conclusion relationship is "If p, then q"

    D. All of the above

    Answer: D. All of the above

    Conditional statements are frequently written in "if-then" form. The "if" clause of the conditional is known as the hypothesis, and the "then" clause is called the conclusion. In a proof, the hypothesis is the information that is assumed to be true, while the conclusion is what is to be proven true. A conditional is considered to be of the form: If p, then q, where p is the hypothesis and q is the conclusion.

(Easy) (Skill 15.3)

82. **Scientific notation can be best described as:**

    A. A research language used by mathematicians and scientists

    B. A method for writing very large or very small numbers

    C. A method of describing data

    D. The results of statistical analysis

    Answer: B. A method for writing very large or very small numbers

    Scientific notation is considered a shorthand method for expressing very large or very small numbers. It uses factors of ten.

(Easy) (Skill 15.4)

83. **When students are checking for the reasonableness of an answer, which problem-solving strategy can be used?**

    A. Draw a diagram

    B. Work backwards

    C. Guess and check

    D. Estimation and approximation

    Answer: D. Estimation and approximation

    Sometimes an exact answer is not needed for checking to see if an answer is reasonable, so estimation and approximation are good strategies to use.

(Easy) (Skill 15.4)

84. **You are teaching your students how to solve problems using measurement. Fluid ounces, cups, pints, and quarts, gallons are all units for what type of measurement?**

    A. Length

    B. Capacity

    C. Weight

    D. Mass

    Answer: B. Capacity

    Fluid ounces, cups, pints, quarts, and gallons are all units of capacity.

(Average) (Skill 15.4)

85. **The four steps of problem-solving are:**

    A. Understand the problem, devise a plan, carry out the plan, write down the solution

    B. Understand the problem, devise a plan, carry out the plan, look back

    C. Devise a plan, carry out the plan, look back, and revise future plans

    D. Understand and carry out the plan, look back, write it up, and revise future plans

    Answer: B. Understand the problem, devise a plan, carry out the plan, look back

    By first understanding the problem, then devising a plan, carrying out the plan, and then looking back, one is able to comprehensively solve a problem.

(Average) (Skill 15.5)

86. **Which of the following is NOT true about the history of mathematics?**

    A. The source of using decimals instead of fractions is attributed to Islamic mathematician Al-Kashi.

    B. Mathematicians in India and from the Mayan civilization were the first to invent the idea of zero.

    C. Calculus and analytical geometry emerged in the 17th century.

    D. Most of the concepts in mathematics occurred in the last 500 years.

Answer: D. Most of the concepts in mathematics occurred in the last 500 years.

Although many modern theorists since the Renaissance era have developed many complex mathematical ideas, many cultures including ancient civilizations have contributed significantly to the field of mathematics.

(Rigorous) (Skill 15.6)

87. **Why are manipulatives, models, and technology used by math teachers?**

    A. To promote interest

    B. To address diverse learning needs

    C. To give hands-on math experience

    D. All of the above

    Answer: D. All of the above

    Some students show more interest in or have a need for concrete, hands-on experience. Manipulatives, models, and technology offer ways to address that in math.

IV. Health/Fitness and Fine Arts

(Average) (Skill 16.1)

88. **Social skills and values developed by physical activity include all of the following EXCEPT:**

    A. Winning at all costs

    B. Making judgments in groups

    C. Communicating and cooperating

    D. Respecting rules and property

Answer: A. Winning at all costs

Winning at all costs is not a desirable social skill. Instructors and coaches should emphasize fair play and effort over winning. Answers B, C, and D are all positive skills and values developed in physical activity settings.

(Average) (Skill 16.1)

89. **Which type of physical education activities would be most likely to help students develop a sense of belonging?**

    A. Solitary activities

    B. Teamwork activities

    C. Competitive activities

    D. Creative activities

    Answer: B. Teamwork activities

    The correct answer is teamwork activities. One of the benefits of participating in physical activities is that students often develop a sense of belonging. This most often occurs in team sports, where students feel a sense of belonging to the team. The relationships developed with others in the process can also create a larger sense of belonging, such as feeling like one belongs to the school community.

(Average) (Skill 16.1)

90. **A positive approach to coaching includes all of the following EXCEPT:**

    A. Instructive, corrective feedback

    B. Repeated demonstration of how to do a task

    C. Frequent encouragement

    D. Positive reinforcement for effort

Answer: B. Repeated demonstration of how to do a task

Although repeated demonstration of how to do a task may be useful at times, it is not considered one of the major elements of the positive approach. Frequent encouragement, validating a student's effort, and giving specific corrective feedback are key factors in this approach.

(Average) (Skill 16.2)

91. **Which of the following is NOT a basic aspect of routine substance abuse treatment?**

    A. Physically and psychologically withdrawing from the addictive substance

    B. Acquiring coping strategies and replacement techniques to fill the void left by the addictive substance

    C. Limiting access to the addictive substance and acquiring self-control strategies

    D. Being placed in an alternative living situation

Answer: D. Being placed in an alternative living situation

Although some students may need to be placed in foster care or a group home situation as part of an overall plan, placement is not a fundamental aspect of substance abuse treatment. Dealing directly with the addiction, both physical and psychological, limiting access to substances, and developing useful coping skills are essential.

(Average) (Skill 16.3)

92. **What is the proper sequential order of development for the acquisition of nonlocomotor skills?**

    A. Stretch, sit, bend, turn, swing, twist, shake, rock and sway, dodge, fall

    B. Bend, stretch, turn, twist, swing, sit, rock and sway, shake, dodge, fall

    C. Stretch, bend, sit, shake, turn, rock and sway, swing, twist, dodge, fall

    D. Bend, stretch, sit, turn, twist, swing, sway, rock and sway, dodge, fall

Answer: C. Stretch, bend, sit, shake, turn, rock and sway, swing, twist, dodge, fall

Each skill in the progression builds on the previous skills.

(Easy) (Skill 16.4)

93. **Which of the following is the best definition of "transfer of learning?"**

    A. How teachers teach students basic facts

    B. Relating learning in physical education to other subjects

    C. Identifying similarities between movements in a skill learned previously and a new skill

    D. The way learning occurs from one year to the next

Answer: C. Identifying similarities between movements in a skill learned previously and a new skill

The transfer of learning is a process in which the teacher clearly links prior learning to the current task or skill to be learned. It is a sequential process that facilitates students' skill acquisition.

(Rigorous) (Skill 16.4)

94. **Which of the following are basic instructional methods for physical educators?**

    A. Cognitive structuring, small-group skill instruction, individual skill instruction, and guided inquiry

    B. Cognitive structuring, small-group skill instruction, individual skill instruction, and testing

    C. Large-group skill instruction, small-group skill instruction, and guided inquiry

    D. Cognitive structuring, problem-solving, individual skill instruction, and testing

    Answer: B. Cognitive structuring, small-group skill instruction, individual skill instruction, and testing

    The physical educator can select from five basic instructional formats: cognitive structuring, large-group skill instruction, small-group skill instruction, individual skill instruction, and testing. Guided inquiry and problem-solving are teaching methods that can be used to facilitate cognitive learning.

(Easy) (Skill 17.1)

95. **The French horn, trumpet, trombone, and tuba are a part of which musical instrument category?**

    A. Stringed Instruments

    B. Brass Instruments

    C. Percussion Instruments

    D. Wind Instruments

    Answer: B. Brass Instruments

    Brass instruments are similar to wind instruments since music from brass instruments also results from air passing through an air chamber. They are called brass instruments, however, because they are made from metal or brass. Common brass instruments include the French horn, trumpet, trombone, and tuba.

(Average) (Skill 17.1)

96. **The quality of sound is the definition of:**

    A. Timbre

    B. Rhythm

    C. Harmony

    D. Melody

    Answer: A. Timbre

    Rhythm refers to the duration of musical notes. Harmony refers to the vertical aspect of music or the musical chords related to a melody. Finally, melody is the tune (a specific arrangement of sounds in a pleasing pattern).

(Rigorous) (Skill 17.2)

97. **In the visual arts, works that project a design from the center axis are said to have:**

    A. Horizontal balance

    B. Radial balance

    C. Symmetrical balance

    D. Asymmetrical balance

Answer: B. Radial balance

Balance is a fundamental of design seen as a visual weight and counterweight, and radial balance is present in works that project a design from the center axis. Horizontal balance is present in works which utilize the picture plane from left to right. Works with symmetrical balance have objects or arrangements on both sides, and works with asymmetrical balance display objects or arrangements on one side or another or are uneven.

(Average) (Skill 17.3)

98. **The process of creativity involves all of the following EXCEPT:**

    A. Independence and choice

    B. A stimulating environment

    C. Clearly defined product outcomes

    D. A playful attitude

Answer: C. Clearly defined product outcomes

Generally, specific goals or predicted outcomes interfere with the creative process. Being open to possibilities and finding different solutions to problems invite creativity. Students respond to environments that encourage them to explore, imagine, and design, determining the outcome along the way.

(Rigorous) (Skill 17.4)

99. **Aesthetic principles vary from culture to culture. Which of the following is NOT an element of Eastern art?**

    A. Universal in nature

    B. Portrays the human figure with symbolic meanings

    C. Conveys a concise, detailed and complicated view

    D. Uses arbitrary choices of color

Answer: C. Conveys a concise, detailed and complicated view

There is an obvious difference in aesthetic principles between works created by Eastern and Western cultures. In attempting to convey reality, Eastern artists generally prefer to use line, local color, and a simplistic view. Western artists tend toward a literal use of line, shape, color, and texture to convey a concise, detailed, complicated view. Eastern artists portray the human figure with symbolic meanings and little regard for muscle structure, resulting in a mystical view of the human experience. In the application of color, Eastern artists use arbitrary choices. Western artists generally rely on literal color usage or emotional choices of color. The end result is that Eastern art tends to be more universal in nature, while Western art is more individualized.

453

(Rigorous) (Skill 17.4)

100. **Which time period of arts do the themes of "Roman mythology, Humanism, and Ancient legends" reflect?**

A. Renaissance arts

B. Baroque arts

C. Mesopotamian arts

D. Middle Ages arts

Answer: A. Renaissance Arts

Renaissance themes include Christian religious depiction (see Middle Ages), but tend to reflect a renewed interest in all things classical. Specific themes include Greek and Roman mythological and philosophic figures, ancient battles, and legends. Dominant themes mirror the philosophic beliefs of Humanism, emphasizing individuality and human reason, such as those of the High Renaissance, which center around the psychological attributes of individuals.

V. Science

(Average) (Skill 18.1)

101. **The best definition of "empirical" is:**

A. Assessment through observations and tests

B. Something that has been scientifically proven

C. Something created by a scientist's hypothesis

D. Observed information

Answer: A. Assessment through observations and tests

Although empirical data may become "proven" at some point or result from a scientist's hypothesis, "empirical" means that a phenomenon is assessed through tests and observations. Simply observing, without a scientific structure within which to organize the data, does not make something empirical, *per se*.

(Rigorous) (Skill 18.2)

102. **Which of the following is an example of scientific evolution?**

A. Giraffes need to reach higher for leaves to eat, so their necks stretch. The giraffe babies are then born with longer necks. Eventually, there are more long-necked giraffes in the population.

B. Giraffes with longer necks are able to reach more leaves, so they eat more and have more babies than other giraffes. Eventually, there are more long-necked giraffes in the population.

C. Giraffes want to reach higher for leaves to eat, so they release enzymes into their bloodstream, which in turn causes fetal development of longer-necked giraffes. Eventually, there are more long-necked giraffes in the population.

D. Giraffes with long necks are more attractive to other giraffes, so they get the best mating partners and have more babies. Eventually, there are more long-necked giraffes in the population.

Answer: B. Giraffes with longer necks are able to reach more leaves, so they eat more and have more babies than other giraffes. Eventually, there are more long-necked giraffes in the population.

Although evolution is often misunderstood, it occurs via natural selection. Organisms with a life/reproductive advantage will produce more offspring. Over many generations, this changes the proportions of the population. In any case, it is impossible for a stretched neck or a fervent desire to result in a biologically mutated baby. Although there are traits that are naturally selected because of mate attractiveness and fitness, this is not the primary situation here, so answer B is the best choice.

(Average) (Skill 18.2)

103. **Which of the following is NOT considered ethical behavior for a scientist?**

    A. Using unpublished data and citing the source

    B. Publishing data before other scientists have had a chance to replicate the results

    C. Collaborating with other scientists from different laboratories

    D. Publishing work with an incomplete list of citations

Answer: D. Publishing work with an incomplete list of citations

One of the most important ethical principles for scientists is to cite all sources of data and analysis when publishing work. It is reasonable to use unpublished data as long as the source is cited. Most science is published before other scientists replicate it and frequently scientists collaborate with each other, in the same or different laboratories. These are all ethical choices. However, publishing work without the appropriate citations is unethical.

(Rigorous) (Skill 18.2)

104. **In an experiment measuring the growth of bacteria at different temperatures, what is the independent variable?**

    A. Number of bacteria

    B. Growth rate of bacteria

    C. Temperature

    D. Size of bacteria.

Answer: C. Temperature

To answer this question, recall that the independent variable in an experiment is the value that is changed by the scientist in order to observe the effects. In this experiment, temperature is changed in order to measure growth of bacteria, so C is the answer. Note that answer A is the dependent variable, and neither B nor D is directly relevant to the question.

(Average) (Skill 18.3)

105. Which of the following sampling techniques is least likely to be biased?

    A. Stratified

    B. Quota

    C. Random

    D. Cluster

Answer: C. Random

A truly random sample must choose events or individuals without regard to time, place, or result. Random samples are least likely to be biased because they are most likely to represent the population from which they are taken. Stratified, quota, and cluster sampling involve subpopulations from which random samples are generally taken.

(Rigorous) (Skill 18.4)

106. Which of the following statistical methods would be most appropriate for analyzing census data to determine the rate of population growth?

    A. Geographic correlation studies

    B. Spatial analysis

    C. Tracking and trend analysis

    D. None of the above

Answer: C. Tracking and trend analysis

Examining time trends in census data is helpful in identifying the growth for a specific area. The other methods mentioned are useful for looking in more depth at specific factors such as socio-economic indicators and rates of death and disease.

(Average) (Skill 18.5)

107. Which of the following data sets is properly represented by a bar graph?

    A. Number of people choosing to buy cars vs. color of car bought

    B. Number of people choosing to buy cars vs. age of car customer

    C. Number of people choosing to buy cars vs. distance from car lot to customer home

    D. Number of people choosing to buy cars vs. time since last car purchase

Answer: A. Number of people choosing to buy cars vs. color of car bought

A bar graph should be used only for data sets in which the independent variable is non-continuous (discrete), e.g., gender or color. Any continuous independent variable (age, distance, time, etc.) should yield a scatter-plot when the dependent variable is plotted.

(Easy) (Skill 18.5)

108. Chemicals should be stored:

    A. In the principal's office

    B. In a dark room

    C. According to their reactivity with other substances

    D. In a double-locked room

Answer: C. According to their reactivity with other substances

Chemicals should be stored with other chemicals of similar properties (e.g. acids with other acids) to reduce the potential for either hazardous reactions in the storeroom or mistakes in reagent use. Certainly, chemicals should not be stored in anyone's office, and the light intensity of the room is not very important because light-sensitive chemicals are usually stored in dark containers. In fact, good lighting is desirable in a storeroom, so that labels can be read easily. Chemicals may be stored off-site, but that makes their use inconvenient.

(Easy) (Skill 19.1)

109. **A student's motor development is influenced by:**

    A. Culture

    B. Environment

    C. Family

    D. All of the above

Answer: D. All of the above

Families and cultures place different emphasis on physical activity. This leads to an influence on a student's motor development. Environment also plays a role, because some students may live close to parks, basketball courts, etc. Other students may not have access to such facilities.

(Easy) (Skill 19.1)

110. **Volume is:**

    A. Area of the faces, excluding the bases

    B. Total area of all the faces, including the bases

    C. The number of cubic units in a solid

    D. The measurement around the object

Answer: C. The number of cubic units in a solid

Volume refers to how much "stuff" can be placed within a solid. Cubic units are one example of something that can be placed within a solid to measure its volume.

(Rigorous) (Skill 19.1)

111. **Which statement best explains why a balance scale is used to measure both weight and mass?**

    A. The weight and mass of an object are identical concepts

    B. The force of gravity between two objects depends on the mass of the two objects

    C. Inertial mass and gravitational mass are identical

    D. A balance scale compares the weight of two objects

Answer: C. Inertial mass and gravitational mass are identical

The mass of an object is a fundamental property of matter and is measured in kilograms. The weight of an object is the force of gravity between Earth and an object near Earth's surface and is measured in newtons or pounds. Newton's second law ($F = ma$) and the universal law of gravity ($F = G \frac{m_{earth}m}{d^2}$) determine the weight of an object. The mass in Newton's second law is called the inertial mass and the mass in the universal law of gravity is called the gravitational mass. The two kinds of masses are identical.

(Average) (Skill 19.2)

112. The following are examples of chemical reactions EXCEPT:

A. Melting ice into water

B. Dissolving a seltzer tablet in water

C. Using a fire-cracker

D. Burning a piece of plastic

Answer: A. Melting ice into water

When you melt ice there is no chemical reaction. Ice and water have the same chemical makeup.

(Rigorous) (Skill 19.3)

113. Which of the following devices is used to regulate the flow of electrical current to achieve a certain output?

A. Conductor

B. Resistor

C. Fuse

D. Circuit breaker

Answer: B. Resistor

Resistors change the amount of electrical current passing through a wire and are used to regulate volume on a television or radio or for a dimmer switch for lights.

(Easy) (Skill 19.4)

114. Which statement is true about temperature?

A. Temperature is a measurement of heat

B. Temperature is how hot or cold an object is

C. The coldest temperature ever measured is zero degrees Kelvin

D. The temperature of a molecule is its kinetic energy

Answer: B. Temperature is how hot or cold an object is

Temperature is a physical property of objects relating to how they feel when touched. Zero degrees Celsius, or 32 degrees Fahrenheit, is defined as the temperature of ice water. Heat is a form of energy that flows from hot objects in thermal contact with cold objects. The greater the temperature of an object, the greater the kinetic energy of the molecules making up the object, but a single molecule does not have a temperature. The third law of thermodynamics is that absolute zero can never be achieved in a laboratory.

(Rigorous) (Skill 20.1)

115. **Which kingdom is comprised of organisms made of one cell with no nuclear membrane?**

A. Monera

B. Protista

C. Fungi

D. Algae

Answer: A. Monera

To answer this question, first note that algae are not a kingdom of their own. Some algae are in monera, the kingdom that consists of unicellular prokaryotes with no true nucleus. Protista and fungi are both eukaryotic, with true nuclei, and are sometimes multi-cellular. Therefore, the correct answer is A.

(Average) (Skill 20.1)

116. **What cell organelle contains the cell's stored food?**

A. Vacuoles

B. Golgi Apparatus

C. Ribosomes

D. Lysosomes

Answer: A. Vacuoles

In a cell, the sub-parts are called organelles. Of these, the vacuoles hold stored food (and water and pigments). The Golgi Apparatus sorts molecules from other parts of the cell; the ribosomes are sites of protein synthesis; the lysosomes contain digestive enzymes. This is consistent only with answer A.

(Rigorous) (Skill 20.1)

117. **Enzymes speed up reactions by:**

A. Utilizing ATP

B. Lowering pH, allowing reaction speed to increase

C. Increasing volume of substrate

D. Lowering energy of activation

Answer: D. Lowering energy of activation

Because enzymes are catalysts, they work the same way—they cause the formation of activated chemical complexes, which require a lower activation energy. Therefore, The correct answer is D. ATP is an energy source for cells, and pH or volume changes may or may not affect reaction rate, so these answers can be eliminated.

(Rigorous) (Skill 20.2)

118. **Angiosperms, the largest group in the plant kingdom, have which of the following characteristics?**

A. The ability to remain dormant for a period of time and still produce plants

B. Have decreased photosynthesis due to their leaf size

C. Rely on single fertilization to reproduce

D. All of the above

Answer: A. The ability to remain dormant for a period of time and still produce plants

The seeds of angiosperms can remain dormant and, later, when water and soil conditions are right, still produce plants. They actually have increased photosynthesis due to leaf size, and reproduce through double fertilization.

(Rigorous) (Skill 20.3)

119. **Identify the correct sequence of organization of living things from lower to higher order:**

    A. Cell, Organelle, Organ, Tissue, System, Organism

    B. Cell, Tissue, Organ, Organelle, System, Organism

    C. Organelle, Cell, Tissue, Organ, System, Organism

    D. Organelle, Tissue, Cell, Organ, System, Organism

Answer: C. Organelle, Cell, Tissue, Organ, System, Organism

Organelles are parts of the cell and cells make up tissue, which makes up organs. Organs work together in systems (e.g., the respiratory system), and the organism is the living thing as a whole. Therefore, the answer must be C.

(Rigorous) (Skill 20.4)

120. **Which of the following types of rock are made from magma?**

    A. Fossils

    B. Sedimentary

    C. Metamorphic

    D. Igneous

Answer: D. Igneous.

Few fossils are found in metamorphic rock and virtually none are found in igneous rock. Igneous rocks are formed from magma and magma is so hot that any organisms trapped by it are destroyed. Metamorphic rocks are formed by high temperatures and great pressures. When fluid sediments are transformed into solid sedimentary rocks, the process is known as lithification. The correct answer is D.

(Easy) (Skill 20.4)

121. **An ecosystem can be described as:**

    A. The connection between plants, plant eaters, and animal eaters

    B. Relationships between a community and its physical environment

    C. The specific environment or place where an animal or plant lives

    D. Organisms that live and reproduce there in an environment

Answer: B. Relationships between a community and its physical environment

Animal and plant communities depend on interactions between each other and with the physical environment in general (e.g., air, water, enriched soil, temperature, and light). The sustaining of life through these interrelationships is called an ecosystem.

(Easy) (Skill 20.5)

122. Which of the following describes the interaction between community members when one species feeds off another species but does not kill it immediately?

A. Parasitism

B. Predation

C. Commensalism

D. Mutualism

Answer: A. Parasitism

Predation occurs when one species kills another species. In mutualism, both species benefit. In commensalism, one species benefits without the other being harmed.

(Rigorous) (Skill 21.1)

123. The theory of "sea floor spreading" explains:

A. The shapes of the continents

B. How continents were named

C. How continents move apart

D. How continents sink to become part of the ocean floor

Answer: C. How continents move apart

In the theory of "sea floor spreading," the movement of the ocean floor causes continents to spread apart from one another. This occurs because crustal plates split apart, and new material is added to the plate edges. This process pulls the continents apart, or may create new separations; it is believed to have caused the formation of the Atlantic Ocean.

(Rigorous) (Skill 21.2)

124. Which of the following is the best definition for "meteorite?"

A. A mineral composed of mica and feldspar

B. Material from outer space that has struck the earth's surface

C. An element that has properties of both metals and nonmetals

D. A very small unit of length measurement

Answer: B. Material from outer space that has struck the earth's surface

Meteoroids are pieces of matter in space, composed of particles of rock and metal. If a meteoroid travels through the earth's atmosphere, friction causes burning and a "shooting star"—i.e., a meteor. If the meteor strikes the earth's surface, it is known as a meteorite. Note that although the suffix –ite often means a mineral, answer A is incorrect. Answer C refers to a "metalloid" rather than a "meteorite," and answer D is simply a misleading pun on "mete." Therefore, the correct answer is B.

(Average) (Skill 21.3)

125. Why is the winter in the Southern Hemisphere colder than winter in the Northern Hemisphere?

A. Earth's axis of 24-hour rotation tilts at an angle of 23°

B. The elliptical orbit of Earth around the Sun changes the distance of the Sun from Earth

C. The Southern Hemisphere has more water than the Northern Hemisphere

D. The greenhouse effect is greater in the Northern Hemisphere

Answer: B. The elliptical orbit of Earth around the Sun changes the distance of the Sun from the Earth

The tilt of Earth's axis causes the seasons. The Earth is close to the Sun during winter in the Northern Hemisphere. Winter in the Southern Hemisphere occurs six months later when Earth is farther from the Sun. The presence of water explains why winters are harsher inland than by the coast.

(Rigorous) (Skill 21.4)

126. **The most abundant gas in the atmosphere is:**

    A. Oxygen

    B. Nitrogen

    C. Carbon dioxide

    D. Methane

    Answer: B. Nitrogen

    Nitrogen accounts for 78.09 percent of the atmosphere, oxygen 20.95 percent, carbon dioxide 0.03 percent, and methane does not make up any of the atmosphere.

(Average) (Skill 21.5)

127. **The Himalayas are an example of which type of mountain formation?**

    A. Dome

    B. Fault-block

    C. Upwarped

    D. Folded

Answer: D. Folded

Mountains are formed when the Earth's crust is impacted by various movements. Folded mountains are the result of folding layers of rock when continents collide. Domes are formed by magma pushing up through the earth's crust but not breaking the surface. Unwarped mountains form when there is an arching of the crust. Fault-blocks occur when shifting plates push rock upward.

(Rigorous) (Skill 21.5)

128. **In the following equation, what does *G* represent?**

    $$F_{\text{gravity}} = G\frac{m_1 m_2}{d^2}$$

    A. The distance between the two masses

    B. The universal gravitational constant

    C. Coulomb's constant

    D. The speed of the object

Answer: B. The universal gravitational constant

The force of gravity is the force that causes objects to fall to Earth. We can feel the force of gravity when we lift something up. The force of gravity also keeps the moon rotating around Earth and Earth rotating around the sun. The universal law of gravity states that there is a gravitational attraction between all objects on Earth determined by the equation:

$$F_{gravity} = G\frac{m_1 m_2}{d^2}$$

where G is the universal gravitational constant and d is the distance between the two masses. Coulomb's constant relates to electrostatic forces between two objects, and speed, or velocity. Finally, statics is the study of physical systems at rest or moving with a constant speed.

VI. Social Studies

(Easy) (Skill 22.1)

129. **Which civilization invented the wheel?**

    A. Egyptians

    B. Romans

    C. Assyrians

    D. Sumerians

Answer: D. Sumerians

The ancient Sumerian civilization invented the wheel.

(Average) (Skill 22.2)

130. **Which of the following is a weakness of "periodization?"**

    A. It is arbitrary

    B. It facilitates understanding

    C. It identifies similarities

    D. It categorizes knowledge

Answer: A. It is arbitrary

The practice of dividing history into a number of discrete periods or blocks of time is called "periodization." Because history is continuous, all systems of periodization are arbitrary to some extent. However, dividing time into segments facilitates understanding of changes that occur over time and helps identify similarities of events, knowledge, and experience within the defined period. Further, some divisions of time into these periods apply only under specific circumstances.

(Easy) (Skill 22.2)

131. **Archaeology is the study of which of the following?**

    A. Norms, values, and standards

    B. Material remains of humans

    C. Genetic characteristics

    D. The historical development of language

Answer: B. Material remains of humans

There are four areas of anthropology:

1. Archaeology—study of material remains of humans

2. Social-cultural—norms, values, standards

3. Biological—genetic characteristics

4. Linguistics—the historical development of language

(Average) (Skill 22.2)

132. **The term** *spatial organization* **refers to:**

    A. Latitude and longitude lines

    B. The alignment of the stars

    C. How things are grouped in a given space

    D. The space between point A and point B

    Answer: C. How things are grouped in a given space

    Spatial organization is a description of how things are grouped in a given space. In geographical terms, this can describe people, places, and environments anywhere on Earth. The most basic form of spatial organization for people is where they live.

(Rigorous) (Skill 22.3)

133. **The process of putting the features of the Earth onto a flat surface is called:**

    A. Distortion

    B. Projection

    C. Cartography

    D. Illustration

Answer: B. Projection

The process of putting the features of the Earth onto a flat surface is called projection. All maps are really map projections. It is impossible to reproduce exactly on a flat surface a spherical object. In order to put the earth's features onto a map, they must be stretched in some way. This stretching is called distortion. Mapmakers are called cartographers.

(Average) (Skill 22.3)

134. **Which shows the relationship between a unit of measure on a map and the real world?**

    A. The scale

    B. The legend

    C. The grid

    D. The compass rose

    Answer: A. The scale

    The scale shows the representation of distance on a map compared to actual miles. For example, one inch on a map might equal 100 miles on the Earth. The legend tells what symbols represent. The grid shows longitude and latitude, and the compass rose tells direction (north, south, etc.).

(Average) (Skill 23.1)

135. **Which of the following is NOT one of the six major themes in geography?**

    A. Regions

    B. Religion

    C. Place

    D. Movement

Answer: B. Religion

The six major themes in geography are: place, spatial organization, human-environmental interaction, movement, regions, and locations.

(Average) (Skill 23.1)

136. **The Northern Hemisphere contains which of the following?**

   A. Europe

   B. South America

   C. Africa

   D. Australia

Answer: A. Europe

The Northern Hemisphere, located between the North Pole and the Equator, contains all of the continents of Europe and North America and parts of South America, Africa, and most of Asia.

(Average) (Skill 23.2)

137. **Which country is considered by some historians to be the oldest uninterrupted civilization in the world?**

   A. Japan

   B. China

   C. Canada

   D. Mexico

Answer: B. China

China is considered by some historians to be the oldest uninterrupted civilization in the world and was in existence around the same time as the ancient civilizations founded in Egypt, Mesopotamia, and the Indus Valley.

(Rigorous) (Skill 23.2)

138. **What is the "Pax Romana"?**

   A. A long period of peace enabling free travel and trade, spreading people, cultures, goods, and ideas all over the world

   B. A period of war where the Romans expanded their empire

   C. The Roman government

   D. A time where the government was overruled

Answer: A. A long period of peace enabling free travel and trade, spreading people, cultures, goods, and ideas all over the world

The "Pax Romana" was a time when the Romans were peaceful and wanted to spread their culture all over the world.

(Easy) (Skill 23.3)

139. **What was the name of the cultural revival after the Civil War that took place in New York?**

   A. The Revolutionary War

   B. The Second Great Awakening

   C. The Harlem Renaissance

   D. The Gilded Age

Answer: C. The Harlem Renaissance

As African-Americans left the rural South and migrated to the North in search of opportunity, many settled in Harlem in New York City. By the 1920s, Harlem had become a center of life and activity for African-Americans. The music, art, and literature of this community gave birth to a cultural movement known as the Harlem Renaissance. The Revolutionary War (1776) occurred prior to the Civil War. The Second Great Awakening occurred in the 1920s, but like the Gilded Age (1878–1889), affected the entire United States.

(Easy) (Skill 23.3)

140. **The Westward Expansion occurred for a number of reasons; however, the most important reason was:**

A. Colonization

B. Slavery

C. Independence

D. Economics

Answer: D. Economics

Westward expansion occurred for a number of reasons, the most important being economic.

(Easy) (Skill 23.4)

141. **The Cold War involved which two countries?**

A. China and Japan

B. The United States and the Soviet Union

C. England and Brazil

D. Afghanistan and the United States

Answer: B. The United States and the Soviet Union

After World War II, the United States and the Soviet Union constantly competed in space exploration and the race to develop nuclear weapons.

(Average) (Skill 23.4)

142. **The year 1619 was a memorable one for the colony of Virginia. Three important events occurred, resulting in lasting effects on U.S. history. Which one of the following is NOT one of the events?**

A. Twenty African slaves arrived.

B. The London Company granted the colony a charter, making it independent.

C. The colonists were given the right by the London Company to govern themselves through representative government in the Virginia House of Burgesses.

D. The London Company sent to the colony 60 women who were quickly married, establishing families and stability in the colony.

Answer: B. The London Company granted the colony a charter, making it independent.

In the year 1619, the southern colony of Virginia had an eventful year, including the first arrival of twenty African slaves, the right to self-governance through representative government in the Virginia House of Burgesses (their own legislative body), and the arrival of sixty women sent to marry and establish families in the colony. The London Company did not, however, grant the colony a charter in 1619.

(Average) (Skill 23.5)

143. **Which of the following is the most accurate definition of a nonrenewable resource?**

    A. A nonrenewable resource is never replaced once used.

    B. A nonrenewable resource is replaced on a timescale that is very long relative to human life spans.

    C. A nonrenewable resource is a resource that can only be manufactured by humans.

    D. A nonrenewable resource is a species that has already become extinct.

    Answer: B. A nonrenewable resource is replaced on a timescale that is very long relative to human life spans.

    Renewable resources are those that are renewed, or replaced, in time for humans to use more of them. Examples include fast-growing plants, animals, and oxygen gas. (Note that while sunlight is often considered a renewable resource, it is actually a nonrenewable, but extremely abundant, resource.) Nonrenewable resources are those that renew themselves only on very long—usually geologic—timescales. Examples include minerals, metals, and fossil fuels.

(Average) (Skill 24.1)

144. **Native American tribes based in Minnesota are governed by:**

    A. Tribal councils

    B. Assemblies

    C. Boards of trustees

    D. All of the above

Answer: D. All of the above

Native American tribes in all states in the U.S. are sovereign nations and have their own governing bodies. They are called by various names, depending on the tribe's choice, and are structured in various ways.

(Easy) (Skill 24.2)

145. **The Bill of Rights consists of which Amendments?**

    A. Amendments 1–5

    B. Amendments 1–10

    C. Amendments 1 and 2

    D. Amendments 1–22

    Answer: B. Amendments 1–10

    The Bill of Rights consists of the first 10 amendments.

(Average) (Skill 24.3)

146. **The ability of the president to veto an act of congress is an example of:**

    A. Separation of powers

    B. Checks and balances

    C. Judicial review

    D. Presidential prerogative

    Answer: B. Checks and balances

    The ability of the president too veto an act of congress is an example of checks and balances. Judicial review is the checks and balances exerted by the judicial on the legislative branch. The system of checks and balances prevents any one branch of the United States government from becoming too powerful and corrupt.

(Easy) (Skill 24.3)

147. **What are the three branches of the United States government?**

   A. Legislative, judicial, international affairs

   B. Legislative, executive, foreign trade

   C. Legislative, executive, judicial

   D. Executive, judicial, state governments

   Answer: C. Legislative, executive, judicial

   There are three parts of the federal United Sates government: legislative, executive, and judicial.

(Average) (Skill 24.4)

148. _____ **is the belief that one's own culture is the central and the superior culture.**

   A. Ethnocentrism

   B. Egocentric

   C. Prejudice

   D. Superiority

   Answer: A. Ethnocentrism

   Ethnocentrism, as the word suggests, is the belief that one's own culture is the central and superior culture. An ethnocentric view usually considers different practices in other cultures as inferior or even "savage."

(Rigorous) (Skill 24.6)

149. **Economics is defined as a study of:**

   A. How scarce resources are allocated to satisfy unlimited wants

   B. Anything that is manufactured to be used in the production process

   C. Anyone who sells his ability to produce goods and services

   D. Decisions of buyers equal to the selling decision of seller

   Answer: A. How scarce resources are allocated to satisfy unlimited wants

   Economics is defined as a study of how scarce resources are allocated to satisfy unlimited wants. Capital is anything that is manufactured to be used in the production process. Market equilibrium occurs where the buying decisions of buyers are equal to the selling decisions of sellers.

(Rigorous) (Skill 24.6)

150. **Laissez-faire capitalism is based on:**

   A. Government ownership of the means of production

   B. Custom, and usually exists in less developed countries

   C. The premise of no government intervention in the economy

   D. None of the above

   Answer: C. The premise of no government intervention in the economy

   Laissez-faire capitalism is based on the premise of no government intervention in the economy. The market will eliminate any unemployment or inflation that occurs. Government needs only to provide the framework for the functioning of the economy and to protect private property.

CPSIA information can be obtained at www.ICGtesting.com
Printed in the USA
LVOW021951030513

332238LV00003B/92/P

9 781607 870760